Rethinking the Rule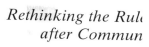
after Commun

GW00368109

Rethinking the Rule of Law after Communism

EDITED BY
ADAM CZARNOTA, MARTIN KRYGIER
AND WOJCIECH SADURSKI

CEU PRESS

Central European University Press
Budapest   New York

Published in 2005 by

Central European University Press

An imprint of the
Central European University Share Company
Nádor utca 11, H-1051 Budapest, Hungary
Tel: +36-1-327-3138 or 327-3000
Fax: +36-1-327-3183
E-mail: ceupress@ceu.hu
Website: www.ceupress.com

400 West 59th Street, New York NY 10019, USA
Tel: +1-212-547-6932
Fax: +1-646-557-2416
E-mail: mgreenwald@sorosny.org

ISBN 963 7326 22 7 paperback

Library of Congress Cataloging-in-Publication Data

Rethinking the rule of law after communism / edited by Adam Czarnota,
Martin Krygier, and Wojciech Sadurski.
    p. cm.
Includes bibliographical references and index.
ISBN 9637326219 (cloth)
1. Rule of law—Europe, Central. 2. Rule of law—Europe, Eastern.
3. Constitutional law. 4. Post-communism. I. Czarnota, Adam W.
II. Krygier, Martin. III. Sadurski, Wojciech, 1950– IV. Title.

KJC4426.R48 2005
340'.11—dc22

2005013594

Preprint by Attributum Stúdió, Budapest
Printed in Hungary by Akaprint Kft. Budapest

Contents

List of Tables

List of Figures

Introduction

ADAM CZARNOTA, MARTIN KRYGIER, AND WOJCIECH SADURSKI

The late 1980s and the 1990s witnessed the dramatic collapses of authoritarian regimes in many different parts of the world, most notably in Central and Eastern Europe and South Africa, but also in other countries, including the Philippines, Chile, and Argentina. In the original euphoria that attended the virtually simultaneous demise of so many dictatorships, there was a widespread belief that problems of "transition" basically involved shedding a known past, and replacing it with an also known future. This was the spirit behind the insistence of the first postcommunist leaders, that they would engage in no more experiments. The miseries of their own immediate histories were in large part the results of experiments gone horribly wrong. They were determined not to repeat them. Their ambition was that the future would be radically different, but not because it would involve new and different experiments. Rather, they had already seen the future at work. in the past and present of successful, normal, Western countries. That future was full of features unfamiliar at home but routine in many other places, in particular liberal democratic politics, capitalist economics, both undergirded by the rule of law, the features of which could be identified by observing successful law-abiding societies and states.

Of course, not everyone was an optimist. It is easy to forget how deep were the apprehensions shared by many at the time. In the postcommunist world in particular, which is the subject of this book, there was fear that legacies of the local past made such a wished-for transition unattainable, or at least extremely difficult and unlikely of attainment. Cultural pessimists (see Krygier 1999) reminded us of the undemocratic, uncapitalist, un*Rechtstaatlich* history of many of the countries in the region, not just from communist times but way before. The more recent deposits left by what Ernest Gellner described as the uniquely Caesaro-Papist-Mammonist character of communism (Gellner 1994: 4), overlaid an uncongenial history with a unique "Leninist legacy" and post-Leninist predicament (Jowitt 1992). Unlike other transitions, the postcommunist one, to be successful, would have to deal with economic, political, legal, and ideological transformations, not just one or the other, and all at the same time (Elster et al. 1998). What was necessary in one domain, say economic transformation, might have conflicted with what was required for another, say democracy; the time it would take for success to be reached in a particular domain differed from that required in the others (Dahrendorf 1990), and yet they were all intertwined.

Opinions differed on the likelihood of a successful transition, the speed it might take, the problems it would face. But there was not much controversy about what it was to start from and how, if things worked out, it should finish. Indeed, in much discussion, the "transition" itself was a kind of residual, empty category: that which occurred between "dictatorship" and "democracy," or "command economy" and "free market," or "despotism" and the "rule of law." The transition would be judged successful to the extent that a "post..." society ceased to look like the deformed chrysalis from which it emerged and came to look like—and develop the organs of—the healthy and wealthy foreign butterflies that it was so anxious to emulate.

It is increasingly becoming evident, however, that "transition" is not merely an empty space between two well known and easily characterized resting-points, but rather a path with highly contested features, many of them unanticipated, to a destination the character of which is far less obvious than once seemed. This has led to an oscillation between two sorts of views, often a tension even in the thoughts of one thinker. At one extreme, in what Wojciech Sadurski with some irony (since he supports such theories) calls simplistic theories, local developments are judged in the light of existing models taken to have been successful elsewhere. On the other end of the extreme, in what he characterizes as fancy theory, transition is taken to be a journey with *sui generis* characteristics and no clearly identifiable destination (see Holmes 1995: 1). And if the problems of transition are unprecedented problems, so the means developed for dealing with them will need to be novel means, and some of the institutions developed in this period will not be available on existing shelves. Thus, as Ruti Teitel, perhaps the best known representative of fancy theory and a contributor to this volume has characteristically observed, "theories of adjudication associated with understandings of the rule of law in ordinary times are inapposite to transitional periods. Our ordinary intuitions about the nature and role of adjudication relate to presumptions about the relative competence and capacities of judiciaries and legislatures in ordinary times that simply do not hold in unstable periods" (Teitel 1997: 2034).

At one extreme, perhaps only a caricature, one would need to know nothing much about the particular society undergoing transition. Rather, it would be sufficient to polish one's models and pack them for export. Of course, no one quite says this, but many attempts to transplant institutions, practices, laws, have foundered on unanticipated difficulties when the graftee of a transplant seems less hospitable to it than the grafter had been. The other extreme would forsake purported lessons, general prescriptions, precedent and experience, and go native. Interesting views occupy neither of these extreme positions, of course, but many are palpably pulled towards one or other, or even to both at once.

Certainly, a powerful case can be made that transitional justice bears systematic differences from what might be called "normal" application of justice, in polities with existing constitutional and political frameworks, with settled laws and practices. For there is an in-built paradox in the contemporary transitions: they are "revolutionary" (in that they lead to a total change of the existing constitutional, political and legal structure), but at the same time they are "reformist" (in that they avoid dramatic upheavals), "evolutionary" (in that they follow a step-by-step, gradualist approach), "legalistic" (in that they pay lip service, at least, to the rule of law), and even "conservative" (in that they include social groups actively engaged in prior authoritarian rule rather than excluding, or even eliminating its representatives). In such circumstances, law is called upon to restrain arbitrariness and secure legitimate expectations, while at the same time being a central instrument for bringing about change.

Doubtless, in circumstances of great flux, institutions of justice have a great deal to do that is not everywhere done. They need to preserve continuity with frameworks of everyday life and law and often with elite arrangements (Roundtable Talks; see Elster 1996) which ushered in the new era, but at the same time, they need to demonstrate an ability to do justice to, and distinguish themselves from, often vicious past legacies. They need to legitimate their own activities, and lend legitimacy to often weak political institutions, which have precious few sources of legitimacy of their own. They need to settle uncertain expectations, while transforming both those expectations and the realities on which they are based.

Moreover, it can be argued not merely that postauthoritarian transitions pose distinctive *problems*, but that they consequently generate distinctive *institutional* innovations that occur in the process of doing transitional justice. Among these can be included the surprising and puzzlingly powerful role of what might be called quasi-judicial bodies (that is, bodies which in many respects look and behave like courts, some are even called courts, but are strictly speaking not conventional courts) in the period of transition. Some of these bodies deal with attempts to build constitutionalism, others are specifically designed to deal with problems of dealing with unsavory pasts. All go into the mix which characterizes the attempts to build the rule of law in societies long unfamiliar with it. Of course, there are important differences between such bodies, but it can be argued that they share common properties of crucial significance: namely, that they all manifest a pattern of practices and structures inspired by traditional courts, and yet in important ways produce non-traditional court outcomes (constitutional courts do not decide cases, truth commissions do not impose punishments, etc.).

The striking emergence of powerful constitutional courts (see Schwartz 2000; *East European Constitutional Review* 1997) on the one hand and various bodies designed specifically for "coping with past" on the other hand, is worth some reflection. And for all the differences between these two types of bodies, we perceive important similarities: in the selection procedures (usually, appointed by parliaments or presidents), relative independence from the executive branches, and quasi-judicial procedures. Most importantly, however, the common function of these bodies is to adjust both the normative structure of legality in transitional society, and public narratives of past and future, to new social expectations and values, without recourse to dramatic, revolutionary means. Constitutional courts do this by introducing major changes in the law through constitutional review which has the form of "interpreting" the constitution (albeit by conjuring with what in Hungary is called [by the Chief Justice] an "invisible constitution" [see Füzér 1996–97; Sajó 1996; Sós 1999]), rather than openly revising the law; on the other hand, bodies such as "truth commissions" (Asmal et al. 1996; Hayner 1995) and so-called lustration courts (Cohen 1995) perform this role by implementing new concepts, new standards of justice. On the one hand, they seek to assuage expectations of the public; on the other, they do so by applying procedural justice to a considerable extent. It remains an open and important question, however, how effectively, fairly, democratically, and in accordance with principles of legality, these novel institutions perform their distinctive tasks.

Fancy theories tend to applaud such bodies, considering them necessary to deal with tasks that are crucial for transition. The paradox of reconciling the revolutionary substance of the transition with the reformist-evolutionary-legalistic-conservative elements outlined above, it is said, created a demand for special institutional structures which would be able to respond to the need for substantial continuity and radical change at the same time. This, they say, is a task of special importance in the unusual but pervasive normative confusion and emptiness after the collapse of one system and the uncertain developments that follow. No political branches of the government (including parliamentary and executive bodies) can perform this legitimating role effectively, due to the generalized dissatisfaction in the societies concerned with politics and politicians. The combination of distrust in politics and a hunger for "justice" makes political branches particularly inadequate in overseeing processes of doing justice in the course of the transition. On the other hand, regular courts are unable to perform this task either, since in many of these countries the judiciary is discredited, often it has been poorly trained, and even when training is adequate it is cramped by the traditional view that courts are only to apply, rather than transform the law. In this vacuum, quasi-judicial bodies enter: bodies which look, behave, and act like courts (for example, in their selection process, adversary procedures, relative independence from the government of the day), but at the same time which have powers traditionally reserved for parliamentary bodies (lawmaking) and executive bodies or conventional courts (vindication of grievances related to the past regime). The hope is that these bodies will be more palatable to the society because they carry little of the stained baggage of traditional politico-legal institutions, and have greater room for maneuver, space for discretion, than regular courts. Yet they share the norm-fashioning role that courts do, and some of the prestige of an idealized vision of law, which has some popular resonance, even when particular legal institutions are not much used or liked. Simplists are unimpressed by these arguments. In the design of political institutions, we are not Robinson Crusoes. There are lessons to be learned from past successes and failures, and too much fancification will deny us their benefit.

This book is concerned to assess, and to draw some of the implications of, the legal developments of these last dozen or so years, specifically as they speak to issues of constitutionalism, dealing with the past, and the rule of law. In each of these areas, which are closely interlinked, there is no doubt that the tensions and novelties of which fancy theory speaks, exist. What their implications are is harder to settle. Fancy theories take them to render transitions *sui generis*. Simplists think that while we are all *sui generis* in one way or another, there are commonalities between us that should not be lost sight of, either. They worry that too much fancy talk will submerge some of the deep and abiding things we have in common: common predicaments, common threats, common capacities and vulnerabilities, and a limited range of possibilities, particularly in matters of institutional design.

Of course, tensions between simple and fancy do not exhaust the issues which these transformations raise, nor do they exhaust the matters discussed in this book. Wherever one comes down in that debate, to which this collection contributes several points of view, the end of communism has generated a quite new range of discussions of the three subjects which frame our contributions. This book is conceived of as an argumentative contribution to that debate, rather than a definitive answer to any of the questions that it raises.

The editors selected participants, among them some of the foremost contributors to the discussion of these themes, and brought them together for a workshop at the European University Institute in Florence, in February 2002. The workshop was intended to stir debate, and so it did. Participants were then asked to revise their contributions in the light of that debate, and each of the editors took primary responsibility for one of the three themes of the collection. In the contributors we invited, in the workshop, and in the editorial process, our concern has been to further debate in these areas. But not to conclude it. In that spirit, each of us has written a substantial introduction to the theme we are responsible for, seeking not merely to introduce the topic but to argue with some of the contributions that we have solicited. But rather than conclude, our volume finishes with Neil Walker's discussion of the new stage in legal transformation which has just begun: the enlargement of the European Union to include eight postcommunist states (we have edited a sequel to this volume, dealing with the impact of enlargement on democracy and the rule of law in new member states. Sadurski, Czarnota, Krygier (2005). Intriguing in its own right, that development reminds us that while there is more than enough to debate in the recent history of the postcommunist world, it is too early for conclusions.

The editors are grateful to the Australian Research Council, the Department of Law of the European University Institute in Florence, and the European Law Centre, University of New South Wales in Sydney for supporting this venture.

BIBLIOGRAPHY

Asmal, Kader, Louise Asmal, and Ronald S. Roberts. *Reconciliation through truth. A reckoning of apartheid's criminal governance.* Cape Town: David Phillip, 1996.

Cohen, Stanley. "Crimes of the State, Accountability, Lustration and the Policing of the Past." *Law and Social Inquiry* 20, no. 1 (Winter 1995): 7–50.

Dahrendorf, Ralf. *Reflections on the Revolution in Europe.* London: Chatto and Windus, 1990.

"Constitutional Courts on Trial." *East European Constitutional Review* 6, no. 1 (Winter 1997): 61–99.

Elster, Jon, ed. *The Roundtable Talks and the Breakdown of Communism.* Chicago: University of Chicago Press, 1994.

Elster, Jon, Claus Offe, and Ulrich K. Preuss. *Institutional Design in Post-Communist Societies: Rebuilding the Ship at Sea.* Cambridge: Cambridge University Press, 1998.

Füzér, Katalin. "The Invisible Constitution. The Construction of Constitutional Reality in Hungary." *International Journal of Sociology* 26, no. 4 (1996–97): 48–65.

Gellner, Ernest. *Conditions of Liberty. Civil Society and its Rivals.* London: Hamish Hamilton, 1994.

Hayner, Priscilla B. "15 Truth Commissions – 1974–1994. A Comparative Study." *Human Rights Quarterly* 16, no. 4 (1994): 597–655.

Holmes, Stephen. "Cultural Legacies or State Collapse? Probing the Postcommunist Dilemma." Paper presented at Collegium Budapest, Institute for Advanced Study, Public Lecture No. 13, November 1995.

Jowitt, Kenneth. *New World Disorder: The Leninist Extinction.* Berkeley: University of California Press, 1992.

Krygier, Martin. "Institutional Optimism, Cultural Pessimism and the Rule of Law." In *The Rule of Law after Communism,* eds. Krygier, Martin and Adam Czarnota. Aldershot: Ashgate, 1999, 77–105.

Sadurski, Wojciech, Czarnota, Adam, and Krygier, Martin, eds. *Spreading Democracy and the Rule of Law? Implications of EU Enlargament for the Rule of Law, Democracy and Constitutionalism in Post-communist Legal Orders,* Berlin: Springer, 2005.

Sajó, András. "How the Rule of Law Killed Hungarian Welfare Reform." *East European Constitutional Review* 5, no. 1 (1996): 31–41.

Schwartz, Herman. *The Struggle for Constitutional Justice in Post-Communist Europe.* Chicago: The University of Chicago Press, 2000.

Sós, Vilmos. "The Paradigm of Constitutionalism. The Hungarian Experience." In *The Rule of Law after Communism,* eds. Krygier, Martin and Adam Czarnota. Aldershot: Ashgate, 1999, 131–48.

Teitel, Ruti. "Transitional Jurisprudence: The Role of Law in Political Transformation." *Yale Law Journal* 106 (1997): 2009–80.

PART ONE
Constitutionalism

Transitional Constitutionalism: Simplistic and Fancy Theories

WOJCIECH SADURSKI

"Transitional constitutionalism" theories come in two main versions: simplistic and fancy. Simplistic theories rely on an intuitive notion that the transition is an intermediary stage between points A and B, where A is the old, sham, communist constitutionalism, with constitutions not really worth the paper they were written on. What constitutes B in this picture is a matter of some controversy, but at least in the eyes of a great majority of constitutional writers and actors in Central and Eastern Europe (CEE), it is identified with Western, liberal-democratic, "actually existing" constitutionalism. Whether the latter is itself a contingent, changing, and contested model, it is something that falls outside the scope of a transitional theory in this first, "simplistic" version. And this slight doubt does not undermine the basic contrast with the second type of theories, the fancy ones, which may be dubbed "exceptionalist" or *sui generis* theories. Their claim is that postcommunist constitutionalism is "transitional," but not in the sense of being an interim space between the two reasonably identifiable points of departure and arrival. Rather, this type has some characteristics of its own which do not collapse into the exigencies of passage from A to B. The transition from communism to whatever-will-follow has characteristics of its own, and cannot be simply measured by the distance already traveled from "really existing socialism" towards one of the forms of mature, liberal-democratic constitutionalism which is discernible in the modern world.

At first blush, there are certainly some good reasons to opt for the former, "simplistic" theory, in which "consolidated" democracies as we know them today serve as a benchmark for judging how far this "transition" has advanced. This, after all, is the intuitive, conventional meaning of "transition": as a phase stretching between the point of departure and the point of arrival. More importantly, this is what the main players in the "transitional" countries overwhelmingly tell us: the discourse of "normalcy" ("no experiments; we want to build a normal country, a normal economy, a normal constitutional rule-of-law") hinges upon the actual standards of real Western states and societies (see, for example, Krygier 1989–90). When people in the CEE countries tell their foreign interlocutors that they want to attain a normal state of affairs, by "normal" they invariably mean a situation corresponding to the (real or imagined) state of affairs in Western Europe or North America.

This, incidentally, illustrates a strange clash of perceptions and ideals between those from within and those from outside: while Western students of transitionalism are skeptical about the idea of borrowing, transplanting, and following Western models, this is usually precisely what the "insiders" want: there is an understandable wariness about pursuing models which have not been successfully tried elsewhere. This, of course, is not to say that these self-perceptions should be taken at face value, and should escape critical scrutiny: they may well be an instance of false consciousness arising when something new and unprecedented is seen, and presented, as merely following an established pattern. Indeed, Claus Offe in his essay on designing institutions for Eastern European transitions identified a characteristic phenomenon, whereby the activity of designing new institutions was deliberately presented as merely an imitation of some successful models (Offe 1996: 213). Such rhetoric may perform certain useful functions, and certainly may help the reformers in having their agenda accepted if it is perceived as merely following well established, successful models from elsewhere. But this perception is not irrelevant, and the voices "from there" should be taken seriously.

This is especially the case regarding the specific topic under consideration in this part of our collection of articles, since the CEE constitutional courts themselves—the central institutions discussed here—have occasionally resisted appeals to "exceptionalism" and adopted the language of "normalcy." As an example, consider an important decision of the Hungarian Constitutional Court of December 1994, which declared the Lustration Law (the law regarding the vetting of political figures) unconstitutional. In its reasoning, the Court relied partly on an argument that a successful transition to a democratic system had *actually occurred* without any need to change the personnel through a lustration process; the upshot was that the alleged purpose of the challenged law (namely, to secure a successful transition) could not apply. The principles to be applied to assess the lustration provisions had therefore to be those applicable to a democratic state based on the principle of the rule of law. The Court drew a clear contrast between the past and the present, separated as they are by "the transition as a historical fact." It made clear that the lawfulness of the Lustration Law should be judged not by reference to the unusual circumstances of transition, but rather by balancing the rights and interests at issue.

In addition, the study of the constitutional texts of CEE suggests that there has been remarkably little experimentation in constitutional design, and that the aim of constitution-makers was to follow the established patterns of Western European constitutionalism. This, of course, is not an argument in favor of a "simplistic" theory of transitional constitutionalism in itself, but at least it suggests that, in the minds of the main constitutional actors in the region, what mattered most was to move to the stage in which their constitutional texts were as similar as possible to those which have been adopted on the

Western side of the continent. Thus the transition consisted of moving to something safe because of its familiarity. In her path-breaking book, Ruti Teitel observes, with regard to transitional constitutionalism (not limited to CEE, of course), a characteristic pattern of adopting new constitutions in two rounds: first, a "disentrenching" constitution, and only then, a less flexible, more stable constitution which would strongly entrench the new norms (Teitel 2000: 191–211). It is significant that this path has *not* been, by and large, followed in CEE. With the exceptions of Poland (with its "Little Constitution" preceding the new one) and possibly Hungary (where the "new" constitution consisted of a patchwork of amendments to the old one), as well as the "restoration constitutions" (as in Lithuania and Latvia, where the point of the first postcommunist constitution was not so much to "disentrench" the old one, but to reassert national sovereignty by adopting, even if for a short time, an another precommunist constitution), CEE constitutionalism proceeded in one step: by adopting a brand new, "non-transitional" constitution relatively soon after the change of system. So in this way, at least, the "exceptionalist" version of transitional constitutionalism has not been vindicated.

There is, finally, another reason why one *might* be reluctant to adopt a *sui generis*, rather than a "simplistic" version of transitional constitutional theory. There is a danger of political relativism, or of a patronizing attitude, in treating the postcommunist transition as not aiming at Western-style democratic goals. No one would, of course, say it in so many words, and undoubtedly such a motive is very far from the actual intentions of those who write about post-communist transitions. But if many of the "insiders" in CEE are irritated by a tendency to adopt a *sui generis* paradigm, it is because they are usually allergic to the sort of relativizing approach which implies that CEE societies are as yet not ripe for democracy. As an example of such an arguably patronizing attitude, consider the views of John Gray, who believes that democratic institutions are not well suited to post-communist societies, and that— at least to many of them, including Russia—"authoritarian political institutions, buttressed by indigenous cultural traditions, seem to offer the best matrix for the emergent civil society" (Gray 1993: 46). Gray's prescription is largely based on his diagnosis that a decisive role in shaping the political life in these societies is played by precommunist traditions which are "hardly those of Western liberal democracy" (Gray 1993: 27). But even apart from the accuracy of such a diagnosis (the testing of which would be beyond the purposes of this introduction), the most worrying aspect of it to Central and Eastern Europeans is that the prescription of authoritarianism which is based on that diagnosis becomes a self-fulfilling prophecy if the policies of the West are shaped by it.

In spite of all that has been said so far, it is clear to everyone who knows the literature on the subject—or even only reads the chapters that follow— that "simplistic" theories of transitional constitutionalism are in disrepute, and that a great majority of writers reject the idea that the development of postcommunist constitutions follows a knowable and determinate trajectory modeled on the Western experience. Most scholars in the field adopt more intellectually ambitious paradigms, which move beyond applying some known templates to postcommunist experience, and, in consequence, invite us to suspend our usual intuitions and convictions (based on Western standards) regarding constitutional democracy.

Within this, as we might now call it generically, exceptionalist paradigm, one can further distinguish between weak and strong versions of exceptionalism. "Weak exceptionalism" declares that the position of postcommunist states is tainted by certain special conditions which render the usual democratic standards inapplicable or only partially applicable: certain crucial factors which are essential to the success of constitutional democracy in the West are missing in CEE. In that sense, weak exceptionalism may be seen as a case of the adoption of a theory of the second-best, which is oriented to identifying the optimal solution when not all the conditions required for the first-best solution are present. As the theory suggests, in such circumstances the next best solution may not be to approximate the first best solution, but rather to design institutions in a way which significantly deviates from such an ideal. It may be regrettable that, for instance, in CEE postcommunist conditions certain factors which contributed to the success of Western democracy are missing, but as the situation is reasonably stable, there is no point in characterizing the success of those newly emerging democracies in terms of the distance that separates them from the more "mature" ones.

In contrast, "strong" versions of exceptionalism abstain from the rhetoric of regret discernible in weak exceptionalism: there is nothing particular to deplore about it; moreover, there may be some important lessons to be drawn from the postcommunist experience that may even be helpful to those in the West. Certain aspects of such strong exceptionalism can be discerned, I believe, in the rich and fascinating essay by Kim Lane Scheppele included in this volume, and are best encapsulated by her assertion that "democracy by judiciary [which has appeared in transitional politics] may be an option that more deeply entrenched democracies may want to consider as well." I do not propose to even begin summarizing the story told by Scheppele, centered as it is around the exciting first decade of the experience of the Hungarian Constitutional Court of which Scheppele is the leading expert and—she probably would not object to such a characterization—enthusiast. All I wish to emphasize at this point is the way in which Scheppele opposes recent postcommunist experience to what she calls the "standard democratic story" based on a purely procedural conception of democracy. The postcommunist experience was based on ideas that, as Scheppele puts it, were "democratic in their own way," and can teach us (as I take Scheppele to imply) that democracy is as much (or perhaps more) a matter of substance as of form, and that democracy is not real until the substance of policies change. Hence, the Hungarian (or, more generally, postcommunist) lesson for all of us is that we should be skeptical of the idea that institutions are democratic in substance as long as they are democratic in form. This, at least, is the case of where there is a transition to democracy in progress: it is not enough to design (and then build) procedurally democratic institutions—it is also important to see to it that they dispense substantively democratic policies.

However, one should be careful not to exaggerate (and I am *not* implying that Scheppele does) the difference between the procedural and the substantive when referring to the claims for democracy made by the inhabitants of the CEE countries. One reading of Scheppele's story which should be resisted is that what was truly wrong with the communist institutions was the substance of the policy-making, while the procedures and the design of institutions were superficially acceptable. They were not, and the frustration and protest of democratic opposition groups were directed both against the policies of the ruling elites and against the deceitful, pseudo-democratic institutions and procedures which dispensed them. When Scheppele says that "the new post-Soviet citizens would not believe that a democracy was real until the substance of previous policies has changed"[1] then she may be misunderstood as advancing a view that the procedures and institutions were not deeply problematic in the eyes of the population. But those procedures, built upon a one-party state (or a dominant-party-plus-satellites state), such as the total centralization of political decisions, uncontested "elections," the absence of press freedom, and state-sanctioned violence and intimidation, did not amount to some pale version of democracy which needed merely to be supplemented with the right "substance": it was a sham democracy, the most laughable elements of which were the "parliaments."

All this may sound obvious, but it is important to spell it out explicitly because the substance/procedure distinction is directly related to the central issue in Scheppele's paper and indeed in all the chapters in this part of the book, namely the role of constitutional courts in the democratic system of postcommunist states. If one adopts a "strong" version of exceptionalism, and draws a conclusion from the postcommunist experience about the primacy of substance over procedure in democratic theory, at least as it is applicable to these countries, then one need not feel any particular compunction about elevating the constitutional courts to the role that they have attained in Hungary, and also in Poland, Slovenia, the Czech Republic, etc. "A democracy run by the [constitutional] court," to use Scheppele's expression, carries in such a case no ironic connotation and is perfectly reconcilable with our notions of democracy—as long, that is, as we substantially approve of the court's decisions, even if (and perhaps, *especially* if) they displace the choices of "procedurally" democratic parliaments. But this is only by virtue of a substantive conception of democracy, where the criteria of substance prevail over those of procedure in judging a system democratic. The democratic (or otherwise) pedigree of a given institution is then of no importance, and we can end up with a system of enlightened absolutism if the non-democratic institution dispenses policies which we favor. But this, let me repeat, would be based on an exclusively substance-based (and, as I have argued, counter-intuitive) notion of democracy. I do not think that such a notion is transmitted to us by the CEE experience.

More often than not, however, "exceptionalist" theories come in "weak" versions, and the essays which follow in this part of the book are no exception. The unusually powerful position of constitutional courts in postcommunist countries is explained (and often justified) by reference to certain specific social and political pathologies (from the point of view of standard democratic theory) prevailing in the postcommunist societies. As a result of these characteristics, we should suspend our usual intuitions (which would normally apply to consolidated democracies) about the proper role of judicial bodies *vis-à-vis* legislatures. These pathologies trigger "second-best" theories of proper institutional design. Both Kim Lane Scheppele and Cindy Skach provide in their chapters remarkably lucid analyses of the weaknesses of social organization, both in terms of "civil society" in general and of party political systems in particular, aimed at explaining why our usual templates, formed in more consolidated democracies, do not apply.

It is in this context that Cindy Skach remarks that the familiar (familiar, that is, to U.S. constitutional scholars) notion of a counter-majoritarian difficulty does not apply to "non-consolidated" states because it presupposes both a strong institutionalized party system and a strong civil society, the two factors largely missing from the socio-political landscapes of CEE. It is interesting to inquire into the status of this argument.[2] Offhand, the fact that in *some* social settings a system of robust judicial review raises the issue of whether the judicial body suffers from a democracy deficit, does not necessarily dispense with the legitimacy problem in *different* contexts, even if the presuppositions for the counter-majoritarian difficulty do not obtain there. For example, we can assert, with Skach, that postcommunist parliaments have a weak claim to legitimacy in representing the majority, but this does not necessarily mean that the claims to legitimacy of constitutional courts are any stronger. Indeed, one could assert that, *precisely in the period of transition*, constitutional courts have even less legitimacy to take important policy decisions than in a more stable system. As Andrew Arato noted some time ago with regard to the Hungarian Constitutional Court: "[J]udicial review does raise problems from the point of view of democratic legitimacy in a normally functioning liberal democracy. These problems, moreover, are inevitably exacerbated by the unavoidable activism in the context defined by *the weak democratic legitimacy of the constitutional document*" (Arato 1994: 274).[3]

So Skach's argument can be better read not so much as about legitimacy as about the value of the outcome: that the constitutional court's activism is conducive to the consolidation of democracy. To use Neil Walker's distinction between "performance legitimacy" (or output legitimacy) and "regime legitimacy,"[4] this is an argument about the former type of legitimacy, understood as the capacity to deliver the goods rather than as a just institutional arrangement in accordance with the criteria of fair representation, appropriate protection of individual and minority interests, etc. To be sure, Walker claims that these two types of legitimacy are closely linked "in the sense that the very institutional matrix whose justness in design and operation is the measure of regime legitimacy is also an important variable in the nurturing of a policy-making environment conducive to the development of 'good' policies and in the effective implementation of those policies which are developed."[5] But this connection seems to be only contingent rather than necessary, and it seems in reality to be less strong than Walker implies. Now going back to Skach's argument, the distinction between regime- and outcome-legitimacy is important because much of the evidence which she supplies is related to the latter, while the general aspiration of the argument (as I read it) is to make a point about the former.

She bridges the gap between the two by viewing judicial review as a response to the failures of democracy—failures which undermine the legitimacy of parliaments. This carries clear analogies with John Hart Ely's theory of judicial review—to which Skach herself expressly alludes. Cindy Skach identifies two such functions of correcting democracy failures in non-consolidated democracies: the function of agenda setting (the "focusing" function) and the "party-building" function. This seems like a very promising theory for supplying the democracy-based grounds for constitutional courts' legitimacy: the task is therefore to examine whether it has actually been vindicated by the practice of these courts in CEE. Their record in these two respects is mixed, to say the least: for various institutional and political reasons, constitutional courts have been largely reactive rather than agenda-setting. They have (with very few exceptions) no powers of self-activation and the moral authority of the judges is often quite moderate, and they have been subject to rather strong and effective pressures by political branches; hence their disabilities in performing the agenda-setting function. When it comes to party-related issues (such as campaign and party financing), the role of the courts has been relatively insignificant so far.

An intriguing case for a "weak exceptionalist" theory of transitional constitutionalism is provided by Kim Lane Scheppele, who argues that the function of the Hungarian Constitutional Court can be easily reconciled with representative democracy because a function of the Court has been to compel the governments to live up to their electoral promises. A constitutional court as an executioner of the voters' actual will against the recalcitrant parliaments and governments—this sounds like an attractive justification for "a democracy run by a court." If indeed it is the case that "what voters voted for was not what they got,"[6] then having an umpire reminding the government about what it was that the voters wanted may be a good democratic idea. The question remains as to whether this justification may be universalized. To test it, one would have to look at the most significant decisions of the courts throughout the region in which the will of parliaments of the time has been displaced, and see whether it was the court rather than the parliament (and the government) who acted in accordance with the voters' wishes as expressed in the directly preceding elections. Scheppele provides some compelling evidence from Hungary (with the Court's overturning the "Bokros package" as the centerpiece of her argument)—but how generalizable is it? Naturally, I cannot undertake such a test here but some powerful counter-examples may be provided, drawing on the cases where the decisions of constitutional courts overturned laws or policies which had been previously approved by the voters. Perhaps the Polish abortion decision of May 1997 is one of the most striking examples of a court invalidating an immensely important law, which clearly enjoyed the support of the voters who had placed the legislative majority in the parliament in the elections which directly preceded the decision.[7] The passage of a liberal abortion law by the center-left majority in 1996 was in accordance with, rather than against, the wishes of the clear majority of the voters. Whatever rationale could be provided for the court's invalidation of this law nine months later, the one which is *not* available claims that the court intervened because "what voters voted for was not what they got." And one can come up with a number of other cases in the region when governments did exactly what they promised they would do, and constitutional courts overturned these policies.

Therefore, perhaps it is better to look at the "output legitimacy" aspect of the constitutional courts' record, as far as their contribution to the consolidation of democracy is concerned. Overall, their record has been—in my opinion—rather mixed, and one should avoid both unrestrained enthusiasm and radical criticism of the courts. They have, by and large, contributed to (what one of our authors, Vello Pettai calls) "democratic norm building"[8] in the process of democratic consolidation, though this contribution has been largely confined to relatively marginal matters (from the point of view of democratic consolidation). It has been partly offset by certain negative consequences of placing the constitutional review mechanism in such a prominent place in the institutional system of postcommunist states. Vello Pettai helpfully cites a number of decisions of the constitutional court from his case-study country (Estonia). In those decisions, the court usefully clarified and fine-tuned the relationship between the president and the parliament, and between the parliament and the government, thus avoiding unnecessary frictions and enabling the system to operate according to the democratic rules of the game. Also, other constitutional courts of the region have made some important contributions to the fine-tuning of the separation of powers although one should be careful to distinguish between "fine-tuning" and "improving." Arguably, some of the postcommunist courts' interventions have made the imbalance between the legislature and the executive even worse (from the point of view of the legislature). As a student of Ukrainian constitutional developments Kataryna Wolczuk notes:

> [W]hile the Presidency was the main initiator of rulings affecting the Parliament (the Supreme Council), the [Constitutional] Court became an instrument through which acts of Parliament were challenged by *ad hoc* Parliamentary minorities… Because of the relative ease with which a group of deputies (often instigated by the executive) could mount a challenge in the Court to a Parliament's decision, and because of the final nature of the Court's decision, referring cases to the Court turned out to be a more expedient way of invalidating a piece of legislation than the orchestrating of Parliamentary campaigns. The cumulative effect of those factors was that while claiming to uphold the separation of powers, the Court became instrumental in eroding legislative power and shifting it to the executive. (Wolczuk 2002: 328)

It has to be conceded, however, that these courts have *sometimes* made important and positive interventions in the operation of the political system. While not specifically in the separation-of-powers area, these decisions have prevented certain political actors from exploiting their position of strength in order to marginalize—or even eliminate from the political scene altogether—more vulnerable actors.

Perhaps the most impressive example of such an intervention by the court is provided by Venelin Ganev in his chapter. The April 1992 decision by the Bulgarian Constitutional Court, in effect, rescued the right of the Turkish-based Movement of Rights and Freedoms (MRF) party to be represented in Parliament, notwithstanding the express constitutional ban on political parties based on national or ethnic grounds. The case (the outcome of which Ganev understandably applauds) is read by him as an example of a "jurisprudence of foxes": that is, a decision which carves out exceptional reasons for departing from the constitutional text. But perhaps a different reading can be provided for the decision, one which does not contain the dangers of *ad hoc* exceptions: this alternative reading suggests that the court engaged in a very ingenious, creative reading of the constitutional text in order to reconcile it with democratic principles. The court reinterpreted the constitutional ban on ethnically based parties as a ban on parties which formally excluded some members on the basis of their ethnic origin, and as the MRF did not contain such exclusions, it was found not to be covered by the constitutional prohibition. Be that as it may, the court acted courageously on the basis of what may be seen as an unstated principle of protecting minority representation within a system of representative democracy—regardless of an outrageous constitutional limitation of such representation.

This particular decision could, of course, be used as powerful evidence for the argument that Cindy Skach develops in the second part of her chapter, namely, that in transitional societies, constitutional courts are crucial elements in shaping the "toleration regimes." But this is just one piece of evidence, and the evidentiary materials on which she relies in her chapter, are drawn from the case of Bosnia and Herzegovina. This is arguably far from being a typical state: in fact it is so exceptional (being the only "consociation" among the postcommunist states; with the constitution *octroyée* by an international community; and with a deliberately internationalized constitutional court) that one would like to support the general proposition with some extra evidence garnered from other postcommunist courts. Alas, the evidence to show that those courts have been importantly instrumental in cementing the "toleration regimes" in those states, particularly those plagued by strong ethnic or religious divisions, is not very easy to come by. Apart from the shining exception of the Bulgarian MRF case, there have been virtually no significant decisions by constitutional courts in CEE along similar lines. In fact, there have been rather few decisions dealing with ethnic/national problems, even in the places where one would expect them. A natural place to look for such cases would be the Baltic states (in particular, Estonia and Latvia, with their large Russian-speaking minorities) but there, constitutional courts have played very little role in imposing a regime which would accommodate the Russians. The case of Estonia, as described in detail in Vello Pettai's paper, is quite instructive in this regard. As Pettai shows, the Constitutional Review Chamber (CRC) was very timid in tackling the Language Act, and fundamentally avoided any principled appeal to minority rights in dealing with the constitutionality of the provisions which arguably discriminated against the Russian minority. The CRC struck down the provisions of the law on the basis of technicalities; the Parliament easily re-enacted the law free of technical defects, and it was only international pressure which subsequently compelled the Parliament to amend the law.

In other postcommunist countries, very few ethnicity-related decisions have been made by constitutional courts, and where they have, they would hardly support the thesis that those courts play a central role in shaping a regime of toleration. For instance, in Romania in 1995, UDMR (the Hungarian minority party), along with some other opposition parties, attempted to introduce into the draft law on education a provision granting a right of the Hungarian minority to have a Hungarian-language state university. They did not succeed in the legislative process, and challenged the bill before the Constitutional Court in an *ex ante* review procedure, but the challenge failed. (Of course one may suggest that it was due to the general weakness of the Romanian Constitutional Court, and that a stronger court would have taken on the legislature more aggressively, but it is an unverifiable speculation). As another example, one could mention a decision of the Ukrainian Constitutional Court of December 1999, in which the court strengthened the constitutional place of the Ukrainian language in Ukraine, and established an affirmative duty on all public bodies to use only Ukrainian throughout the country (even though in the Eastern and Southern regions the Russian language is widely used both in private and public contexts).

Of course, the ethnic/national dimension is not the only aspect of difference; the religious is another. But again, constitutional courts in CEE have not been, by and large, active fighters for religious tolerance based on the separation of state and religion. In the country in which the churches (or one should say, *the* Church) are the strongest, Poland, the Constitutional Tribunal has been anything but a champion for accommodating difference, and time after time it has caved in to the Catholic Church's pressure. Invalidating crucial provisions of the (relatively liberal) Abortion Law (a case referred to above); upholding the introduction, by ministerial decree, of religious teaching in public schools; upholding the ban, in the Broadcast Law, on expressions offensive to Christian values—all these decisions were seen, rightly, as establishing a privileged position for Roman Catholic faith, and amounting to discrimination against other religions or non-believers.

This is not to say that the constitutional courts have not made positive contributions in the shaping of the accommodation of difference, but rather that the conception of the role of these courts, as outlined by Skach, is perhaps more of a program for the future than a description of the past and the present. The positive potential of these courts has to be compared to the negative consequences of elevating them to such a prominent role in the political system. For one thing, there is a very real danger of producing pathologies in the incentive structures for the other political actors: when the legislative process is "in the shadow of judicial review," there is a high likelihood that legislative irresponsibility will result. Kim Lane Scheppele herself gives an example of one particular provision of the Bokros package which raises the suspicion "that the Parliament... very much wanted the Constitutional Court to strike down this law."[9] This, in Scheppele's narrative, is an isolated and non-typical episode but, in my own reading of the story of judicial review after the fall of communism, it points to a much more serious threat to the integrity of legislative process than many enthusiasts of constitutional judicial review are willing to concede:[10] namely, the generation of legislative irresponsibility. This occurs when the very awareness of possible review makes legislators less attentive to constitutional rights, with the possible result that a sub-optimal law will never be invalidated. Another negative consequence could be legislative apathy in the implementation of constitutional rights (along the lines: "if something is wrong, the court will remind us of it"). The very existence of judicial review can also have a negative educational effect; it may help to generate the perception that the rights discourse is an obscure activity reserved for lawyers, and that deliberation about the political values that give rise to specific articulations of rights is something over which neither the population nor its elected representatives have any control. As Ronald Dworkin (himself, of course, a leading proponent of robust judicial constitutional review) puts it, "[t]here is little chance of a useful national debate over constitutional principle when constitutional decisions are considered technical exercises in an arcane and conceptual craft" (Dworkin 1996: 31).

> This last point indicates that, contrary to conventional views, a robust constitutional review mechanism may be harmful to, rather than supportive of, the values of constitutionalism. If by "constitutionalism" one understands a state of affairs in which the rules and values entrenched in a constitutional text penetrate public discourse and public practice, that is, when the fact that a particular rule is constitutionally recognized weighs heavily upon the arguments and motivations of political actors (including the citizens when they act in public roles: as voters, members of political parties, etc.) then, ironically perhaps, strong constitutional review conducted by judges may restrict, rather than broaden constitutionalism so understood. This is because there is an understanding emerging that a broad range of issues are decided on "legal" (constitutional) grounds, with qualified lawyers having a privileged understanding of the "true" meaning of those grounds, because "legal craftsmanship is essential to decode the meaning" of the constitution.[11] When, to take an extreme example, the legal permissibility of abortion is decided by a contest of different legal understandings of the concept of *Rechtsstaat* (as was the case in Poland), rather than by public debate about what the constitutional values of life, privacy, non-discrimination, dignity, etc. dictate, then obviously the incentives for the general public to argue in constitutional terms are eroded. Constitutional arguments are then seen as an external constraint upon public discourse (a constraint policed by constitutional experts sitting on the constitutional court) rather than as an integral part of that discourse.

The general public and its representative, the parliament, are then socialized into the rules of the division of labor in which they are expected to argue in terms of their interests and preferences while the court looks after constitutional standards. The correlative implication is that these other political actors—and the general public—are relieved of a duty to takme constitutional concerns into account, and even if they occasionally do, they may be proved mistaken by a small body composed of constitutional experts. This is a fiasco, rather than a triumph of the ideal of constitutionalism.

Whether, and to what degree, this somewhat catastrophic prophecy will follow the operation of a system of judicial review is, obviously, a context-sensitive matter, and will depend on a great number of specific political, institutional, cultural and other variables which differ from country to country. From this point of view, a detailed discussion of one particular system of constitutional review, that of Estonia supplied in the chapter by Pettai, is very instructive, especially when contrasted with a system which in many respects is diametrically different, namely that of Hungary as described in the chapter by Scheppele. To many observers, the powers of the Estonian CRC will look disappointingly weak when compared to the Hungarian Constitutional Court. However, when viewed from the perspective of the impact of judicial review upon the ideal of constitutionalism, they may display some important institutional precautions against the establishment of "democracy by judiciary." As the description provided by Pettai shows, the dangers of policy distortions brought about by judicial review[12] are minimized by a number of institutional devices, which result in a "very narrow constitutional review mechanism." Perhaps the most important of these is the narrow list of agents authorized to initiate constitutional review: when there is no possibility for a group of members of parliament to challenge the law, there is no opportunity for a legislative alliance to be formed between the constitutional court and the parliamentary opposition. Other important institutional factors which need to be considered include whether there is a power of self-activation by the constitutional court, whether there is a power to find constitutional omissions, whether there is an *ex ante* review of bills before their final adoption by the parliament, etc.

Of course, formal institutional design is only one among a number of important variables; differences in prevailing judicial doctrines and recognized styles of judicial reasoning are equally, if not more, important. From this point of view, the identification of two opposite styles of judicial reasoning: a "jurisprudence of hedgehogs" and a "jurisprudence of foxes" in the chapter by Venelin Ganev is extremely interesting. As Ganev sees it, the "constitutional jurisprudence of hedgehogs" consists of an attempt by the judges of a constitutional court to articulate a unitary vision of a single hierarchy of values which rests upon a coherent set of principles. One possible danger of such a style of judicial reasoning, which Ganev identifies, is that this may bind the courts too strongly in the future, in the "post-founding" period. However, one should perhaps observe that, in the context of the general reluctance of European constitutional courts to rely upon their own precedent and upon the doctrine of *stare decisis*, this danger is somewhat minimized. Apart from this, one needs to be careful not to blend together two forms of principled judicial decision-making: the "jurisprudence of hedgehogs" (to use the Berlin-inspired terminology of Ganev's chapter), which may often be a laudable attempt to bring about a degree of doctrinal coherence by appeal to general principles on the one hand, and constitutional hubris which is exemplified by (what Ganev calls) "normative overshooting." This is characterized by an appeal to more general and vague notions, when an appeal to more specific constitutional rules would be perfectly sufficient. The former ("jurisprudence of hedgehogs") does not seem to be deplorable *per se*; it is the latter ("normative overshooting") which reveals the excesses of judicial activism and leads to the replacement of the legislative will by the preferences of the court's majority.

Perhaps the most extreme case of such constitutional hubris is the Hungarian Court's idea of an "invisible constitution."[13] The Court used this idea to legitimize its displacement of parliamentary choices, alluding to respect for paramount values drawn from an ideal, as opposed to the textual, Constitution. Obviously, such values may only be identified by those with the requisite specialized knowledge. This "normative overshooting" consists of invoking the most general available principles even when some more specific rules would do the job. An example comes from a 1990 decision in which the Hungarian Constitutional Court proscribed trade unions from representing employees without their consent.[14] In its argument, the Court relied on the concept of "human dignity," when in fact it could have easily held that the specific constitutional clauses dealing with the rights of unions "to safeguard and represent the interest of employees," only authorize representation with consent. Such "normative overshooting" is dangerous, because the more general and vague the constitutional ground for review is, the more controversial is the subsumption of a given decision within the scope of this constitutional principle, and therefore the wider the scope for the Court to disguise its own preferences as the application of an "objective" constitutional rule.

The concern that Ganev expresses with regard to the "jurisprudence of hedgehogs" is connected with the passage from the "founding" to a "non-founding" period in the process of development of the legal systems discussed here. The fear is that the habits, styles of reasoning and discourses, which were understandably developed in an extraordinary "founding" stage, will weigh heavily upon, and become detrimental to, the period of "normalcy." This is linked with a broader concern which I have with regard to exceptionalist theories of transitional constitutionalism: that they have the potential to become self-perpetuating truths. By acting upon them we may actually postpone the advent of "normalcy," and prolong the suspension of our usual intuitions regarding the principles of the separation of powers and democratic legitimacy, such as those encapsulated in the quotation from Robert Dahl, recalled by Cindy Skach: "a system in which the policy preferences of minorities prevail over majorities is at odds with the traditional criteria for distinguishing a democracy from other political systems" (Dahl 1957: 283). Suppose we agree that objective social and political factors weaken the argument for parliamentary supremacy in transitional democracies because of a weak civil society and because of a weak party political system—two factors among a number of conditions which render the arguments for parliamentary supremacy meaningful. By acting on this diagnosis, we contribute to the perpetuation of this state of affairs, by further disabling the parliaments, and by entrenching a strong role of constitutional courts. By doing this, we institutionalize those very conditions which led us to doubt the role and legitimacy of parliaments in the first place.

This, in its extreme, may be seen as entrenching the idea of a constitutional court as an enlightened ruler, and of the people as not mature enough to rule themselves. If, as the exceptionalist theories suggest, the outcomes of elections in postcommunist states do not mean all that much because democracy is associated by the citizens more with a substantive change of policies than with procedural and institutional changes,[15] then indeed we might as well settle for the legislative dominance of an unelected body which we know will confer on us better laws and better policies than the parliament. If, as the exceptionalist theories imply, the legislative majority does not represent adequately any significant majority of the electorate, because of extreme party polarization and/or the weakness of civil society,[16] then indeed why should we take the legislative majority seriously?

The attitudes and habits formed by such conclusions cannot but have a further disabling, demoralizing impact upon the capacities, sense of responsibility, and seriousness of voters and parliaments alike.

NOTES

1 Scheppele, this volume.

2 Skach, this volume.

3 Emphasis as in original.

4 Walker, this volume.

5 Ibid.

6 Scheppele, this volume.

7 Decision K 26/96 of 28 May 1997 of the Polish Constitutional Tribunal, striking down certain key provisions of the statute of 30 August 1996 on family planning, protection of the fetus, and the conditions of termination of pregnancy.

8 Pettai, this volume.
9 Scheppele, this volume.
10 This danger figures nowhere in the best book-length description of postcommunist judicial review so far, namely Schwartz 2000.
11 The words in quotation marks are from Eisgruber 2001: 1. They do not represent Eisgruber's conception of the grounds of judicial review, but the one which he opposes.
12 For an analysis of policy distortions caused by judicial review, see Tushnet 1999: 57–70.
13 The concept of "invisible constitution" was coined by the (then) Chief Justice of the Hungarian Court, László Sólyom, see Sólyom and Brunner 2000: 41.
14 Quoted in Halmai 1994: 116.
15 See Scheppele, this volume.
16 See Skach, this volume.

BIBLIOGRAPHY

Arato, Andrew. "Constitution and Continuity in the Eastern European Transitions: The Hungarian Case (Part Two)" in *Constitutionalism and Politics*, ed. Grudzińska-Gross, Irena (Bratislava: Slovak Committee of the European Cultural Foundation, 1994), pp. 271–88.
Dahl, Robert A. "Decision-Making in a Democracy: The Supreme Court as a National Policy-Maker." *Journal of Public Law* 6 (1957): 279–95.
Dworkin, Ronald. *Freedom's Law*. Oxford: Oxford University Press, 1996.
Eisgruber, Christopher L. *Constitutional Self-Government*. Cambridge, Mass.: Harvard University Press, 2001.
Gray, John. "From Post-Communism to Civil Society: The Reemergence of History and the Decline of the Western Model." *Social Philosophy and Policy* 10 (1993): 26–50.
Halmai, Gábor. "Comment: The Constitutional Court of the Republic of Hungary." *East European Case Reporter of Constitutional Law* 1 (1994): 116–18.
Krygier, Martin. "Poland: Life in an Abnormal Country." *The National Interest* 18 (1989–90): 55–64.
Offe, Claus. "Designing Institutions in East European Transitions" in *The Theory of Institutional Design,* ed. Goodin, Robert E. (Cambridge: Cambridge University Press, 1996), pp. 199–226.
Schwartz, Herman. *The Struggle for Constitutional Justice in Post-Communist Europe.* Chicago: University of Chicago Press, 2000.
Sólyom, László and Georg Brunner. *Constitutional Judiciary in a New Democracy*. Ann Arbor: The University of Michigan Press, 2000.
Teitel, Ruti. *Transitional Justice*. New York: Oxford University Press, 2000.
Tushnet, Mark. *Taking the Constitution Away from the Courts*. Princeton: Princeton University Press, 1999.
Wolczuk, Kataryna. "The Constitutional Court of Ukraine: The Politics of Survival" in *Constitutional Justice: East and West*, ed. Sadurski, Wojciech (The Hague: Kluwer Law International, 2002), pp. 327–48.

Democracy by Judiciary.
Or, why Courts Can be More Democratic than Parliaments

KIM LANE SCHEPPELE

In the remarkable "decade plus" that has followed the remarkable year of 1989, democratic theory has undergone a revival. The collapse of the Soviet Empire brought with it an outpouring of writing on democracy, its nature, its structure, its inevitability. "Transitology," the study of the transition to democracy, has emerged as a specialty within the discipline of political science (see, for example, Linz and Stepan 1996; Elster et al. 1998; O'Donnell et al. 1986; O'Donnell et al. 1988), becoming popular when those who once studied the totalitarian or authoritarian regimes of Latin America, Southern Europe, or Eastern Europe found themselves (happily, but uneasily) stuck without a model for understanding what had happened so rapidly to their previously impervious governments. Cold War scholarship in the West has been replaced by a "one model fits all" conception of empirical democratic theory, where the formerly authoritarian and totalitarian regimes of the South and East are now put in the same theoretical framework as the governments of the North and West, with variables varying of course (see, for example, Lijphart 1992; Sartori 1994; Von Mettenheim 1997). Democracy is all the rage these days, in theory and in practice. It's very nearly the only game in town.

But the strong theoretical frameworks that the new democratic analysts bring to their work have blinded them to the genuinely new innovations that Central and Eastern European institution-builders have created, and to the new conceptions of democracy that have come with them. In particular, the transitologists, captured by the conventions of first-world empirical political science, have assumed that all democracies must have the same small set of moving parts and to pass roughly through the same stages on their way to a broadly similar endpoint. Accordingly, democratic institutions are seen as more or less "developed" or "consolidated" on their way toward building functioning democracies, but what it means to be a functioning democracy is the same ideal for all. To paraphrase Tolstoy, every functioning democracy is pretty much alike, but dysfunctional democracies are miserable each in their own way.

In this chapter, I would like to challenge the conventional picture of ideal democratic institutions, focusing in particular on the political innovations brought about by the new (and newly aggressive) constitutional courts in the newcomer democracies. I want to suggest that there may be some times when strong constitutional courts are more democratic than elected parliaments and elected executives. As I will argue, this is in part a function of institutional design. Constitutional courts can be structured so that they have better access than the more conventional elected branches to what democratic publics want from democratic politics. But the democratic role of constitutional courts is also in part a function of the role of long, detailed, and substantively thick constitutions in modern political life. Constitutions written before any of the current politicians know what their positions would be may in fact have more widely supported provisions than the narrowly self-interested legislation that comes later, once there are more clearly vested interests to protect. Constitutions may in fact be better signs of what democratic publics want from their governments than legislation, and so aggressively enforcing constitutional provisions to the detriment of ordinary legislation may be what democratic publics actually prefer and what democratic publics expect democracies to provide.

While I argue that this was true in the 1990s in Hungary, where I did four years of fieldwork in the 1990s, I think that democracy by judiciary may be an option that more deeply entrenched democracies may want to consider as well. Though this form of government has appeared in its strongest form in transitional polities, I do not believe that it should be limited to them currently or even in the long run. The form may have more general uses.

To see how this new form of democratic governance may work, we need first to explore what is usually meant by a democracy in what I will call the "standard democratic story." The standard democratic story is a tale of elections and elected officials as the central features of governance. This account usually confines courts to the sidelines. After all, courts are legendarily counter-democratic (or counter-majoritarian), because they have judges who are not directly elected, who have longer terms of office than ordinary politicians, and who have no regularized way to collect broader public input, focused as they are on narrowly presented cases. As I will show, these *usual* features of courts are not *necessary* features of courts, and changing the structures of courts may well improve their democratic potential, particularly in places where elections and inter-election mechanisms of communication between voters and representatives break down.

So—to the standard democratic story.

The problems with applying this standard story—a story about democratically substantive outcomes being connected to democratically typical processes—to Central and Eastern Europe are numerous. The specifics of their history are different, and so too are the institutions, promises, and possibilities with which they have begun to construct democratically responsive regimes. The main problems with applying the standard democratic story in the postcommunist part of the world can be divided into (a) problems with elections; and (b) problems in communication between elections. But in Central and Eastern Europe, there has also been a potential solution: thick constitutions.

PROBLEMS WITH ELECTIONS

In the older established democracies (the ones where the standard democratic story best applies), "civil society" organizations and political parties grew gradually at the same time as democratic institutions expanded their reach and responsibilities. Some of these intermediary organizations (intermediate between state and citizen) were moral and religious, others were based on independent trade unions and other groupings emerging from the pursuit of economic interests, still others depended on more specifically political agendas. Political parties, reasonably well differentiated from simple interest groups, came to take on relatively stable programs supported by a core of electors. The specifics of elections depended on which leaders' and parties' platforms appealed to the most voters. Their votes would be aggregated through methods that varied from one polity to the next, but systems of electoral representation (however different from each other) quickly became naturalized in most consolidated democracies.[6]

The typical pattern in the West was for the franchise to expand into an already-mobilized population, whose interests were quite organized and whose institutions were ready for political action, if need be. As Tocqueville's famous assessment of America reported, America was already socially organized by the time he came to take a look, and this was one of the secrets of America's democratic success (Tocqueville 2000). And as Robert Putnam's more recent historical study of Italy has also argued, the stability and success of democratic institutions has been associated with the development and growth of civil society there as well, where the regions with the deepest histories of civic organization also have the most stable and democratic politics (Putnam 1993). What Italy and America share, on Tocqueville's and Putnam's accounts, are electoral systems that do not have to invent from scratch reasonable devices for the mobilization and aggregation of interests; a socially mobilized population stands a better chance of growing political parties that in fact reflect interests than a population that is fragmented and disorganized.

In addition, even in established democracies with well-functioning party systems, elections may be controversially conducted and their outcomes may be contested. There are many ways that elections may misfire, so that the mere fact of having elections is no guarantee that the government so elected in fact has a popular mandate.[7] In fact, given the professional quality of opinion manipulation through polling and media coverage in experienced democracies, it is often unclear that even a well-functioning election machinery in an experienced democracy actually produces a match between popular interest and political victory. Not only is the choice of candidates functionally made by party officials (even if primary elections leave something for rank and file party members to do), but also the official political platforms and hot campaign issues may have relatively little to do with actual governing policy.

Perhaps no one knows this better than those who lived under Soviet rule. There were, of course, elections for public office—even (by the time of *perestroika*) contested elections.[8] But the choices were limited. There was no real organized opposition, and access to the ballot was tightly controlled. The voter was not guaranteed of seeing her real political preferences represented on the ballot in any form, and the government that took office after the election was guaranteed to hold a monopoly on policy, even if the popular vote were itself divided. The elections did not address the bigger questions—how the party/parties arrived at its/their platforms, how the set of candidates was itself determined, and which interests would be represented in the set of electoral choices. By the time the voters came to vote in Soviet regimes, much of what they might have voted for was already taken off the table.

In Central and Eastern Europe, civil society was either decimated or colonized by the only party there was. Official unions, youth groups, and women's groups responded to the call of the Party. Other formal or public groups were illegal or discouraged. The Party might have been internally diverse (as it surely was in the last days of the Soviet Empire both in the Soviet Union and in Central Europe), but its public face still appeared quite unified. Most citizens' interests and desires were not deeply connected to these structures, which were seen as belonging to a public realm of official compliance rather than to the private realm of the satisfaction of needs (see Fehér et al. 1983). Instead, informal friendship networks occupied the space of social organization and provided not only social solidarity, but also scarce goods.[9]

Building democratic institutions that can mobilize electorates whose interests are well-specified and well-represented is extremely difficult if there is a vacuum of public social institutions. As a result, in the post-Soviet political space, political parties are often friendship networks gone public, rather than a group of relative strangers united by a common substantive commitment or brought together by a common set of interests. The consequence is that the platforms of political parties are not very stable. Groups of friends may disagree quite a lot over what their circle should do if it gets into power, and this disagreement is communicated to the general public in the form of vague, weak, or non-existent party platforms. Politicians, even those who are central to their party, quit their original parties and join different ones when their friendship ties unravel. The general public who may be voting for these parties can hardly be expected to be more loyal.[10]

Added to this is the fact that while it is now legally possible, most people in the post-Soviet world have no time to form voluntary interest groups outside of the new party structures, because they are busy accumulating multiple jobs for pay in economies gone haywire. If your official job cannot possibly provide the income to support you, you have to spend your time outside your official job doing something else that will pay you to survive. Volunteerism, as a result, is nearly non-existent in these societies. The calls by Western democrats to develop civil society organizations have been met with much interest, but little response, because the most mobilizable population is already stretched too thin. Since the political changes, political parties occupy nearly the whole sphere of organized interests, because they are the only organizations that can pay people to work for them.[11] But these parties are not mobilized primarily to serve a broader constituency. Party officials are primarily interested in promoting themselves and their friends in the new opportunity channels which, when elected, they want to close to all others. And if loyalty can be bought by employment (this is the familiar world of political patronage), one may not necessarily expect parties to reflect broader interests than simply maintaining power for power's sake. The structure of interests and its representation is not stable as a result, and so the new democratic institutions of parliaments, prime ministers, and presidencies are often built on sand.[12]

In Hungary, clearly one of the democratic success stories in postcommunist Europe, elections have been characterized by a high degree of professionalism in the actual conduct of the vote and its tally,[13] but many Hungarians are critical of the fact that the mostly state-controlled broadcast media tend to be deployed in favor of the governing party, and so opposition parties have a harder time getting their message out during the campaign. In addition, Hungarians associated with the opposition parties during the 1998–2002 term of Prime Minister Viktor Orbán believed that his government was self-consciously engaged in a campaign to reduce the number of parties from the previous relatively stable five or six parties in Parliament down to only two or three, guaranteeing Orbán's Hungarian Civic Party if not the government, then at least the only obvious opposition. These tactics involved fomenting scandal among coalition partners and splitting the opposition by working under the table with one of the opposition parties to prevent the opposition from ever reaching a common stance against the government of the day. That made the opposition look weak and ineffective, which had the further effect of marginalizing the smaller parties among the opposition. The outcome of the 2002 election shows the results: for the first time, Hungary had only four parties represented in the Parliament, one with only a tiny fraction of the seats. Several other parties dropped off the political map by failing to reach the 5% parliamentary threshold. In other post-Soviet countries, the election stories are typically worse.[14]

It is no wonder, then, that the legitimacy of the new elective institutions is not very high in the post-Soviet world. These institutions do not always represent the interests of the public, because the mechanisms through which such interests would be aggregated and expressed are not well-established at election time. Forces well above the level of the ordinary voter control the options, and the options are often not very good. This can be seen in the general decline of voter turnout in the region.[15] If one happens to be in a circle that has converted its friendship network into a political party, then one may have more faith in the legitimacy of elective institutions. But if one is outside of those circles, it is hard for one's voice to be reliably heard. Extensive cynicism in these new electorates is the result.

The newly democratic post-Soviet publics could be forgiven for thinking that the changes that democratic reform brought were less revolutionary than they might have imagined. Given the lack of fit between parties and voters at election time, it would not be surprising if elections failed to represent voters with candidates who shared their views. But the assumption, crucial to the standard democratic story, is that institutions are democratic in content if they are democratic in form. This assumption does not always meet with widespread faith in the countries of the former Soviet world. The low esteem in which both executives and parliaments are almost everywhere held in the former Soviet world stands as proof of this. Much higher in the confidence scheme are the totally new institutions, like constitutional courts and ombudsmen, whose substantive commitments to democratic values give them a basis for their power. As a result, it may be that what matters in the post-Soviet world is not only a formal commitment to the results of the flawed elections in the new democracies, but also a substantive commitment to democratic values.

PROBLEMS OF REPRESENTATION BETWEEN ELECTIONS

In consolidated democracies, representatives develop a number of mechanisms for staying in touch with voters between elections in order to represent their views. Or at least they should, because elections are blunt instruments for communicating nuanced views about concrete policy options. Even when candidates represent real choices for voters, stable party structures, and no corruption, votes at election time are votes for a package deal of positions on issues. Perhaps voters vote for a candidate from Party A because they like the party's position on taxes, even while they dislike its positions on foreign policy. So even if Party A is elected with many voters who feel this way, there may be a mandate for the tax policy but no mandate for the foreign policy. Moreover, issues that loom large at election time may change their context or shape by the time they are seriously debated, and a voter's vote in an election may not reflect the view of that very same voter when the issue is raised in concrete form. Between elections, representatives must figure out how much support they have for each of the positions they take, or run the risk of losing the next time.

In democracies of long-standing consolidation and the history that typically goes with them, the institutional practices that keep representatives in tune with voters between elections were not accomplished all at once, but instead developed slowly over decades, even centuries. As constituencies grew in size, so too did staffs, bureaucracies, and mass-mediated methods of constituent contact. In the U.S., for example, representatives and senators in the U.S. Congress have ever-growing personal staffs, both in Washington and at home, who handle constituent communications and constituent requests. Moreover, the committees on which they serve have increased staffs to research alternatives, including the public acceptability of them. In Britain, the Prime Minister's Question Time allows members of the House of Commons to address the Prime Minister directly before a national (even international) television audience, right down to questions from various backbenchers about individual constituents' problems that the backbenchers have been called upon to solve. Not that these mechanisms completely address the problem of how to maintain ongoing contact with interested publics between elections, but they help.

In newcomer democracies, however, these mechanisms are often not in place. Hungary, though one of the models for democratic development in the first post-Soviet decade, provides an example of how these mechanisms of inter-election responsiveness simply are not there. Members of the Hungarian Parliament don't have personal offices, let alone personal staffs. Instead, they camp out in their overcrowded party suites in the Parliament building or in their committee offices in the White House several blocks away when the

Parliament is in session. And, in lieu of offices, Hungarian MPs have cell-phones, so that those who need to reach them, can. If MPs make contact with constituents at all, they do so directly without the benefit of a large interme-diary organization (except perhaps for a local party office), which often means that they cannot maintain direct constituency contact at all. And when MPs vote in the Parliament, it is not based on figuring out what their own con-stituencies want, but instead typically on what their party has told them to do on particular issues, often without personal knowledge of the issues at all.

Hungary has the benefit of a set of professional polling companies, both connected with the political parties and with the press, so that public opin-ion on major issues is generally known. But the connection between specific representatives, or even specific political parties, and the public opinion of those who vote directly for them is not necessarily close.

And that is not even the worst of the between-elections issues. Given the instability of the party mechanisms in Central and Eastern Europe since the changes, it is often the case that party members, even visible and apparent-ly central party members, bolt their parties for others. Or parties split, cre-ating new party fractions in the parliament, a state of affairs that usually caus-es all of the subsequent party fractions to lose at the next election, functionally destroying the party. Or parties break down over leadership questions, leav-ing entirely ambiguous who actually rightly controls the party caucus or the party offices. Since many political parties in Central and Eastern Europe are just friendship networks gone public, it is not surprising that there is tremen-dous volatility of membership when political disagreements turn into per-sonal fights. These personnel shifts are one reason why the policies of the governments themselves are often not stable, predictable, or connected to campaign promises.

In Hungary, there have been four multiparty elections since the political and constitutional changes of 1989. In each election, Hungarians voted in governing parties which had not been in the previous government. In fact, Hungarians voted whenever they could for a dominant political party that had not previously been in the government at all, if possible, a complete new-comer to political power. By 2002, there were no such parties left, so Hun-garians elected the dominant parties in opposititon to the then – current one. As a result, each election was more of a negative mandate than a positive one. Each election was a fresh opportunity for Hungarians to "throw the bums out." That was generally because each governing coalition governed differently from the way it said it would at election time, and Hungarians expressed their distrust and anger at the polls the next time.

The continual cycling of parties in government at election time in Hunga-ry shows a certain lack of confidence in political leaders and the jobs that they have done between the last election and the current one, because no single governing party has ever been voted into two successive governments in the first post-Soviet decade-plus of Hungarian politics. In 2002, for the first time, a previous coalition government was voted back into office, but by the narrowest margin in post-Soviet Hungarian electoral history. This result occured because Hungary now has what is basically a two-party system, with the Socialists on the left and the Hungarian Civic Party on the right of the political spectrum. Only the much-diminished Free Democrats survived as a substantial third party in the Parliament in the 2002 elections. By the time of the 2002 elections, there was only one viable political party left if one wanted to get rid of the one then currently in place.

Between Hungarian elections, every single elected government has broken its most distinctive and popular campaign promises in light of intervening events. No wonder voters generally report being disillusioned with both elections and with the governments so elected.

SOLUTIONS: THICK CONSTITUTIONS

Soviet-style regimes were, obviously, hugely different from Western democracies both in the Soviet time and in the post-Soviet period as well. But the differences were more in content than in superficial form. There were (superficially) elected officials running the government. But the *content* of Soviet-style policy was radically undemocratic. Specific abuses were characteristic of the Soviet-style regimes: the lack of attention to the citizen as a bearer of rights, to the citizen as the author of her/his own life, to the citizen as an individual whose divergent political views deserved as much respect as their conforming ones. There were also abuses of culture, of the environment, of privilege. To see whether the new regimes of multiparty elections in the postcommunist world are substantively different from the old regimes of single-party domination, one needs to look not just at the form that the new institutions take, but also at their content.

Those who are emerging from the Soviet political space have an idea of democracy that comes from longing for it rather than from having a history of it. As a result, they may have a more *substantive* sense of what it means to have a democracy than do those who have had the luxury of living always in a democratic regime. This may be especially true where the old communist parties recycled themselves as socialist or new communist parties and where, as a result, the new elections feature many of the same old faces. The transition from the Soviet-style governments to more genuinely democratic ones, then, must be signaled by some more radical break, more of substance than of personnel. The institutions might retain the same superficial appearance— no one wanted to abolish parliaments and elections. Instead, reformers wanted to change the number of parties and the independence of the voters who voted for them, thereby strengthening both parliaments and elections. But, as we have seen, this did not always happen. Elections are a necessary but not a sufficient condition of a democratic regime. Something more is necessary.

In fact, the new post-Soviet citizens would not believe that a democracy was real until the *substance* of previous policies had changed. The new constitutions not only guaranteed this, but also gave these institutions more radically democratic *content* through the "thickness" of post-Soviet constitutions. The new constitutions are quite detailed and specify not only how the new democratic institutions are to operate procedurally but also how they are to govern substantively. These new constitutions provide answers to questions that are, in older constitutional democracies, given by legislation alternatively than by constitution (or rather, by procedure rather than by substantive limits on policy).[16] Thick constitutions take a great many policy choices out of the hands of the remodeled political institutions, and lodge them instead in a higher law. From guaranteeing avenues of access to government to providing substantial social safety nets, constitutions in the post-Soviet world dictate to the new parliaments what policies they should have.

In many of the countries of the post-Soviet world, these newly constitutionalized issues have been given over for safekeeping to the special competence of the newest political institution in these postauthoritarian worlds— the constitutional courts. Though these courts vary widely in their bravery, powers, and successes, they have been the primary marker that the new political orders are very different from the old ones. And it is the constitutional courts in many newcomer democracies that are the most popular and the most trusted institutions in the new political order.

As I will argue, I believe that this means that the new voters of Central and Eastern Europe want the postcommunist polity to show its commitment to change by committing itself to a thick *substantive* vision of the new democratic state. This vision has been provided in the sharpest outline not by parliaments and executives, but by the sudden and radical expansion of the role of judicial review taken on by activist constitutional courts.

The place where these developments proceeded the farthest and the fastest was in Hungary, so I will turn to the more specific materials on Hungary to continue my argument.

CREATING A COURTOCRACY: AN OVERVIEW OF HUNGARY'S
CONSTITUTIONAL DEVELOPMENT

For most of the period after the Second World War, Hungary was a state on the edges of the Soviet Empire in two ways. First (and most obviously), it was on the edges of the Soviet Empire *geographically*, which has enabled Hungary to move in the 1990s from a position firmly in "Eastern Europe" to an aspirational position in "Central Europe." Being next to and historically linked with Austria, which is now a member of the European Union, was critical to this "un-edging" of Hungary through the 1990s, as it hurtled as fast as it was allowed toward joining the EU itself. Second, Hungary was on the edges of the Soviet Empire *politically* as well during the Soviet period, since Hungary had one of the more liberal regimes in the former Soviet world and had already engaged in quite a lot of economic, legal, and political reform before 1989. Economic pluralism came with a series of reforms in the mid-1970s. Political pluralism came as a number of Communist Party members tried to separate government from party in the 1980s. Both processes were already relatively far along by the time of the Roundtable that negotiated the transition to formal economic and political pluralism.

Throughout the Soviet period, Hungary's courts retained a certain positivist legalism that shielded them from much direct political interference, and private-law lawyers and academics enjoyed a substantial amount of room for maneuver especially at the end of that era. Public law lawyers and academics were more politically compromised, as were the specialized political courts. Through the later days of the Soviet period, intellectuals, too, were given more room for maneuver. As one of my friends in Hungary put it, "[a]s long as we published in journals and in jargon, they didn't care what we said." These liberalizing tendencies meant that Hungary had an educated elite that was accustomed to having ideas that were not already colonized by the Party. Even the Party was not fully colonized by the Party by the end.

Even before the dissidents called the government to negotiate multiparty elections and a transition to more open politics in 1989, there was a split within the Hungarian Communist Party between the reformers who wanted to separate the government from Party control (and who were remarkably far along in doing so) and the more conservative Party officials who insisted on keeping the political lid on. The transition moved as smoothly as it did in Hungary in part for demographic reasons; the hard-liners were reaching retirement age and were being pushed aside in retirement as 1989 neared. The reformers, younger people with more open minds, clearly had the upper hand. The calls for a new constitution, replacing the Stalinist-era Twentieth Law of 1949 (as the Hungarian Constitution was then called), came as early as in 1987, when the then-new Minister of Justice Kálmán Kulcsár (himself a distinguished Marxist sociologist of law who was to become a born-again liberal) ordered his ministry to prepare one. By early 1988, substantially before it was clear that the Central and Eastern European states would be allowed to move out of the Soviet orbit, a new constitution was in circulation and introduced in the Parliament. It still outlined a People's Republic, but proposed many changes that would make the state significantly more autonomous from the Party. These substantial internal reform attempts were overtaken by the Roundtable Talks that started in spring 1989 between the Party and the democratic opposition.[17] The Roundtable Talks succeeded in producing what amounted to a wholly new constitution in 1989, accepted by the still-communist Parliament several weeks *before* the fall of the Berlin Wall. The Constitution was again changed through another large series of amendments in 1990, when there was still widespread consensus about the direction of the new democracy. Those changes wiped away the remnants of the compromises with socialism that the former dissidents had made.

The new Hungarian Constitution created a new Constitutional Court, which turned out to be the most revolutionary part of the new institutional structure. The Constitutional Court opened for business on 1 January 1990, five months before the first multi-party elections, and it was immediately deluged with petitions from ordinary citizens, demanding that their rights be recognized.[18] The Court operated from its opening day as if the transition had already happened, and it started striking down laws as inconsistent with the new Hungarian Constitution at a rapid rate. These were all, after all, communist-era laws, many of which could be expected to be inconsistent with a new, basically liberal, constitution.

After the first election, as Hungary hurtled through the early years of transition, most citizens experienced not just the early heady sense that the sky was the limit, but also the vertiginous sense that there was no limit to how far things could drop. The transition produced 13 daily newspapers in Budapest alone, covering a wide range of political viewpoints, as well as a multitude of new political parties. The first elections saw a large turnout and a lot of enthusiasm for the new political changes. A center-right government was elected, in which the Hungarian Democratic Forum was the lead party. But the Parliament quickly fell into squabbling about the new symbols of state, spending a huge amount of time fighting about whether the Holy Crown of St. Stephen should be part of the national seal, while leaving much structural change on the back burner. When they weren't debating the Holy Crown, MPs were trying to find suitable methods for expressing revenge against the previous communist leaders. But neither nationalist symbolism nor political score-settling were popular with the electorate, which seemed to want substantive reform. There was a public disillusionment with politics almost immediately, and the popularity of the first government plunged accordingly.

On the economic side, the transition brought a tremendous influx of foreign capital, along with a tremendous influx of foreigners. But the transition also brought a startling drop in family incomes for those who were not part of the new globalized economy. The transition also created a sharp rise in inflation and unemployment. For those on fixed incomes, the shock was severe. While in the socialist times there was not much opportunity to take upside risks, there was also little chance that one would experience a severe downside risk. Life may have provided few economic opportunities, but it also protected everyone against sudden economic shocks. In the new world of political changes, there might have been a more robust politics, but there was also an increasingly desperate economics going on at the same time.

Into the middle of this picture in which politics did not live up to its advance billing and in which economic expectations were dashed, came the Constitutional Court. The Court had spent its first few months before the first election and a substantial amount of its caseload shortly after the first election dismantling many of the dysfunctional leftovers of the communist state. The Court required that the Ministry of Justice no longer control the court system and that there be judicial review of every administrative decision. The Court ordered the state surveillance system to be disabled by mandating that there could no longer be a personal identifier number to which all state records would be attached and by introducing a strong system of data privacy. The Court abolished death penalty and some late communist-era taxes. The Court required that the state not be allowed to appeal cases against the wishes of the parties to a lawsuit. The Court was very active in a great many different areas, and in general its decisions were both followed and respected.

But the Court did not stop by striking down communist-era laws as inconsistent with the new Hungarian Constitution. The new legislation coming out of the newly elected Parliament fared little better. Looking over the Parliament's effort to return farmland to its previous owners, the Court refused to go along. Instead, the Court required that reprivatization of, or compensation for, previously nationalized property, if it were to be done at all, had to treat all former owners identically, thereby taking the issue out of the area of special pleading in the Parliament where the farmers had the government's ear.[19] Ditto with the Parliament's effort to bring former communist officials to justice for violating the rights of political opponents. The Court said that Parliament could not take political revenge on the former communists who preceded them, because retroactive punishment violated the new rule of law. The Parliament tried to hang onto the state-owned media to use it to propagandize for the new government. The Court demanded that the government give up control of the broadcast media in the name of freedom of the press.

The Constitutional Court Act gave Hungarians virtually barrier-free access to the Court to ask that laws be stricken as unconstitutional, so nearly every one of the major new laws was challenged. The Hungarian Constitution literally says that "anyone" may file a petition with the Constitutional Court of Hungary if she believes that a law is unconstitutional. There is no requirement of standing, the demonstration of a particular injury, or any personal connection with the challenged law at all. A person does not even have to be a citizen to file a petition with the Court, nor does the petitioner need to have a lawyer represent her before the Court. In a country of 10.5 million people, the Court received between 1500 and 2500 petitions a year, some with many signatures.

The Court generally took a broad view of its mandate to review the constitutionality of entire laws if any part of the law were challenged. Moreover, the Court had the power to review laws before and during their discussion in Parliament, upon request by any of a set of listed officials, so the Court was free to give advisory opinions in the midst of the legislative process.[20] And once a law was passed, *anyone* could challenge it on an abstract basis, whether they had a personal stake in the challenge or not. Perhaps, most surprisingly, the Court was also given the power to declare that Parliament was acting "unconstitutionally by omission," which meant that the Court was able to declare that Parliament had violated the Constitution by *failing* to pass a law that the Constitution required the Parliament to pass. The Court could therefore order the Parliament to pass laws that, in the view of the Court, were necessary to realize the promises of the new constitution.

The Constitutional Court decided roughly 300 cases per year, which meant that it had a presence great and small in many areas of political life. By contrast, the first elected Parliament was quite visibly stalled in passing new laws to make a symbolic and real break with the communist past because it was caught up in symbolic politics that quickly made the Hungarian public cynical. Moreover, the parties that were in the first governing coalition, the Hungarian Democratic Forum, the Christian Democratic Party, and the Smallholders, were elected as political liberals, but they governed as nationalists. They barely began economic reform and did little to dismantle the state apparatus, still unchanged from the communist time. The media remained in state hands, as did most economic assets. Reforms that had been promised at election time didn't even make it onto the agenda of the Parliament. The Christian Democrats followed no discernible Christian agenda.[21] Only the Smallholders maintained a consistent and recognizable party orientation, though they had a small constituency. As a result, the first elected government engaged in reform efforts usually (and sometimes only) at the prodding of the Constitutional Court, which used its substantial powers to order the Parliament to pass new laws on a wide range of topics. The Parliament was ordered to pass a law on minority rights, on freedom of the broadcast media, on environmental protection. If the Parliament was tied up in internecine struggles, the Court tried to break the deadlock.

By the time of the second elections in 1994, the public was quite fed up with the government that it had previously elected. The Democratic Forum went from being the dominant party in Parliament to being one of its smaller fractions. The Christian Democrats nearly disappeared. Only the Smallholders survived in Parliament, but not in the government, and then only because they alone among the governing parties had tried to cater to their base, the small farmers. If they hadn't been successful in getting legislation passed and approved by the Constitutional Court to benefit their constituency, it wasn't because they hadn't tried. But in the second elections, the former communists (the Hungarian Socialist Party) won an absolute majority of the seats in Parliament. Even though they didn't have to, they went into coalition with the liberals (the Free Democrats), and so together the two parties had 72% of the votes in Parliament. Surely with this strong majority, the elected branch could act to live up to its substantial electoral mandate—or so it seemed.

While it was true that the second Parliament was far more effective than the first in terms of passing laws that substantially reformed the political and economic structures and in carrying through on those laws, it is also the case that the Socialist-Liberal government rather quickly moved away from their political base as well. The Socialists (the ex-communists) had campaigned on a platform of "expertise in government," and it was clear that the people who voted for them did so because they missed the good old days when things were more stable. Their constituency wanted reform—but they also wanted a guarantee of a social safety net and a restoration of order as it had been. But inflation continued to be high and, while unemployment came down in Budapest, it did not abate in the countryside. There was a growing gap between rich and poor, and a growing number of poor. The new government brought neither expertise nor stability to the country.

During this time, the Constitutional Court maintained its activism by striking down laws and ordering the Parliament to draft new ones that it had not yet gotten around to working on. But in the interviews I conducted between 1994 and 1996, it was clear that the other branches of government were quite willing to defer to the Court, even in cases where the government or Parliament disagreed with the policy choices implicit in the Court's rulings. There were virtually no voices of dissent within the other government branches from the proposition that the creation of a rule of law state required that all Court decisions be promptly and completely followed. "We are a country of lawyers," said one leading member of the Parliament, whose favorite new law had just been struck down, going on to state that the rule of law required that not a single decision of the Court go unenforced.

As a result of these extraordinary developments, the Court moved into a position where it was for all intents and purposes running the country. If one looked at the Parliament's agenda at any given moment, a large fraction of it was taken up with mandatory revisions, or with demands for new laws that the Court had thrown the Parliament's way. On a whole range of issues, the Parliament's first attempts to set policy were struck down as unconstitutional, forcing the Parliament to go back to the drawing boards.

In the first six years of the Court's operation, the Court nullified about *one-third of all the laws* brought before it for examination. Some of the early decisions struck down communist-era laws, the later decisions struck down the new laws passed by the elected parliaments at about the same rate. The Court, apparently proud of its record, produced an official booklet in Hungarian, German, and English, complete with pie charts showing the rate at which they struck down challenged legislation. The Court even published its statistics divided helpfully so that one could compare the rates of unconstitutionality found in communist and postcommunist legislation. They were the same.

In creating the Constitutional Court, the Hungarian National Roundtable had effectively created a new governmental system that was not presidentialism or parliamentarism (the usual two choices), but instead a "courtocracy." Through the mid-1990s, the Constitutional Court was for all intents and purposes running the country. Or at least the Court had as much power in the Hungarian system as the President has in France or the Parliament in the UK. Neither governs alone, though each has the last word. If presidentialism identifies the president as the strongest power in government, and parliamentarism identifies the parliament as the institution that has the most weight in policy making, courtism (or courtocracy) identifies the judiciary as the branch with the most power and the final word. Though in Hungary only the Parliament could make laws, the Constitutional Court always had the last say, and the Court struck down laws early and often, sending them back to the Parliament with explicit instructions on how the laws had to be rewritten. Moreover, since the Court had the power to order Parliament directly to pass laws on subjects that it had not yet considered, a great deal of the Parliament's agenda turned out to be simply complying with Court decisions. Hungary was more nearly a country run by a court than it was a country run by any other institution.

This is what I mean to point to when I say that presidentialism and parliamentarism are not the only forms of democratic system on offer, as the political scientists customarily claim. It is logical to think that the third branch—courts—could also be as dominant in some sorts of democratic governments as presidents and parliaments can be. What seems to get in the way of this idea, however, is the persistent view that courts are undemocratic, therefore unsuitable for being the lead institution in a democratic polity. But whether a court is democratic or not, is an empirical question, not an *a priori* claim.

In many ways the Hungarian Constitutional Court turned out to be a more democratic institution than the Hungarian Parliament for a number of structural and historical reasons. To see how this process worked, I will take up in more detail the most pressing and controversial set of cases that arose for both the Parliament and the Constitutional Court in the mid-1990s, because it is in the interplay between Parliament and the Constitutional Court in specific cases that one can see why the Court was arguably more democratic than the Parliament. In the example I will discuss, the "Bokros package cases," the Constitutional Court's decisions were critically important because the shape of the transition hung on the answer.

PARLIAMENT VS. COURT: HUNGARIAN DEMOCRACY UNDER PRESSURE OVER SOCIAL RIGHTS

Hungary's constitution, written in 1989 and 1990, included a lot of social rights. While some commentators have asserted that these were "leftovers" from Hungary's Soviet-era constitution, it turns out that many of the social rights provisions were new. Lawyers working on the constitutional subcommittee of the Roundtable process in 1989 had copied into the new Hungarian Constitution provisions from international human rights documents (particularly the International Covenant on Economic, Social and Cultural Rights). The primary social rights provisions in Hungary's constitution is Article 70/E, which states that Hungarians "shall be entitled to social security; they shall be entitled to provision necessary for subsistence in case of old age, illness, disablement, widowhood, orphanhood, and unemployment through no fault of their own." With this constitutional language, the Court has a lot of text to back up a claim that government spending to provide for certain social rights is constitutionally required. With that text as its mandate, the Court entered a battle with the Parliament in 1995.

The people hardest hit in the economic transition were pensioners and others who were dependent for their livelihoods on social benefit payments (for example, family allowances and sick pay). Though the constitutional protection seemed strong, the Parliament did not provide enough money to keep increasing any of these payments along with the inflation rate, especially not pensions. The Court largely went along with the Parliament at first, siding with the Parliament against challenges from citizens (primarily pensioners) who said that their real income was declining because pensions had not been raised with the level of inflation.[22]

But then the political background for the Court's social rights decisions changed dramatically when the social benefits system went from being attacked by inflation to being directly attacked by the Parliament. The Parliament acted following from a rather heavy-handed threat of the International Monetary Fund to shut down its office in Hungary and leave the country unless the new socialist-liberal government passed an economic austerity program that began to get a handle on Hungary's massive deficit. Since it was a large fraction of the state budget in Hungary, social benefits had to be included in the cutbacks.

At first, the socialist-liberal government elected in 1994 refused to cave in to IMF pressure, because the Socialists, who had run on a platform of social stability, balked. For about six months, the government held out against the IMF threats and tried to proceed on a course of slow but steady economic change. Through that time, the government maintained its public support. The government's strategy was to encourage the growth of small private businesses, while restructuring and selling off state-owned companies, but to do this while keeping the system of social security payments in place. Current deficits were justified in terms of investing in future growth and having compassion for a panicked population. But this rationale was not persuasive to those giving the loans.

When the IMF's patience ran out at the end of 1994 and the shutdown of their Hungarian office was imminent, the Hungarian government did the only thing it could do under the circumstances—it began to talk compromise. One finance minister resigned in protest. But the new Socialist-party finance minister, Lajos Bokros, was a born-again free marketeer with relentless determination to get the budget in line with international expectations. By March 1995, the government had proposed a new budget that took aim at social programs in a major way.

Leading the list of cutbacks was a near-total repeal of the popular system of child supports, starting with pregnancy benefits, continuing through infant benefits and state-supported maternity leave for new mothers in the first three years after they gave birth to a child, paying a child care allowance until the child reached school age, and then guaranteeing every family regardless of income a regular monthly payment for each child below the age of 18 living in the family (the *családi pótlék* system).[23] The government proposed that such benefits be subjected to a means test, though they were quite unclear about how such means tests were to be conducted, or what the level was below which such benefits would be guaranteed.[24] In addition to this, sick-leave benefits, once state-supported, were to be largely cut from the state budget and not paid for by the state until after an employee had been sick for 25 days. Employers were ordered to make up the difference, again with no time to adjust.

The new package, nicknamed the "Bokros package" after the very visible and photogenic finance minister, was proposed in March, passed in May, took effect in June and the immediate and harsh cutbacks were scheduled for 1 July 1995. The law, consisting of 157 paragraphs each amending another pre-existing law, went through Parliament so fast that it is doubtful that many MPs understood what they were voting for on the final ballot. Certainly, the interest groups one would expect in a well-functioning democracy were nowhere to be found. There were almost no organized public protests; the bill sailed through Parliament with very few organized objections. Pensioners, poor families, people with chronic illnesses, pregnant women and others had a good reason to lobby the Parliament to spare them the changes. But the bill sped unchecked through Parliament even though the majority party in the Parliament had campaigned less than a year before that it would never do this. Right after the package became law, it was immediately brought to the Constitutional Court for review by a number of petitioners.

While the "Bokros package cases" (as they came to be called) were special in many ways, in fact, this pattern was common for major legislation in Hungary. And it shows why the Court is arguably more democratic than the Parliament even though the judges are not directly elected. Hungarians understand that they have to be mobilized in large numbers to affect the Parliament and even then they are not likely to be successful. But, mostly because of the difficult economic conditions, Hungarians have no time to volunteer to work for interest groups that would defend their interests. They are too busy working six jobs to have time for something that doesn't pay them. Therefore, the most organized interest groups are the political parties themselves, because they are the only groups that have money to pay a staff to organize political support for various causes. But the political parties change once they come to power, partly because they run vague or unrealistic campaigns, and partly because the strongest pressures once they get into office are either from the minority parties that enable the coalition to govern (as in the 1990–1994 period), or from external institutions that have some leverage on Hungarian domestic policy (as in the 1994–1998 period). Either way, the majority parties in Hungarian governments since 1989 have found that they have to compromise their election platforms to keep their governments from falling, and that means doing something other than what they said they would do. The political parties in power are often, as in the Bokros package cases, allied with the very side of the policy issue that they campaigned against. Where is an alienated public to go?

This is where the Constitutional Court has come in. It is relatively easy for people to approach the Court to challenge a law that reflects something other than what they wanted. All that is necessary to activate the Court's jurisdiction in the case of an already enacted statute or other legal regulation is for

someone—literally, in the Constitution, "anyone"—to write a letter to the
Constitutional Court that challenges this legal regulation in light of some provision of the Hungarian Constitution. This does not require a lot of mobilization or great numbers. Lone individuals can file petitions without demon-
strating any broader constituency or, perhaps more importantly, without
taking the time to organize a substantial opposition. Sometimes there are petition drives and the Court gets petitions signed by a great many people.
More often, however, petitions come from people acting alone, though an
upsurge of petitions to the Court can demonstrate that a lot of people are
angry about a particular government action. Regardless of whether a petition has the force of numbers behind it or not, the Court is mobilized to act
because it has no discretion to refuse to hear a validly posed constitutional
question even if submitted by a single person, writing alone.[25]

The Bokros package was challenged by nearly all of the opposition political parties, by a series of nascent interest organizations representing interests that had been affected by the law, and by a number of individuals. The
Court sprung into action, dividing up the petitions among the judges so that
almost all the chambers were working on a piece of the Bokros package case
at the same time. They did this because there was only a two-week window
between the time that the law passed and the time that benefits would have
been cut to nothing.

In those two weeks, the Constitutional Court judges reviewed as much of
the law as they could. But since the cuts to social benefits were due to take
effect on 1 July, the judges decided to announce the first round of decisions
while petitions were still coming in and before they had had a chance to review
the entire law. The Court called a rare public session to announce its first set
of decisions on 30 June 1995, on the very eve of the Bokros package cuts. So
the judges donned their robes, paraded into the Court's auditorium and read
the decisions from the bench.[26] In five separate decisions, the Court struck
down major parts of the austerity program unanimously while upholding the
law only against a purely procedural challenge to the form of its enactment.
Two of the decisions were constitutionally uncontroversial, one saying that
budget shortages could not count as a reason for failing to enforce the Court's
prior decisions about the abolition of the personal identity number[27] and
another saying that people could not be made to pay taxes into the social
security system if they could not then get the benefits out at some later stage.
That left two decisions, one dealing with the system of child supports and the
other dealing with the sick-leave question, that required the government to
stop in its tracks. Nine other decisions were to come later in the fall, but the
first round of decisions set the tone the Court would take when dealing with
the cutback of social rights.

The most important of the first set of decisions focused on the system of child supports (43/1995 [VI.30]). The Court declared that the law cutting these benefits was unconstitutional primarily because the cuts violated the central constitutional principle of *legal security*. The Hungarian Constitution does not mention the principle of legal security explicitly, but the Court in its prior decisions had said that the principle of legal security is the most important idea contained within the broader concept of the rule of law, which *is* explicitly contained in the Hungarian Constitution. Legal security implies that the law must be predictable, that it cannot be changed without following appropriate procedures, and that it not be used to unsettle expectations without adequate warning. In the case of the Bokros package, it meant that the government could not cut social benefits so quickly. The system of pregnancy benefits, maternity leave, childcare supports, and child payments had to be kept intact precisely because people counted on them, and if the government were to change these benefits on which people relied, the government had to give notice, introduce the changes gradually, and give people a chance to adjust their lives to the new reality. These changes, because of the speed with which they had been enacted, had been made in an improper manner, the Court ruled.

Turning to consider the sick-leave cuts, the Constitutional Court ruled that they were also unconstitutional, and for much the same reason. The Bokros package mandated that the government would pay no sick-leave for citizens until they had been sick for 25 days in a year. The package created a group of people who were entirely left out of the social welfare system at precisely one of their most vulnerable moments, either because they were unemployed, or because they worked for a group of employers who had been previously exempted from the need to pay their employees' sick pay. In this case, the Court agreed that a category of beneficiaries protected under the second part of Article 70E—the sick—could be guaranteed a specific level of benefits as a matter of social right. Just what the level of guarantee was, the Court did not say. But in the instance of sick pay, where all citizens paid into the social security system through mandatory taxes and where the social security system was supposed by Article 70E to cover the specific group of beneficiaries (the sick), the Court agreed unanimously that the Constitution contained enforceable social rights that the Parliament could not abrogate.

The general public was strongly in favor of what the Court did. Five days after the Court's decision, a poll found that 89% of the public had heard of the decision and that overwhelming majorities (84% of those who had voted for the parties in the government and 90% of those who hadn't) believed that the Court made the right decision in the Bokros cases.[28] That same poll also showed significant distrust of politicians.

The Bokros package was brought to a halt, much to the consternation of the IMF. But the IMF, not willing to urge a government to ignore its own high court decisions,[29] strategically backed down and settled for a budget-cutting plan that left social spending alone. The Court's series of decisions in the fall striking down more provisions of the Bokros package continued the same pattern.

The Hungarian Parliament did not respond by changing the Constitution, though that was theoretically possible as a way of getting around the Court decisions. The government in power had a 72% majority in the Parliament, and a one-time two-thirds vote of a single Parliament was all that was needed to change the Constitution. The government could have, but didn't, overrule the Court by removing the constitutional provisions on which the Court relied for its most sweeping decisions, Article 70E.[30] Instead, the government set about trying to comply with both the Court decision and the IMF by finding money from other sources to fill in the budget deficit. The government, as a result of this, sped up the privatization program, hurrying to put state-owned property on the international market. The income generated through the sale of state assets went to pay off the international loans more quickly than the loan terms required, thus making Hungary independent of the sort of international influence that caused the government in spring 1995 to pass a radical austerity program.

The government also tried to comply with the Court's decisions by changing the social benefits program within the limits that the Court had outlined. The government was ultimately able to phase out the universal coverage of the family benefits program, once they had a workable means-testing program in place to satisfy the Court. In the Bokros package cases, the Court sharply reigned in what the Parliament could do and the Parliament complied. In terms of who had the largest and most final say in Hungarian politics through the 1990s, it was clearly the Constitutional Court, with strong public approval.

A DEMOCRACY RUN BY A COURT

What should we make of this rather extreme case in Hungary, where the Court often struck down legislation, ordered the Parliament to pass laws and generally set the direction of state policy for nearly a decade? If one takes the standard democratic story, then it appears that Hungary was deeply undemocratic, since policy came from a branch with limited electoral accountability and the elected branches were constantly forced to change direction by an aggressive and activist court. Hungary was, in short, a courtocracy. But was it democratic?

16 For example, post-Soviet constitutions typically specify a large number of rights, including social rights. Instead of leaving the shape of a welfare state up to the elected branches, these constitutional provisions seem to sketch out the substantive goals to be achieved. Also, post-Soviet constitutions frequently include provisions that regulate the central bank, the military, the central audit office, the national prosecutor's office, ombudsmen, ministries, and the judicial system. By putting these things into a constitution rather than into ordinary legislation, constitution-drafters took both the shape and content of government out of the realm of ordinary political decision-making.

17 For a thorough and excellent account of the Roundtable Talks in English, see Tőkés 1996. For more on the Roundtables in Hungary and elsewhere in the postcommunist world, see Elster 1994. The transcripts of the Hungarian Roundtable have since been published (in Hungarian) in Bozóki et al. 1999.

18 In one of the first major cases determining the constitutionality of an unpopular new tax that the communists tried to impose on their way out of power, the Constitutional Court received about 35,000 signatures on petitions to overturn the tax (in a country of 10.5 million people). Clearly, many people had high hopes for the Court.

19 The Smallholders' Party was the only party in the first coalition government that did relentlessly attempt to satisfy the political demands of its specific constituents, who were displaced farmers and people from rural areas. But they were in a minority in the country generally, and to the Constitutional Court, it was not fair that they should get more in the compensation laws than others whose representatives did not stand up for them.

20 The Court later decided this was a bad idea and got the Parliament to change the law.

21 In fact, one of the party leaders during an interview I did with him in 1995 admitted he had a pro-choice view on abortion because his wife and daughters would hate him if he didn't—but he didn't know whether to tell his party colleagues or not. He hoped simply to avoid the issue by preventing it from being brought up in Parliament.

22 Actually, this is not quite true. For the first five years of the Court's operation, there was a steady group of four dissenters (out of 9 judges at that time) who resolutely stood up for social rights and who believed that the Court should order pensions, in particular, to be increased so that they could keep their real value. The dissenters kept losing, but just barely. So the majority view of the Court was not unanimous. The social rights cases before the Bokros package cases (that are the subject of this section) had a large number of 5–4 decisions, something that was quite unusual in the Hungarian Constitutional Court which tended to have unanimous opinions about nearly all other matters.

23 The reaction of most Westerners to this generous system is often incredulity. But the incredulous should know that Hungary has no tax breaks for families as do most West European and North American systems, and so much of this subsidy for children might be thought of as a different way of accomplishing a state subsidy to families with children. There was no parallel plan in Hungary to institute tax breaks for families with children to compensate for the removal of child allowances when the cuts were proposed.

24 Means tests were very difficult to do in Hungary since people's official income and their real income were often very different. Because marginal tax rates were so high (48% for private sector employees), people had great incentives to keep their incomes out of any official registry. This of course complicated the problem of tax payments and budget deficits, since money earned off any official books couldn't be taxed and therefore the state was always tempted to raise taxes on that small fraction of income that it could see, further driving people to get paid off the books. And of course, those

limited sources of revenue limited the state's ability to pay for social benefits to people who seemed, from their official records, to be poor. Means testing was the obvious answer, but also a symptom of the problem. Those most successful at avoiding state taxes would appear to be most deserving of state relief.

25 The Court has discretion in two other senses, however. (1) The Court can refuse to see the constitutional challenge in a badly framed petition, and therefore turn it down for failing to state a constitutional question. Or the Court can reach for a constitutional subject in a petition that doesn't quite say it, thereby allowing themselves to reach issues that they are eager to address. There is some interpretive room for the Court to construct its caseload by reading petitions narrowly or broadly. (2) Because there was no legal regulation that said that the Court had to decide cases in the order in which they came in, or even by some definite time limit, judges could put petitions that they did not want to reach at the bottom of a pile in someone's office, not formally rejecting it, but not exactly getting around to it, either.

26 Normally, judges simply instruct that a decision be published and they issue a press release describing the decision. Only one or two decisions a year warrant this sort of robed formal announcement where the decision is literally read from the bench.

27 The Bokros package included a number of quite extraneous and irrelevant budget cuts, which happened to include axing the money for compliance with a number of Court decisions that the President of the Court felt particularly strongly about. The fact that cutting money to enforce Constitutional Court decisions was even in the budget at all as a separate item (when it had never been so before) indicated to some observers that the Parliament set up the law *precisely so that* the Constitutional Court would strike it down. Though I could not get any of the MPs to whom I talked to admit it, I must say I share the suspicion that the Parliament, with its back to the wall, very much wanted the Constitutional Court to strike down this law. That complicates the analysis about democracy in this paper because I think that the Bokros package cases are actually an instance where the Court did exactly what the Parliament wanted, but I don't think this is fatal to my larger argument about courtocracy. With the Court as the most powerful institution in government, the Parliament could predictably count on not having to take responsibility for a bad law.

28 Poll results were reported in the *Magyar Hírlap,* 5 July 1995. Interestingly enough, the poll also asked citizens what should be done to raise the money that the Court decision now required. 34% said to tax the rich, 30% said to decrease other state expenditures, and 25% said to decrease the income of politicians.

29 At least publicly. Behind the scenes, the judges at the Constitutional Court got phone calls from the World Bank representatives in Hungary, asking whether their economists might come over and explain economics to them. While some of the judges listened, no one was affected in their views, because the Court continued the same unanimous attack on the Bokros package in the fall when it reviewed the rest of the provisions. Some of the judges were outraged by these phone calls, seeing in them a deliberate attempt to manipulate the Court and compromise its independence.

30 Actually, though this was theoretically possible, it was made more difficult than it otherwise would have been because the government had agreed with the opposition parties on special parliamentary rules for drafting a new constitution, a process that was just getting underway. The government wanted a new constitution because the 1989 constitution said in its preamble that it was a temporary constitution, to be replaced by a permanent one after the "transition" was over. The government didn't have elaborate plans for changing the text, and certainly leaving social rights out of the text was not really a live option. But in order to get the agreement of the opposition parties to

Choper, Jesse H. *Judicial Review and the National Political Process.* Chicago: University of Chicago Press, 1980.

Comisso, Ellen. "Is the Glass Half Full or Half Empty? Reflections on Five Years of Competitive Politics in Eastern Europe." *Communist and Post-Communist Studies* 30, no. 1 (1997): 1–21.

Crawford, Beverly and Arend Lijphart, eds. *Liberalization and Leninist Legacies: Comparative Perspectives on Democratic Transitions.* Berkeley: University of California Press, 1997.

Dahl, Robert A. "Decision-Making in a Democracy: The Supreme Court as a National Policy-Maker." *Journal of Public Law* 6, no. 2 (1957): 279–95.

Dworkin, Ronald. *Law's Empire.* Cambridge, Mass.: Harvard University Press, 1986.

Ekiert, Grzegorz. "Democratization Processes in East Central Europe: A Theoretical Reconsideration." *British Journal of Political Science* 21 (1991): 285–313.

Eisgruber, Christopher L. *Judicial Review as a Democratic Institution.* Unpublished manuscript, n.d.

Ely, John Hart. *Democracy and Distrust: A Theory of Judicial Review.* Cambridge, Mass.: Harvard University Press, 1980.

Elster, Jon, Claus Offe, and Ulrich K. Preuss. *Institutional Design in Post-Communist Societies: Rebuilding the Ship at Sea.* Cambridge: Cambridge University Press, 1998.

Flemming, Roy B., John Bohte, and B. Dan Wood. "One Voice Among Many: The Supreme Court's Influence on Attentiveness to Issues in the United States, 1947–1992." *American Journal of Political Science* 41, no. 4 (1997): 1224–50.

Friedman, Barry. "The History of the Countermajoritarian Difficulty, Part One: The Road to Judicial Supremacy." *New York University Law Review* 73, no. 2 (1998): 333–433.

Gellner, Ernest. *Nations and Nationalism.* Oxford: Blackwell, 1983.

Gross, Jan T. "The Burden of History." *East European Politics and Societies* 13, no. 2 (1999): 285–87.

Habermas, Jürgen. *Between Facts and Norms: Contributions to a Discourse Theory of Law and Democracy.* Cambridge, Mass.: MIT Press, 1999.

Hall, John A., ed. *Civil Society: Theory, History, Comparison.* Cambridge: Polity, 1995.

Hayden, Robert M. *Blueprints for a House Divided: The Constitutional Logic of the Yugoslav Conflicts.* Ann Arbor: University of Michigan Press, 1999.

Huntington, Samuel P. *The Clash of Civilizations and the Remaking of the Modern World.* New York: Simon and Schuster, 1996.

Kitschelt, Herbert, Zdenka Mansfeldova, Radoslaw Markowski, and Gábor Tóka. *Postcommunist Party Systems: Competition, Representation, and Inter-party Cooperation.* Cambridge: Cambridge University Press, 1999.

——. "Federalism and Secession: At Home and Abroad." *The Canadian Journal of Law and Jurisprudence* 13, no. 2 (2000): 207–24.

Kymlicka, Will. *Politics in the Vernacular: Nationalism, Multiculturalism, and Citizenship.* Oxford: Oxford University Press, 2001.

Laver, Michael. "Government Formation and Public Policy." *Political Science and Politics* 33, no. 1 (March 2000): 21–23.

Lijphart, Arend. *Democracy in Plural Societies: A Comparative Exploration.* New Haven: Yale University Press, 1977.

——. *Patterns of Democracy: Government Forms and Performance in Thirty-Six Countries.* New Haven: Yale University Press, 1999.

Linz, Juan J. and Alfred Stepan. *Problems of Democratic Transition and Consolidation.* Baltimore: Johns Hopkins University Press, 1996.

Mainwaring, Scott and Timothy R. Scully, eds. *Building Democratic Institutions: Party Systems in Latin America.* Stanford: Stanford University Press, 1995.

Michelman, Frank I. *Brennan and Democracy.* Princeton: Princeton University Press, 1999.

Mishler, William and Reginald S. Sheehan. "The Supreme Court as a Countermajoritarian Institution? The Impact of Public Opinion on Supreme Court Decisions." *American Political Science Review* 87, no. 1 (1993): 87–101.

Nagel, Robert. *Constitutional Cultures: The Mentality and Consequences of Judicial Review.* Berkeley: University of California Press, 1989.

Nino, Carlos Santiago. *The Constitution of Deliberative Democracy.* New Haven: Yale University Press, 1996.

Peretti, Terri Jennings. *In Defense of a Political Court.* Princeton: Princeton University Press, 1999.

Ponnuru, Ramesh. "Supreme Hubris: How the Court Overrules the Constitution." *National Review* 31, (2000): 28–31.

Putnam, Robert D., Robert Leonardi, and Raffaela Y. Nanetti. *Making Democracy Work.* Princeton: Princeton University Press, 1993.

Riker, William. *The Theory of Political Coalitions.* New Haven: Yale University Press, 1962.

Rose, Richard, William Mishler, and Christian Haerpfer. *Democracy and its Alternatives: Understanding Post-Communist Societies.* Baltimore: Johns Hopkins University Press, 1998.

Sartori, Giovanni. "Political Development and Political Engineering." *Public Policy* 17 (1966): 261–98.

Schöpflin, George. "Postcommunism: The Problems of Democratic Construction." *Daedalus* 123, no. 3 (1994): 127–42.

Schwartz, Herman. "Eastern Europe's Constitutional Courts." *Journal of Democracy* 9, no. 4 (1998): 100–14.

Scheppele, Kim Lane. "Democracy by Judiciary." Paper presented at the Conference on Constitutional Courts, Washington University School of Law, 1–3 November 2001.

Skach, Cindy. "Constitutional Courts and Democracy." Paper presented at the annual meeting of the American Political Science Association, 31 August–3 September 2000.

———. *Constitutional Justice: Judicial Review in the Modern World.* In preparation, n.d.

Stepan, Alfred. "Modern Multinational Democracies: Transcending a Gellnerian Oxymoron" in *The State of the Nation: Ernest Gellner and the Theory of Nationalism,* ed. Hall John A. (Cambridge: Cambridge University Press, 1998), pp. 219–39.

Sunstein, Cass R. *One Case at a Time: Judicial Minimalism on the Supreme Court.* Cambridge, Mass.: Harvard University Press, 1999.

Teitel, Ruti. *Transitional Justice.* Oxford: Oxford University Press, 1999.

Thayer, James Bradley. "The Origin and Scope of the American Doctrine of Constitutional Law." *Harvard Law Review* 7 (1893): 129–56.

Transition Report 1999: Ten Years of Transition. London: European Bank for Reconstruction and Development, 1999.

Tushnet, Mark. *Taking the Constitution Away from the Courts.* Princeton: Princeton University Press, 1999.

Walzer, Michael. *On Toleration.* New Haven: Yale University Press, 1997.

Wesolowski, Wlodzimierz. "The Nature of Social Ties and the Future of Postcommunist Society: Poland after Solidarity" in *The State of the Nation: Ernest Gellner and the Theory of Nationalism,* ed. Hall, John A. (Cambridge: Cambridge University Press, 1998), pp. 110–35.

Foxes, Hedgehogs, and Learning:
Notes on the Past and Future Dilemmas
of Postcommunist Constitutionalism

VENELIN I. GANEV

In a memorable paragraph, Alexander Bickel once described the Justices of the Warren Court as "rationalists coming after men of faith" (Bickel 1978: 14). The immediate objective of these distinguished jurists was to unshackle American constitutionalism from its attachment to doctrinaire traditions. Their powerful ambition was to articulate a vision of societal advancement through rational reform. And their broader goal was to re-evaluate inherited constitutional principles from the point of view of progressive reason.

Rushed onto the political scene almost half a century later, the first Justices in postcommunist Eastern Europe could not but behave *both* as "rationalists" and "men of faith." Easy choices were not available to them. For example, they had *to create* a constitutional tradition rather than transform an existing one, an endeavor that necessarily involves cultivating faith in the new normative order. They did not have to spur a conservative political establishment into action, but *to contain and regulate* an intractable, largely spontaneous process of political change—hence for them the articulation of norms and values limiting political action was as important as the commitment to reforms intended to restore "reasonable normalcy." And they had to operate in an intellectual milieu where, for perfectly understandable historical reasons, commitment to the "ultimate values" of liberal democracy was treasured much more than belief in "progressive reason."

As they were trying to explicate the meaning of the past, then, Eastern European Justices were both re-affirming articles of faith and engineering into existence a set of rational practices. And this process involved an element of "learning": members of constitutional courts became skilled at constructing certain kinds of arguments that would allow them to come to grips with historical legacies. In this chapter, I will try to find a place for this analytical theme—how and what the Justices learned when addressing the problems of the past—into the broader scholarly discourse on constitutional reform in Eastern Europe.

The phenomenon of "political learning"—cogently defined by Nancy Bermeo as "a process through which people modify their political beliefs and tactics as a result of severe crisis, frustrations and dramatic changes" (Bermeo 1992: 273)—is hard to pinpoint and yet impossible to ignore. Clearly, it may have a beneficial impact on postcommunist jurisprudence: as Andrew Arato has recently argued, "learning from the past" may become "conscious and fruitful for constitutionalism." But—as Arato himself perspicaciously acknowledges—this process may also lead to "too much learning," in other words it may engender, rather than alleviate, problems within the constitutional system (Arato 2000: 253–54). It is this second, less appealing aspect of learning that I would like to explore. In a nutshell, my argument runs as follows. Compelled by the circumstances to address and resolve an array of issues pertaining to the past, Eastern European Justices developed certain modes of argumentation, styles of reasoning, and mental habits that allowed them to carry out their difficult task. As postcommunist societies move to a "post-founding stage," however, these mental habits and preferred styles of argumentation may prove to be less than fully adequate to the needs of evolving constitutional orders. In particular, I will argue that the process of "learning from the past" limited the impact of judicial review as a reflexive mechanism and impeded the development of what might be called "constitutional equity." Some "unlearning," then, might be good for the integrity and functionality of constitutionalism in Eastern Europe.

More broadly, I advance two claims, one empirical and the other analytical. On an empirical level, I suggest that "the lasting legacy" of the early stages of postcommunist jurisprudence is to be found not only in concrete answers to specific controversies, but in enduring "constitutional manners" and persistent "styles of reasoning" acquired in the immediate aftermath of 1989. Put differently, the outcomes of constitutional litigation constitute one, albeit very important, element of the courts' overall impact on the constitutional system—the rhetorical strategies employed by the Justices and the manner in which they justify their decisions also shape the dynamics of institutionalized interactions in young democracies. On an analytical level, I suggest that Eastern European democracies, young although they might be, are by now (at the beginning of the 21st century) in a position to draw upon an array of accumulated constitutional experiences. Therefore, it might be time for scholars to look beyond the political, scientific, and jurisprudential concerns that frame the study of "constitutional founding" in a postcommunist context, towards a more careful examination of the problems of "post-founding" constitutional review. From that vantage point, the problem of "too much learning" is not a pathological manifestation of constitutional underdevelopment—it may be considered one of many aporias that distinguish constitutional maturity.

THE CONSTITUTION OF THE HEDGEHOGS, OR JUDICIAL
REVIEW AS A REFLEXIVE MECHANISM

What is the most appropriate way to characterize the past from the point of view of the post-totalitarian constitutionalism? What is the constitutional meaning of 1989? And, given the orderliness and legality of the "transition," how is the present political order different from the one left behind? These questions haunted postcommunist jurisprudence: whatever their predilections for "restraint" or "activism," Justices in all postcommunist countries had to grapple with similar conundrums. And, under such pressure, these Justices rapidly became conversant with what might be called—borrowing a metaphor from Isaiah Berlin—"the constitutionalism of the hedgehogs." According to Berlin, the hedgehogs know "only one big thing": they "relate everything to a single central vision," to "one system more or less coherent in terms of which they understand, think and feel," to "a single, universal, organizing principle in terms of which alone all that they are and say has significance" (Berlin 1994: 22). The creation of a constitutional discourse focused on the task of "coming to terms with the past" is, in an important sense, a hedgehog's pursuit. This pursuit is inevitable and necessary at a time when entire societies are trying to grapple with the tensions between a largely intact legal order and a dramatically changed political order, to comprehend the ramifications of "the non-radical founding" that occurred in 1989, and to meet the challenge of "constitutionalizing" the impulse for sweeping change. It is only understandable that under these historical circumstances, Justices will resort to a "jurisprudence of difference," or a sustained effort to articulate a unitary vision about a single hierarchy of values resting on a coherent set of principles which would make it clear to everyone that "the new order" has severed the umbilical cord with the infamous past. And yet, as postcommunist polities develop and become more complex, the constitutionalism of the hedgehogs may fall short of expectations of political actors and social constituencies—and the jurisprudence of difference may remain silent when confronted with the challenges of the "post-founding" era.

Let me illustrate my contention with two examples. Reflecting on the legal dimensions of the *ancien régime,* the Czech and the Hungarian Courts reached decisions that are, in important respects, diametrically opposed. Nonetheless, in both countries important attributes of "the constitutionalism of the hedgehogs" began to emerge as their Justices attempted to "come to terms with the past."

The Czech Constitutional Court was the only one in the region that had to decide whether the communist regime was "lawless" or not—and the Justices answered in the affirmative. Let me say clearly and emphatically that I share the Czech Justices' moral intuition—the "people's democracies" established in Eastern Europe after the end of World War II were inhumane and, at times, unabashedly terroristic. At the same time, the style of reasoning that underpins the Justices' decision may serve as an example of "the jurisprudence of difference." All the arguments the Justices invoke revolve around the issue how "the present" is different from "the past"—and how the invocation of "ultimate values" may yield unambiguous answers to constitutional conflicts.

The concrete case that prompted the Czech Court to pass a legal verdict on the past stemmed from a controversy regarding the constitutionality of a special declaration adopted by Parliament that denounced the communist regime as "lawless." Affirming the constitutionality of the declaration, the Court did consider the substantive issue at hand, namely whether the former system was indeed "lawless." Its argument rests on two distinctions and an idiosyncratic interpretation of an important legal concept.[1] First, the Justices alleged that the *ancien régime* was "formally rational," while the new Czech democracy is "substantively rational": "The starting point of our Constitution is the substantive-rational conception of legitimacy and the law-based state." In other words, communist authorities were only concerned with the legal form of their political decisions—and therefore these decisions ought to be considered as unjust "even though they are wrapped in the cloak of law." Second, they asserted that the declaration—which, among other things, posited that statutes of limitation did not run between 1948 and 1989—is "declarative" and not "constitutive," and therefore it does not violate the principle of non-retroactivity of criminal law.[2] With regards to "legal certainty"—the argument that tampering with statues of limitations may endanger the legal certainty enjoyed by citizens living under the rule of law—the Justices maintained that "the legal certainty of offenders is, however, a source of legal uncertainty to citizens (and vice versa). In a context of these two types of certainty, the Constitutional Court gives priority to the certainty of civil society, which is in keeping with the law-based state."

Upon closer scrutiny, these distinctions and interpretations cannot stand. To begin with, the attempt to invoke the Weberian categories of "substantive" and "formal" rationality in order to drive a wedge between communist and postcommunist political orders is somewhat misleading. Max Weber defined a "substantively rational order" as one where "decision of legal orders is influenced by norms different than those obtained through logical generalization of abstract interpretations of meaning" and hence predominance is accorded to "ethical imperatives... and political maxims" (Weber 1978: 657). And he clearly and unambiguously identified "socialism" as a political system resting on substantively rational premises. The rise of socialism, Weber argued, is intimately linked to "the growing dominance of substantive natural law doctrines in the minds of masses and even more in the minds of their theorists from among the intelligentsia" (Weber 1978: 873).[3] Clearly, the dichotomy between "formal" and "substantive" constitutional orders cannot serve as an analytical tool for distinguishing modern Czech democracy from the regime that immediately preceded it.

The problem with the other distinction, between "declarative" and "constitutive" norms is that the Czech Court plays upon the ambiguity of the term "declarative." Strictly legally speaking, a "declarative act" is one that has no immediate legal consequences but illuminates the nature of legal relations that existed prior to the passage of the act. In the Justices' interpretation, however, it apparently means an act announcing a verifiable truth. Hence the Court could refer to the former meaning when asserting that the document is constitutional because it does not introduce criminal legislation retroactively, and to the latter meaning when contending that the same declaration does indeed legally discontinue the statutes of limitation from running in the 1948–1989 period. The act of parliament is treated as a declaration of truth about the *ancien régime,* a declaration that opens the door for criminal persecution of a particular group of wrong-doers.

With regards to the distinction between the legal certainty of perpetrators and legal certainty of civil society, one may point out that this is a false dilemma. From the point of view of "substantive postcommunist constitutionalism," all citizens must enjoy "certainty." And the designation "perpetrator of crimes" must be determined in accordance with the rules of the new order, rather than in accordance with the status enjoyed by groups of individuals under the *ancien régime.*

In affirming the constitutionality of the declaration, a decision was reached that was perhaps shared by the majority of citizens in the Czech Republic— and is in line with the moral sentiments of enlightened public opinion around the world. At the same time, its rhetoric and choice of specific arguments steered constitutional jurisprudence in a particular direction—towards persistent efforts to explicate the normative vision informing the new polity— that might obfuscate rather than illuminate the constitutional dilemmas facing Czech political actors.

The Hungarian Court also had to address the question of the legal nature of the former regime—but it reached for a rather different substantive conclusion: it affirmed the legality of the acts of the former regime (in particular of its economic measures) and affirmed the principle of "legal continuity" that bridges the gap between "before" and "after."[4] For example, according to the Justices, communist nationalizations were legally valid and therefore former owners did not have a "right" to be compensated for their losses. The state may decide to launch compensation programs—but such programs ought to be considered a manifestation of the sovereign will of the new parliament rather than the fulfillment of a moral obligation to redress the injustices of the past.[5] More broadly, there is ample evidence suggesting that the first Justices of democratic Hungary espoused a "basically positivist view" according to which the *ancien* and *nouveau régimes* constitute "a single continuous legal tradition" whose fundamental uninterruptedness must be explicitly recognized (see Halmai and Scheppele 1997: 162).

This does not mean, however, that Justices do not come again and again to the question of how, even if continuity is recognized, the present is different from the past. In fact, at times they seemed afflicted by a strange kind of "continuity guilt": having affirmed the continuity, the Court is then compelled to explore the normative dimensions of difference that set the new regime apart from the old. As the most prominent "founding father" explains, the jurisprudence of the Constitutional Court rests on "a clear hierarchy of fundamental rights" that "is not based on positive law" and "at the pinnacle of which are the rights to life and human dignity" (Sólyom 2000: 5). In other words, the affirmation of "legal continuity" goes hand in hand with a large-scale theorizing about the unified hierarchy of normative principles that sustains the post-totalitarian constitutional order.

One particular corollary of this trend might be called "normative overshooting": faced with the choice of framing a concrete dispute either as a matter of ultimate values, or in more technical, legalistic terms, the Justices habitually embrace the former option and forego the latter. Two examples illustrating my contention may suffice. When discussing the relevance of the principle of "legal stability" for welfare reform, for instance, the Hungarian Justices simply asserted that the concept of "legal certainty" is "the most important conceptual element of a rule-of-law system" (Sólyom 2000: 41). This blank statement clearly bespeaks a willingness to refract the questions put before the Court through the prism of higher normative principles rather than the specifics of policy-making and concrete constitutional rights. Professor András Sajó's charge that the Court has succumbed to "populist material justice" and thus "killed" welfare reform may be a bit harsh (cf. Sajó 1996). But it undoubtedly illuminates the downside of "the jurisprudence of difference"—the ambition to take the moral high ground when a more focused discussion of options and alternatives might have been more helpful.

The second example of "normative overshooting" is the Court's decision in the "trade union representation case."[6] Rather than referring to the principles of labor law, or even the notion of representation, the Justices invoked "the right to human dignity" in order to strike down the challenged norm. Assessing this approach, even commentators sympathetic to the Court were forced to admit that "the decision to rely on the admittedly extra-textual right to human dignity... signals that the Court does not see a need to link its interpretation to the text of the Constitution" (see Klingsberg 1992: 80). "Normative overshooting" results in a hortatory affirmation of a single hierarchy of values and virtually no guidelines pertaining to the constitutional implications of labor law legislation.

In order to understand fully the implications of "the constitutionalism of hedgehogs" that Justices have learned to use with some dexterity, a reference to Niklas Luhmann's discussion of types of "reflexive mechanisms" might be helpful. According to Luhmann, "reflexive mechanisms" articulate meanings that structure the expectations of actors and render "manageable" complex and multi-layered social interactions (cf. Luhmann 1985: ch. 4). At times, these mechanisms serve the purpose of articulating the difference between "before" and "after."[7] Under such circumstances, the articulation of meaning may focus, hedgehog-like, on the invariant bases of institutionalized politics, absolute values and basic principles. And this trend, according to Luhmann, may lead to problems in a constitutional system: the reiteration of basic principles may prove to be an insufficient guarantee of order; the invocation of absolute values may not be instructive enough to guide the process of continuous structural variation; re-affirmation of invariant bases may exclude too little and not contain sufficient indications of the respective utilizable solutions. That is why it may be possible to envisage an alternative function of judicial review as a "reflexive mechanism," namely one centered on the operationalization of concepts (for example, "legal continuity"), decisions about decision-making (for example, under what conditions statutes of limitation may be extended retroactively), and positing of norms about norm-making (for example, the normative criteria against which the constitutionality of labor laws will be evaluated). Once integrated in the jurisprudence of Eastern European democracies, this novel form of reflexivity may generate a new range of options that these societies may consider, and propel the process of institutionalization of the branches of government.[8] The discourse on ultimate values and uplifting visions will, no doubt, continue to exert its irrepressible appeal on Justices, scholars, and commentators. But this discourse should be supplemented by a more reflexive (in a Luhmannian sense) approach towards the complex institutional and political problems that beset evolving constitutional systems.

THE CONSTITUTION OF THE FOXES:
SHOULD JUDICIAL REVIEW BE AN INSTRUMENT
OF CONSTITUTIONAL EQUITY?

The political discourse on "equity" has a venerable tradition that goes back at least to Aristotle. He defined "equity" as "correction of law owing to its universality" and also asserted that "the equitable is just."[9] In essence, "equity" is the imperative to avoid the application of general principles in concrete cases if this application will result in an unjust outcome—or, to quote a contemporary scholar, it is "the practice of doing particularized justice, when the just result is not required by, or contrary to, the result required by the set of applicable rules" (Solum 1994: 123). And there is a shared understanding that in a modern political system it is the courts that should mitigate the harshness of abstract rules on specific occasions—as Hamilton put it in *Federalist* 80, it is "the peculiar province of courts" to "relieve against hard bargains," in other words to handle situations where a strict application of the letter of the law will cause "undue misfortunes" to individuals (Madison et al. 1987: 449). It is only understandable then, that the articulation of some notion of constitutional equity, of the relation between legitimate rules and justifiable exceptions, should be counted among the main jurisprudential tasks of newly established constitutional courts.

At first glance, it would seem that Eastern European Justices are well positioned to engage in deliberations about constitutional equity. On the one hand, these courts were new institutions that had to apply novel principles to unpredictable situations. On the other hand, and perhaps more importantly, they had to make their first steps in a situation that was, unquestionably, "exceptional": radical changes were reshaping all aspects of social and political life, "the multiple transitions" generated intractable dilemmas almost on a daily basis, and an array of exigencies seemed to require immediate and decisive executive action. Amidst this almost unmanageable turbulence, the Justices were repeatedly confronted with the question what "exceptional departures" from general rules and principles may be constitutionally acceptable. More often than not, however, Justices ground their decisions on the interpretation of past events rather than on a careful exploration of the normative dimensions of exceptionality.[10] Fixation on the past may explain why constitutional equity is yet to become a principled practice in Eastern Europe. To invoke Berlin's imagery once again, when dealing with exceptions, the Justices at times behaved like "foxes" who "pursue many ends, often unrelated and even contradictory," espouse "ideas that are centrifugal rather than centripetal," seek to move on "many levels without... seeking to fit them into, or exclude them from, any one unchanging... unitary inner vision" (Berlin 1994: 22). The "constitutionalism of foxes" may yield outcomes that are eminently desirable and wise. But it is bound to leave underdeveloped the theoretical foundations of constitutional equity in postcommunism—a defect that may decrease the capacity of the constitutional system to absorb conflicts when the variety of issues confronting postcommunist societies become even more variegated and complex.

An analysis of the most famous decision of the Bulgarian Constitutional Court might illustrate the problematic nature of the "constitutionalism of foxes." In early 1992, the Bulgarian Justices had to pass a judgment on the

constitutionality of the Movement for Rights and Freedoms (MRF), the political organization of ethnic Turks in the country. The history of the case is as
follows. After the collapse of the communist regime on 10 November 1989,
multiparty elections for a Great National Assembly were held. The elections
were won by the former communists who openly embraced nationalism as
their new credo. The majority managed to engineer the passage of a constitutional provision banning "political parties formed on ethnic basis" (Article
11.4). In the meantime, the MRF had been duly registered as a political party
by the Sofia City Court, and was therefore allowed to participate in national electoral contests. Invoking the newly passed constitutional provision, the
former communists petitioned the Court, asking the Justices to declare the
MRF unconstitutional. In a landmark decision, the Court rejected the petition and affirmed the constitutionality of the MRF.[11] Let me make it clear—
the decision of the Court was a wise, just, and effective one. It convinced the
Bulgarian public that the MRF is, and should be accepted as, a legitimate
participant in the national political process and thus represents a major step
towards ethnic reconciliation in the country (and the consolidation of what
has been called "the Bulgarian ethnic model"[12]). At the same time, it may
be considered as an example of the constitutionalism of foxes—and as such,
it displays the limitations inherent in this mode of legal reasoning.

The main challenge with which the Court had to cope was how to refuse
to apply the scandalous Article 11.4 in the case of a party that was clearly
formed on an ethnic basis. In order to justify its departure from an emphat-
ic constitutional rule, the Court engaged in a historical analysis that passed
through three steps. First, the Court looked into the recent past and reiterated the well-known truth that the Muslim minority in Bulgaria was subject
to systematic, bloody repressions by the communist regime in the 1980s.
Second, the Court asserted that the formation of the MRF must be construed
as a legitimate response against these repressions. The Justices pointed out
that "the very formation of the MRF occurred in a concrete historical moment"
marked by the rise of political pluralism. It was an "immediate consequence
of the acts perpetrated by the totalitarian regime against a part of the Bulgarian
citizens" and the rise of the MRF is "a natural reaction" to these campaigns.
The Court duly noted that the governing documents of the party explicitly
refer to the "specific ethnic and religious basis" of the Movement. "Language"
(Turkish) and "religion" (Muslim) are among the markers mentioned by the
Movement's founders when they described the intended audience of their
party. The program clearly contains provisions that contradict *both* the communist constitution effective when the Movement was organized (1990), and
the postcommunist constitution adopted in 1991. Nevertheless,—and this is
the third step of the argument—the Court concluded that the leading consideration should be *"the moment in which the Movement was formed, and*

the context in which it was formed," and not the fact that many of its characteristics are indisputably proscribed by Article 11.4. In other words, the Court
revived what might be called—following W. James Booth—a "memory of
injustice" in order to justify a departure from a constitutional norm (Booth
2001: 780). And the logic of the argument implied that such departures might
be justified through a historical inquiry designed to alleviate the injustices of
the recent past.

While—let me repeat again—the result of this line of reasoning is perfectly
legitimate and constitutionally desirable, the argument of the Court suffers
from ad-hocishness and a lack of analytical depth. More specifically, the reference to unique historical circumstances does not spell out the general principles that may justify departure from constitutional rules. And there is evidence that by resolving this case by means of introducing "a constitutional
exception," the decision did not generate two specific kinds of positive consequences associated with constitutional equity: increased predictability of
the system of rules, and overall adherence to constitutional norms.[13]

*Levels of unpredictability in the constitutional system remain high: it is
not clear what, if any, other minorities will benefit from "the exception."*
Despite the categorical decision of the Court in the MRF case, it is still uncertain how minority organizations will be treated in light of the constitutional
ban on ethnic parties. Recently the Court declared a party purporting to represent the "Macedonian" minority unconstitutional, even though there were
serious reasons to believe that it should be allowed to exist—and though some
evidence of injustices perpetrated against this minority might be easily
adduced. At this moment, there is a lack of clarity regarding the considerations that the Court might rely upon when assessing the constitutionality of
minorities other than the Turks.

*In the absence of clearly articulated guidelines for equitable solutions
to constitutional problems, basic norms of the constitution may be endangered
when the Justices "carve out" the constitutional terrain of exceptionality.*
Clearly, when disregarding the constitutional ban on ethnic parties, the Court
acted as a champion of a politically prosecuted and repressed minority. It is
less certain what other exceptions—in addition to *de facto* lifting the ban of
Article 11.4—the Court may consider legitimate in light of its laudable objective, namely the rectification of past injustices. Several months after the MRF
case, the Parliament passed a decision invalidating all contracts signed by
Turks forced to depart from Bulgaria in the mid- and late 1980s—a legislative measure that allowed these involuntary emigrants to reclaim property
they were coerced to sell at very low prices. This act encountered the objection that contracts concluded under duress may be invalidated by means of

ordinary litigation (and thus declared void by Courts and not Parliament), and therefore the passage of a general law is an inadequate measure that retroactively interferes with legally valid contracts. To this the Court pointed out that the legislators' ultimate objective is the "rectification of ills inflicted as a result of a condemnable state policy." And to the argument that the retroactive tinkering with contracts violates property rights, the Justices responded: "the rights of buyers should be disregarded because they are incompatible with the purpose of the law."[14] Thus the Court found itself on a slippery slope towards accepting as constitutional even exceptional measures that pose palpable threats to constitutional rights (such as the right to property)—a form of quasi-equitable jurisprudence that brings incoherence, rather than coherence, in the constitutional system.

To the arguments outlined above one may add the—unfailingly pertinent—claim that the expansion of equitable remedial powers, which transforms the courts into major actors who not only block the enforcement of questionable provisions, but also prescribe the implementation of substantive policies towards large groups, may in the medium and long run undermine the authority of the Justices—authority that ultimately rests on their reputation as more or less impartial and competent guardians of the constitution.[15] As Aristotle himself pointed out, the line that separates the practice of dispensing equity and judicial arbitrariness is thin and elusive, and therefore judges who habitually disregard "laws properly enacted" incur the risk of being regarded as actors whose "judgment is obscured by their own pleasure or pain."[16]

Needless to say, the foregoing analysis is not intended to cast doubt on the continuing and at times unquestionably successful efforts of constitutional courts in Eastern Europe to find ways to reconcile the application of general rules with the suspension of these rules in concrete cases. But it does seek to alert us to the fact that the circumstances under which Justices should engage in the practice of equity remain ill-defined. What are the conflicting principles that call for an equitable decision? What are the general rules that must prevail? Why is deviation justified? How is it likely to affect future behavior? How are exceptions reconciled with the rule of law? More often than not, courts might be expected to identify victims rather than principles of justice and equity—and thus opportunities to explicate the tensions between equity and the rule of law was passed unheeded. Behind the ultimately desirable outcome of this case lies the agility of foxes—and not the tempered passion of a virtuous judge.

CONCLUSION

One of the peculiarities of the centuries-old debates about the rule of law and constitutionalism is that even though these debates usually conjure up universal categories and aim at general conclusions, they are inescapably linked to local concerns and experiences. After all, Judith Shklar characterized one of the most monumental tracts on the subject, Albert Venn Dicey's *Introduction to the Study of the Law of the Constitution* (1939) as "an unfortunate outburst of Anglo-Saxon parochialism" (Shklar 1998: 26). That is why I would be the first to deny any generalizability to my notes on postcommunist constitutionalism. I do think, however, that the foregoing observations may help us both put the courts' past successes in context and anticipate the future problems of judicial review in Eastern Europe.

Most of the Justices in most of the countries have clearly learned how to adjudicate.[17] They know that sometimes the invocation of ultimate values may bring a conflict to an end, motivate politicians to behave in a law-abiding manner and pacify unruly publics. The Justices have hammered out demonstrably workable solutions to complex problems. Perhaps most importantly, they have—as Wojciech Sadurski put it—"affected the political discourse and infused it with constitutional considerations" and thus made transgressions of basic constitutional principles more costly for unruly politicians (Sadurski 2000: 473). In sum, constitutional courts have produced a rich and diverse body of jurisprudence that forms the solid basis of fledgling constitutional orders in postcommunist Europe.

At the same time, the courts may be considered prisoners of their own success. The lessons they have learned while "coping with the past" may be a deficient compass for societies moving in new, unpredictable directions. To stick to those lessons—for example, to insist that the articulation of a unitary normative vision may provide answers to all constitutional controversies, or that the re-evaluation of the past may provide guidelines for justifiable departures from general rules—would be a strategy that needs to be critically re-assessed.

And the reason for that is that there are new lessons to be learned. For example, the mechanism of judicial review is yet to become one of the motors that may propel postcommunist polities from "negative" to "positive" rule of law,[18] or from "obstructionist" versus "enabling" constitutionalism (Holmes 1995: 302). More concretely, the Justices will have to find ways to oversee the implementation of various constitutionally relevant policies. As several observers of the postcommunist political scene have noted, the degree of "ruleness" decreases rapidly the further below the constitutional level one descends (see, for example, Örkény and Scheppele 1999). It is not immediately clear what the Justices may do to alleviate this problem, but a more sustained attention to the problem of increasing the constitutional system's capacity for generating binding decisions may help.

More generally, the strange mixture of "constitutionalism of the hedgehogs" and "constitutionalism of the foxes" renders difficult the development of a broader *constitutional culture* that revolves around "a web of interpretative norms, canons and practices."[19] Dominique Rousseau once observed that "although the Courts calm political life, they must not lull it to sleep" (Rousseau 1994: 268). Ritualistic invocation of supreme principles may, indeed, increase the level of boredom in the political domain. More importantly, however, vague announcements of ultimate values may foreclose debates—if the Justices behave as oracles, then the venues for participation in constitutional debate may be locked as the gates of a heavenly city.

Hannah Arendt once argued that the very fact that we consider "concern for stability" and "exhilaration for creativity" antithetical is a manifestation of that peculiar malaise, "the loss of revolutionary treasure" (Arendt 1963: ch. 6). When coping with the past, the courts have been able to display creativity without endangering the stability of democracy. But if their success is to endure, the courts will have to reinvent themselves as actors whose reason is not constantly endangered by upsurge of faith. And the most formidable challenge in this process of re-invention will not be the heated struggle with political competitors and anti-constitutional forces. The most formidable challenge for Eastern European Justices will be to avoid falling prey to their own achievements—and to adjust to the consequences of their own successful interventions during the "founding" era.

NOTES

1 Hereafter I have relied on the official English translation of the court's decision, available at http://www.concourt.cz/angl_ver/decisions/doc/p-19–93.html.
2 The parliamentary decision on the statute of limitations clearly had implications for criminal law insofar as it would make it possible to prosecute individuals for crimes committed during the period in question irrespectively of whether or not the statutes of limitation passed by communist authorities had already elapsed.
3 For Weber's views on socialism, see also Weber 1994.
4 On the "legal continuity theory," see Sólyom 2000: 31. This theory was articulated in the famous "compensation cases," both of which are included in that volume (pp. 108–17 and 151–58).
5 This view is discussed at length in the "compensation cases."
6 Published in the collection of decisions quoted above, note 4, pp. 105–107. The Court had to evaluate the constitutionality of a Labor Law provision that empowered Trade Union activists to represent employees even in the absence of an explicit consent on the part of the latter.
7 For an analysis of this mode of reflexivity from a theoretical perspective, see Luhmann 1995: 443.

8 On these benefits of reflexivity, see Preuss 1996: 17.

9 Aristotle, *Nicomachean Ethics*, V.10.

10 For more on this issue, see Ganev 1997.

11 See *Reshenija I opredelenija na Konstitutzionnija sud 1991–1992* [Decisions and Rulings of the Constitutional Court, 1991–1992], pp. 67–98.

12 On the peaceful character of ethnic relations in Bulgaria, see Zheljazkova 2001.

13 Hereafter I draw on Solum 1994, note 21.

14 See *Reshenija I opredelenija na Konstitutzionnija sud 1991–1992* [Decisions and Rulings of the Constitutional Court, 1991–1992], p. 205.

15 For an excellent discussion of the risks inherent in the expansion of equitable remedial powers, see McDowell 1982, especially part 1, pp. 15–50.

16 Aristotle, *Rhetoric*, 1354a-b.

17 This is, in a nutshell, the general conclusion reached by Herman Schwartz in his pathbreaking study (Schwartz 2000).

18 On "negative" and "positive" rule of law, see Selznick 1999.

19 I borrow this definition of constitutional culture from John Ferejohn, John Rakove, and Jonathan Riley (Ferejohn et al. 2001: 18).

BIBLIOGRAPHY

Arato, Andrew. *Civil Society, Constitution and Legitimacy.* Oxford: Rowman and Littlefield, 2000.

Arendt, Hannah. *On Revolution.* New York: Viking, 1963.

Berlin, Isaiah. "The Hedgehog and the Fox" in *Russian Thinkers*, eds. Hardy, Henry and Aileen Kelly (London: Penguin Books, 1994), pp. 22–81.

Bermeo, Nancy. "Democracy and the Lessons of Dictatorship." *Comparative Politics* 24, no. 3 (1992): 273–91.

Bickel, Alexander. *The Supreme Court and the Idea of Progress.* New Haven: Yale University Press, 1978.

Booth, W. James. "The Unforgotten: Memories of Justice." *American Political Science Review* 95, no. 4 (2001): 777–91.

Dicey, Albert Venn. *Introduction to the Study of the Law of the Constitution.* London: Macmillan, 1993.

Ferejohn, John, John Rakove, and Jonathan Riley, eds. *Constitutional Culture and Democratic Rule.* Cambridge: Cambridge University Press, 2001.

Ganev, Venelin I. "Emergency Powers and the New East European Constitutions." *American Journal of Comparative Law* 45, no. 3 (1997): 585–612.

Halmai, Gábor and Kim Lane Scheppele. "Living Well is the Best Revenge: The Hungarian Approach to Judging the Past" in *Transitional Justice and the Rule of Law in New Democracies*, ed. McAdams, A. James (Notre Dame: University of Notre Dame Press, 1997), pp. 155–84.

Holmes, Stephen. "Constitutionalism" in *The Encyclopedia of Democracy*, ed. Seymor, Martin Lipset (Washington D.C.: Congressional Quarterly, 1995), pp. 299–306.

Klingsberg, Ethan. "Judicial Review and Hungary's Transition from Communism to Democracy: The Constitutional Court, the Continuity of Law, and the Redefinition of Property Rights." *Brigham Young University Law Review* 1 (1992): 41–144.

Luhmann, Niklas. *A Sociological Theory of Law*. London: Routledge and Kegan Paul, 1985.

——. *Social Systems*. Stanford: Stanford University Press, 1995.

Madison, James, Alexander Hamilton, and Jay, John. *The Federalist Papers*. Harmondsworth: Penguin, 1987.]

McDowell, Gary L. *Equity and the Constitution: The Supreme Court, Equitable Relief and Public Policy*. Chicago: University of Chicago Press, 1982.

Örkény, Antal and Kim Lane Scheppele. "Rules of Law: The Complexity of Legality in Hungary" in *The Rule of Law after Communism*, eds. Krygier, Martin and Adam Czarnota (Aldershot: Ashgate, 1999), pp. 55–76.

Preuss, Ulrich K. "The Political Meaning of Constitutionalism" in *Constitutionalism, Democracy and Sovereignty: American and European Perspectives*, ed. Bellamy, Richard (Aldershot: Avebury Publishing, 1996), pp. 11–27.

Reshenija I opredelenija na Konstitutzionnija sud 1991–1992 [Decisions and Rulings of the Constitutional Court, 1991–1992]. Sofia: BAN, 1993.

Rousseau, Dominique. "The Constitutional Judge: Master or Slave of the Constitution?" in *Constitutionalism, Identity, Difference and Legitimacy: Theoretical Perspectives*, ed. Rosenfeld, Michel (Durham: Duke University Press, 1994), pp. 261–284.

Sadurski, Wojciech. "Conclusions: On the Relevance of Institutions and the Centrality of Constitutions in Post-Communist Transitions" *Democratic Consolidation in Eastern Europe: Institutional Engineering*, ed. Zielonka, Jan (Oxford: Oxford University Press, 2000), pp. 455–74.

Sajó, András. "How the Rule of Law Killed Hungarian Welfare Reform." *East European Constitutional Review* 5, no. 1 (1996): 31–40.

Schwartz, Herman. *The Struggle for Postcommunist Justice in Postcommunist Europe*. Chicago: University of Chicago Press, 2000.

Shklar, Judith. "Political Theory and the Rule of Law" in *Political Thought and Political Thinkers*, ed. Hoffman, Stanley (Chicago: University of Chicago Press, 1998), pp. 121–37.

Selznick, Philip. "Legal Cultures and the Rule of Law" in *The Rule of Law after Communism*, eds. Krygier, Martin and Adam Czarnota (Aldershot: Ashgate, 1999), pp 1–16.

Solum, Lawrence. "Equity and the Rule of Law" in *Nomos XXXVI: The Rule of Law*, ed. Shapiro, Ian (New York: New York University Press, 1994), pp. 120–47.

Sólyom, László. "Introduction to the Decisions of the Constitutional Court of the Republic of Hungary" in *Constitutional Judiciary in a New Democracy: The Hungarian Constitutional Court*, eds. Sólyom, László and Georg Brunner (Ann Arbor: University of Michigan Press, 2000), pp. 1–64.

Weber, Max. *Economy and Society, Vol. II*. Berkeley: University of California Press, 1978.——. "Socialism" in *Max Weber: Political Writings*, eds. Lassmann, Peter and Ronald Speirs (Cambridge: Cambridge University Press, 1994), pp. 272–303.

Zheljazkova, Antonina. "The Bulgarian Ethnic Model." *East European Constitutional Review* 10, no. 4 (2001): 49–54.

Democratic Norm Building and Constitutional Discourse Formation in Estonia

Vello Pettai

Introduction

Democratic consolidation—in perhaps its most essential meaning—represents a process of learning new rules of the political game and developing long-lasting institutional relationships. To the extent that such consolidations often include totally new constitutions, the process is magnified even further. Political actors are placed in a situation where their behavior according to a new set of rules must gradually nurture new democratic norms; the letter of constitutions must be cultivated into a longer-term discourse of constitutionalism.

While most attention in the literature on democratic consolidation has been focused on centre-stage politicians—meaning politicians in the executive and legislative branches—, the ways in which judicial bodies and more specifically constitutional review mechanisms have contributed to democratic norm building has attracted much less interest.[1] To be sure, the reality is that center-stage politicians do most of the "democratic consolidating" by setting precedents through their everyday institutional interactions and decisions. Such precedents might be as little as accepting defeat on a parliamentary bill, or handing over government to the opposition after an election. In addition, these politicians are generally the ones who need "consolidating" the most, for if democracy breaks down it will probably be because of these same politicians, not because of the judiciary. No court has ever staged or even precipitated on its own a *coup d'état*.

At the same time, democratic consolidation cannot adequately take place without a deeper and more authoritative sense of constitutionalism being formed. It is this more profound consciousness of what a constitution means as an organic system that constitutional review mechanisms often help to rear. By playing the role of watchdog—or as is more often the case, by allowing other institutions to call this process forth—, constitutional courts often drive home certain points about democratic politics and government much more profoundly that any single political actor's action might otherwise. In the struggle between different and often equal political players, the transgressions of one over another are generally not solved well by some kind of more powerful or retaliatory action by the player transgressed against. Institutional or political tugs-of-war may, of course, maintain a semblance of balance-of-power for a certain period of time. However, such deadlocks are more like-

ly to end eventually in an earthquake of political tension, and quite probably in democratic breakdown itself. Instead, longer-term lessons tend to be
learned as well as more recognized procedural outcomes reached when disputes are settled by separately standing judicial bodies. The weight that is
carried by the decision of such a body will usually seep much deeper into
political actors' psyches, and it is this that therefore represents the most meaningful facet of democratic consolidation.[2]

It is no great discovery, therefore, to say that constitutional review mechanisms matter for democratic consolidation. Yet, it becomes a much more
difficult question to elucidate what are some of the *archetypical* institutional or political disputes which constitutional courts in consolidating constitutional systems may be called upon to adjudicate. To what extent can we begin
to aggregate and generalize the exact democratic norm building experiences
of different constitutional courts in the postcommunist countries of Central
and Eastern Europe? What kinds of legal-procedural and/or rights questions
have arisen in these constitutional systems, which constitutional courts have
had to help consolidate? Are there any patterns discernible purely in terms
of "frequency" of different kinds of disputes? In turn, amongst similar kinds
of constitutional disputes *across* countries, can we distinguish similar legal
thinking or constitutional discourses in the opinions of different constitutional courts, or have varying legal cultures begun to evolve? Do the constitutional courts in the region tend to think the same or differently?

Having raised all of these questions, the reader will surmise that this chapter will not be able to answer all of them. Rather, they are raised as part of
a broader context-setting exercise and with an eye to indicating what kind of
comparative conceptual framework I aim this chapter to contribute to. In this
sense, what follows is a presentation of the "frequencies" of different kinds
of institutional/political disputes which have arisen in the constitutional court
of one particular Eastern European case, Estonia, and thereafter a broader
reflection upon the constitutional discourse which this experience has fos-
tered. It is hoped that from here more cross-national, comparative studies
might be possible, which in turn would lead to a generalized picture of the
process of democratic norm building via constitutional review mechanisms
in Central and Eastern Europe.

To say that democratic consolidation involves learning to play by new rules
of the political game means in operational terms learning to work and respect
the basic tenets of constitutional law. Thus, the question of democratic norm
building via constitutional review mechanisms creates in its own way an interesting nexus between political science and constitutional law. As noted above,
the full scope of democratic consolidation cannot be ascertained without
assessing the degree to which constitutional legal principles have taken root
in a political system. By the same token, constitutional law likewise cannot

operate in a vacuum; its function is (perhaps more than any other branch of law) deeply embedded in the political science and normative theory dimension of democratic consolidation.

In this chapter I take predominantly a political scientist's view on these issues. More specifically, I should note that the categories, according to which I present the different democratic norms encountered in the Estonian case, are derived somewhat endogenously or inductively. Clearly, more rigorous application of exogenous or deductive constitutional legal theory would produce a different kind of analysis. Succinctly put, however, I will raise five broad categories of democratic legal norms, which have repeatedly arisen in the ten-year case history of the Estonian Constitutional Review Chamber. These are: separation of powers, breach of powers, fundamental rights and freedoms, minority rights, and public policy making.[3]

I will present and discuss some of the more characteristic court cases which have embodied each of these norms, and I will conclude each subsection with an assessment of how much each norm has been developed by the sum of individual cases.[4] Before proceeding to this full-scale analysis, however, a brief introduction to the Estonian Constitutional Review Chamber (CRC) itself is in order.

ESTONIA'S CONSTITUTIONAL REVIEW CHAMBER

Estonia's "constitutional court" is in reality a five-member sub-division of the 19-member Supreme Court; hence its formal designation as a "chamber." It is one of the four chambers of the Supreme Court, the remaining three being the criminal, administrative, and civil chambers. The uniqueness of the CRC is that its chairman must always be the chief justice. Thus, its status is higher than that of the other three chambers, although it is still embedded within the Supreme Court as a whole; it is not a separate entity as in France or Germany. The origins of this particular arrangement lie in the constitution-making process Estonia underwent during 1991–1992, immediately after its breakaway from the collapsing Soviet Union. This leap to freedom in the midst of the attempted putsch in Moscow in August 1991 was accompanied by a bold decision to immediately convene a new constitutional assembly for the drafting of a fresh constitution.

While the assembly's deliberations were protracted over such things as the mode of election for president, the need for some kind of constitutional review was never disputed. Instead, according to the protocols of the assembly, the only concerns raised were in regard to the mechanics (Roosma 1997; Peep 1997). In the end, Estonia's new constitutional review mechanism came to stand on three main avenues of constitutional appeal—the president, the legal chancellor, and the lower courts—all leading to the Constitutional Review Chamber, which would have final decision-making authority.[5] The system is thus a concentrated one (as opposed to a diffuse one), along the lines of those adopted in Germany, France, or Italy.[6]

Of the three institutions that can appeal cases to the CRC, the legal chancellor is the most unconventional within constitutional law. The idea for such a post was derived from Estonia's 1938 constitution and also resembles a similar institution in Finland. More specifically, the legal chancellor is responsible for monitoring all legal acts in the country—from the parliament to the government, all the way down to local municipalities—from the express point of view of their constitutionality. Procedurally, if the legal chancellor believes a legal act is in violation of the constitution, he must call on the body that passed the legislation to rectify the discrepancy, or within twenty days he may file a petition to the Constitutional Review Chamber for the act to be annulled.

In the case of the lower courts, their role in constitutional review is quite standard. If in the process of hearing a case a court comes to the conclusion that a particular legislative act is unconstitutional, it must dismiss the law from consideration in the case and rule without it. Thereafter, an appeal is filed immediately with the CRC, which must review the case within two months. Thus, the appeal is made on behalf of the lower court, and does not involve in any way the original parties to the case. It is the court which argues its case against the respective executive or legislative authority that originally adopted the legal act.

Lastly, the president's prerogative *vis-à-vis* constitutional review is the only one which is expressly pre-emptive or *ex ante*. Under Article 107 of the constitution, the president has the responsibility for promulgating laws adopted by parliament. However, if the president believes a bill is unconstitutional, he or she may refuse to promulgate it and return it to parliament for reconsideration. If the parliament passes the law again in its identical form, then the president must sign the legislation, or he or she may appeal to the CRC for a ruling on the law's constitutionality.

Since its inception in May 1993 through 2002, the CRC issued a total of 64 decisions. As indicated in *Table 1*, the most active year for the CRC was 1994, when 11 cases were considered, although subsequent years such as 1998 and 2000 also featured many cases. While initially the president as well as the legal chancellor took the lead in submitting cases, the lower courts began to be more active in 1995 by using their constitutional review prerogatives, and by 1997 they had moved ahead of the other two institutions. The *Riigikogu* was challenged the most by these actions, since formal laws were contested on 36 separate occasions. The executive (both government and individual ministers) was challenged 19 times, and local governments 9 times.

In terms of the five categories discussed below, it is difficult to draw up an

Source: Author's calculations.
* In some cases, more than one type of legal act was contested.
** The total number of cases here is higher as in some instances the CRC struck down only part of a legal act, while declaring another to be constitutional.

		1993	1994	1995	1996	1997	1998	1999	2000	2001	2002	TOTAL
Appeals made by	President	2	3	–	1	–	2	–	–	–	–	8
	Legal chancellor	2	6	–	1	–	3	–	3	–	1	16
	Lower courts	–	2	4	2	3	5	3	7	7	7	40
Total rulings		4	11	4	4	3	10	3	10	7	8	64
Type of legal act contested*	Law	2	7	3	2	–	6	2	4	3	7	36
	Government decree	–	2	–	2	2	2	1	3	2	–	14
	Ministerial decree	–	1	1	–	–	1	–	1	–	1	5
	Local government legislation	2	2	–	–	1	1	–	2	–	1	9
Ruling of the CRC**	Act declared unconstitutional	3	9	2	3	2	8	2	5	5	6	45
	Act already repealed by the time of the CRC's ruling	–	2	–	1	–	2	1	3	1	3	13
	Act declared constitutional	1	1	2	1	1	–	1	2	1	2	12

Table 1. Appeals heard by the Constitutional Review Chamber, 1993–2002.

exact distribution, as many cases involved numerous principles at once.[7] Nevertheless, it is safe to say that cases involving breach of powers predominated. This was understandable, since four possible institutional actors (the parliament, the government, individual ministers, and local governments) and their legal acts could all come under this category. Still, in each of the categories important arguments were made about the place of democratic norms in governance.

SEPARATION OF POWERS

Estonia's adoption of a new constitution in 1992 was a decisive step toward building a new and comprehensive democratic order. At the same time, the decision also created an entirely unknown and untested institutional configuration. Not only were the parliament, government, and courts all expected to become serious institutions (in contrast to the old Soviet ones), but in addition, the new constitution created several new offices, including a presidency, a legal chancellor, and an auditor general. Thus, on the one hand, the constitution went about laying down a general foundation for the separation of powers by declaring in its Article 4 the following: "The activities of the *Riigikogu*, the President of the Republic, the Government of the Republic, and the courts shall be organized on the principle of separation and balance of powers." At the same time, it was clear that many details would still have to be settled, both through additional legislation as well as simple precedent. Where agreement could not be reached as to these details, the CRC was frequently called upon to arbitrate. In the sections that follow, I will examine two important institutional axes: first, the president vs. the parliament, and second, the parliament vs. the government.

President vs. parliament

In any political system, an essential division of power is that which exists between the president and the parliament. During the work of the Constitutional Assembly of 1991–1992, there were considerable debates as to whether Estonia needed a president, and if so, what prerogatives he or she should have. This was a sensitive issue, since Estonia's first experience with democracy during the 1920s and 1930s had foundered precisely as a result of debates regarding presidentialism vs. parliamentarism. In 1920, Estonia's first constitution had instituted a strongly parliamentary, but likewise unstable regime. After 1934, the country turned to the other extreme, when Konstantin Päts, a caretaker prime minister, staged a coup and thereafter installed a presidential regime. By 1992, the question had become whether the new constitution and its constitutional review mechanism would succeed in finally striking an adequate balance.

In the event, the new constitution created a largely ceremonial presidency, but which included a limited power of veto in the area of legislation. In September 1992, a special presidential election was held, at the end of which Lennart Meri, a writer, filmmaker, and former foreign minister, was elected to office. Meri was an excellent choice for his stately demeanor and strong commitment to democracy; however, he was also well known for his independent-mindedness and political self-assurance. As a result, he had a keen awareness of his institutional prerogative, as well as of his powers of institutional precedent sitting as the first president. Indeed, Meri was the first of Estonia's three constitutional oversight institutions to appeal a case to the CRC, just two months after the Chamber was formed.

Through 2002, the CRC heard four major cases concerning the president's institutional powers. In each case, the issue involved laws which the *Riigikogu* had attempted to pass in order to flesh out practical procedures and relations involving the president. Meri, however, sought to block what was to his mind over-regulation of these matters, and in general he was victorious. His most celebrated victory came in June 1994, when he vetoed an attempt by the *Riigikogu* to regulate the presidency in general through a Presidential Procedure Act. In this case, the law sought to lay down the procedure (mentioned in Article 109 of the constitution), whereby the president would be authorized to issue decrees with the force of law in special situations where the parliament was prevented from coming together. The law stated that first the speaker of parliament would have to certify that the parliament was unable to come together, and that second the prime minister would have to confirm that there was a "matter of urgent state need" at hand, which required legislation by presidential decree. President Meri argued that these two specific modalities (not mentioned in the constitution) infringed on his constitutional rights and duties as head-of-state in such situations, and were thereby unconstitutional. The CRC agreed with the president and struck down the law. Subsequently, the *Riigikogu* was so deterred from touching the issue again that a Presidential Procedure Act was not put into effect until Meri left office.

Parliament vs. government
A second type of separation of powers concerns the relationship between parliament and government. This issue was first raised in November 1994 based on a case brought by the legal chancellor. The legal chancellor protested against the *Riigikogu* Procedure Act (or basic rules of order in parliament), which allowed MPs to serve concurrently on the executive boards of major state-owned firms. The boards were intended to supervise general management at the few enterprises still left in state hands, both during and after large-scale privatization. Having MPs in particular serve on the boards was seen as a way of securing political consensus for the management of state assets. Yet, the

legal chancellor saw the issue as a conflict of interest between the legislative and executive branches. He argued that because the MPs were receiving remuneration for their work and were viewed on a par with board members drawn directly from the executive branch, they were in fact working simultaneously as members of both branches of government, and were therefore in violation of Article 4 of the constitution. In its ruling, the CRC agreed with the legal chancellor's case, saying that "[a]ny situation of conflict of interest, in which a state employee simultaneously fulfils essentially contradictory tasks as well as seeks contradictory objectives, can precipitate deficiencies in the execution of his official responsibilities as well as create the pre-conditions for corruption. Conflicts of interest must be avoided in all state institutions."[8]

Still, the issue was a delicate one, since it contained important practical implications. According to Article 64.2 of the constitution, if a member of parliament assumes a position in any other branch of government (except cabinet positions), he or she automatically forfeits their seat in parliament. Thus, if this provision were strictly adhered to and the CRC decided to rule against the parliament, the result would have been to throw out automatically a large number of MPs from the parliament and bring chaos to the legislature's work. Instead, the CRC set an important precedent by granting the MPs one month in which to make their choice between the parliament and the executive boards. Although the Constitutional Review Chamber Procedure Act that was in force at the time did not expressly allow for such time-delays, it was clearly warranted in this case.[9]

Breach of powers

In a consolidated democracy, an essential norm of governance involves rule of law and a respect by political institutions of their constitutionally mandated prerogatives. Such institutions must develop a clear understanding of both the kinds of issues they are allowed to regulate, as well as the procedures by which they may wield that power. Where such powers are breached, there is a possibility for not only institutional conflict, but also delegitimation of the political system as a whole. In a broad sense, therefore, it is often up to a country's constitutional review mechanism to reinforce these norms when they are violated, and thereby contribute to creating overall confidence in the constitutional system.

In Estonia's constitution there are a number of important principles about how questions of policy are to be legislated and by whom. Firstly, Article 104 lists a total of 17 specific laws or domains in relation to which the *Riigikogu* can pass laws only with an absolute majority of its members. These include the state budget, various electoral laws, laws relating to the structure of the Estonian government, as well as other state institutions. Any law pertaining to these areas which is passed without such a majority is unconstitutional. Secondly, if a particular aspect of any one of these domains is by chance legislated within the context of some other law (which needs only a simple majority to pass), such an act can also be found unconstitutional. Thirdly, the constitution contains several paragraphs on fundamental rights and freedoms as well as other institutions' rights, which stipulate that restrictions on these rights can only be legislated by a law, not by any other legal act such as a decree. Any attempt to regulate these areas through other such means is equally unconstitutional. Fourthly, Articles 87.6 and 94.2 state explicitly that the government of the republic, as well as cabinet ministers, shall issue regulations and orders "on the basis of and for the implementation of law." This means that the government can issue decrees only on the basis of specific paragraphs in law authorizing it to do so. Moreover, these paragraphs must be explicitly cited in the text of the decree. As it will be seen below, this was a particular area of focus for the CRC during the 1990s, as many government decrees during the early years of Estonia's new constitution were sloppily drafted and thus unconstitutional. Lastly, local authorities are also bound by national law when adopting regulatory ordinances in two main domains: taxation and fundamental rights and freedoms. Where municipalities overstepped these boundaries or adopted regulations not sanctioned by law, the CRC struck them down. In this section, therefore, I will review four types of breach of power, involving the parliament, the government, individual ministers, and local governments.

Parliament
An important principle that the CRC repeatedly sought to enforce during its first years concerned the *Riigikogu*'s constitutional responsibility to fulfill its legislative duties. This referred to the parliament's obligation to adopt laws and decide matters delegated to it by the constitution, instead of passing them off to the executive to decide. In one of its earliest decisions, the CRC made this argument very clear. In November 1993, President Meri challenged the *Riigikogu*'s adoption of the Tax Regulation Act.[10] In the original law, the *Riigikogu* had authorized the Minister of Finance to scrutinize and define the nature of taxes levied by local governments on their territory. While the CRC struck down the law on the principle of local government autonomy, it also noted that the law was an attempt by the parliament to delegate to the executive a job (defining local taxes), which the constitution had specifically assigned to the legislature (Articles 113 and 157.2). Thus, the CRC did not shy away from admonishing the parliament based on the latter's obligation to fulfill its legislative functions. Moreover, in 1994 the CRC reiterated this stance in connection with an appeal by the legal chancellor concerning a law

regulating surveillance activities by the police.[11] Again, the *Riigikogu* had attempted to pass on the modalities of authorizing such surveillance to the
Security Police Board, although it included within these rules a requirement
that the consent of a justice of Supreme Court must also be obtained. Nevertheless, the CRC ruled that such circumstances had to be spelled out specifically
in law; otherwise they would violate basic rights and freedoms. *Inter alia*, the
CRC stated "[t]hat, which the legislature has been authorized or obligated to
do by the Constitution, can not be delegated to the executive branch, even
temporarily or under the possibility of control by the judiciary."[12]

Government
A second institution, which was caught more than all others breaching its constitutional powers, was the government and its individual ministers. Of the
CRC's 64 cases through 2002, executive-branch breach of power was at issue
in at least 19 of them. Of these, the issue was raised most notably in December 1996, when a 1994 government decree regulating the import of vodka was
challenged by the Supreme Court's Administrative Law Chamber in a criminal case.[13] At issue was the fact that although the decree referred to Estonia's
Consumer Protection Act of 1993 as its basis in law, the text itself did not actually cite a specific paragraph from the law. Thus, the decree was formally
unconstitutional. Although in the months that followed the decree's adoption
the *Riigikogu* amended the Act to authorize the government to take action in
the specific sphere of vodka importing, the CRC ruled that such initial violations of constitutional law could not be legalized *post hoc*, and were in any
case a dangerous sign of legal arbitrariness. The justices argued that on the
one hand, "[t]he objective of the right given to the Government of the Republic
to issue decrees is to reduce the burden on the legislature and to hand the
technical specification of norms over to the government, so as to guarantee
flexible administrative activity as well as to avoid the overburdening of laws
with useless individual regulations. At the same time, the circumscription of
executive power by law is necessary for maintaining control over the democratic nature of exercising state power, and for preserving general legal order
as well as protecting constitutional rights and freedoms."[14] Thus, while the
two aspects were significant, the latter was constitutionally more important.

Likewise, in March 1999 the CRC clipped the government's wings after the
latter had attempted to restrict the right to free enterprise by banning the sale
of brand-new consumer appliances at municipal markets.[15] The regulations
had been part of a general government endeavor to channel the sale of consumer appliances into licensed retail stores. However, ruling on two separate
cases brought by lower courts (in which the defendants had been fined by local
authorities for violating the government decree), the CRC found that fol-

lowing Article 31 of the constitution on free enterprise such restrictions could only be legislated by law. The relevant point in the decree was therefore declared unconstitutional.

Ministers

The issue of government ministers (or, in some cases, their department heads) overstepping their legal prerogatives arose in the CRC only 4 times during its first ten years. In all of these cases, the respective decrees were declared unconstitutional, although in one case the decree was rescinded before the CRC handed down its ruling. For example, in January 1995 the CRC heard a lower court appeal involving a 1994 decree issued by the Minister of Interior concerning residency permits for non-citizens.[16] Although the lower court had ruled that the decree was unconstitutional because a section of it violated the principle of rule of law (Article 10), the CRC ruled instead that the decree was actually unconstitutional because Estonia's respective law on aliens did not explicitly authorize the Minister of Interior to issue such decrees; only the full government had actually been authorized. Thus the ruling was an important case where the CRC sought to correct an error which had slipped by not only the lower court, but also the legal chancellor.

Local government

Lastly, the CRC was called upon to adjudicate alleged breaches of power by local authorities. Within this category, it is interesting to note that all of these appeals have been raised so far by the legal chancellor, and not for instance by the local courts. During his 1993–2000 term in office, Eerik-Juhan Truuväli had to deal in particular with the Tallinn city authorities, appealing first a case in 1994 regarding the capital's decision to begin booting illegally parked cars, and again in late 1998 after the city began charging a fee for cars entering the municipality's old town.[17] In both cases, Truuväli argued that Tallinn had overstepped its legal bounds, since neither the booting of cars nor the charging of what he alleged was a tax on vehicles entering the old town had been authorized by national legislation. These two Tallinn decisions therefore constituted a breach of power. Naturally, in the opinion of the city as well as many residents, both practices were seen as essential measures for controlling traffic in and around the city center. Nonetheless, the legal issues predominated for the CRC, which ruled in the legal chancellor's favor and struck down the Tallinn decisions on both occasions. Indeed, in the latter instance, the effect was immediate in that as soon as the ruling was announced, newspaper reporters in cars tried to force their way into the old town for free, and city authorities were left pondering as to what measures they could take to curb the traffic some other way.

RIGHTS AND FREEDOMS

For average citizens in a democratic state, an even more direct threat than government breaching its powers is a violation of fundamental rights and freedoms. Democratic rule is instituted not only in order to install accountable government, but also to afford its citizens opportunities for self-expression and self-realization. Naturally, the precise range of these rights is a question open to each society to decide for itself. However, those rights that are accorded must be protected against infringement by constitutional institutions, and where these fail, they must be further upheld by constitutional review mechanisms.

In Estonia's constitution, Chapter 2 is devoted to a whole series of fundamental rights, freedoms, and duties.[18] While many of these are clear-cut, the CRC was nonetheless called upon several times during the 1990s to adjudicate or give more substantial meaning to a number of these rights. This process has concerned three, more specific roles: (1) the legal-technical defense of rights; (2) the fundamental defense of rights; and (3) the proportionality of punishment.

Legal-technical defense of rights

In a number of instances, the legislative acts which the CRC struck down on legal-technical grounds, also concerned various rights and freedoms. As a result, the CRC's action was in favor of not only legal propriety, but also the defense of constitutional rights. For example, the CRC's ruling in January 1994, striking down the *Riigikogu*'s attempt to authorize the Defense Police to engage in surveillance activities, was based on the grounds that such activities must be spelled out in law and not delegated *carte blanche* to a part of the executive. This was in part a technical argument; however, as one Estonian scholar of the CRC has written, the decision also established important principles with regard to rights protection, since: (1) the term "law" used in the restriction clauses of the Fundamental Rights and Freedoms Chapter of the Constitution has to be interpreted as an act of the *Riigikogu*; and (2) the restrictions to the fundamental rights and freedoms are unconstitutional if they are not provided for in a way detailed enough to enable the subjects of law to determine their conduct on the basis of informed choice (Roosma 1997: 60).

Likewise, the CRC applied this principle in its March 1999 ruling, concerning the right of individuals to sell brand-new goods at local markets, for in that decision the CRC said that the constitution allowed for such restrictions to be placed, but that these had to be legislated by law, not government decree.[19] The CRC also indirectly defended rights and freedoms when it overturned a 1996 decision by the city council of the small town of Valga to impose a curfew on minors moving about late at night, since such restrictions had to be first sanctioned by national law.

Fundamental defense of rights

A more serious case of fundamental rights, however, arose with the passage of a Police Service Act by the *Riigikogu* in May 1998. This law allowed police commanders to transfer a rank-and-file officer to another department or precinct without the officer's consent, even if that entailed an additional change in residence for the officer. President Meri promulgated the law in early June. However, in mid-September, the legal chancellor launched an appeal to the CRC charging that the provision regarding officer transfers violated Article 34 of the constitution, which guarantees the right of legal residents to "choice of residence." According to the legal chancellor, this principle was completely inviolable, since the constitution does not state (as it does regarding, for example, the right to free enterprise) that this right can be circumscribed by the law. Thus, even though the *Riigikogu* had attempted to legislate the flexible transfer of police officers via a full-fledged law, the CRC agreed with the legal chancellor that this was not enough and that such a restriction of rights was unconstitutional in whatever form.[20]

In May 1996, President Meri also raised the issue of fundamental rights when he challenged the *Riigikogu*'s passage of the Non-Profit Organizations Act. The law, as originally passed by parliament, excluded the right of minors to register non-profit organizations. According to the president, however, this decision was in violation of Article 48 of the constitution, which states that "[e]veryone has the right to form non-profit undertakings and unions." More specifically, since the constitution does not expressly restrict this right to adults or allow it to be circumscribed in any way by law, the *Riigikogu*'s action had no legal basis. On this score again, the argument was about basic rights, and the CRC concurred with the President.[21]

Proportionality of punishment

A third category involving the defense of rights emerged during 2000–2001, when the CRC ruled in two specific cases that laws passed by the *Riigikogu* had established punishments, which were too automatic and hence too severe in relation to the seriousness of possible infractions. In the first case, the CRC threw out a section of the Alcohol Act, which mandated that stores, which had been caught selling alcohol to minors, would automatically have revoked their license to sell alcohol.[22] The specific case involved a small kiosk owner in Tartu, whose employee had sold a bottle of beer and a pack of cigarettes to a 15-year-old boy. Even though it was clear that this incident had been only a minor violation of the law, the owner's entire alcohol license was invalidated. Similarly, in 2000, a retired ex-Soviet military officer and former employee of the KGB had been denied the prolongation of his residency permit when amendments made to Estonia's Aliens Act no longer allowed him to even apply for one.[23]

In both of these cases, the issue at stake for the CRC was the precise meaning of Article 11 of the constitution, which states that "[r]ights and freedoms may be restricted only in accordance with the Constitution. Such restrictions must be necessary in a democratic society and shall not distort the nature of the rights and freedoms restricted." In particular, the CRC argued that this article also meant that parliament could not mandate automatic degrees of punishment for certain violations of law, if there was a danger that such punishments would go beyond the proportionate degree of damage caused to public order or societal interest. Rather, the chamber maintained that parliament had to leave the executive branch of government a degree of maneuver in order to decide cases where extenuating circumstances warranted lesser punishments or the approval of some administrative application. In the case of the Alcohol Act, local governments would have to be given the right to simply warn store owners who violated the law, while in the case of the Aliens Act, the Minister of Interior had to be accorded the right to grant a residency permit to ex-military officers if, for example, they had immediate family residing legally in Estonia or had shown themselves to be otherwise law-abiding residents.[24]

Minority rights

A narrower domain of fundamental rights and freedoms concerns the rights of national minorities. In Estonia especially, questions of ethnopolitics have occupied a prominent place within the country's democratic transition and consolidation, mostly because the Soviet Union's policy of encouraging migration among Russians and other Slavs to the outlying republics had resulted for Estonia in a precipitous drop in the share of the native Estonian population.[25] By 1989, the "Russian-speaking population"[26] in the republic topped 30%, and Estonia appeared to have become a bi-national Estonian-Russian country. It was therefore this fear which motivated much of the Estonian nationalist movement during the *perestroika* period. Most significantly, however, a major turning point in this ethnopolitical struggle came with the development of a new political argument, which stated that because of the Soviet Union's illegal takeover of the Baltic states in 1940, Estonia was not legally bound to offer automatic citizenship to the Soviet-era immigrants, even though the vast majority of them happened to be Russian-speakers. After independence, it was this doctrine, adopted as the basis for Estonia's citizenship policy, which henceforth caused problems for the country in terms of minority rights.

Although the Estonians' argumentation was eminently juridical in that it related purely to the consequences of an illegal foreign occupation, its practical consequences in terms of the political marginalization of a large share of the minority population were severe. For example, it created an entire class of people known as "non-citizens," who even in 2002 still amounted to 20% of the population. At the same time, the Constitutional Review Chamber's role in possibly mitigating this policy was hampered by three factors. First, the CRC itself was not formed until summer 1993, when the Supreme Court was finally fully appointed. Second, because the rationale for the citizenship policy was so deeply embedded in Estonia's more fundamental notion of being a *restored* state, rather than a Soviet successor republic, any challenge to the policy itself would have called into question this broader legal principle and was therefore highly problematic. Lastly, given that Estonia's constitutional review mechanisms passed through the president, the legal chancellor, or the courts, it was unlikely that any of these institutions in and of themselves would attempt to confront the entire legal basis of the Estonian state. Yet, barring any move by these players, the CRC itself could not come into play.

Conflict resolution
Nevertheless, the CRC was called upon in two important instances to rule on ethnopolitically charged matters. Indeed, in mid-1993, the CRC was instrumental in resolving one of Estonia's most serious ethnopolitical conflicts: a threat of secession by the two mostly-Russian towns of Narva and Sillamäe in Estonia's northeast. Although for all intents and purposes this intervention was more to diffuse the tension itself, rather than actually promote minority rights, its importance in terms of building the credibility of the CRC was indisputable. The conflict was ignited by Russian opposition to a new and controversial Aliens act, which threatened to revoke many non-citizens' (and thereby a great number of Russians') right to residency in the republic. Ostensibly, the act was meant to create a process whereby non-citizens would be able to apply for new Estonian-issued residency permits. However, because the law offered no assurances that current non-citizen residents of the republic would be guaranteed a new residency permit, the measure evoked fears among Russians that Estonian authorities would now use the law to further deny Soviet-era immigrants of their residency, on top of citizenship. In opposing this legislation, a number of local authorities in Narva and Sillamäe decided to resort to what they saw as their last card—calling a referendum on territorial autonomy. After some intense political mediation by moderate Russian leaders from Tallinn, as well as officials from the Organization for Security and Cooperation in Europe (OSCE), a compromise was struck in which the Estonian government agreed not to interfere with the balloting, while the local Narva and Sillamäe authorities agreed to accept a future ruling from the Constitutional Review Chamber as to the referendums' constitutionality. The deal eventually held, since the referendums took place in

mid-July without major incident, while immediately thereafter the legal chancellor submitted an appeal to the CRC to declare the referendums unconstitutional.

For the CRC, the autonomy issue was clearly one with important ethnopolitical consequences which it could not easily overlook. Although the referendums themselves had already been somewhat discredited by news reports indicating widespread procedural errors during the poll, the Estonian government was still keenly interested in having the actions themselves struck down by the CRC. This was made easier by the fact that both the Narva and Sillamäe authorities had themselves formulated their decisions in a contradictory legal matter, leaving the way open for the CRC to dismiss the referendums on essentially technical grounds.[27] Additionally, the CRC noted that although both the constitution (Article 154) as well as Estonia's Local Government Organization Act gave municipalities the right to decide matters of local importance, the question of territorial autonomy was fundamentally a national one, which local governments could not raise unilaterally. Thus, based on these two arguments, the CRC threw out the Narva and Sillamäe referendums, and in turn the two local governments accepted the rulings.

Minority rights protection
The Narva and Sillamäe rulings instilled a lull in Estonia's ethnopolitical debates until 1998, when the CRC was called upon again, and indeed twice, to decide whether the Estonian parliament had the right to institute Estonian language requirements for electoral candidates running for national and local legislatures. In specific terms, the amendments would require candidates to attest before the national electoral commission that they had a so-called "high" or professional command of Estonian. The problem was that such requirements would be a clear violation of Article 25 of the International Covenant on Civil and Political Rights, which Estonia had ratified already in September 1991. Thus, the test for Estonia's constitutional review mechanism would be, first, whether any of the three appellate institutions would single out this particular violation as the basis for a claim, and second, barring any such move, whether the CRC would itself bring this international obligation into play. In the event, neither scenario came to pass, and in a major test of minority rights, the language requirements for electoral candidates were actually left to stand (at least from the constitutional point of view).

In adopting its original law in November 1997, the *Riigikogu* (along with the sitting government at the time) had been motivated by nationalist desires to make sure that no non-Estonian-speaking person could be elected to parliament or a local council, where he or she would not be able to perform their duties because of insufficient language skills. The solution was therefore to amend Estonia's Language Act. In the end, these amendments consisted of two dimensions, the first concerning language requirements for electoral candidates, and the second mandating a tightening of Estonian language proficiency requirements for non-Estonian employees in both the public and private sectors. Since both of these changes were controversial for the Russian-speaking community, President Meri soon came under pressure to veto the amendments. Yet, in his decision to actually do this, Meri relied on legal technicalities, not minority rights based considerations. First, he argued that the language requirements for state- and private-sector employees had been worded too vaguely, and that they therefore violated Article 11 of the constitution on the principle of restricting rights only within the limits of democratic society. Secondly, President Meri claimed that because the task of controlling an electoral candidate's knowledge of Estonian would according to the law be assigned to the executive branch (specifically the Minister of Education), this provision would constitute a serious violation of the separation of powers (Article 4), since the executive would potentially be able to harass these candidates later on if they were elected members of parliament. In neither case did Meri assume any recourse to Article 25 of the ICCPR. His conviction was that the language requirements were fundamentally just, but juridically incorrect.

After the *Riigikogu* adopted the amendments anew without any changes, President Meri appealed his veto to the CRC. Yet, in its February 1998 ruling, the CRC too retained an essentially nationalist stance, for although it struck down the amendments to the Language Act, it did so precisely on the basis of the legal-technical arguments, and rejected most of the rights-based considerations.[28] Indeed, in dismissing the latter, the CRC cited not only Article 6 of the constitution (on Estonian as the official language), but also very interestingly the constitution's Preamble, which declares as one of the fundamental goals of the Estonian state "the preservation of the Estonian nation and culture through the ages." For the justices this was an important principle, based on which the state had the right even to circumscribe the linguistic rights of minorities. Moreover, the CRC attempted to link the issue to effective democracy by arguing that "Article 1 of the Constitution declares that Estonia is a democratic republic. Democracy fulfils its objective only when it functions. One pre-condition for the functioning of democracy is that those individuals who exercise power understand wholly what is happening in Estonia and use in their dealings one communicative system. Thus, in a representative democracy as well as in the business of the state the establishment in Estonia of a requirement to use Estonian language is in harmony with the public interest, as well as justified from the perspective of historical-derived circumstances."[29]

In November 1998, the CRC reiterated this stance after the issue came up again via a lower court and in relation to the specific case of a local government deputy.[30] Although in this new ruling the CRC acknowledged the argument that any restrictions of rights have to comply with Article 11 of the constitution on democratic norms, it continued to believe that the goal of protecting the Estonian nation and culture (as stated in the constitution's Preamble) was an overriding concern, and that language requirements had merely to avoid being too excessive. As regards Article 25 of the ICCPR, the CRC was again silent on the issue, even though the original defendant in the case had actually cited this provision at his trial. It would not be until November 2001 that the *Riigikogu* would agree to rescind the language requirements as a result of pressure from an entirely different source, the OSCE. In this respect, a complete structure of minority rights protection, which would rely both on national and international legal principles, had yet to fully sink in.

PUBLIC POLICY MAKING

As it is evident from the previous sections, two of the most important domains of constitutional review involve institutional prerogatives and the protection of fundamental rights and freedoms. In contemporary debates over constitutional theory, however, a third area of judicial influence has emerged in relation to public policy making. With the evolution of judicial activism in many countries, constitutional courts have often become involved in adjudicating (and essentially deciding) important public policy issues hitherto determined solely by the executive and legislative. This trend has raised concerns, however, that the courts are "distorting" policy by removing it from the domain of direct public control (within the executive and legislature), and transferring it to the judicial arena, where the public has less check. The issue is a significant one for postcommunist countries, since as a rule these states have been faced with important, and oftentimes controversial socio-economic reforms. In the event of adroit manipulation by political actors or simple activism by the courts, such policies can easily become "distorted."

With regard to this danger, Estonia's system of constitutional review offers few worries in the sense that cases can be brought to the CRC by only three particular institutions. The consequence of such a system is to limit the type and range of cases brought to the CRC, in addition to focusing them more on legal, rather than political arguments. Indeed, in the CRC's first ten years of existence, there were only five clear-cut instances in which government-initiated and parliament-approved public policies were overturned by the CRC.[31] To be sure, in three of these five cases the CRC interpreted the issue as one of "rightful expectations," since the state had attempted to reverse policies and procedures which individuals had come to expect would continue, and they were therefore placed at a disadvantage when the state suddenly

ciple of rightful expectations. In its ruling on the issue, the CRC agreed with the applicability of Article 10 in this case, and in addition noted the relevance of Article 12 on the equality of individuals before the law. The CRC said that even if the government and parliament had wanted to avoid further social injustices by abolishing the right to compensation, the reversal of policy to the detriment of those still within the policy implementation process was itself a larger social injustice. Likewise, the CRC ruled in March 1999 that the abrogation of claimant rights for spouses of children of legal owners was a comparable violation of due process. Although officials in charge of restitution policy were disappointed by their defeat, as well as fearful that the CRC's decisions would re-open claims processed in the meantime on the basis of the new amendments, there was nothing they could do but to follow the rulings and deal with the new situation.

Direct policy intervention
If in the previous two cases the CRC had based its opinions mainly on the question of consistency in policy and not of policy itself, in 1995 the chamber mounted a more serious challenge to policy-making when it considered a lower court appeal regarding housing privatization.[34] At issue was a provision in the Housing Privatization Act of 1993, which mandated that all Soviet-built apartments would be made eligible for privatization by their occupants, regardless of whether the apartment had been built by the state, a municipality, a state enterprise, or certain semi-state cooperatives, which also frequently provided housing for their workers. The law was aimed in particular at this last category of apartments, since in many cases the cooperatives had claimed these dwellings as their corporate property, and had therefore refused to privatize the apartments to their inhabitants for anything less than full market value (and not the voucher scheme mandated by the state). When in 1994 one such cooperative, known as the ETKVL, went to court over the issue, the Tallinn City Court ruled that the cooperative was indeed not obliged to privatize its apartments on general terms, but rather that if the state placed such demands upon it, the cooperative could demand just compensation for such expropriation of property.

After hearing the case in April 1995, the CRC sided with the lower court (and the ETKVL), and struck down the disputed provisions of the Housing Privatization Act. In its decision, the chamber noted that "[t]o force one subject of private law to hand over its property to another subject of private law can not be considered [a legitimate] pursuit of public interest."[35] The ruling thus vindicated the ETKVL's position, while the state's scheme for housing privatization was dealt an important setback. In resolving the dispute, the CRC took a legal stance, denying the state's prerogative to freehandedly reorganize property relations despite the fact that just a few years earlier all property had essentially belonged to the state. Moreover, the CRC was unmoved by arguments in favor of allowing property reform to be quick and decisive so that the country would have a faster transition to a market economy. On the contrary, it refused to allow the property rights of these cooperatives to be fudged, since such enterprises (and in particular the apartments they had built with their own resources) were now essentially private and therefore protected by the 1992 constitution.

In response to its setback, the *Riigikogu* returned to the drawing board and in December 1995 adopted a new law mandating the same privatization of apartments, but this time offering cooperatives such as the ETKVL the chance to take the state privatization vouchers they were set to receive and to use them to privatize other land belonging to them. In this way, some sort of meaningful compensation would be offered to the enterprises involved, while also allowing for the privatization process to encompass the initially left-out tenants. The issue reflected a deep commitment on the part of several members of the *Riigikogu* to find a just solution to the privatization problem and to avoid being thwarted by the CRC's earlier ruling. Yet, their proposed alternative did not satisfy Legal Chancellor Eerik-Juhan Truuväli, who in June 1996 launched a new appeal to the CRC, this time claiming that the new compensation scheme still fell short of the market value of these apartments and was therefore unjust.[36] Yet, in resolving this second round of debate concerning housing privatisation, the CRC was now obliged to approach the issue from a different angle, since in this case the appeal came from the legal chancellor and was therefore an instance of abstract judicial review. This fact altered, in particular, the CRC's standpoint toward the legal chancellor's claim that the compensation being offered by the new privatization scheme was unjust. On the contrary, ruled the CRC, only the cooperatives themselves could contest through the regular courts the amount of compensation being offered. Abstract judicial review could not be used in this case. Moreover, the CRC noted the fact that since the *Riigikogu* had now tried twice to resolve this privatization question, there seemed to be a legitimate public interest at stake, which the Chamber was not in a position to dispute, especially under conditions of abstract review. As a result, the CRC backed away from challenging the *Riigikogu* again, and instead it denied the legal chancellor's appeal.

In this respect, the CRC appeared to be developing a sensitivity for public policy issues, and in early 2000 it again shied away from getting too involved in such matters when it rejected another appeal by the legal chancellor questioning a pair of budget cuts enacted in August 1999 as part of an austerity budget. In this case, which was transferred to the full Supreme Court, the debate opened with doubt being cast over whether the legal chancellor even had a right to contest individual allocations in budgetary legislation. Although a majority of the court found in favor of the legal chancellor's right to appeal, the justices made a clear attempt to avoid getting caught up in policy matters again by citing a renewed unwillingness to deal with abstract judicial review.[37] They stressed that even if certain budget cuts would appear to threaten policy programs prescribed by law, such claims could only be judged based on specific evidence *post hoc*; it could not be determined *a priori*. Although three justices ended up dissenting from the majority's opinion, the full court denied the legal chancellor's appeal and the supplementary state budget law was declared constitutional.

DISCUSSION

In relation to one of the main, and perhaps most thought-provoking issues raised by this volume—whether and to what extent "quasi-judicial" institutions in postcommunist countries have altered traditional understandings of the rule of law—, the experience of the Estonian Constitutional Review Chamber has arguably not been overwhelming. In part, this has been because of the limited breadth of Estonia's constitutional review mechanisms. As it has been discussed earlier, appeals to the CRC are restricted to just three institutions—the president, the legal chancellor, and the lower courts—, which means that the CRC itself cannot play a very autonomous role in democratic norm building, unless these appellate institutions themselves decide to undertake the effort. In the event, while all of these three actors have at times raised difficult constitutional issues for the CRC, they have also shied away from other cases of proactive constitutional legal activity, for example, in the case of minority rights. In this respect, the Estonian CRC is not just a single phenomenon or player; it must be and can only be studied in relation to its other organic parts, that is, its appellate institutions. The CRC is not so much a constitutional court as it is merely a part of a multifaceted constitutional review mechanism; and from this perspective, given the complexity of the mechanism, the end result is not necessarily "revolutionary" from the standpoint of altering conceptions of the rule of law. Instead, it aims to consolidate traditional principles of democracy, and even more specifically, parliamentary democracy.[38]

In consequence, the focus of this chapter has been on the contribution of the CRC to more conventional dimensions of democratic consolidation, that is, democratic norm building. I have delineated these norms along five different categories of constitutional law and sought to assess the degree to which practice within Estonia's constitutional review mechanism has raised these categories. With regard to the first category—the separation of powers—, the essence of this debate has really been around delineating the powers of the presidency, since in the minds of most Estonian politicians Estonia is a parliamentary republic and must definitely remain so. While Estonia's first president Lennart Meri never attempted to alter this basic principle, his concern for not allowing his office to become completely inconsequential led to several early cases being fought in defense of presidential prerogative (in particular in cases where the constitution had not spelled out all the details of some presidential function). Naturally, the full scope of the presidency would emerge from many other political interactions separate from the CRC; and in some cases disputes were resolved before the CRC was necessary. But to the extent that the institutionalization of a separation of powers would include a more recognized delineation of institutional prerogatives, the CRC did contribute to making the presidency a much more tangible institution.

A second important effect of the CRC was to promote a greater awareness of legal complexities and legal propriety by adjudicating a considerable number of cases in which legal acts were struck down because of breach of powers. These cases encompassed a range of different institutional players, although most often they concerned the executive branch of government. Naturally, to have less than twenty governmental or ministerial decrees be challenged in the course of ten years is not a very high number in proportion to the thousands of such acts passed since independence. Nonetheless, the CRC's actions in this realm could be considered important for three reasons. The first was that by establishing these precedents, plaintiffs (and their lawyers) would know that recourse in some cases of bureaucratic injustice could be had from challenging the very legality of governmental or ministerial decrees. This would strengthen the public perception of rule of law. Secondly, based on the CRC's actions, governmental and ministerial officials would know that the basis for any act, which they wanted to draft, would have to be first confirmed in law, or else the likelihood was high that it would eventually be challenged. Lastly, with respect to parliament, the CRC's rulings regarding breach of powers helped to sensitize MPs to their duty to make decisions concerning legal norms that only parliament had the responsibility to do.

Regarding the protection of fundamental rights and freedoms, it could be argued that this domain was probably one of the most difficult to develop in the postcommunist countries because of its nuanced character. If generating respect for a legal-bureaucratic order (by drafting, for example, legal acts with a correct basis in law) was something, which by and large had similarities with any bureaucracy and was therefore not an especially novel concept, then the nurturing of a judicious sense of rights protection was likely to be a more demanding endeavor. In Estonia's constitution, there were two articles in particular (Articles 10 and 11) which required further elaboration and interpretation by the CRC. Because these articles were above all declarations of principle, they were obviously designed to provide flexibility and breadth for the protection of rights. They would be the principles which would help fuse the remaining list of rights into an organic and mutually reinforcing whole.[39] Thus, by using these articles as the basis for numerous rulings, the CRC contributed to forging an integrated rights system. Again, its precedents would seep back down into the legal calculations of not only the CRC's appellate institutions, but also legal scholars and perhaps average citizens.

More narrowly in terms of minority rights, however, the CRC had shown itself to be primarily a means to de-escalate crises, but not to actively defend minority rights. Neither it, nor the three main constitutional review channels had sought to play a role where they would question the ethnopolitical policy itself, or raise awareness about minority well being. Perhaps it could be argued that none of these institutions was as yet ready to take on such a weighty issue, when they themselves had only recently been created. Given the sometimes tense struggle Estonia had just waged over independence, nationalist sentiment was still pretty high among all Estonians. Yet, it was also significant, for example, that amidst the tension of the Aliens Act crisis, Estonia's politicians (both Estonian and Russian) were able to recognize the conflict-resolution role that the CRC could still play. They were able to immediately work through their institutional options and come upon a formula, where Narva and Sillamäe would be able to organize their symbolic referendums, but thereafter respect the ruling of the high court. Had the Estonian government decided simply to reject the referendums as illegal without seeking recourse to any other institution such as the CRC, the impression of having blatantly ignored the two towns' grievances would have been palpable. Rather, the politicians had enough confidence in and respect for the judicial institutions they had created in order to use them as part of the political conflict resolution process.

Finally, public policy issues have also become a part of democratic norm building in Estonia to the extent that principles of rightful expectation or policy consistency have been raised. Of course, these norms may perhaps be too much to demand of countries that are simultaneously undergoing rapid and fundamental socio-economic change. Indeed, in Estonia's case many of the drafters of the country's constitution believed that the state should be offered as much leeway as possible to conduct social and economic reforms, since otherwise economic recovery would never take root. Hence the conviction with which the *Riigikogu* insisted on its right to renationalize all Soviet-era housing in order to carry out effective housing privatization. At the same time, it is interesting to note that as Estonia's constitutional system has evolved, the legal chancellor has gradually taken on the role of public policy watchdog (Maveety and Pettai 2005). This is perhaps no surprise, since of Estonia's three channels of constitutional appeal, the legal chancellor is clearly the most flexible, for he can receive suggestions and input from all levels of society. In addition, he has more time (than, for example, the president) to consider different cases. Thirdly, following the adoption of a new Legal Chancellor's Act in 1999, this office was also given new ombudsman functions, which included the right to question public officials about citizen complaints. All this meant that the legal chancellor had the potential to become a more active player. Nevertheless, it remained the case that Estonia's overall constitutional approach was cautious on public policy issues. The CRC was thus not likely to develop any kind of activist stance in this domain, either.

In sum, the constitutional discourse which one could begin to discern from the Estonian Constitutional Review Chamber's first ten years of rulings, was one that stressed above all legal propriety and the protection of rights and freedoms. In areas which were less of a focus for the CRC (such as public policy and separation of powers), there had been some discussion of altering Estonia's constitutional review system in ways which would open up the scope of this system for such additional domains. For example, proposals were made to split off the CRC from the Supreme Court and make it into a freestanding constitutional court. In turn, the functions of this court would be widened to include settling direct institutional conflicts (for example, between the president and the parliament) or electoral disputes. In the event, however, a new coalition government which came into power in January 2002 explicitly declared its opposition to creating a separate constitutional court. As a consequence, a new Constitutional Review Chamber Procedure Act finally adopted in March 2002 focused only on elaborating the CRC's role in adjudicating institutional and electoral disputes. As noted above, the new law also granted constitutional appeal authority to local government councils. However, here also this right was strictly limited to matters of local government policy. Thus, Estonia's constitutional review mechanism remained a fairly cautious one, aimed mostly at maintaining the stability and functionality of the parliamentary regime.

The author would like to thank Wojciech Sadurski and Peeter Roosma for insightful comments on previous drafts of this chapter.

NOTES

1 The lacuna is evident in, for example, Mainwaring et al. 1992; Di Palma 1990; Linz and Stepan 1996; but also even Elster and Slagstad 1988.
2 Quite admittedly, this view of democratic consolidation adheres to the "standard democratic story" that Kim Lane Scheppele criticizes as idealised in her contribution to this volume. While I agree with her argument that in Eastern Europe there may be additional notions of democracy emerging (which, for example, call for an activist constitutional court in addition to standard democratic institutions), I would maintain that

Maveety. Nancy and Vello Pettai. Government Lawyers and Non-judicial Constitutional Review in Estonia." *Europe–Asia Studies* 57, no. 1 (2005): 93–115.

McWhinney, Edward. *Supreme Courts and Judicial Law-Making: Constitutional Tribunals and Constitutional Review.* Dordrecht: Martinus Nijhoff Publishers, 1986.

Peep, Viljar. *Põhiseaduse ja põhiseaduse assamblee* [The Constitution and the Constitutional Assembly]. Tallinn: Juura, Õigusteabe Aktsiaselts, 1997.

Pettai, Vello. "Estonia's Constitutional Review Mechanisms: A Guarantor of Democratic Consolidation?" Working Paper, RSC No. 2000/59, Florence: Robert Schuman Center, European University Institute, 2000.

———. "Estonia: Positive and Negative Engineering" in *Democratic Consolidation in Eastern Europe, Volume 1: Institutional Engineering*, ed. Zielonka, Jan (Oxford: Oxford University Press, 2001), pp. 111–38.

———. "Ethnopolitics in Constitutional Courts: Estonia and Latvia Compared." *East European Constitutional Review* 11/12, nos. 4/1 (2002): 101–105.

Roosma, Peeter. *Methods of Constitutional Interpretation in the System of Checks and Balances: Development and Practice of Constitutional Review in Estonia.* MA thesis. Budapest: Central European University, Legal Studies Department, 1997.

———. "Constitutional Review under 1992 Constitution." *Juridica International* 3 (1998): 35–42.

———. "Protection of Fundamental Rights and Freedoms in Estonian Constitutional Jurisprudence." *Juridica International* 4 (1999): 35–44.

Schneider, Henrich. "Relations Between State Bodies in Implementing Constitution." *Juridica International* 3 (1998): 10–24.

Schwartz, Herman. "The New East European Constitutional Courts" in *Constitution Making in Eastern Europe*, ed. Dick, Howard A. E. (Washington D.C.: The Woodrow Wilson Center Press, 1993), pp. 163–207.

Taagepera, Rein. "Estonia's Constitutional Assembly, 1991–1992." *Journal of Baltic Studies* 25, no. 3 (1994): 211–32.

PART TWO
Dealing with the Past

Between Nemesis and Justitia:
Dealing with the Past as a Constitutional Process

ADAM CZARNOTA

The subject of this part of the book is one of the most controversial topics that arise in post-dictatorships, usually referred to as dealing with the past. This problem cannot be reduced to dealing with the remnants or legacies of former communist regimes.

In the Western legal tradition, law was not a tool for dealing with historical justice. It was a well-designed tool for coping with injustice on smaller scales. At the same time in Western culture, another concept of historical justice was present but conceptually separated from normal justice. That distinction was represented by two different goddesses dealing with justice. In Ancient Greece, these were *Dike* and *Themis*; and in Ancient Rome, *Nemesis* and *Justitia*.

The first dealt with the historical and/or divine dimensions of justice, quite often referred to as providence or fate. Realization of that dimension of justice was left in God's hands. It appears that criteria for that type of justice were perceived as different from those applied and developed by human reason. Realization of that type of justice was left to other times, usually outside human time. It was about the apocalyptic character of total justice. Nemesis was presented as the goddess of justice and revenge, a personification of that goddess's wraths and punishment. That is beautifully presented in the intriguing engraving, *Nemesis,* by Albrecht Dürer.

Themis and Justitia were goddesses of the human dimension of justice. In their administration of justice, they were more understanding of, or softer to, human errors. They are usually presented as blind in the application of justice, which shows on the one hand commitment to principles of human justice, impartial application of law. At the same time, that blindness shows the limitation of justice embodied in human legal systems. Those limitations of human legal systems are due to limitations of human knowledge. How can we do justice when our knowledge about events and especially past events is limited? That is why human legal systems contain so many principles which limit justice to the past, such as statutes of limitations, the presumption of innocence, etc. But that is only part of the issue. Another is the apocalyptic character of the Nemesis- and Dike-type justice. Up to the present, there was no attempt to approach legally the process of political and social change. That was a matter of fate and divine justice. The demand for legal redress for the communist past is based on a refusal to accept blind fate.

It seems to me that in discussions of the extremely complicated problem of dealing with the past, the line is still, as it used to be, between those who have a limited concept of human justice—as represented by Justitia and Themis—and those who look from the point of view of historical justice, Justice with a capital "J" based on principles considered universal in time and space, which have to be implemented regardless of social costs.

In my short introduction to this part of the book, I argue that "dealing with the past" is based on a combination of two perspectives and that the process of building bridges between these two perspectives requires a new approach in legal thinking and in institution-building. A combination of two very different strategies and institutions is needed in order to deal with the wrongs of the past. The traditional legal approach is not satisfactory, and we can observe the creation of a new type of quasi-judicial institutions designed to deal with the past. The problem of "transitional justice" or "dealing with the past" is not for itself only. It is about the future of those societies. The problem of coming to terms with the communist past in postcommunist societies is constitutive for these societies. It is a constitutional problem for the new postcommunist system. The different approaches to the problem have had an impact on the form and structure of new regimes in the region.

The problem of dealing with the past unfortunately is not only theoretical, notwithstanding that it is fascinating to theoreticians. Relations between dealing with the past and theories of regime change, relations to the rule of law, can and should be discussed as shown in the collection of contributions in this part of the book.

Is the problem discussed here universal in character or specific to postcommunist societies? Each society that has undergone a transition from one to another regime has faced the problem of "dealing with the past." Particularly societies in transition from dictatorial to democratic regimes. But even in those transitions, the main problem was how to deal with the mass violation of human rights. So, the issue was mainly for criminal law. More complicated are problems faced by the South African transition from apartheid, since the problem of beneficiaries of the regimes and redistribution of property rights, and not only gross violations of human rights, have to be dealt with.

It is true that a universal problem faced by all societies in transition from authoritarian rule is how to build a democratic and human rights observing culture. In this context, the problem of dealing with the past as a constitutional process for all societies in transition from authoritarian rule is a universal one. The specificity of "dealing with the past" in postcommunist societies is the enormous complexity of the problem, due to the peculiarity of the communist system. One of the most visible legacies of that peculiarity is the need to cope with the problem at the same time as rebuilding the entire institutional setting.

From the practical point of view, dealing with the past can be divided into four parts: (1) relations between new and old regimes; (2) the problem of decommunisation and lustration; (3) the problem of retributive justice for crimes committed under the former regimes; and (4) the problem of restitution of property after communism. The specific type of communism and specific form of exit from communism determined the relationship between old and new regimes and policies in relation to "dealing with the past."[1]

Apart from Romania, the transfer of power in other Central and Eastern European former communist states was peaceful and through negotiations. Old communist elites still in control of the state apparatus decided to co-opt representatives of the illegal opposition. The two most spectacular Roundtable Talks were in Poland, which set up the model and then in Hungary. Other countries at least tried to follow the established pattern. The very fact of negotiations between representatives of communist ruling elites and representatives of the opposition provided the former with legitimacy which had been denied to them from the beginning of the regimes. Roundtable Talks morally compromised representatives of the former opposition who took part in negotiations. In other words, communist elites due to the negotiations got some social capital at the expense of the opposition.

Naturally, in the process of negotiations, communist elites tried to guarantee for themselves impunity and immunity, as well as the best position in future regimes. At the peculiar historical moment when the negotiations took place, nobody thought that communism would collapse so quickly and oppositional elites were ready to strike a deal. The Roundtable Talks established a junction point between the old communist and new postcommunist regimes. In other words, agreement achieved in Roundtable Talks established a base for legal continuity between regimes, with consequences for the new legal and political order. Symbolically, a new law-governed state, as stated in amendments to the constitutions, was born as a legitimate child of a communist regime installed against law. Old communist regimes which operated with no respect for law posthumously received legitimacy that has been denied them since 1944.

New, postcommunist regimes tried to address the problem of continuity and at the same time stress discontinuity, by adopting, with rather small results, a policy of a so-called "thick line" between present and past, as it was termed by the first noncommunist prime minister in postcommunist Central and Eastern Europe, Tadeusz Mazowiecki. The idea was to integrate all citizens in the process of building a new political and social order after communism, and at the same time to stress that it will be a new political and social structure, not simple continuation of the former regime.

It has to be stressed that in different countries different approaches to the past were adopted, but in all of them inconsistently and with varying results. Probably, it is possible to make some generalizations that depend upon the type of exit from communism. The later the exit took place and the less organized the opposition was, the more radical the rhetoric, though not necessarily the policies. Nevertheless, in all countries, the problem exists and the new ruling elite faced the issue of doing justice to the past. The question, which nearly all societies asked themselves was the following: Which is better—to draw a thick line, and cut off and forget the past; or to face the problem of wrongdoings committed in the past?

This is an important moral question and answers have been different in different societies. To a great degree, the answer actually given depended upon the balance of political forces within the political elite. Usually, in each postcommunist society, there were mixed answers, which means that some policies were adopted to cope with at least some elements of the difficult past.

The issue is not any type of strategy of dealing with the past, but legal strategies of dealing with the past. Law represents authority and law also possesses its own authority. Law can authoritatively condemn or authoritatively vindicate. Law is not a stranger to the issue of dealing with the past. In the essence of law are experiences from the past and the correction of wrongdoings from the past. Law as a system of norms and institutions is a mechanism for systematic remembrance and forgetting. During the two-thousand-year history of the Western legal tradition, a very impressive arsenal of techniques has been developed, to remember but also to forget. Just to mention a few: statutes of limitation, *nulla poena sine legem, nulla crimen sine legem.* What is important is the fact that law possesses authority, and the authority of law approves remembering as well as forgetting. It means that individuals and groups can remember and not forgive, but it is impossible to start a new legal action. That peculiar character of law, its authority, plays an important role in all possible strategies for dealing with the past.

After the change of regimes due to loss of war or negotiations, new elites always faced the problem of what to do with the wrongdoings of the past. The question is not so dramatic when the collapse of regimes was due to revolution or defeat by an external power. The outcome is always condemnation of the past and imposition of the victors' justice. Often, criminal law is used in order to show the criminal character of the former regime and show trials play the role of education for the new political and social community.

More interesting problems of dealing with the past are faced by the new political elites when the change of regimes is done through negotiations. On the one hand, the old power is being recognized as a partner, and usually is interested in granting itself general amnesty for wrongdoings in the past. On the other hand, there is a pressure for justice and revenge coming from below and from some factions within the new political elites. The legal strategies adopted are never perfect, but we can evaluate them from the above perspective—their contribution to new normative values.

In all postcommunist countries, there is always a combination of retributive justice (criminal trials, lustration, and decommunisation) with restorative justice (restitution of property, usually called reprivatization, and rehabilitation of victims). Surprisingly, I do not know of any political and legal strategy which was focused on the creation of public discussion about the mechanism of operation of the communist regimes and involvement of every person in sustaining that regime. In other words, a focus not on revenge and stigmatization only, but on public truth telling and reconciliation—real coming to terms with the past by the entire society; overcoming the decisive division in society. It is an interesting question why there was no single attempt to stimulate an open public debate about the involvement of citizens in the operation of communist regimes. The only such attempt in the former communist world of Central and Eastern Europe was the *Enquête Kommission* in the Federal Republic of Germany (see McAdams 2001: 88–123).

There is no doubt that those who committed crimes during the former regimes should face the law and also punishment. At the same time, criminal law cannot play the role of public truth telling and reconciliation. Mark Osiel (1997), an American socio-legal scholar, wrote a book in which he tried to show on the basis of Argentinean examples that criminal show trials (not in the Stalinist sense, but according to rules of law) are able to implant liberal values in society and especially the observance of human rights. He follows the theory of Emile Durkheim (1997) that in modern societies based mainly on organic solidarity (division of labor), the function of criminal law is the reinstatement of basic accepted values in society.

I have doubts, for there are limitations of criminal law and criminal procedure, and these are not such a bad thing. Opening up the procedure would also open the space for abuse of law. Even the author at one point confirms that criminal law plays a limited role.

Communist regimes were based on control of society not only through the party cells in all factories and organizational units, but also through permanent surveillance by the secret police and its collaborators. The scale was not the same in each country in the communist camp, some barracks were under more relaxed surveillance, but nevertheless, the so-called "problem of the files" exists. Legal strategies adopted by particular countries vary. The most radical was the strategy adopted in the ex-GDR. Each person, and not only citizens, has a right to have access to his/her own files with names of the secret collaborators not erased. From the media we learn about the personal tragedies when brother spied on brother and a husband on his wife. It is true that such a strategy cleans up the atmosphere, but I do not think that it stimulates public discussion about the mechanisms of the past and our involvement in sustaining the regime. It still has a private character. It is a private citizen having access to his/her file through the so-called Gauck Agency. In one of the interviews given to the Polish weekly magazine *Wprost*, Joachim Gauck said that "there is only one way to finish the problem with the files," meaning the way adopted by Germany. Possibly, it could stop the use of files in political battles and for short-term political gains, but it does not have a healing potential for the entire society.

Other countries, such as for instance Poland, adopted a middle-of-the-road approach. This approach is based on sequestration of the archival records of the secret services in the Institute for National Remembrance. Each citizen has a right to apply to have access to his/her file, but the decision is taken on the basis that the applicant has been victimized. Only applicants recognized as victims of the regimes will be granted access to the files. At the same time, "victim" status is very broad and plays a role of positive lustration. Again, there is a private character—no national debate.

Other legal strategies, such as decommunisation and lustration, also play a very limited role in societies dealing with the past. I can understand security reasons behind lustration of state officials, but generally the entire process of lustration has failed everywhere. It has been used mainly in political battles and for political gains. Lustration and decommunisation also play the role of curtailing discourse on the operation of the communist system. Instead of serious societal discussion, they limit the discourse by showing a few scapegoats. Of course, the level of responsibility of the members of the *Politbüro* was higher than that of the members of the Communist Party, but if we think about facing the difficult past "in the service of life," to use Nietzsche's phrase, all levels of responsibility and operation of the system must be objects of the process of societal discussion. The question remains: Is it possible in the case of the former communist past? Well, in some parts of the world there were attempts to do precisely that. I mean the so-called truth commissions and especially the most comprehensive process of facing the difficult past by the society in South Africa in the institutional form of the Truth and Reconciliation Commission.

It appears that unwillingness to adopt a strategy of public debate dealing with the past in postcommunist societies is caused by the character of communist society. The communist system was characterized by moral compromise, changes of role from perpetrators to victims and again to perpetrators. A lack of morally clear borders, change of roles, moral compromises engaged in by all but a few righteous ones, all create a situation in which dealing with the past in the form of public cleansing cannot be done by the generation which grew up during communist times.

That does not mean that it cannot be tried in the form of creation of a new type of legal institution which will accommodate elements from both Nemesis and Justitia—dealing with the past as a constitutional process is possible only in such a way. The restriction of dealing with the past only to traditional legal mechanisms, based mainly on criminal law and retributive justice, are not good tools. There is a need for a new type of quasi-judicial institution.

Law, as a mechanism for systematic remembering and forgetting in dealing with the past, should always be in the service of life—for a better present and future. The best way is to deal with the past as part of a constitutional process. As the moral and political philosopher, Hanna Pitkin says, constitutions are not only something that we *have* but they are also what we *are* and more importantly something that we *do*. By *do* she made reference to "the action or activity of constituting—that is, of founding, framing and shaping something anew" (Pitkin 1987: 168). Legal facing and dealing with the difficult past is part of "what we do"—reshaping our societies and ourselves.

GUIDE TO THE CONTRIBUTIONS IN THIS SECTION

The question about learning from the past in "dealing with the past" is the object of Luc Huyse's chapter on "Transitional Justice in Belgium, France, and the Netherlands after World War II: Innovations, Transgressions, and Lessons to Be Learned." Luc Huyse is a distinguished Belgian expert on the problem of dealing with the past, especially in postwar Belgium, France, and the Netherlands. He has also done a lot of empirical research on reconciliation. No surprise that he approaches the problem from a transitional justice perspective. In this chapter, Huyse focuses on the use of tools characteristic for retributive justice.

Saying that *historia magistra vitae est* has limited truth. We can learn something from the past but not necessarily apply that learning in a positive sense in new postcommunist circumstances. The lessons from history described in the first part of Huyse's paper are that there are plenty of variables which limit the range of strategies for dealing with the past; that the choices made by elites are within that limited spectrum and they are political choices; that law was used instrumentally with consequences for its prestige and for the sense of justice.

In the second part of his paper, Huyse stresses two variables as the most important for understanding the differences in policies applied towards the wrongdoers from the communist past: the "exit situation" and the "legacy of the past." He stresses that the effect of these variables was completely different in Central and Eastern Europe than in postwar Western Continental European countries. In regard to the "exit situation," he draws our attention to the way political power was transmitted, and to the role of the international community. As to "legacies of the past," two elements mentioned by

Huyse should be noted: the length of the former regime and its impact on blurring the distinctions between victims and accessories of the regimes, and "experiences society has with the various strategies of dealing with the past," Huyse's suggestion, that experiences of the show trials of the 1940s and 1950s should be taken seriously in analysis of contemporary choices, is a valid one.

The chapter by Hubert Rottleuthner and Matthias Mahlmann, "Models of Transition—Old Theories and Recent Developments," is composed of two parts. The first, about the model of transitional justice, is more abstract and theoretical, while the second addresses the problem of transitional justice in three transformations in modern German history.

The chapter starts with the fundamental question of an adequate theoretical model for social transformation and transitional justice. The authors claim that social contract theory is a useful tool for the analysis of transitional justice, since it is a holistic model of society with a stress on driving forces of transformation, and provides us with a means of normative evaluation of the social change.

A crucial problem for any "dealing with the past," or as some prefer to say, "transitional justice," is the idea that societies are the product of intentional creation by individuals as historical agents. That idea, formulated by social contract theories, presupposes the responsibility of individuals for their action. Rottleuthner and Mahlmann start by stressing the necessity of a human concept of justice in the above-mentioned form of Themis or Justitia, not a fatalistic or divine concept of justice. The second theoretical question discussed by the authors is the problem of normative standards used in "dealing with the past," They distinguish three possibilities: universal standards, local standards without claim to universality, and the internal standards of the old normative order.

In the second part, the authors guide the reader through the drama of transitional justice in Germany in the last century. They show the specificity of the situation after World War II and after 1989. They show how and why courts applied the first (universal) and the third (internal) model of normative standards in criminal cases after 1989.

In their conclusion, the authors state that transitional justice can be reconstructed in social contract theory terms only to a limited degree. They also forcefully present a defense of the natural law position on transitional justice by claiming that universalistic moral standards positivized in human rights catalogues can be applied in "dealing with the past." They also state that it is possible to sanction certain types of past conduct *ex post*. That means, according to the authors, that retroactive justice in some cases is permissible and justifiable.

They also touch the problem of relations between political will and courts as the main tool of dealing with the past. Rottleuthner and Mahlmann's critique of flaws in transitional justice in Germany after 1989, which was conducted mainly by the court system, is close to the present argument that dealing with the past must be treated as a constitutional process.

The chapter by Claus Offe and Ulrike Poppe, "Transitional Justice After the Breakdown of the German Democratic Republic," includes more than is promised in the title. The authors deal with policies adopted or sponsored by state actors such as the government, the judiciary, and special agencies established by law to deal with "transitional justice" in relation to the former German Democratic Republic. They discuss and describe the three major strategies adopted in "dealing with the past": criminal trials, the Gauck Agency, and the Commission of Inquiry of the German *Bundestag* (*Enquête Komission*). That peculiar comprehensive strategy of "dealing with the past" in Germany is put in the social and political context of the former GDR and unified Germany, which predetermined some policy choices. They also put the special case of Germany's way of dealing with the past into the Central and Eastern European postcommunist context. It is possible to say that they provide a theoretical framework for analysis of different policies for dealing with the past. Offe and Poppe are right that peculiar temporal features characterize any policies of dealing with the past in transition from authoritarian to postauthoritarian regimes. That temporal dimension is the threefold reference to the past, the present, and also the future. That reference is crucial for the problem of transitional justice. That temporal reference represents universalistic features of dealing with the past or transitional justice. The authors also sketch another element of a universal framework for an analysis of transitional justice policies: as focused on victims or perpetrators and as legal sanctions or political sanctions. A partial "decision tree" concerning wrongdoings under the old regime also provides a very useful analytical tool. After that what follows in their chapter is an analysis of the specificity of German "dealing with the past" within the above-described theoretical framework.

Grażyna Skąpska, in her study of restitution of property in Central and Eastern European postcommunist countries, "Restitutive Justice, Rule of Law, and Constitutional Dilemmas," stresses the complexity of that aspect of the process of doing justice to the past. She discusses the problem of restitution of property expropriated first by the Nazis and then by the newly installed communist masters. Skąpska's study has empirical and theoretical dimensions. On the empirical level, she discusses the scale of expropriations in detail, and legal and extra-legal frameworks of expropriations. Then she discusses the legal measures and policies adopted in postcommunist countries regarding the restitution of property. On the theoretical level, she discusses the impact of the restitution issue on the necessity of reconciling traditional conceptualizations of rule of law.

Skąpska suggests that private property, which is an object of a restitution claim, should not be treated as a commodity only. That private property possesses a moral dimension as well. That moral dimension of expropriated property makes the issue of restitution so important for the new moral, social, and political order of postcommunist societies. That moral dimension is connected with the possibility of bringing in a moral impulse for societies under the transformation process. She is right in claiming that choices made in relation to restitution of property are constitutional choices in the broadest sense.

In the study, Skąpska shows the limitation of a narrow and formal concept of rule of law, that due to "alienating justice" and "alienating injustice" effects as an outcome of the conventional, legal approach to restitution of property, puts the very promise of the rule of law under question, one of the crucial guiding ideals of postcommunist transformation.

Skąpska's study shows the complexity and peculiarity of the issue of legal redress of past injustices in postcommunist societies. It also shows the need for design of new legal institutions which will be able to take into account the peculiarity of the restitution of property. In dealing with the past in postcommunist countries, a sort of "responsive law" is needed.

She also shows that reversing the historical injustice in postcommunist property rights distribution, when beneficiaries of the expropriation system are at work defending their vested interests, is extremely difficult. Nevertheless, the issue cannot be left untouched, put aside by a "thick line," because postcommunist societies need some "organic solidarity," some moral impulses for social life, and that can be achieved only by facing the issue of past injustices.

Renata Uitz's contribution, "How Far Does Transitional Justice Stretch? Judicial Review for Dealing with the Past in Democratic Transition," is not focused on transitional justice from the point of view of criminal law, but takes a constitutional law perspective. She asks about the legal relevance of knowledge and sensitivity towards the past from the point of view of constitutional review, or whether it is possible to claim that ignorance about the past in the approach of constitutional courts was used as a tool for upholding the role of the courts.

Uitz provides the reader with comparative analyses of constitutional court decisions in cases involving dealing with the past in South Africa and Hungary. Her sophisticated analysis of constitutional cases is a valuable contribution to the problem of dealing with the past as a constitutional process. According to Uitz, South African and Hungarian constitutional courts share the same feature in decisions on constitutionality of legislation directly dealing with the past, namely both courts did not analyze in detail the past addressed by the legislation.

In her analyses of the activity of the Hungarian Constitutional Court, Uitz states that the court tested legislation designed for dealing with the past many times, and did that in detail. In the field of retributive justice, the court, as a matter of principle, rejected all measures for retroactive criminal justice to prosecute offenders not punished under the *ancien régime*. Interestingly, in the area of restitution of property, the constitutional court "emphasizes the great discretion of the legislative." It looks as though two different principles were adopted by the constitutional court in relation to two spheres of "dealing with the past."

According to the court's jurisprudence, transitional justice legislation cannot be exempted from constitutional review, and the court was not going to establish special standards for transitional justice legislation. In the case of restitution of property, as Uitz shows, the Hungarian court in its concept of rule of law relied on legal continuity, and as a consequence adopted a rule that restitution has no other ground than the political decision of the government. A second concept of *novation* allowed the court to make a line between the past and the future. The court's interpretation of novation shows discontinuity. In effect, the two premises allowed the court to test and uphold the transitional legislation in relation to property restitution. The *ex gratia* nature of compensations and novation plays the role of a historical bridge between the past and the future.

Uitz draws the reader's attention to the problem that many cases which do not look *prima facie* as involved in dealing with the past are actually so involved, as long as the problem of legal rules preserved from the previous regime preserving the past are concerned. Constitutional cases involve more than abstract questions about law but have to do with rights and interests from the former regime. Constitutional courts in postcommunist states determine constitutionality with the past in mind. That does not mean that they do detailed analysis of the communist past.

Uitz rightly stresses that there is a crucial difference between taking that past as fact within other facts for consideration, and taking the past in the form of preserved constitutional interests. In that second approach, the structure from the former communist regime became part of the new normative order in the process of creation. This chapter is another contribution to the broad problem of dealing with the past as a constitutional process.

Closing remarks

The contributions discussed above are pitched at different levels of abstraction. Some, such as those of Offe and Poppe, and Reuttleuthner and Mahlmann, are more theoretical; others, such as those of Skąpska, Uitz, and Huyse, more empirical. Some of them, like Uitz's, represent a predominantly legal analysis, while others follow a social science approach. The aim to put these differing approaches together in one section of the volume was to show the complexity of the problem of "dealing with the past": that there were no simple solutions and easily available legal tools and strategies of proper approach to the past; that the problem of dealing with the past in postcommunist transformation itself has peculiarities not shared by other transitions to democracy; that legal tools available in the warehouse of the Western legal tradition are not adequate for that type of justice.

We try to show readers different perspectives in approaching the problem. Different from the point of view of disciplines: jurisprudence, sociology, political science, and also different in their normative dimension. The problem itself requires not an inter-, but a trans-disciplinary approach. The problem of "transitional justice" is one of the crucial problems facing contemporary social sciences and is awaiting future elaboration. The five contributions of this section not only fulfill this role, but also provide a stimulating and interesting read.

NOTES

1 See the very illuminating book by Pavel Câmpeanu (2004), in which the distinguished Romanian sociologist shows the links between the ways in which communism was installed, and the ways in which it ended; and moreover, between the ways in which it ended and the future development of postcommunism.

BIBLIOGRAPHY

Câmpeanu, Pavel. *Ceauşescu. Lata odliczane wstecz* [Years counted backwards]. Warsaw: Wydawnictwo Iskry, 2004.
Durkheim, Emile. *The Division of Labor in Society*. With an introduction by Lewis A. Coser, translated by W. D. Halls. New York: The Free Press, 1997.
McAdams, James A. *Judging the Past in Unified Germany*. Cambridge: Cambridge University Press, 2001.
Osiel, Mark. *Law and Collective Memory*. New Brunswick: Transaction Publishers, 1997.
Pitkin, Hanna. "The Idea of a Constitution." *Journal of Legal Education* 37 (1987): pp. 167–69.

Transitional Justice in Belgium, France, and the Netherlands After World War II: Innovations, Transgressions, and Lessons to Be Learned

LUC HUYSE

The specific focus of this book is on postcommunist Europe. But a more general aim is to debate widespread institutional developments in postauthoritarian states throughout the world. Transitional justice policies in the aftermath of World War II show many such institutional innovations and are, consequently, an attractive domain for comparative analysis and discussion.

One of the major problems in examining recent cases of regime transitions in general and of transitional justice activities in particular is the too short amount of time that has elapsed since they developed. It is, for example, actually impossible to judge success or failure of newly designed instruments, such as truth commissions. Here too lies the importance of looking back at what happened more than half a century ago and reflecting on the long-term effects.[1]

PART I
TRANSITIONAL JUSTICE IN POSTWAR BELGIUM, FRANCE, AND THE NETHERLANDS[2]

A striking similarity in the policies of Belgium, France, and the Netherlands was the outspoken desire, especially evident in the months just before and after the Liberation, to expel with great speed and firmness the collaborators from their societies. A much heard expression was that "there was no place left for those who had betrayed their country." A second resemblance lies in the tendency—especially in the early stages of the operation—to judge the population under absolute standards of good and bad. Sensitivity to the many shades of gray between "black" and "white" was very low indeed.[3] The result of those policy choices was that the purge affected extremely large numbers of citizens and that severe sanctions hit them. The number of unpatriotic citizens who suffered state-induced punishment in one or another form was about 80,000 in Belgium, 130,000 in France, and 110,000 in the Netherlands. Or, for every 100,000 inhabitants, 963 for Belgium, 309 for France, and 1250 for the Netherlands.[4] Those who served prison sentences numbered 48,000 in Belgium, 38,000 in France, and 51,000 in Holland.[5] However light the sentence, imprisonment was almost always accompanied by other sanctions: a fine, confiscation of personal goods, police supervision after the end of the prison term, the obligation to reside in a specific town. In Belgium, damages had to be paid to the state, out of the marital goods or by the heirs if necessary. Fifteen thousand Dutchmen suffered the loss of nationality. The three countries also introduced some form of "national indignity" that implied a series of civic disqualifications and a prohibition on some kinds of professional activity. This sanction was in most cases an extension of a prison sentence. It was, however, also used independently as a "milder" punishment for the "small fish." As such, it was applied to 22,000 Belgian, 50,000 French, and 56,000 Dutch collaborators. In addition, special measures were taken to purge the national and local public administrations.

EXCEPTIONAL TIMES, EXCEPTIONAL POLICIES

"Times of transition are, almost by definition, exceptional. The procedures used in dealing with the past also tend to be exceptional. Second-best arguments come to the forefront, together with considerations of practicality and expediency" (Elster 1998). Elster's statement also applies to the policies Belgium, France, and the Netherlands conceived and implemented in their dealings with those who collaborated with the German occupying forces. Unusual measures appeared in two sequential episodes: the period of massive prosecutions (1944–1947) and the gradual reintegration of the convicted (1947–1950).[6]

– Innovating punishment –
Retributive justice underwent substantial changes through the introduction of uncommon judicial techniques and of quasi- and non-judicial ways of dealing with the friends of the Nazis.

Judicial developments – *Force majeure* and intense time pressures have been invoked to justify exceptional legal techniques.[7] Retroactive criminal legislation was introduced through interpretive modifications of prewar laws. Shortly after the liberation of the country, the Belgian *Cour de Cassation* ruled that all the legislative measures taken by the government-in-exile had full legality, including the law that in December 1942 had considerably broadened the scope of the criminal legislation on collaboration. The argument was that the government had not created new rules, but had only interpreted an existing body of penal arrangements. In France, Peter Novick writes, despite "the breadth of the existing statutes, and the desire to avoid retroactivity, there was general agreement concerning the need to 'interpret' some of the provisions of the prewar Code. Accordingly, legislation was enacted by the Comité Français de la Libération Nationale 'to facilitate the Court's interpretation of the prewar texts'" (Novick 1968: 143). In the Netherlands, retroactivity was clearly present in the reintroduction of capital punishment. In addition, newly created sanctions, such as police supervision after the prison term, were defined as administrative, not criminal in nature. They were, technically speaking, not retroactive.

The three countries also espoused the principle of collective guilt. People were disqualified, not considering them one by one, but for their membership in a collaborationist group. In the Netherlands, all members of pro-German military movements (and their spouses) automatically lost their Dutch citizenship. The Belgian government decided to strip the rank-and-file of pro-German organizations collectively of their political and of many of their civil rights. Claus Offe notes that in such case the defendants "are not—or only marginally—given a legal chance to invoke excuses that might exonerate them individually. Even if they are given this chance, they will be forced to collect evidence to prove their innocence, so that the burden of proof is reversed" (Offe 1992: 195). In addition, curtailing of the right of defense took place through restrictions of access to appeal courts and of contacts between lawyers and their clients and in the form of prolonged internments.

Lay judges participated in the activities of the tribunals that tried the collaborators. France included members of the resistance movements in two of the newly created key institutions of the purge, the *Cours de Justice* and the *Chambres Civiques*. The Dutch set up some thirty-five Special Courts, with two of the five judges being army officers. For the lesser cases, tribunals were created and staffed by two patriotic citizens and one professional judge. The Belgian government-in-exile and its immediate successors turned to the already existing military courts and made them competent for the trial of collaborators. Three of the five members in every court were army officers. Belgium, finally, introduced the possibility of plea bargaining—a completely "foreign" technique in most European countries.

Quasi-judicial techniques – For many collaborators, punishment came via traditional (special or military) court outcomes. At the same time, mechanisms were set in motion for sanctioning the "small fish," those who remained outside the court system because their collaboration had been petty or was of a purely political nature. These mechanisms operated autonomously, be it "in the shadow of the law," as is demonstrated by two Belgian examples.

Two-thirds of those who were accused of political collaboration did not appear before the courts, but were registered on a very special list, published regularly in the official gazette (*Belgisch Staatsblad/Moniteur Belge*). Registration, which was planned as a sort of summary proceedings, implied the loss of a series of political and civil rights. It was the military prosecutor, and he alone, who decided which persons were sent to the courts and who was to take the more informal route to disqualification. Tens of thousands of Belgians were registered, learning their fate after notification in the gazette. The procedure was judicial in a double sense: it was a member of the judiciary who steered the process and appeal before a civil court was possible. But in many other aspects, the practice receded from normal procedural justice.

A second technique linked lustration in private organizations (professional and cultural associations, labor unions, sport clubs, etc.) with state-induced repression. A decree law of 19 September 1945 stipulated that private lustration was a ground for being put on the prosecutor's list, automatically resulting in political and civic disqualification.

Non-judicial measures – In Belgium, civic disqualification was not only the product of a court decision or of being put on the prosecutor's list. Every citizen who wanted to take up a certain profession, or start a business, or receive an exit visa or a driver's license, or enroll as a student at a state university, etc. had to show a so-called certificate of patriotic behavior.[8] Issuing such a document was the prerogative of local authorities (the mayor or the head of the police). Up to two years after the Liberation, the denial of the certificate could not be appealed.

Purging the civil service was, in each of the three countries, a question that was dealt with in large part by the administration's hierarchy. Legislation, regulating these procedures, was scarce.

– Organizing the return into society –[9]

One year after the Liberation, arguments were heard in favor of a controlled reinsertion into society of the convicted collaborators. The idea was that a prolonged expulsion of such a large group of citizens was not without considerable ambiguity. There was no guarantee, it was said, that its effects would be merely beneficial for the re-established democratic state.

The policy shift was based on a variety of considerations. Some were of a politico-strategic nature. It was feared that the ex-collaborators would be driven into social and political isolation. This in turn could result in the creation of subcultures and networks, which would almost certainly become hostile towards democracy. It was also felt that a lengthy exile of one particular category of collaborators, namely administrative and managerial manpower, risked to be very counterproductive as it could endanger the badly needed political and economic reconstruction of the country. In addition, the prisons had to cope with an over-population and the many thousands of political criminals exerted an untenable pressure on public resources. Other motives were of a politico-moral order. All governments viewed clemency— the moral category that opened the door to reintegration—as a way to correct and efface shortcomings of the judicial process. One such shortcoming was the considerable inequality that had arisen, because punishment had been much harsher in the first months after the war than one or two years later. Measures of magnanimity were also seen as a way of making reconciliation between the good and the bad citizens possible. The need for closing the ranks was one of the main arguments of advocates of amnesty laws. The latter consideration was prominent in France, mainly because of the many doubts about the status of the Vichy regime and its followers.

The *obstacles* to reintegration were manifold: detention, deprivation of nationality, of office and of political and civil rights, financial sanctions such as the confiscation of money and goods, denial of war-damage retribution and of military pensions. The height of the hurdles varied. It depended on the size of the sentence, for example, the length of the detention and the impact (in terms of time and scope) of the deprivation of rights.

The *measures* the authorities could take were of a great variety: amnesty, release on parole, reduction or remission of detention and of financial sanctions, restitution of nationality, of office and of civil rights, rehabilitation. An overview is given in *Table 2*. Some of these actions were a prerogative of Parliament, others of the head of state, the executive, or the prison administration. Judicial procedures were an exception here. They were needed only in the case of rehabilitation.

Measure	*Scope*	*Effect*	*Initiative*	*Decision taken by*
amnesty	collective	abrogates crime and punishment	mostly legislature	mostly legislature
pardon	collective/ individual	total/partial remission of penalty	executive/convict	B and NL: King/Queen F: President
provisional release	individual	interrupts execution of sentences	prison administration	prison administration
conditional release/ parole	individual	grants early release under conditions	several authorities	several authorities
rehabilitation	individual	wipes out conviction and puts end to future consequences	convict	judiciary

Table 2. Varieties of reintegration measures.

Belgium – From mid-1946 onwards, convicted collaborators could benefit individually from conditional release. By the end of 1949, about 25,400 of those convicted had been released on parole. Reduction of sentence was also possible through an individual petition for pardon. Between 1946 and 1953, 15,400 collaborators saw their prison time at least once reduced via this way.[10]

France – Policy here was developed along two paths. The first was parliamentary and resulted in the production of three so-called amnesty laws. Presidential pardon was the second way:

1. On 16 August 1947, the French Parliament voted a law that granted a collective amnesty to youngsters who had committed minor acts of collaboration and to civil servants who had suffered the lightest disciplinary punishment. In May 1949, President Auriol, in a public address, presented a new amnesty bill as a badly needed way to reconciliation between the France of Vichy and the France of post-1944. It took Parliament almost two years to pass the bill. The law of 5 January 1951 had a far-reaching impact on the population in detention. The law also returned *la dignité nationale* to approximately 50,000 persons. A third and final law, voted on 6 August 1953, ended the loss of political and civil rights for all and made individual amnesty decisions possible for the convicts whose prison sentence was less than 15 years.
2. In the meantime, the French presidents made full use of their right to grant pardon. Such an action, in the summer of 1948, gave back all rights to more than one third of those who had been struck by disqualification.

The Netherlands – The policy here was developed along three paths:

1. Conditional release (after completion of two thirds of the sentence) has been applied to convicted collaborators from the very start of the transitional justice operation. In addition, the Dutch authorities have made early release available on a larger scale through successive waves of individual and collective pardoning.
2. In 1953, a law granted the 15,000 collaborators who had lost the Dutch nationality the right to make an individual demand for reinstatement. In the years that followed, some 8000 men and women took advantage of this opportunity.
3. The question of the return of political rights was not dealt with in an explicit way. Since the duration of this sanction was limited to 10 years, almost all collaborators won back suffrage in the second half of the fifties. Almost all these mechanisms were, strictly speaking, not real innovations.

They existed in a more or less similar form before World War II. What was new and truly ground-breaking was the size and the speed of their mobilization in an operation that was set up to reduce the unwanted effects of the many novelties in prosecuting, sentencing, and otherwise punishing the former collaborators.

EVALUATING POSTWAR TRANSITIONAL JUSTICE INNOVATIONS

Any evaluation has to start with the identification of the measure against which to judge success or failure. At the time of the Liberation, the stated goal for the evolving transitional justice was that it had to be "swift, severe and fair." Proceeding that way was the one and only route to a reunified and reconciled population and, in the long run, to a sound and balanced dealing with the past. This was, in the official rhetoric of the time, the political basis on which exceptional procedures for punishing the collaborators were grounded.

Success or failure?[11]

Swiftness and severity were attained. Equity was the problem. Most of the innovations in the area of punishment considerably reduced traditional rule of law guarantees.[12] The use of non-professional judges in special courts was one source, among many others, of grave risks. Such judges are easier targets for pressure by the executive, the media, and public opinion. Fidelity to legality and the rule of law, if it is imbued in the minds of members of the judiciary, is a strong safeguard against political and partisan use of the judicial process. It looks plausible to hypothesize that lay judges, particularly in the context of a regime transition, are badly equipped to offer resistance against the intrusion of the executive and of other societal forces in their activities as prosecutors. The purge in the civil service and the technique of the certificate are other examples of rule of law violations: their result was improvisation, unpredictability, and great inequality in the sanctions that were handed out.

The effect of some of these lapses from important legal norms was partly corrected by the innovative use of existing reintegration instruments. In addition, elite-inspired and -induced silence on the legal transgressions kept the episode for many years out of the public debate. But it is clear that the passage of time has not fully exorcised the ghosts of the past. Collaboration and the purge that followed still haunt these nations' collective memory.[13]

Belgium – The commotion here is like a chronic disease for which there is no actual treatment. It involves the war years of whole sections of the population (the Flemish and francophones, Catholics and non-Catholics).

Because official reintegration policies failed, many collaborators developed the tendency to rely heavily on networks of "colleagues" and sympathizers. Sometimes these networks became breeding grounds of bitterness, revanchism, and anti-Belgian and anti-democratic ideas.[14] They also created a "victim culture": the belief that collaborators had fallen victim to victors' justice. Reconciliation, publicly acknowledged, between the "heirs" of the resistance and of the collaboration is still absent.

The Netherlands – In this country, emotion is like a fire that intermittently flares up. Years of silence alternate with periods of heated unrest. The commotion is always centered on individuals and the course of the event is predictable: the discussion involves the quality of the trials and of the official policy towards the collaborators. There is an explanation. The purge was dealt with in silence, hidden from the public. An open debate was avoided by restricting the flow of information and by emphasizing the urgent need to close ranks. Those who had sympathized with the enemy were "treated" by professionals: judges, civil servants, professors of criminal law or criminology, probation officers, and psychiatrists. From the seventies on, though, the forced silence (a state-imposed "memory hole") on collaboration and the purge could not be kept intact. The grounds on which the postwar verdicts were based had not become part of the collective memory, which again and again led to embarrassing questions of "how" and "why."

France – France, too, is still suffering from its 1940s. The course of the fever chart is closely linked to such events as a book (on Mitterand's war past, for example), a movie, a TV-program or, most prominently, a new trial (as in the case of Barbie, Papon, and Touvier). The disease is similar to what happens in the Netherlands: a slumbering neurosis that flares up around specific incidents and individuals. Yet there is a difference: the debate moves almost always from the case of an individual to the nation's conduct between 1940 and 1944. There is a second resemblance between the Netherlands and France. Up to the seventies, a sort of compelled amnesia existed. But, as Henry Rousso (1990) writes, the mirror finally broke and obsession replaced repression of emotions.[15] History took revenge.

PART II

TRANSITIONAL JUSTICE IN POSTCOMMUNIST EUROPE

Post-1989 transitional justice in Central and Eastern Europe has, compared with what happened in Belgium, France, and the Netherlands after World War II, run a very different course.

have received great attention in the first debates on screening. The Hungarian President has asked the Constitutional Court to review two articles of the February 1993 law (on the lifting of the statute of limitations) for their conformity with Article 7.1 of the European Convention of Human Rights and with Article 15.1 of the International Convention on Civil and Political Rights. A strong motive for not neglecting the signals coming from abroad was the possibility that violations of rule of law codes might compromise the country's membership of the Council of Europe.

The legacy of the past

A most important feature of an authoritarian regime is its duration – The time factor counts in a variety of ways. If the life of a criminal regime is short, questions with regard to the statute of limitations (and the hesitation they stir up) are unlikely to arise. A second consequence relates to the survival of pre-totalitarian, viz. democratic structures. The communist regimes in Central and Eastern Europe lasted for forty years. Judging their abuses made the lifting of the statute of limitations almost inevitable and the production of firm proof troublesome. This has lead to discussion and debate, and has slowed down decision-making on crime and punishment. In addition, almost none of the institutions of the precommunist past survived. The legal culture, created by communism, was firmly established and has proven to be hard to eradicate. Another aspect of the long length of the communist regimes is that complicity or, at least, accommodation pervaded most of the population and did so for several generations. Communist society was gradually accepted because of the workings of socialization, isolation, and a system of rewards and punishments. Indeed, authoritarian regimes, particularly if they stay in power for long years, tend to blur the distinction between being victimized and being an accessory. Large parts of the population are casualties of the totalitarian use of continuous indoctrination and ideology and may have collaborated in state crimes. The result is that drawing the line between good and bad citizens becomes extremely difficult. Such a situation, that was almost absent in the postwar European countries, considerably decreases the urge to start a full-blown punishment operation.

The post-transitional conflict between legal systems – A crucial problem in postcommunist transitional justice has been provoked by the real or potential conflict between the legal legacy of the past and the laws and regulations of the new or reconstructed democracy. As Tina Rosenberg writes, "[p]eople can only legally be prosecuted for crimes that were illegal at the time of the commission. The truly hated acts of eastern European regimes—the secret police shadow, the censorship, the political criteria for all decisions—they were the very basis of the system" (cited in Boraine et al. 1994: 95). A defendant might argue, Offe writes, "that he was unaware of the now alleged criminal nature of the acts of which he is accused; given the fact that he has been brought up in a regime that pardons and in fact mandates acts (now deemed criminal) for the sake of higher political purposes, he had no reason to doubt the rightfulness of what he had been doing" (Offe 1992: 199).

Type of authoritarian regime – Communist Czechoslovakia, Hungary, and Poland are examples of what the French call *une collaboration d'Etat*: a state apparatus of a domestic origin accepting an imported or imposed order. Judging such a regime is an intricate assignment for the successor elites. It permeates large segments of the political and civil society, both in terms of the institutions and of the population. A full purge of the country would cause, in the words of Offe, "a veritable witch-hunt, thus creating permanent and bitter cleavages rather than healing the wounds the past has left behind" (Offe 1992: 197). The judiciary, too, has been, wholly or in part, closely associated with the outgoing regime. Thoroughly cleansing this corps would most likely cripple the criminal justice system. In addition, the nature of the totalitarian system in the countries of Central and Eastern Europe tended to diffuse responsibility for abuses. "Hundreds of thousands of people," Aryeh Neier writes, "were implicated in the administration of repression and similar numbers were victims of repression. It was often the case that people simultaneously implemented and were victims of repression" (cited in Boraine et al. 1994: 4). All these circumstances may be called upon to explain why dealing with the past in Eastern and Central Europe has been ambiguous in its content.

In addition, atrocities against the life and property of men and women occurred predominantly in the late 1940s and during the 1950s. In most cases, such as in Hungary where a 30-year statute of limitations exists, criminal proceedings regarding the most reprehensible human rights abuses are thus precluded by reason of lapse of time. The passage of time may have blurred the memories of what happened. In addition, during the last two decades, the violence was more psychological than physical in nature. "The main instruments of control over society," as Wiktor Osiatyński (a constitutional lawyer associated with the University of Warsaw) says, "switched from terror and repression to primarily economic control, control of the media, control of association and of rights" (cited in Boraine et al. 1994: 60). This may have led to a more moderate attitude towards those held responsible. Moreover, the communist regimes were not in all aspects viewed and perceived as completely negative. Many, for example, appreciated their policy with respect to education and health care. Antecedent regimes thus differ in their actual performances, but so also do the perceptions and interpretations of them.

Transitional Justice After the
Breakdown of the German Democratic Republic

CLAUS OFFE AND ULRIKE POPPE

New political regimes are never built on a *tabula rasa*. Hence any new regime must establish some relationship to the actors and subjects of its predecessor regime. Also, it must establish reasons supporting the nature of this retrospective relationship. The retrospective relationship must be justifiable in terms of the new regime. While new authoritarian regimes may be able to repress and destroy the traces and memories of its predecessor regime, this option is precluded in new democracies. The latter must deal, in order to secure their viability and credibility of their principles in the future, with past injustices through means and procedures that are consistent with presently valid standards of justice, such as the rule of law and equality before the law. This threefold temporal reference to the past, the present, and the future is constitutive of the problems of transitional justice in new democracies. This chapter is about how these backward-looking practices evolved in unified Germany with regard to the past of the now defunct state of the German Democratic Republic (GDR) and the dominant actors of this state, as well as its victims.

We deal here with "policies," that is, initiatives taken and strategies chosen or sponsored by state actors (governments, the judiciary, and special agencies constituted by law), not the numerous exclusively civic actions in which conflicts are carried out among family members, by social and political movements, within occupational groups or the media. Policies of transitional justice can focus upon perpetrators and on victims. They can also consist in formal legal procedures or the conditioning of discretionary moves taken by political actors. A matrix that is made up of these two dimensions can help to group the numerous policy options available in this field *(Table 3)*.

	PERPETRATORS	VICTIMS
legal sanctions	criminal punishment 1 3	restitution/compensation 2 4
political sanctions	disqualification from public sector employment	"recognition"

Table 3. Types of responses to past injustices.

Box 1 represents all those cases where criminal law procedures are applied to perpetrators. The rules and decisions governing this field of activities include those governing the resources spent on investigation; decisions concerning the statutes of limitation and the time frame of prosecution; kinds of actors and acts that are to be prosecuted; and rules concerning amnesty and dismissal from prison.

Box 2 concerns victims and the legal entitlements they are endowed with regard to restitution of property, compensation of suffering, and incarceration. Note that the satisfaction of seeing former oppressors formally punished can be an externality of Box 1 activities that belongs here.

Box 3 contains all the practices by which state policies shape and condition the fates of alleged perpetrators within civil society without directly ordering specific outcomes. For instance, perpetrators are banned from public sector employment or must pass special screening before being eligible for public office. Such information can be issued publicly or conveyed to specific target recipients, with some probability implied (and intended) of the persons in question becoming targets of civic and political disqualification. The sanctions following upon such exposition remain largely (except, within limits, for the sector of state employment itself, as in the case of lustration) a matter of how friends, customers, employers, relatives, local communities, the media, etc. respond to what has been made public or specifically conveyed to them about particular acts and actors. This type of sanctioning can be termed "civil disqualification." Other policies belonging in this category include the state-sponsored establishment of documentation centers, exhibitions, research activities, investigative commissions, and the like.

Finally, Box 4 contains the role assigned by policy makers to victims' associations, state-sponsored confrontations, encounters and exchanges between former perpetrators and their victims, and claims against perpetrators granted victims by the state. The typical goal (and not just the side effect, as in Box 1) of policies belonging here is to offer recognition to victims of the old regime and to help them to develop a sense of trust and belonging to the newly constituted political community.

We concentrate here on state-sponsored activities focusing on agents of the old regime, that is, on phenomena belonging to Box 1 and Box 3. The practices thus categorized are intended to deal with the morally, legally, economically, and politically relevant residues of the old regime and the persons who made up that regime. These practices of coping or coming to terms with recent history have a history of their own. We proceed as follows. First, we follow the main nodes, or branching points, in the history of dealing with the past of the GDR and its relevant residues. The question is the following: What choice of policies was adopted in these fields? These policies include those initiated by the pre-unification regime in the GDR that began to form to much the same logic as corporate capitalism creates the need for an army of investment brokers. In either case, the role people play is mandated by systemic requirements and cannot fully be reduced to their personal intentions and moral qualities. State socialism is an opportunity structure that imposes constraints, allocates incentives and premiums, and inculcates preferences which are all not of anyone's deliberate making and free choice. How is it possible to come to terms with these "faceless" arrangements in terms of personal guilt and culpability?

On the other hand, such a "systemic" view of the past is deeply unsatisfactory for actors that are external to the system in time and space. For the past regime lives on, not just in the memories and continued suffering of victims, but also in the visible and suspected position of privilege and influence that members of the old elite and their functionaries continue to enjoy. Many of them have been able, or are suspected to have been able, to "convert" the resources acquired under the old regime into present status and advantage. The old regime has its traces and residues within the new. What present actors can act upon is no longer the institutional order of the old regime, or its "structure." That order has gone anyway. The only thing to deal with that remains is persons who are known to have done certain things or suffered certain things. The failure to deal with these residues, or so it is believed at least by the victims themselves and those who feel solidarity with them or indignation over their victimization, would stand in the way of an effective integration of both actors and sufferers into the new political order unless these events are properly dealt with by the new regime. In order to cope with either of the two continuities—the continuity of memory and indignation and the continuity of impunity and influence—, the present reading of the history of the now defunct system of state socialism is bound to shift to an "activist" mode. In an epistemic gestalt switch, personal responsibility is now being emphasized and systemic causation played down, and actors are now being looked upon in terms of personality traits such as heroism, moral weakness, guilt, awareness, deliberate action, and opportunism, rather than in structural terms such as social roles, built-in constraints, and preferences shaped through indoctrination and manipulation. Those who used to be (and to think of themselves) as "functionaries" of the regime are now, after that regime's end, being reconstituted as responsible and potentially culpable agents.

Many people both inside and outside the defunct empire of European state socialism believe that this type of political and economic order was a profoundly unfortunate period in the history of the societies affected by it, as state socialism deprived huge populations of the measure of well-being and happiness, as well as of the benefits of a civilized and liberal political order, that they could have attained in the absence of the state socialism. Let us assume, for the matter of argument, that this proposition is both meaningful and true. In retrospect and after the old regime went under, it is unlikely for the reasons just mentioned that the gap will any longer be attributed to impersonal forces and structures causing a historical disaster. Such a "structuralist" view of the past may well be the preferred reading of history of those whose acts are now being explored and perhaps punished. On the other hand, the preferred reading of victims (as well as of the proponents of the new regime) tends to be that the entire malaise of the past system can be accounted for in terms of crimes committed by identifiable and responsible persons, among whom many survived the breakdown of the old regime.[1] As this question remains contested, and as the discourse concerning the question cannot be concluded by authoritative fiat in a liberal society, the first problem is to reach a workable agreement between all sides involved on the range of acts and actors within the old regime to which the notion of moral or criminal guilt and punishment should be held to be applicable.

THE POLITICS OF BUILDING INTERPRETIVE FRAMES

Unoriginally, the notion of "responsible agency," and hence the answer to the question just raised, is a social construct. Let us distinguish two polar types of such constructs. One is the "weak" frame which denies, and the authors and proponents of which may be actually quite strongly interested in denying, the possibility of linking outcomes to causal acts of internal actors ("internal" regarding both space and time) who have been sufficiently autonomous and knowledgeable to be culpable. Adherents of this frame tend to look upon the negative experience of state socialism in terms of a fateful and anonymous historical disaster, perhaps even mitigated by some favorable accomplishments. This disaster emerges, according to this reading, from the synergism of innumerable actors, past and present, internal and external, well-intentioned, unknowing, and only marginally criminal by intention and effect. In other words, the "disaster" component, according to the proponents of this type of interpretive frame, is held to approach 99 per cent.

The polar opposite is a "strong" frame which claims, and the proponents of which may be equally interested in claiming, that most of the negative outcomes can actually be traced back to personal actors who are demonstrably legally and, at least, morally responsible for the damage they have inflicted upon others (as well as themselves). Adherents of this frame tend to favor criminal prosecution, as well as other retroactive methods of dealing with unjust acts committed in the past that the new regime must cope with. To be sure, most empirical cases of interpreters dealing with the past must be located "in between" these polar opposites. But the distribution of frames across observers is far from random. The individually preferred interpretive frames may differ across countries, across generations, across types of disasters/crimes under scrutiny, across time, across political orientation, biographical experience, institutional location, and professional identity. As a result of this plurality of orientations, frames are essentially contested, and the contest is unlikely to be resolved by compelling arguments coming from philosophical analysis, historical research, legal scholarship, or political expediency.

To what extent were actors and acts actually "internal" ones? And if they are to be held external, are they external in space or in time? Answers are far from obvious. Why was it that the exculpation was rarely used (or, at any rate, rarely accepted) in the case of the GDR, that much of the disaster must be attributed to external rather than internal actors? This excuse has been widely used in the Polish case. It might have been used regarding the GDR regime as well, given the fact that the sovereignty of the East German state was a limited one (contrary to what the GDR leadership itself postulated at the time) to the end within the framework of the Warsaw Pact and the Council of Mutual Economic Aid (CMEA), with the Soviet leadership playing a dominant and generally decisive role. The excuse of external agency was actually invoked by defendants in the trial conducted against the *Politbüro* members accused of being responsible for the border regimes and the lives lost under this regime. These defendants claimed that they were just following Warsaw Pact orders, without any possibility to escape. This attempted exoneration was rejected by the court on account of its dubious factual premise and the moral inconclusiveness of the claim that the defendants were actually "coerced" to comply. However, the argument of ascribing the wrongdoings of the past regime to the coercion of an external actor was, and still is, much more widely in use in the GDR's neighboring countries, most obviously in Poland, than in Germany itself. This difference can be explained by the fact that any externalization strategy would be blunted, in the German case, by the obvious consideration that the control of the Soviet Empire over East German politics was itself caused by the war of aggression originating from Germany, and Germany's subsequent defeat. In other words, it is only to Germany that the condition applies that the agents of external coercion were originally caused, enabled, and seemingly justified by previous internal actors. This consideration deflates the value of any depiction of the past as a history of collective victimization. One might speculate that the latter intellectual scheme is more likely to emerge in a Roman Catholic as opposed to a Protestant culture with its basically individualist background assumptions.

Concerning the question of the causal attribution of outcomes to internal and external actors, and more precisely: actors being internal or external in either space or time, a complex matrix could be drawn which links categories of interpreters to their respective most favored interpretations. For example, opposition activists having fought the old regime, together with many courts involved in prosecuting members of the old regime, would typically reject the old elite's claim of having been coerced by forces external in space. In the eyes of these interpreters, rulers and other agents making up the old regime are held to have been sufficiently unconstrained by external actors and hence autonomous and responsible for their acts. At the same time, these interpreters would certainly be prepared to recognize the role of causal forces that were external in time, namely the Nazi regime and its war of aggression. In contrast, the interpretive frame prevailing in Poland is significantly different in that the attribution of deplorable outcomes to responsible actors was unequivocally based upon the notion of some unjustified foreign rule of the Soviet Union, without many criminal forms of cooperation being focused upon, of which significant numbers of internal actors could now be justly accused. For attempts to scrutinize the elite of the former regime and its supporters are widely seen in Poland as a dangerously divisive move that could undermine the sense of national unity and pride.

These two examples may just serve as an illustration of the link that exists between the location of actors in a field of interests and meanings, on the one hand, and their preferred frame of interpretation, on the other. The framing of agency and the causal attribution of outcomes to agents is not conditioned by factual evidence and disinterested analysis alone. There is a discursive "politics" of framing. Pragmatic considerations of acts that would have to follow from the adoption of a particular "reading" of the old regime, and strategic responses to these acts that must be anticipated from affected groups, will all play a role in the formation of interpretive frames. For instance, pragmatic considerations such as the following ones may play a role in the motivation of those favoring a "weak" frame:

a) The anticipation that attempted legal activism in prosecuting crimes committed under the old regime is likely to be obstructed (or even actively and violently fought)[2] by alienated agents within the state administration and the judiciary.

b) The anticipated need that the expertise of those liable to criminal prosecution will be indispensable for the reconstruction of the political and economic order, with the implication that tactical lenience should be allowed to prevail.

c) The anticipation that the quality of the available evidence will not be sufficient (perhaps due to the control members of the old apparatus have gained or even maintained over these documents) to enter into effective criminal prosecution.

d) Proponents of the new regime may also wish to protect themselves by protecting key actors of the old regime from criminal prosecution, the underlying reasoning being that if such prosecution were to result in significant penalties, representative actors of the new regime could be blamed in retrospect for having cooperated with (or at least not duly resisted suggestions aiming at cooperation coming from) those whose eventual demise from power had caught them by surprise.

These and similar considerations may all play a role in discouraging the building of a "strong," actor-centered frame built upon the presumption of evident links between outcomes, on the one hand, and autonomous and knowledgeable (and hence potentially culpable) actors, on the other.

Conversely, the adoption of a "strong," or agency-centered frame that would allow for the attribution of most of the negative outcomes to internal actors who are held fully responsible, is also driven by values, anticipations, and interests. Relevant considerations of this kind include the following:

a) Proponents of the "strong" frame may be motivated by the desire to respond to the emotional needs of victims and to win over those who have suffered under the old regime to accepting the rules and principles of the new regime.

b) There are also invariably less lofty motivations for the adoption of a strong frame and its punitive practical implications. One of them results from the fact that coping with acts committed in the past is always embedded in present-day political conflict. For instance, if a governing political party A manages to demonstrate and publicize the fact that actor X has been involved in objectionable activities under the old regime and, furthermore, that this very same actor is now associated with or enjoys the support of opposition party B, this is likely to yield a competitive advantage for party A in future electoral campaigns. The obvious retaliatory move that party B is likely to resort to is scrutinizing the elite personnel associated with party A for similarly reprehensible actors or acts. Political competition may also be conducted in terms of a moralizing conflict over meta-norms, with the typical accusation being that political parties on the left are disposed towards practicing inappropriate leniency to crimes committed under the old regime.

c) Other political goals served by the adoption of a "strong" frame include the attempt of restoring some international reputation of a country (such as Germany) that has been widely accused in the past, from the outside as well as from within, for having failed to punish the perpetrators of the Nazi regime as vigorously and consistently as was called for moral reasons. This type of motivation follows the rule of "this time we are determined to do it right."

d) Also, the somewhat triumphalist goal can be served of engraving the fact into the memory of the present and future generations that "we," the liberal democracies of the West, have won the Cold War and that the merciless prosecution of the old regime's elites is mandated by the need to consolidate the new state.

e) More respectably perhaps, the goal to be served by adopting a version of the "strong" frame is to immunize future actors against the dangers and temptations of relying on or complying with authoritarian rule, and to make irreversible the transition to a liberal and democratic form of political regime.

f) Finally, a strong frame, together with its practical punitive implications, can be advocated because it serves the political, juridical and scholarly interests of those who are committed to shed as much light as possible on the internal dynamics of the old regime; for criminal trials afford the unique opportunity to gather data because courts can (1) force strategic actors to testify before a court and to submit to the scrutiny of criminal investigation; and (2) in most cases, to testify under oath.

The adoption of a "strong" frame in Germany after 1989

The two lists of motivations, both of them incomplete, highlight the complexity that is involved in adopting either the weak or the strong frame, or any mixed position "in between." Yet, the actual trajectory that can be observed in the case of the GDR and its retrospective treatment within unified Germany is easy to summarize. A dominant coalition emerged in which actors and motives converged on adopting a modified version of the "strong" frame. The German case of retroactive justice resulted in a more activist strategy concerning the pre-1989 regime of the GDR and its actors than is the case in any of the other postcommunist countries. Why was this so? Let us review how the various pros and cons that we have identified above figured in the German formation of a policy concerning transitional justice.

The presence of a substantial welfare gap, both material and immaterial, that had accumulated throughout the forty years of history of the GDR was taken for granted at the end of the year 1989 not only (trivially) by West German political elites and the former GDR's opposition forces, but also by the political and economic leadership of the GDR itself. There was literally nobody who would claim publicly that the old regime deserved any credit any longer in terms of its economic sustainability or political legitimacy. Similarly pervasive was the consensus that this grim reality of moral and economic bankruptcy must be largely accounted for in terms of internal agency, as no external scapegoats were available. These internal actors were seen to be accountable (in the sense specified above). This accountability was recognized by all sides involved, including the state party SED and most of its leadership. The latter, however, was somewhat selective in its recognition of accountability and guilt, taking exception, for instance, regarding the border regime and the lives lost under this regime, which were attributed to external coercion originating in Warsaw Pact structures. Otherwise, the recognition of failures and mistakes, though not universally of a criminal nature, was unequivocal.

The state party's preparedness to engage in self-blame is less curious than it might appear at first sight. For the leadership of the SED, soon after the breakdown of its regime renamed into the PDS, was bound to appreciate that its political future was contingent upon some credible measure of distancing itself from aspects of its political past and that of selected elements of its former leadership.[3] At the same time, the insistence of the leadership upon the logic of "mistakes" having been committed by identifiable individuals rather than structural patterns of state socialism having caused an inescapable disaster allowed leaders and masses alike to preserve their belief in the viability of some future form of state socialism, one in which such mistakes were to be avoided.

There was thus no relevant voice raised in the GDR between November 1989 and the end of its statehood on 3 October 1990 that would have raised principled objections to the prosecution of at least some of the violations of rights that were instigated, sponsored, tolerated, and condoned by and under the old regime. More than that: there was a broad if highly diverse and diversely motivated advocacy in favor of legal sanctions of these violations. Nor were there, at least during the initial phase of the process in 1989–90, significant objections to actually embarking upon a course of criminal sanctioning. Virtually all the reasons suggesting the adoption of a "weak" frame, as summarized above, were absent, as well as all the reasons supporting the adoption of a strong frame present. The focus of the criminal prosecutions initiated in 1990 (that is, before unification) was not on the old regime's acts of repression, but on illegitimate appropriation of economic resources (through corruption) and of political resources through the falsification of local elections that had demonstrably occurred on a large scale in May 1989 (Marxen and Werle 1999: 235).

To elaborate, no substantial fears arose (contrary to the actual subsequent experience of a substantial nostalgic backlash spearheaded by the PDS) that juridical activism in dealing with violations of the defunct regime would alienate relevant parts of the East German population and thus exacerbate divisions within the postcommunist society of the GDR. With the exception of the core of the state party and the most loyal parts of its constituency, virtually all political forces, and particularly so both the former opposition within the GDR and the political elites of the Federal Republic, expected a rapid process in which, for both political and economic reasons, the vast majority of the people of the GDR would be persuaded to adopt a loyal attitude to the principles the West German state is based upon, and eventually to unification. At the very least, and with the prospect of unification becoming rapidly more concrete, committed supporters of the old regime were expected to be incapable of playing any significant role anymore in the future of unified Germany. There was no perceived need to extend any leniency towards them out of political prudence. To the contrary, it was widely perceived that juridical *in*action would have grossly frustrated the internal opposition forces in the GDR and their allies within the emerging party system.

Similarly, the concern that the personnel of the state apparatus, including the judiciary, would feel alienated by a strategy of judicial activism and would try to obstruct the process appeared unfounded. To be sure, there were various attempts and initiatives launched by *Stasi* officers and other agents of the old regime to intimidate, threaten, and "punish" the new authorities, as well as to join forces with West German and other gangs involved in organized crime (Richter 1996: 254ff.). But no case is documented in which these networks (often referred to as *Seilschaften*, or mountain climbers connected by a rope) actually succeeded in effectively interfering with the orderly conduct of politics, administration, or justice. For the functionaries of the old regime, incentives to adapt to the new conditions were significantly more powerful than incentives, as well as opportunities, to fight the new regime. This can be explained by the fact that it must have been evident to officials of all ranks and branches of the state apparatus (in sharp contrast to both the post-1945 situation in Germany and the situation prevailing in all other postcommunist countries) that acts betraying faithfulness to the politics and principles of the old regime would be responded to by the new regime through disciplinary measures and ultimately the removal of opponents from their position. Such removal would involve the consequence for those affected of losing their career prospects, particularly as a virtually unlimited supply of substitute personnel could be mobilized and moved in from West Germany. This configuration of power relations has actually led to highly opportunistic behavioral responses that are proverbially referred to by comparison to a chameleon, a reptile that is able to quickly adjust to the color of its environment, or to the *Wendehals*, a bird capable of turning its head by 180 degrees without breaking its neck. The term also alludes to the transition (*Wende*). Scores of those who were involved in *Stasi* activities were dismissed and replaced by either substitutes who could be recruited locally or, particularly in cases where the newly adopted West German institutions required new kinds of expertise and professional knowledge, by temporary substitutes brought in from the West.

Finally, there was also no reason to believe that the databases for criminal prosecution would turn out to be insufficient for criminal prosecution in either quantity or quality. To the contrary, and after the Citizens' Committees had largely succeeded during the winter of 1989–90 in obviating local *Stasi* officials' attempts to destroy or hide files, a vast official data archive was organized through an act (*Stasi-Unterlagengesetz*, StUG) passed by the German Federal Parliament (*Bundestag*) in December 1991. No other postcommunist country has at the disposal of its authorities a comparable wealth of data that would be, on top of it, equally well protected from the interference of interested parties.

All of these considerations do not yield a single point of view that could serve as an objection to the strategy to juridical activism in dealing with the violations of rights committed under and with the approval of the old regime. The adoption of a "strong" frame was made more likely in the case of the GDR by the circumstances just discussed than was the case in the other post-communist regimes, where these favorable conditions did not apply, certainly not to the same extent.

Yet, in the early nineties arguments against adopting the "strong" frame, at least in its radical version, do play some role in the case of the GDR, too. These arguments are based upon doubts that a justification for vigorous retroactive transitional justice can be found that is consistent with both legal principle and historical precedent. Concerning the latter, the comparison with the transitional justice that was practiced in Germany after 1945 works both ways. On the one hand, one can argue that what went wrong then must be corrected now. But on the other hand, the argument cannot be dismissed that after scores of leading politicians, state functionaries, and intellectuals who were deeply involved in the Nazi regime went unpunished after 1945, why should it be right to adopt tough strategies of criminal prosecution against those whose crimes were on the whole of an indisputably smaller scale? If anything, these and other doubts have increased in their weight and significance since the beginning of criminal prosecution in late 1989. In a nutshell, or so we wish to argue, the arguments supporting the adoption of a "strong" frame lost much of their force in the process, giving way to doubts, disappointments, and even regrets as the process unfolded. The questions which must be coped with in the process are momentous indeed. Who is to be sanctioned for what acts, by what methods, and on the basis of what kind of justification?

ACTS AND ACTORS

The welfare-diminishing acts by which the GDR regime has deprived its cit-izens of rights as well as of material resources are numerous (for the most detailed account, cf. Marxen and Werle 1999: 3–140). Beginning with viola-tions of the right to life inflicted upon people killed at the border and as polit-ical enemies of the regime, actors within the state apparatus of the GDR have systematically violated, based upon the official instruction, justification, and toleration of the regime's representative elites, virtually every human and civil right recognized in civilized nations.[4] Cases in point are the systematic repression of free communication and information; the denial of the right to communicate and to move across borders; coercive internal relocations, abductions and (in some cases) subsequent killings of persons from foreign countries;[5] the denial of property rights and the program of forced agricultural collectivization; ideological indoctrination of the entire population; the violation of the physical integrity of athletes through routinely administered doping programs; the far-reaching denial of the right to associational life within civil society; large scale spying on people suspected of oppositional activities; and the unjust sanctioning of such activities through criminal punishment and the practice of *Zersetzung*.

These violations of rights were undisputedly of an "internal" origin. The excuse that political repression, including criminal punishment for acts of political opposition and dissent, were ordered by representatives of the Soviet government (such as the Soviet Military Tribunal) active within the territory of the GDR had entirely lost its foundation by about 1955. All repression after that early date was largely home-made. There were between 250,000 and 300,000 political prisoners sentenced during the entire history of the GDR. As late as during the period 1979 to 1989, the average number of people sentenced for political acts (including alleged economic "crimes" and requests to obtain a permit to leave the country) was 5000 cases per year. The number of those whom the actors within the repressive state apparatus considered "hostile elements" and therefore prosecuted has been much larger than the number of those who actually adopted a "hostile" position by engaging in organized, religious network, or movement forms of opposition and resistance. The latter figure is estimated, as late as in the mid-eighties, as "a few thousand" people. The difference between the two figures—say 250,000 and perhaps 5000—is partly explained by the fact that very often people who were sentenced to prison terms were "bought free," at a rate of about DM 100,000 per capita, by West German authorities—an act which implied their "dismissal" from GDR citizenship and transfer to West Germany. This act also provided the GDR government not only with the opportunity to "earn" substantial amounts of revenues, but also with the unique chance to get rid of and to permanently externalize much of the opposition. While authoritarian regimes often run the risk of increasing the ranks of their opponents by employing repressive means against them, the GDR had exempted itself from this dialectics of repression.

The apparatus of repression that was designed to deter oppositional activities and investigate political "crimes" was sizable indeed. Recent estimates of the number of people active in the state security apparatus cite 91,000 full time (*hauptamtliche*) and another 174,000 "unofficial" employees and collaborators.

But there is no obvious reason to restrict criminal prosecution to those actors who demonstrably were involved in the repression of activities of citizens that were perfectly legal according to the letter of the GDR's laws. In addition to such repressive acts, there were other damages inflicted and losses implemented by the leadership of the GDR. As far as the collectively detrimental destruction (or inefficient allocation) of resources (as opposed to the violation of rights) is concerned, massive environmental poisoning must be mentioned, as well as the decay and rotting of buildings and entire historical cities that was allowed to occur due to lack of repair and maintenance, the waste of items of the so-called *Volksvermögen* ("peoples wealth") through the deficiencies of the system of management and planning, and the illegal appropriation of economic resources by members of the elite and privileged strata.

How can these acts be accounted for in terms of the above conceptual analysis? The answer to this question is far from certain. On the one extreme, few commentators would probably describe the system of state socialism as it was established in the German Democratic Republic after 1949 as anything coming close to a criminal conspiracy of self-serving power holders intentionally and knowingly causing the economic malaise and civilizational decline from which the GDR irremediably came to suffer. Between the extremes of unequivocal criminal guilt and equally unequivocal innocence, there is a huge gray zone where both the questions of fact ("who did what or ordered it to be done?") as well as questions of legal principle ("which norms and procedures should apply and what kinds of excuses of a defendant must be recognized?") are often exceedingly hard to settle. That is to say (using the criteria of guilt mentioned above, namely violations of rights and interests, absence of justification, absence of excusable ignorance, and absence of coercion), most actor's who were positioned at some point within the vast apparatuses of political, military, economic, and cultural control thought of their own action most of the time as either justified by valid norms, or as desirable outcomes.

But even if not, they may have felt caught in such a dilemma that one and the same act appeared mandated in view of one norm or utility, while lacking justification in terms of another principle or rule of a roughly equal salience. Perpetrators may also have been unaware (and perhaps inexcusably so) of the consequences of their action. Furthermore, they may have felt "forced" to do what they were doing, with the alternative possibilities implied that the "force" was real, that it was just imagined in order to calm the actor's conscience, and that it was real but with relatively mild sanctions being attached to non-compliance so that actual compliance appears more a matter of opportunism rather than coercion. Other possibilities include the fatalistic type of compliance based upon the agent's full awareness that there is no valid justification for doing what he is supposed to do, but that non-compliance is, at the same time, perfectly inconsequential, as "if I don't do it, someone else will."

But not only are terms such as "justified," "aware," and "forced" highly ambiguous and contested. To be sure, the gray zone does not cover the entire range of objectionable acts committed by officials and servants of the old regime. Large numbers of cases can be cited in which power holders have intentionally, arbitrarily, and freely violated the rights, destroyed the life plans, and inflicted damage upon fellow citizens in ways and to an extent that must be described as deeply cynical and often positively sadistic. Also, opportunism was widespread and practiced with good conscience under a regime that put a premium upon conformism and obedience rather than the exercise of autonomous moral judgment. At the other extreme, the honest belief, on the part of "perpetrators with good conscience," that compliance was justified by the ideals of social justice and international peace was also part of the picture. Even within the limited segment of the overall malaise of state socialism in which negative outcomes can be traced to personal actors, it appears exceedingly difficult to disentangle the varieties and mixes of all of these motives, cognitive states, and interested interpretations, narratives, rationalizations, and excuses by which those under accusation may defend themselves. Even more difficult is the attempt to assign criminal guilt to actors and to do so in conformity to procedures which live up to the requirements of rule-of-law principles, such as non-retroactivity.

The overall malaise of state socialism is much larger than the total of damages and suffering which identifiable actors inflicted upon concrete victims. The ways in which potential well-being and happiness was obstructed by the state socialist regime of the GDR fall roughly into three categories. One is the violation of civil rights, as just specified. A second one is the erection and maintenance of a system of economic management that, while implementing in its distributional effects a pattern of authoritarian and paternalistic egalitarianism covering all *Werktätige* ("working people") and their families, implied a relative waste of economic resources (including the waste inflicted through economic corruption and privileges of the ruling elite) and a lag in productivity which was partly caused by the mode of integration of the GDR economy into the CMEA system. Third, the ruling ideology, together with the monopolistic control it exercised over the school system, the media, the arts, sciences, and virtually all other institutional sectors of society, imposed a regressive cognitive culture. The doctrines of the ruling ideology, as promulgated by the monopolistic party, can be held responsible not just for providing justifications for the practices in the two other realms of civil rights and economic efficiency, but also for blocking and paralyzing much of the intellectual, moral, and perhaps even esthetic potential, sensibility, and creativity of the citizenry of GDR (notwithstanding the major artistic accomplishments achieved by the GDR's often oppositional writers, painters, and musicians).

Now, the disastrous effects of the two latter categories of deprivation, the economic and the cultural, are not easily accounted for in terms of individual acts and actors as in the case of the first. Conversely, if the past of the state socialist regime is primarily looked at through the prism of criminal law and its logic of processing illicit acts and their consequences through attributing them to individual actors according to legal rules, this practice would seem to involve a somewhat selective attention to damaging acts that are potentially punishable according to standards of criminal law. For this perspective implies the framing of the deprivations caused by the old regime as something that is primarily committed by agents within the repressive state apparatus (the *Staatsicherheit*, the courts, and the police); conversely, it de-emphasizes those deprivations which largely cannot thus be attributed, namely the "systemic" ills of the apparatuses of ideological control and economic (mis)management. The question can be asked (but cannot possibly be fully discussed in the present context) whether the worst deficiencies of the past regime were actually its systematic violation of human and civil rights and not, to an equal or even greater extent, its equally systematic mismanagement of economic resources or its imposition of a rigidly ideological cognitive culture.

Is it right to conclude that if only the GDR had paid greater respect to civil rights, the realities of the GDR society would have become more tolerable, as its economic and ideological deficiencies alone would have been less objectionable? At any rate, this is a point of view that implicitly seems to be endorsed if we were to approach the problem primarily in terms of acts for which identifiable actors are legally responsible and punishable for having violated human and civil rights of citizens. This is a question on which the two authors of this paper remain somewhat divided. The more strictly and scrupulously legal procedures are applied, the more legitimate complaints about the damages the old regime has inflicted are likely to remain outside the realm of retrospective sanctioning, as the full range of damages inflicted cannot possibly be processed through the narrow channels of orderly criminal prosecution. Given the constitutional provision that prohibits retroactive punishment according to *nulla poena sine lege,* not the wrongs of the regime, but only the violations of the regime's own (at least nominally valid) norms can be the object of criminal prosecution. What can be sanctioned is thus not the "normal" operation of the system, but its excesses. The question arises whether this implicit demonstration of the impotency of criminal law will actually contribute to the intended purpose of its administration, namely the cultivation of trust in the rule of law. By implication, many harmful acts that were typical of the practices of the old regime cannot be prosecuted due to the lack of one or more prerequisites of formally correct trials (about which more in a moment). Conversely, some categories of crimes are relatively easy to bring to trial, although they may in no way constitute a distinctive characteristic of the state socialist regime. Examples are ordinary white-collar crimes (for the commission of which the economics of currency reform and unification provided plentiful opportunities) or the doping of athletes.

These complications have led to the formation of a multi-tiered system of state-sponsored *Aufarbeitung der Vergangenheit*, or working on the coming to terms with the past (as the somewhat ambiguous term can be translated that was adopted from the retrospective debates of the 1950s). The highest level of this multi-tiered system comprising legal, historical, and political strategies consists in regular criminal proceeding, initiated by a special prosecutors office (the ZERV and the Sta II—to be discussed in the following section). The next level is the complex set of activities which unfolded on the basis of the act of 1991 (*Stasi-Unterlagengesetz*) and which were conducted by the agency set up by this law, commonly referred to as the Gauck Agency after the name of its president. While the initiation of criminal procedures is only part of this agency's mandate, it does focus upon individual actors on either side of the repressive transaction, and sanctions the perpetrators of repressive acts through exposure and (indirectly) civic disqualification. A further step away from formal sanctioning and criminal procedure is the *Enquête Kommission* (inquiring commission set up by the *Bundestag* on 20 May 1992). This commission was assigned the truly formidable task of "working on the coming to terms with the history and consequences of the SED dictatorship in Germany." This commission focuses in its work not so much on individuals and their responsibilities, but upon institutions and power relations. Finally, there are a number of proposals for state-sponsored activities, such as the setting up of research and documentation centers, and educational activities, which are intended to serve the deeper understanding, as well as a wider awareness of the nature of the state socialist regime. We now proceed to discuss the activities on these four tiers in turn.

CRIMINAL TRIALS

Whether or not to employ criminal law was a question that was settled from the beginning in political terms and under the impact of political contingencies. There was nothing "natural" or automatic in the reliance on criminal proceedings initiated against the former state's elites. To wit, there are a series of "ifs" which would have excluded criminal prosecution as a viable option. Had either the old regime in its desperate struggle for survival taken recourse to massive violence (following the Chinese example of 4 June 1989), or had the opposition turned violent during or after the breakdown of the old regime, nothing would have remained in terms of an agenda of criminal prosecution. For in the first case, the system's breakdown might at least have been postponed, thus making the prosecution of its crimes impossible for the time being. In the second case, a kind of revolutionary "justice" would have taken its course, which arguably might have made formal criminal prosecution unnecessary at a later point. Furthermore, such prosecution would have been renounced as an option under the conceivable circumstances of a *transición pactada*, where the forces of the old regime (or its sponsors in Moscow) would have remained strong enough to negotiate a general amnesty for themselves as a precondition of conceding their removal from office and power.

Thus, the question of applying criminal justice has been treated as a political question in the GDR after November 1989 and (beyond the end of the GDR's life span) in unified Germany. The overall preference was, from the beginning of the breakdown of the old regime onwards, in favor of prosecution, with initially at best a marginal support for the alternative of drawing a "thick line" or amnesty. As early as on 18 November 1989, the SED-controlled legislature installed a committee of investigation that was mandated to inquire into cases of abuse of official powers and corruption, as well as the falsification of election results. On 22 November, a police officer was sentenced to a 14-month prison term for having badly beaten up a GDR citizen. In December, several members of the SED *Politbüro* and party officials of regional headquarters were arrested, and subsequently more than half of the members of *Politbüro* were arrested for some period of time. After the parliamentary elections of 18 March 1990, the second plenary session of the *Volkskammer* debated on 12 April the need for prosecuting regime crimes; this need was endorsed by members of all parliamentary groups. This determination to prosecute regime crimes was also emphasized by the GDR delegation negotiating the terms of the Unity Treaty with its West German counterpart. As a consequence, the mandate for prosecution was enshrined in the Unity Treaty that came into force on 3 October 1990.

This very broad consensus has generated a path dependency of judicial activism, as the new all-German legislature and political elites could not possibly fall back behind this stated policy goal of the *Volkskammer*, the democratically legitimate parliament of the GDR elected on 18 March 1990, as well as obviously also of the majority of the population. Courts in unified Germany considered themselves in possession of a mandate to embark upon criminal prosecution of "regime criminality" not because of their own authority to do so (which would have smacked of "victors' justice"), but because of *Verfolgungskontinuität*, or continuity of a prosecution that was originally initiated by the (democratic) GDR, and which now became a legacy to be honored by the court system of unified Germany.

Why was criminal prosecution considered to be worth the effort, in spite of the difficulties that arguably might have been foreseen even at the beginning? Three lines of argument have been offered to show why criminal punishment must be attempted. One is the familiar argument that perpetrators must be punished in order to deter them or others from committing similar crimes in the future. This argument has been dismissed as a non-starter in the case of GDR *Regierungskriminalität* as, thanks to unification and the evident moral as well as economic breakdown of the old regime, there will be no conceivable opportunity for incriminated actors or others to commit comparable crimes within a newly erected state socialist regime at any point in the future (Jakobs 1992). At best, there can be a preceptorial effect of attaching moral and juridical disapproval to the old regime as a whole and the principles it was based upon.

A second argument in support of criminal prosecution takes the point of view not of perpetrators (or potential future perpetrators) who must be deterred, but the victims who must be integrated and (at least) symbolically compensated. Apart from the potential conflict between the objectives of administering justice in strict conformity with standards of procedural fairness, on the one hand, and the provision of emotional comfort and satisfaction to victims, on the other, the argument presupposes that this reconciliation can actually be achieved within the constraints of the rule of law principle and ordinary criminal proceedings. Much of the later evidence that was perhaps not foreseeable at the point of unification suggests that this is not the case and that, to the contrary, victims are often deeply irritated and offended by the fact that very few and relatively mild sanctions have actually been implemented. This applies all the more as the reverse side of the medal of criminal prosecution is acquittal of those against whom no sufficient case can be established—with the implication being, much to the anger of victims, that perpetrators have often received a virtual stamp of innocence when being acquitted from criminal prosecution due to lack of sufficient evidence against them. Even worse, German courts of appeal have decided that even though a particular crime was defined by the criminal code of the GDR but only nominally so (because it had never been actually applied to relevant cases, for example, of homicides committed at the border), it is inadmissible to prosecute a case on the basis of that (pseudo) norm because doing so would violate the principle of non-retroactivity.

A third set of considerations in support of criminal prosecution takes the point of view neither of the perpetrators nor their victims, but, as it were, of the corporate interest of the German criminal law system itself. The argument is that after the German court system has failed to prosecute most of the government crimes of the Nazi regime, and after it has been rightly and severely criticized for this failure, this is the opportunity to do things right and to restore the (self)respect of the court system. At any rate, what must be avoided at all cost is committing the same mistakes again.

None of the major political actors making up the post-unification German party system, not even the PDS, could afford to oppose criminal prosecution as an instrument of dealing with the personnel of the old regime. Any such opposition would have been scandalized by political competitors as proof of inappropriate permissiveness and leniency. The awareness of this potential charge applies with particular force to the (Social Democratic) German Left, as it is the Social Democrats who are now being remembered for initiatives they had launched in the mid-1980s which aimed at a closer cooperation with the SED and resulted in a paper co-authored by representatives of the two parties. Also, the political Right (as well as some media supporting it) were not always able to resist the temptation of the following argument: as the Left has stigmatized the early history of West Germany as being under the shadow of Nazi continuities, conservative forces must now strike back by exposing the Left for its continuing intellectual affinities with state socialism. At any rate, during the first half of the nineties, the denunciation of (aspiring) political elite members in East Germany for alleged *Stasi* collaboration was a tactic applied by either of the two major political parties of the West. As the Christian Democrats (in their infamous "red socks" electoral campaign of 1994) accused the Social Democrats of being irresponsibly open to collaboration with SED/PDS elements, so the Social Democrats exposed their major electoral competitor of harboring in their ranks important elements of the Eastern CDU, an institutional ally (within the GDR National Front) of the SED. These tactical moves, however, were clearly not appreciated and rewarded by either Western or Eastern voters. To be sure, these initiatives were not aimed at bringing state criminals to criminal justice, but at disqualifying individuals from political elite positions.

However, and coming back to criminal prosecution proper, a demanding set of conditions must be met in order to conduct criminal justice under rule-of-law principles. Six of these conditions can be distinguished which are needed for the prosecution and eventual sentencing of a defendant. Each of them is associated with some thorny questions. Let us briefly review these conditions and related problems, without, however, going into any detail of the vast technical legal literature that has emerged in recent years on these issues (cf. Isensee 1992; Jakobs 1992; Lüdersen 1992; Schaal and Woell 1997; Stark et al. 1992; Marxen and Werle 1999).

First, a valid and specific norm must be found that identifies some act in question as a crime. The problem here is the question of retroactivity, as the legal norm must have been valid *already* at the point the act was committed *and* must have actually been operative as a norm applying to all acts and all actors. That is to say, a rule is actually a rule only if it is not a rule where arbitrary exemptions from the rule are being made and can be expected as a rule. Also, the norm must *still* be applicable at the point of the opening of criminal prosecution, as opposed to being inapplicable due to some statute of limitation. The solution found in the case of the GDR is that only those norms that were enshrined in the criminal codes of both of the states concerned, the German Democratic Republic and the Federal Republic of Germany, were relied upon for criminal prosecution. If either of the legal norms provided for a milder punishment than the other, that was the one to be adopted for the trial. The statute of limitation was suspended, as some crimes actually punishable under GDR law were arbitrarily not prosecuted by the authorities. The clock was restarted so that all crimes committed between 1949 and 1990 could be prosecuted for a period of 10 years, ending on the 10th anniversary of unification on 2 October 2000. As an exception, the prosecution of homicides remains open until October 2030. Some acts, such as practices of *Zersetzung*, were actually, in spite of the often significant damages inflicted upon victims, technically no more than minor misdemeanors. For instance, breaking into the apartment of a citizen was punishable under GDR law only if the act had been committed repeatedly.

Second, the act violating a criminal norm must be proven to have actually taken place. The availability of evidence differs according to categories of crimes. Given the vast quantity of violations of rights committed by members and collaborators of the Ministry of State Security of the GDR, as well as the opaque organizational context in which these violations have been committed, the problems of producing viable evidence were massive (Marxen and Werle 1999: 228). Furthermore, and in order to avoid the politically divisive appearance of "victors' justice," the courts have tended to impose very stringent requirements upon admissible proof (ibid.). Some acts that could be proven to have taken place on the basis of documents, such as the tapping of the telephones of citizens, could not be prosecuted as they were not punishable under GDR law.

Third, the author of some particular act, the perpetrator, must be identifiable. Similar difficulties apply as in the previous point. If acts could be identified, they could not be linked to the authors of such acts, or vice versa with potential actors, such as prison guards. Also, the courts tried to avoid another potential objection, namely that of focusing upon the hierarchically inferior actors (for example, in the cases of border homicides), while letting their superiors off the hook.

Fourth, in most cases some concrete damage must demonstrably have been caused by the actor's act. Fifth, the actor must have been aware of the illicit nature of his act. And sixth, the actor's excuse of having been coerced must be invalidated.

The kinds of criminal activities, however, that were to be investigated and, wherever possibly, subsequently brought to trial were sharply limited. They included six major categories of crimes: (1) homicides committed by border guards; (2) violation of court procedures and defendants' rights, as well as arbitrary sentences according to GDR law; (3) economic crimes, mostly committed in the context of unification; (4) killings and abductions committed by agents of the Ministry of State Security; (5) extortion of property of persons who were allowed to leave the GDR; and (6) miscellaneous crimes such as falsification of election results, administering anabolica and other drugs to athletes, etc.

What is conspicuously missing from this list are huge numbers of cases where individual citizens became the objects of "disorganizing" measures (*Zersetzungsmassnahmen*) initiated by *Stasi* agents who would not just spy and report on their victims, but also interfere with their (work, family, social, sexual, educational, etc.) lives with exquisite viciousness. An internal book of instructions issued by the Ministry for State Security in 1985 recommended to collaborators, as methods of operative intervention, practices such as "finding out about personal weaknesses of persons and fabricating compromising materials," "promoting distrust and mutual suspicions among members of groups," engaging in the "deliberate splintering, paralyzing, disorganization and isolation of hostile-negative forces," or "undermining the self-esteem of persons by organizing failures in their professional and social life."

Considerable resources were made available for the formidable task of implementing criminal justice under these constraints and with the foreseeable order of magnitude of cases. These resources included a specialized criminal investigative agency for the inquiry into government crimes of the GDR, as well as white collar crimes committed in the process of unification, the *Zentrale polizeiliche Ermittlungsstelle für Regierungs- und Vereinigungskriminalität* (ZERV), set up in Berlin in 1994. The ZERV was designed to employ a staff of as many as 300 police investigators and to perform its task until the end of 1999. Its director, who retired at the end of 1998, was a senior West Berlin police officer, Manfred Kittlaus, who started his career as a prominent and controversial figure in the political police of West Berlin. The specialized resources for criminal prosecution also included a special prosecutor's office, the *Staatsanwaltschaft II* (StA II), founded on 1 October 1994, which was to open criminal proceedings based upon the investigative results of the ZERV. It was headed by the eloquent and strongly committed state attorney Christoph Schaefgen and designed to employ as many as 65 attorneys as special prosecutors. To complicate matters further, it must be mentioned that apart from the two centralized agencies operating out of Berlin, there were also specialized departments of the state attorney's offices in the five new states which pursued the investigation of local and regional government crimes.

The vast resources, however, that were to be made available to the two Berlin-based agencies, never became fully operational. Given the centralist structure of the GDR, many of the crimes in question were to be investigated in (East) Berlin, the capital of the defunct state. But given the federal structure of the old (and now, subsequent to unification, enlarged) Federal Republic, the costs to be spent on investigation and subsequent trials were to be jointly borne by the (old) federal states. Although the Prime Ministers of the states had agreed, as early as in May 1991, to contribute substantial resources to the national task of criminal prosecution, this agreement was honored, according to the heads of both the ZERV and the StA II, with symptomatic reluctance.

Both Mr. Schaefgen and Mr. Kittlaus have complained vividly that their hands were partially tied by the unwillingness of the West German states to honor their contractual commitments. There were also complaints voiced by the two that the possibilities the Unity Treaty and German courts allowed for in terms of criminal prosecution of GDR government crime were severely limited. The account that Kittlaus gave in several interviews prior to his retirement at the end of 1998 was the following: as resources were limited and rule of law guarantees made prosecution difficult, very few perpetrators were actually sentenced. But also inversely, as the "success in court" that any police agency depends upon as a measure of its performance was so disappointing, the *Länder* governments, the media, and the (West German) public soon lost much of their interest in the entire enterprise of criminal prosecution and failed to provide the necessary support and material resources. Kittlaus complains about a "certain lack of interest in our work" (*Die Welt*, 30 November 1998).

The quantitative yield of the efforts of the ZERV and the StA II has been unimpressive indeed. As of 31 March 1999, 22,765 investigations were opened, leading to just 565 criminal court cases. Verdicts were reached in 211 cases, of which just 20 cases resulted in actual prison sentences. As a rule of thumb, less than a tenth of one per cent of all investigations resulted in prison sentences. Border guards who were sentenced in court for having committed intentional homicides were, almost without exception, punished with suspended prison terms. Serious crimes such as more than 20 presumed commissioned murders perpetrated by the GDR Ministry of State Security could not be tried because the actual perpetrators could not be identified. Legal experts (Marxen and Werle 1999: 253) have offered the highly plausible counter-factual speculation that, had the democratic GDR existed for longer than it actually did, the criminal prosecution its government and court system had initiated during its short span of life would have resulted in considerably more numerous and more severe sentences than was actually accomplished by the unified German system.

Not only has the juridical outcome of criminal proceedings remained very limited. Also the interest of the national public (more than three quarters of which are former West German citizens) in the data that became available and in the unmasking of acts and actors in the GDR remained remarkably moderate. But media interest in the juridical (the ZERV and the StA II) as well as broader historical databases (the Gauck Agency and the *Enquête Kommission*) was at best short lived. The issue of transitional justice has played a somewhat marginal role in Germany, at least a much smaller one that it would have played in a separate and permanent democratic successor state of the GDR. A widely shared feeling in the West is that, as it cannot be done right, and as so much effort has led to so little outcome, it shouldn't be done at all—"it" being the attempt to come to terms with the old regime by the means of criminal justice. This lack of a vigorous interest of Western elites in criminal prosecution is attributed by former activists of the citizen movement to a measure of latent complicity of segments of the old Federal Republic with elites of the old GDR. In case government crimes had been prosecuted more energetically and successfully, these Western elite segments (which extend not just to Social Democrats) would be exposed and embarrassed for having sought collaboration with positively criminal counterparts in the East.

Concerning ordinary citizens, the vast majority of Germans have never come close to being threatened by (to say nothing about being co-opted or hired by) *Stasi* or other criminal institutions of the former GDR. Also, given the highly precarious economic and labor market situation that prevails in most of the new *Länder*, there are more urgent matters perceived to be worthy of worrying about than the ugly realities of the defunct SED regime and its acts of repression. Here, the unique German constellation plays a role that consists in the fact that the transition from state socialism took place in the form of national unification. While the future of the ongoing integration of the former two German states is widely understood to be a problem of the entire German society, economy, and polity, the past of the former GDR is perceived as a matter of mainly regional interest.

The somewhat complacent and disinterested attitude of much of the (West) German public may also have to do with the perception that, in contrast to at least the Latin American and South African cases of transitional justice, but arguably also those of some other Central and East European countries, the state crimes in the GDR were of a relatively (!) mild nature. Apart from the killings on the border since August 1961 (estimated at up to 1000 cases), homicide cases were not numerous and mostly a matter of the distant past of the

1950s, often attributed to the Soviet occupation forces rather than internal actors. At any rate, passionate feelings of hatred and painful memories of past suffering and losses are certainly intense with the direct victims, but by far not as widespread in the new *Länder* as they are in the successor regimes of terrorist military dictatorship such as Chile or Argentina. Also, the crimes of the SED dictatorships are clearly less horrendous, by orders of magnitude, than the crimes of the Nazi regime that are and remain the central focus of any reading of German history of the 20th century. It is almost as if so much attention is absorbed by the Nazi regime that little remains to be spent on the East German SED dictatorship. The arguably lopsided distribution of attention and interest is further conditioned by the widely shared perception that it is neo-Nazi ideology and mobilization which constitutes a persistent threat to liberal democracies, whereas dictatorial state socialism, particularly after the end of the Soviet Union, enjoys much less of a prospect for renaissance.

Three players of very different size and significance are active within this discursive field of German transitional justice. First, the forces of the old GDR regime (now being led by the well organized successor party PDS that contends rather successfully for the position of the second largest party in several of the new *Länder* as well as the former East Berlin). These forces have understandably very limited interest in having any light thrown on the dark side of the state socialist state; they are rather busy in "renormalizing" that state retrospectively. Second, the forces of the former GDR opposition that have been the main target of state repression and pursue an interest in criminal sanctions, as well as in engraving the malaise of the old regime and of the suffering it has caused into the nation's collective memory, mainly for preventive and reconciliatory purposes. This category is by far the least numerous and resourceful of the three. To be sure, it is supported by (relatively small) numbers of West German politicians, academics, and intellectuals who, for a variety of motivations, consider the in-depth exploration of the state socialist regime's crimes a national priority. But it is also the case that former opposition activists and their insistence upon vigorous practices of transitional justice cannot claim representativeness for the GDR population in general, as the vast majority of this population had been "neither for nor against" the old regime or willing to undergo risks by offering opposition or even resistance. This majority of the GDR's population was understandably reluctant to support a process as a result of which it would have been exposed as having engaged in practices of opportunistic adjustment. On the other hand, some limited support for tough measures of criminal justice can be motivated by the wish to unload one's own feelings of guilt upon individuals within the leadership. Thirdly, and by far most important, the forces of the West German political party system that managed to organize a grandiose political takeover in the period between the first (and last) free elections on 19 March 1990 and the final dissolution of the GDR on 3 October of that year.

Within this triangular configuration of forces, the citizen movements of the GDR, which credit themselves with having brought down the regime through their peaceful "revolution" in November 1989, have been deprived of any distinctive and visible political role. Many of the activists have been absorbed into the Eastern wing, itself highly precarious concerning their political fates in the new *Länder*, of the Green party (*Bündnis 90*). Others turned to the Social Democrats (SDP). In contrast to some other postauthoritarian cases of transition, the opponents and targets of the old regime do not, as a coherent political formation, play any significant role in the new regime, although dozens of former opposition activists are now holding important political and other positions across the entire political spectrum and within a variety of institutional sectors. But there is hardly any charismatic figure (such as Václav Havel or Bishop Tutu) nor movement (such as the *Madres de la Plaza de Mayo* in Buenos Aires) in Germany which would represent a credible and authentic account of the suffering that was caused by the old regime and the moral demand for sanctions and rehabilitation.

To summarize the experience from criminal prosecution, the dilemma is the following: the more scrupulously the tools of criminal justice are being employed for the sake of legitimacy, the less effective the sanctioning mechanism becomes. In spite of the extension of the statute of limitation to 1999 adopted by the German legislature, it is now clear that the yield of the efforts of prosecution in terms of criminal sanctions will remain extremely limited. It also became evident that the interest of political and juridical elites, the media, and the public in general in issues of both punishing and rehabilitation has been declining. At the same time, the successor party PDS and its constituency have perversely profited from what could be read as an implicit demonstration that virtually nothing can be shown to be wrong with the old regime in terms of criminal law. Also, the following dilemma is evident: the maximum that can possibly be done within the constraints of rule of law and non-retroactivity is still way below the minimum that would have to be done in order to satisfy the small but vocal groups of those who have suffered most under the old regime.

As a result of the sobering experience of criminal justice, two overall developments took place in the course of the 1990s. For one thing, disappointment and frustration spread among those who were interested in criminal prosecution because of the difficulties of conducting "successful" trials. Second, procedures other than criminal prosecution were increasingly relied upon and proposed as a method of sanctioning actors of the old regime and a means to come to terms with its residues.

ADMINISTERING ARCHIVES: THE GAUCK AGENCY

While the due process of criminal prosecution often runs into the problem that acts are known to have taken place while the authors of those acts cannot be identified with the degree of accuracy that is called for by rule of law principles, the problem the Gauck Agency is mandated to solve is the reverse one. Here, particular actors (as defined by their organizational affiliation, the duration of this affiliation, and hierarchical position within the GDR state apparatus) are to be sanctioned without the need to prove that they have committed particular acts or inflicted a particular damage to specific fellow citizens. Sometimes, and that is doubtless one of the legislative intentions behind the StUG, the information made available by the agency will lead to third party sanctioning of the persons to whom this information pertains. The nature of these indirect sanctions, as well as the procedural principles applied, is quite different from ordinary criminal law. While in criminal law a court makes a decision (that can be appealed under most circumstances) which, if upheld, causes a state-organized sanctioning (fines, imprisonment), the sanctioning that is merely triggered by the Gauck Agency and the law it is based upon (StUG) is implemented through an independent decision of third parties and their autonomous practices of disapproval and disqualification. The agency exercises influence, not authority, over the severity and incidence of sanctions. The output of the agency's activity is, in other words, not a sentence, but a flow of information addressed to (or selectively made available to) particular actors. What happens as a consequence of the dissemination of information is beyond the authority and responsibility of the agency to determine. Arguably, the most significant and most effectively cathartic of these consequences are those that take place in a framework of private encounters between former oppressors and the victims who have found out about them and their activities from the *Stasi* files. These intense and often painful confrontations cannot be ordered by administrative fiat, nor can they be monitored by state agencies or the public. Hence these types of sanctions are caused, but not controlled by state authorities.

Apart from the cases in which the information collected by the agency serves the initiation of criminal prosecution, the impact of the information made available upon the person the information is about remains to be determined by actors outside of the court system. Even if public sector agencies execute the sanctions, they are not mandated by (criminal) law to do so. For instance, upon learning that a particular person has been an unofficial collaborator of *Stasi*, that person's employer may or may not refuse to employ or dismiss the person in question. To be sure, the law of 1991 (StUG) that establishes the Gauck Agency provides for the possibility to appeal in labor courts the negative consequences that private or state actors draw from the information obtained. What these courts, however, determine is not whether or not the claimant has committed particular objectionable acts, but whether or not these alleged acts provide sufficient reason to the respective employer for dismissal or discrimination in hiring. All the agency itself does is make accessible information to large but specified categories of actors who are entitled by law to receive such information, parts of which can (and are in fact likely to be) used as reasons for sanctioning by public or private sector recipients.

Thus the agency can best be described as a hybrid of a public archive (distributing information) and an investigative agency triggering punishment. It differs from the first in that the information made available is, at least in part, intended to trigger the action of third parties, and it differs from the latter as crimes are not proven according to the strict procedures of criminal law, the presumption of innocence does not apply, and practical repercussions, such as civic disqualification, are not apportioned by state-controlled procedures and institutions (such as fines and prisons). It is for this hybrid nature of the Gauck Agency that it has always been controversial between those who appreciate its alleged "lustration"[6] effect of coming to terms with a painful past, and those who find it violating one of the most fundamental principles the new regime is supposedly based upon, namely the rule of law with its implications of non-retroactivity, the presumption of innocence, and a guaranteed access to the court system (Brandenburger 1995).

The agency enjoys a legal monopoly over the information contained in the vast files the old regime's repressive agencies have left behind.[7] The law regulates in much detail how the wealth of information is to be used, that is, what kind of information is to be made accessible to whom, upon whose initiative, and in what form. Categories of recipients include those of the people subject to observation, third parties, the observers themselves, their actual or potential employers, and the general public which is to be served through extensive research, documentation, and educational activities. One of the purposes of the agency's information output is to provide data bases for criminal prosecution. Also, the agency conveys information to public sector agencies on people to be hired for public office. In this case, the agency initiates the flow of information "without being requested to do so" by eventual recipients. In other cases, it provides information upon request, particularly in the hundreds of thousands of cases when people turn to the agency in order to find out what has been reported upon them, and by whom. Some people may be relieved to learn that nothing has been reported upon them and that the respective suspicions they may have held against others were unsubstantiated. Some people may learn that other people (including apparent friends, family members, superiors, neighbors, colleagues, etc.) have actually reported on them, and what—truthfully or otherwise. Others may learn that employees (or people considered for jobs) have been involved in spying activities. And still others may just benefit by forming an enlightened judgment about the grim realities of the day-to-day operation of the old regime. Finally, some of those being affected by the decisions others draw from information obtained through the agency may feel that the files on which the information is based grossly misrepresent the realities of their own past. In this case, complaints of incorrect information, unjust exposure, and unfair sanctions third parties initiate in response to the data obtained tend to be particularly bitter. These complaints are difficult to process in court. Even if claimants' dismissals from jobs can be reversed through favorable decisions of labor courts (as has often been the case), the substantive question of whether or not the person in question has actually done what the files seem to document is often impossible to settle in court, as the files do not allow such proof by strict rule-of-law standards. Hence the danger that *aliquid semper haeret.*

The consequences of the agency's activities of gathering and distributing information have been as highly diverse as the evaluation of these consequences remains controversial. Giving victims access to their files, as well as making them aware of the actors who helped to generate these files, is widely agreed to have an often shocking and painful, but generally cathartic function. Such favorable evaluation is also often attached to the research and educational function of the agency, although concerns have been voiced that research on important matters of recent history should be left, in the interest of academic freedom, to academic institutions rather than being performed by state-operated agencies. Sanctions initiated against spies and collaborators are more intensely contested, not just from the point of view of those directly affected by these sanctions. Critical observers have taken issue with two kinds of perverse effects of the poorly controlled process of "civic" sanctioning. For one thing, people may be sanctioned (for example, through dismissals or the demolition of their reputation) who have not, by any standard of fairness or proven evidence, deserved to be punished. For another and conversely, large numbers of people who have deserved to be sanctioned (at least according to the standards that make up the agency's *raison d'être*) actually manage to escape punishment. There is an abundance of examples of either of the two cases. While the first category, the "false positives," is hard to prove, the false negatives (failure to sanction persons who have deserved such sanctions according to the letter of the Unity Treaty) are problematic in terms of their effects upon the emotions of victims.

Not only are people who are dismissed from public sector employment because of uncontested *Stasi* involvement perfectly free to try their luck (as a rule, successfully) in the private sector. It is also the case that whether or not public sector workers (such as policemen) are actually dismissed or denied employment as a consequence of relevant information supplied by the agency is a matter that is often determined not by the charges raised against them, but ultimately by the contingencies of local and sectoral labor markets and other discretionary considerations entertained by public sector employers. For instance, 7300 persons, or 12 per cent of the 62,680 policemen employed as civil servants (that is, in the highly privileged and secure status of German *Beamte*) by the state governments of Berlin and the five new *Länder* are known to have been working for the Ministry of State Security as regular or unofficial collaborators *and* have been re-employed in spite of the fact of this being known (*Frankfurter Allgemeine Zeitung*, 14 February 2000). The proviso of the act of 1991 that sanctioning must take place on a case-by-case basis has allowed them to appeal successfully to labor courts, claiming excuses such as young age or merely reluctant involvement in *Stasi* activities. But often it was not even necessary for them to initiate such an appeal, as state governments, to an extent that differed from state to state and from ministry to ministry, chose to ignore the files and extended clemency to police personnel applying for jobs according to the demand and supply situation that prevailed at the time in particular labor markets. Such inconsistency and unevenness of the implementation of sanctions is sometimes taken as proof of the harmlessness of the practices of the Gauck Agency, or, more precisely, of the third parties that put to use the information acquired through the agency. But instead of such benign assessment, the opposite conclusion can well be drawn, because the rule-of-law principle is severely violated when—even in the highly sensitive field of police services—the rule that *Stasi* involvement must be sanctioned is frequently, arbitrarily, and opportunistically suspended.

Exploring the Past: the Commission of Inquiry

A third instrument for performing the "work of coming to terms" (*Aufarbeitung*) with the GDR past is, besides the criminal courts and the Gauck Agency, the Commission of Inquiry of the German *Bundestag*. It was chaired by Rainer Eppelmann, a member of parliament and deputy of the CDU who is, like Gauck, a theologian and opposition activist from the former GDR. The commission's statutory mandate was to explore and evaluate major institutional sectors and policy areas of the defunct regime and its history of 40 years. The focus is thus not upon actors and acts, but upon structures, events, strategies, and developments which cannot be attached to individual actors. In a little more than two years of intensive work (from Spring 1992 to Summer 1994), the Commission held 76 sessions, heard the testimony of politicians, GDR opposition activists, academic experts, and victims. It commissioned dozens of detailed analyses of experts. The major themes of inquiry were the power structure of the old regime, the role of the state socialist ideology, the role of the repressive state apparatuses, the policies towards the West German state and intra-German relations, the role of organized religion within the GDR, forms of oppositional activities, the Ministry of State Security, and policy considerations concerning the question of how to deal with the legacies and memories left behind by the "two dictatorships in Germany" in the 20th century. This major and comprehensive project resulted in the publication of 18 volumes (15,187 pages) of testimony, documentation, analysis, and political evaluation, plus two plenary debates of the *Bundestag*. A follow-up commission has been installed that is charged with inquiring into the problems and prospects of German unification.

If the Gauck Agency is a hybrid of an archive and a criminal court, the Commission, headed by Eppelmann, can perhaps best be described as a hybrid of a political conference and a huge research project on contemporary history. In the very first paragraph of the introductory note to the 18 volumes, the president of the *Bundestag* tries to refute the suspicion that what is being published here is an "official," if not a "partisan" and "preceptorial" writing of history. Such suspicion is not supported by the politically diverse composition of testimony and expertise, but, if anything, by the virtually exclusive focus upon the repressive nature of the regime, as well as the intention to appreciate the suffering of victims and to draw lessons which are capable of "strengthening democratic consciousness." Unsurprisingly, the arguably less objectionable institutional sectors of the regime (such as its health system) do not figure at all in these volumes. More curiously, the economic and ecological disasters the old regime has left behind are generously bypassed, except to the extent they triggered the activity of oppositional movements. Due to the sheer quantity of the materials printed here and also due to the relatively early stage of scholarly exploration of the GDR regime at which the volumes were compiled, the attention these 18 volumes were able to generate has been neither widespread, nor lasting.

ADDITIONAL POLICY OPTIONS

The three policies of transitional justice discussed so far—criminal prosecution, *Stasi* archives, historical inquiry with educational purposes—have accomplished a great deal in making the past transparent, defining a normative perspective as to why its essential features must be rejected, and in affording comfort and satisfaction to victims. However, in unified Germany as a whole, the topic of coming to terms with the state socialist past is of an almost marginal significance. It was the past of a fraction of the nation, and the vast majority has no personal and direct access to the realities of that past. Moreover, the *present* problems of the new *Länder*, ranging from record rates of unemployment to high levels of violent xenophobia to manifest signs of poor political integration as indicated by the strong electoral performance of PDS, seem to largely absorb the attention that can be mobilized for the affairs of the new *Länder*. Frustration with the failure of both the courts and the Gauck Agency to sanction those responsible for the old regime to the extent that had been hoped for seems to have contributed to a loss of attention and support for these forms of transitional justice.

Even at the early stage of 1990–91, before (in December 1991) the law was passed that established the Gauck Agency, alternative approaches in addition to criminal prosecution and civic disqualification were widely discussed in the East German public. Among these alternatives, the idea of holding "tribunals" stood out. Such tribunals, as opposed to criminal courts, would be made up of national and international experts and prominent figures whose moral qualities were undisputed. Instead of punishment or even revenge, their function was conceived to be moral condemnation without individual verdicts, with the hoped-for consequence of a society-wide catharsis and the sharpening of moral sensitivities in the public-at-large. The attractiveness of this idea was seen in the possibility that East Germans themselves, rather than West German legislators and judges, would be given the chance of initiating autonomous acts of finding out the truth and hence of self-purification. But in the absence of charismatic figures (such as Václav Havel or Bishop Tutu) in East Germany who would be able to perform this highly visible and potentially intensely controversial role, it was feared that the practice of tribunals might do more harm than good, because of the suspicion of arbitrariness that tribunals in general as practices of informal justice are likely to trigger (cf. the essays in Schönherr 1992). The concern was that justice cannot be done, at least not widely recognized as such, if it is done, by "self-appointed" and therefore possibly biased judges. Nor was it clear how tribunals could induce significant actors to give truthful and comprehensive testimony, which is a matter that courts can perform through formal investigations, hearings, and oaths and that even the South African Truth and Reconciliation Commission (TRC) could perform through its mandate to grant impunity in return for true testimony. In fact, tribunals have never been tried as a form of coming to terms with past injustices (except in the context of military defeat, as in Nuremberg), whereas tribunals seem to perform best if the injustice under scrutiny is a present one (as in the case of the Russell Tribunal investigating the American war in Vietnam in the seventies).

As a final possibility, "amnesty" is being proposed, sometimes in a fuzzy sense that shades into amnesia, as neither the clarification of acts and responsibilities, nor the consent of the victims or their representatives ("forgiveness") is consistently deemed a prerequisite by proponents of amnesty. In 1998–89, that is, immediately prior to the conclusion of the ZERV and the

StA II, the former GDR civil rights activist Friedrich Schorlemmer (another Protestant theologian) advocated amnesty in 1999 as the lesser evil, given the inconsistencies, disappointments, and emerging conflicts over criminal and other forms of sanctioning practices. But amnesty can also be viewed as a necessary condition to motivate actors of the old regime to enter into forms of communication, confession, and critique of the old regime that they would never consider appropriate under the threat of criminal punishment or civil disqualification. There are various forms of amnesty, some of which are the opposite of amnesia. Amnesty can be used as an alternative to criminal prosecution or as a subsequent step. Furthermore, if amnesty is obtained individually (rather than collectively or categorically), if it must be applied for by individuals (rather than granted unilaterally by the state), if it is limited to less serious categories of crimes (excluding all homicides), and if it is granted as a reward for truthful confessions and the public expression of regret, it might well function as a serious instrument of achieving transitional justice and its intended effect, namely the "reconciliation" (meaning just the recognition that all fellow citizens are entitled to the enjoyment of equal rights) of the citizenry of new democracies and thus the stabilization of the new regime. Such reconciliation and stabilization is probably the uncontroversial standard underlying the ongoing controversies over the appropriate methods of administering transitional justice.

NOTES

1 This emphasis on concrete individual actors who can be held responsible for systemic properties is also illustrated by the reversal of the role of party and party members in the 1945 and 1989 cases. In 1945, the Nazi party was outlawed by the occupying powers, but many of the ranking party members were allowed to pursue their juridical, political, or administrative careers. After 1989, the party was allowed to continue to exist, but members were screened before they were (re)admitted to professional or administrative positions.
2 The most dramatic case that corroborated reasons for fear were the attempted *carapintada* revolts in Argentinean barracks. Compared to them, the Spanish case of a military officer invading the parliament with a gun in 1981 remained a minor and isolated incident.
3 This is in marked contrast to military authoritarian regimes who can resist—as well as have every reason to resist—even gestures in the direction of criminal proceedings being adopted. After their demise, they are interested in wholesale amnesty. After all, they are not based upon a political party whose electoral fates are at stake, in case no such prosecution would be forthcoming.
4 Though interestingly, not every violation of civil rights was actually tolerated by the regime's officals. When two *Stasi* officers decided that it would be a helpful idea to actually kill two opposition activists by making them victims of what was designed to appear a fatal traffic accident, they were accused and sanctioned by the superiors for

going much too far and for planning to commit criminal acts. Details of the case, as well as of the failure of the German court system to prosecute even this extreme case, are reported in *Der Spiegel,* No. 47, 22 November 1999, pp. 72–76.

5 The number of abductions from West to East, both executed and attempted, is estimated to be 600 to 700 cases. Just one of these cases resulted in a single person being sentenced to prison.

6 It is worth noting that the term "lustration" is in no way etymologically related to the words "lux," "lucere," or "enlightenment," as is sometimes claimed in defense of the practises associated with "lustration." Instead, the term comes from a Latin root that means "ritual cleansing."

7 In a comparative perspective, it must be noted that the investment in information gathering and research that went into the elucidation of politics and society of the GDR is probably unparalleled by any other case. This is so because skilled manpower, numbering several thousand people, was quickly made available by the West German government after the breakdown to do the job. Also, the chances of interested parties and actors of the old regime destroying sources and concealing information were probably slimmer than in all other cases. Given these unique opportunities for throwing light on the matter, it is sobering to see how much remains in the dark.

BIBLIOGRAPHY

Borneman, John. *Settling Accounts: Violence, Justice, and Accountability in Postsocialist Europe.* Princeton: Princeton University Press, 1997.

Brandenburger, Maren. "Stasi-Unterlagen-Gesetz und Rechtsstaat." *Kritische Justiz* 28, no. 3 (1995): 351–69.

Deutscher Bundestag, ed. *Materialien der Enquête-Kommission 'Aufarbeitung von Geschichte und Folgen der SED-Diktatur in Deutschland'.* 18 volumes. Baden-Baden: Nomos Verlag and Frankfurt: Suhrkamp, 1995.

Elster, Jon. "Coming to terms with the past. A framework for the study of justice in the transition to democracy." *Archives Européennes de Sociologie* 39, no. 1 (1998): 7–48.

Gauck, Joachim. *Die Stasi-Akten. Das unheimliche Erbe der DDR.* Reinbek bei Hamburg: Rowohlt, 1992.

Günther, Klaus. Der strafrechtliche Schuldbegriff als Gegenstand einer Politik der Erinnerung in der Demokratie" in *Amnestie oder die Politik der Erinnerung in der Demokratie,* eds. Smith, Gary and Avishai Margalit (Frankfurt: Suhrkamp, 1997), pp. 48–89.

Jakobs, Günther. "Vergangenheitsbewältigung durch Strafrecht? Zur Leistungsfähigkeit des Strafrechts nach einem politischem Umbruch" in *Vergangenheitsbewältigung durch Recht,* ed. Isensee, Josef (Berlin: Duncker and Humblot, 1992), pp. 37–44.

Lampe, Ernst-Joachim, ed. *Die deutsche Wiedervereinigung. Band III: Die Verfolgung von Regierungskriminalität der DDR nach der Wiedervereinigung.* Köln and Berlin: Carl Heymanns Verlag KG, 1993.

Lüdersen, Klaus. *Der Staat geht unter—das Unrecht bleibt? Regierungskriminalität in der ehemaligen DDR.* Frankfurt: Suhrkamp, 1992.

Marxen, Klaus and Gerhard Werle. *Die Strafrechtliche Aufarbeitung von DDR-Unrecht.* Berlin: de Gruyter, 1999.

Misztal, Barbara. "How not to deal with the past: Lustration in Poland." *Archives Européennes de Sociologie* 40, no. 1 (1999): 31–56.

Offe, Claus. *Varieties of Transition*. Oxford: Polity Press, 1996.

Pampel, Bert. "Was bedeutet 'Aufarbeitung der Vergangenheit'?" *Aus Politik und Zeitgeschichte* B, nos. 1–2 (6 January 1995): 27–38.

Richter, Michael. *Die Staatssicherheit im letzten Jahr der DDR*. Weimar: Boehlau, 1996.

Rosenberg, Tina. *The Haunted Land. Facing Europe's Ghosts after Communism*. New York: Vintage, 1995.

Sa'adah, Anne. *Germany's Second Chance. Trust, Justice, and Democratization*. Cambridge, Mass.: Harvard University Press, 1998.

Schaal, Gary and Andreas Wöll, eds. *Vergangenheitsbewältigung*. Baden-Baden: Nomos, 1997.

Schönherr, Albrecht, ed. *Ein Volk am Pranger? Die Deutschen auf der Suche nach einer neuen politischen Kultur*. Berlin: Aufbau, 1992.

Schwartz, Herman. "Lustration in Eastern Europe." *Parker School Journal of East European Law* 1, no. 2 (1994): 141–72.

Smith, Gary and Avishai Margalit, eds. *Amnestie oder Die Politik der Erinnerung*. Frankfurt: Suhrkamp, 1997.

Stark, Christian, Wilfried Berg, and Bodo Pieroth, eds. *Der Rechtsstaat und die Aufarbeitung der vor-rechtsstaatlichen Vergangenheit*. Berlin: Walter de Gruyter, 1992.

Tucker, Aviezer. "Paranoids may be persecuted: post-totalitarian retroactive justice." *Archives Européennes de Sociologie* 40, no. 1 (1999): 56–103.

Unverhau, Dagmar, ed. *Lustration, Aktenöffnung, demokratischer Umbruch in Polen, Tschechien, der Slowakei und Ungarn*. Münster: Lit Verlag, 1999.

Wassermann, Rudolf. "Zur Aufarbeitung des SED-Unrechts." *Aus Politik und Zeitgeschichte* B, no. 4 (22 January 1993): 3–12.

Models of Transition—Old Theories and Recent Developments

HUBERT ROTTLEUTHNER AND
MATTHIAS MAHLMANN

HOLISM, TRANSITION, AND MORAL-LEGAL ASSESSMENT

There are many social phenomena that have been described as transformations. Some are empirical phenomena in the social world, others are—while being supposed to be real life phenomena—perhaps nothing else but the constructs of theorizing scientists that do not stand the test of empirical verification if considered seriously.

The process of transformation in Central and Eastern European countries since the end of the 1980s is without doubt and in contrast to some historical constructs fundamental: the constitutions, the whole political system, the economic structures, the civil society, and elites have been the object of radical change. In this context, holistic approaches to theory construction are often pursued that take societies as a whole, in contrast to individual actions, describable as a unity in some unifying terms. Holistic approaches have a long tradition in theoretical constructions that mostly dealt, however, with historic processes of epochal dimensions.

Classical accounts of such holistic approaches in political philosophy are well-known. To take just some examples: Rousseau tried to describe the formation of the world of the *ancien régime* in terms of a pessimistic evolutionary development without teleology, that drove man out of the state of nature of an isolated quite deprived being into the social world and its corruption, circumstances that are only partly overcome by the creation of a new society based on special historical circumstances and a social contract (Rousseau 1964 [1755]). Hegel provided an ambitious theory of evolution that attempted to prove the inner necessity of a dialectical development of world history to the presence of the Absolute, via different stages of consciousness of freedom, embodied to a considerable degree in the post-1817 Prussian state (Hegel 1976 [1821]). Marx and Engels followed Hegel in this theoretical ambition, proposing that history driven by material forces proceeds through the stages of a primitive, slave holder, feudal, and capitalist society to socialism and communism (Marx 1859). Today, there are still big theories of transformation pursued, such as Niklas Luhmann's attempts to force heterogeneous historical circumstances under the unifying concepts of systems theoretical construction. In the latter case, history proceeds through the stages of a segmentary and a stratified society to a functionally differentiated society.[1]

Historically less ambitious are other accounts of social transformation that deal only with the change of a period of 200 years, for example, describing the evolution of societies from a feudal political and economic agrarian order to an industrial and service society. In current sociology and political theory, there are attempts to describe modern developments in terms of holism by trying to capture the essence of a historical social setting by taking up some new social phenomena to describe a whole society, for example, the idea that modern societies are risk, leisure, communication, event, consumer, or fun societies.[2] In contrast, the term "class society" is rather outmoded. Common to these approaches is the theoretical move that makes a sometimes rather marginal property of a social setting its decisive new feature. There are further forms of holism, like the politico-legal classification of whole societies as monarchy, republic, democracy, dictatorship, *Rechtsstaat*, etc. These concepts are often used in accounts of social transformations.

In all these contexts, the question and problem of justice might arise. Is the development perceived or described as a development to more justice, to the realization of a normative ideal, or at least to a better state of affairs? The normative assessment of the past mostly means its condemnation. The achieved new state is, from the perspective of the dominant agents of social change, regularly an embodiment of progress. (This does not necessarily mean, however, that a continuous historical development is assumed. There is often room in these historical interpretations for regressions: the Republic of Weimar was interpreted by the Nazis to be such a regression in comparison to the better times of the Empire. Conversely, after 1945, the Nazi epoch was interpreted as an atavistic regression below any civilized standards.)

The object of the evaluation and sanctioning from an ex-post perspective are individual acts or the social system as a whole as a dictatorship, totalitarian regime, *Unrechtsstaat*, or "rogue state." The evaluation of the social system is often derived from the sum total of the individual crimes. In addition, some background interpretations and understandings of the regime as a whole and its legitimacy play a considerable role in assessing individual actions.

There is good reason to be skeptical of holistic descriptions of societies that tend to underestimate the complexity of social phenomena. There is even more reason to be skeptical about the grand theoretical attempts that try to provide scientific explanations of the transformations of societies from one of these states to another. These attempts tend to have rather limited explanatory merits if really scrutinized in detail. The price paid for the appearance of great theoretical power is often little historical accuracy. Historical content is sometimes the first victim of this kind of theory construction, be it in Rousseau, Hegel, Marx, or Luhmann. As to modern evolutionary theories, it is often the era of Fascism and National-Socialism that somehow fails to fit into the theoretical design.

To keep these weaknesses—the lack of empirical foundation, the over-simplification of social complexities by holistic descriptions and the limited explanatory power of evolutionary theories—of accounts of historical transformations in mind might be useful when dealing with the concrete kind of transitional justice, in the widely established technical sense of the word that is of concern here, and the normative questions it implies. In this technical sense, transitional justice refers to the problems of the ex-post legal treatment of state crimes or, to use the term of one of the expert countries of the 20th century in this respect, Germany: *Systemunrecht*. It might be useful to fortify us against the seduction of rash ascription of attributes like *Unrechtsstaat* or "rogue state" to certain regimes, or of delivering grand theories of transformation to democracy and the problems of justice implied. Instead, it might encourage us to discuss the problems with a clear sense of responsibility to historical detail and differentiation of the various cases considered.

Consequently, the following remarks are intended to pursue a rather limited and modest task. They seek to question whether one of the core theoretical constructs of the social, political, and legal philosophy of modern times, the construct of a *social contract*, provides tools to understand the problems of transitional justice posed today, especially by the social transformations after the collapse of communism in the Eastern European countries and in Russia, but equally posed by other transformations of the past and present, be it the establishment of a democratic order after a dictatorship in Chile or Argentina, or in Spain, Portugal, Greece, and South Africa. The question is interesting because a theory of a social contract is a theory of social transformation: the contract brings a society from a regularly not too idyllic state of nature to the formation of a "Body Politick" to use the terms of the possibly most influential theorist of contractualism, Locke (Locke 1690: § 14, 276–77). In principle, this transformation poses exactly the question of interest in the context of transitional justice in the sense explained above: how to deal with the past, and more precisely, with the crimes of the past? The paper will explore whether or not theories of social contract have anything to say about the problem pursued, and if so, what. As we will see, the retrospective on contract theory will bring out, among other things, a core problem of transitional justice: is there some absolute standard of justice before and beyond a concrete social setting or is any standard of justice dependent on an existing social framework? There are other ways to clarify the implications of this problem, but it will be argued that contractualism is one as well.

The paper will then address some recent problems of transitional justice, more precisely of the German example, which is instructive because Germany had to face the problems of transitional justice in a very radical manner at least three times in the last century: after the fall of the monarchy in 1918, after the end of Fascism in 1945, and after the end of the German Democratic Republic (GDR) in 1989. It might seem inappropriate to connect Nazi actions to any notion of transitional *justice*. One should not forget, however, that in 1933 there was a fourth radical change in German history that offers insights into how a regime can deal with what it regards as the crimes of the past. The answers were very different indeed under these varying circumstances and teach a lot about the ethical basis, political perils, and historic significance of transitional justice.

Social contract and the problem of transition

A classical form of a theory of transformation of societies is social contract theory. It combines holistic descriptions of societies with accounts of the driving forces of transformation and a normative evaluation of the development.

The so-called argument of contractualism (Kersting 1994; Macpherson 1962) assumes two basic social states: a state of nature, *status naturalis*, and an established politically order, the *status civilis*. The progress from one state to the other is mitigated by at least one social contract of a varying nature and content, depending on the theory concerned. The transformation of the state of nature into the *status civilis* is interpreted as a decisive normative progress. The *status civilis* either provides, unlike the *status naturalis*, for the first time normative order,[3] or at least improves the protection of the conceptualized pre-social natural law.[4] Mostly the move from the state of nature is interpreted—as demanded by instrumental reason—as a rational choice of agents trying to pursue their personal interest in self-preservation and utility-maximation. The move can be conceptualized differently, too. For Kant, for example, it is a moral duty, imposed by practical reason, to leave the state of nature (Kant 1968 [1797]: Volume VI, § 44). The goal of the process of transformation is the establishment of some kind of political order, and more concretely, a state. Regularly, courts play an important role in this order. Other institutions, like an executive or a parliament are, however, conceptualized as well (c.f., for example, Locke 1991 [1690]: chs. X–XIV).

The various theories differ in many aspects. To name just a few: the kind of state of nature described differs significantly depending on the source of inspiration of the author. One author might use images of a civil, religious war of his time. Others might refer to imperial wars. Sometimes travel reports about primitive, "natural" societies play an important role in painting a picture of the *status naturalis*. The contracts conceptualised are different in kind and number—there might be for example a contract conferring power to one authority, a contract uniting the society or a contract with the rulers imposing obligations on them, or a combination of these kinds of contracts. And—

to mention a last feature of possible difference—evidently the *status civilis* differs considerably from author to author. It might be an authoritarian order (for example Hobbes 1986 [1651]), a constitutional monarchy (Locke 1991 [1690]), or a republic (Rousseau 1964 [1762]).

The idea of a contract implies several assumptions:

1. Most importantly, it implies an individualization and secularization of political legitimacy. It frames the idea theoretically that social arrangements are not made by God but by human beings.
2. At least in the moment of the contract the members of the society form in a crucial respect one homogeneous body: they are united in the will to establish a new political order.
3. Interestingly, the transformation in contract theory is not regarded as a process. It is not a development in time, but rather a construction happening in a logical or legal second. In no theory of social contracts are the problems of transformations through time discussed.

These are familiar observations to contract theory. Let us now turn to the question what contract theory has to say about the problem of transitional justice, and the question how to deal with the past.

In Hobbes' theory, the answer seems to be clear—the normative concepts of right and wrong, just and unjust, are an original product of the *status civilis*, they have no meaning in the state of nature: "To this warre of every man against every man, this also is consequent; that nothing can be Unjust. The notions of Right and Wrong, Justice and Injustice have there no place. Where there is no common Power, there is no Law: where no Law, no Injustice" (Hobbes 1986 [1651]: 188). In consequence, there is no normative standard immanent to the state of nature. Any evaluation would be the application of normative standards that simply did not exist in the state of nature.

This kind of ethical skepticism is of course current in modern theory as well. To quote Jacques Derrida as an influential author beyond contractualism: "The origin of authority, the foundation or ground, the position of law can't by definition rest on anything but themselves, they are themselves a violence without ground. Which is not to say that they are themselves unjust, in the sense of 'illegal.' They are neither legal nor illegal in their founding moment. They exceed the opposition between founded and unfounded, or between any foundationalism or anti-foundationalism" (Derrida 1992: 14). Other contractualists clearly conceptualize normative standards independent of the social contract. The prime example is of course Locke's pre-social natural law: "The *State of Nature* has a Law of Nature to govern it, which obliges every one: And Reason, which is that Law, teaches all Mankind, who will but consult it, that being all equal and independent, no one ought to harm another in his Life, Health, Liberty, or Possession" (Locke 1991 [1690]: § 6, emphasis as in original).

The contract theories discussed help to clarify some implications and to formulate several problems of transitional justice:

1. The background assumption of the pursuit of transitional justice is the idea—formulated for the first time in modern history by contract theory—that societies are the product of the intentional creation of individuals as historic agents. If one tends to believe in a different model of social evolution driven forward by super-individual forces, say the predestination of God or an impersonal, unchangeable fate, transitional justice, i.e. the imposition of normative standards to action of individuals in the past, seems not to make any sense. The idea of transitional justice presupposes the responsibility of individuals for their actions and to a certain degree for the actions of the community they live in.

2. The social contract theories pose the additional question whether in the process of transformation after 1989 there was ever a moment of homogeneity of political intentions and aspirations, such as in the imagined event of making the social contract. For Germany, this was hardly the case, especially as any attempt to launch a process of new constitutionalization of the new republic were blocked from the outset. The famous Roundtable Talks or the elections in 1990 were hardly an equivalent to a new social contract of all Germans in the East and West. The revolution in East Germany, however, did not lack a democratic profile.[5]

3. The transition after 1989 was interpreted as in contractualism as a progress towards democracy and the rule of law after a period of dictatorship and totalitarianism. The transition after 1989, however, did not take place in a logical second as in the theories of social contracts—not surprisingly so, as these theories are concerned with legitimation, not with real time social change as mentioned above. It is still very much in progress and will take surely many more years. The things achieved, such as for example the creation of new judicial structures, were the product of painful efforts.

In addition, the core problem of transitional justice, the question that motivates the great schisms in the political, historical, and legal evaluation of the historic events after 1989 and that forms one of the great problems of practical philosophy, can be nicely framed by contract theory: are there any normative, "natural" standards beyond and independent from a particular, established social order, as natural law theorists like Locke assert? And if so—what do they consist of? Are they evident to everybody or just to an enlightened few? Or are there no such standards, is any concept of right and wrong, of just and unjust, nothing but the product of a social order as Hobbes (echoed by Derrida) asserts, dependent on the existence of this social order and perishing with it in the event of historic change? If the latter is the case—how can one such order legitimately judge another, being as contingent and relative as the object of its evaluation? Why should its values be supreme and not the ones of the order that has perished?

Given this problem, a society faced with the problem of dealing with the past of a different social order can choose between three options—or blend some of them into each other:

1. It can assert universalistic standards not relative to social and historical circumstance and judge the perished order accordingly. These standards can be derived from natural law, or—in the modern legal context—from public international law, most notably the human rights covenants or principles of international criminal law.
2. It can apply its own standards without asserting their universalistic nature.
3. It can accept the relativity of all normative standards and can in consequence refrain from evaluating the old order by other than internal standards of this order itself.

Of course, the apparent selection of one of these options can be nothing but the disguise of the pursuit of quite another strategy to deal with the problem of transitional justice. One might claim, for example, to choose option 3 and apply internal standards, which in effect, however, are reinterpreted according to the principles of the new order. Which course of action Germany took after 1989 will now be the object of further scrutiny.

THE GERMAN EXAMPLE

As mentioned above, German history is particularly rich in examples of transitions from one political regime to another. Clearly, the core interest of questions of transitional justice in Germany is the post-1989 period as the most recent example. But in order to avoid loosing the historic perspective and the normative yardsticks it provides, a brief look backwards to the other German examples of transitions seems not inappropriate.

Transitional justice: 1918, 1933, and 1945
Potentially, the year 1918 could have set a precedent for transitional justice in Germany. The monarchy fell, a short-lived revolution was staged, a new republic was created. Without doubt there were possible objects of transitional justice. The German monarchy was not a liberal state but took state action against political opponents, most notably the Social Democrats. It is

not far-fetched to assume that the newborn republic might have tried to seek justice for the victims of these measures. In addition, the question of the responsibility of German political elites for the war was highly contested. There was, however, hardly any action against the key figures of the old regime, and little legal prosecution took place. Continuity, not change was the key interest of the new republic to bolster its widely doubted legitimacy. The most important example of transitional justice in this period is perhaps the *Leipziger Prozesse* of German war crimes based on the criminal law clauses of the Treaty of Versailles from 1921 onwards (Schwengler 1982). The victorious Allies required the German government to try the defendants in German courts. In these trials, in principle, German criminal law was applied by German courts, with hardly any convictions, however. In addition, some of the more severe convictions were overturned later.

As mentioned before, it is surely not evident to associate the Nazi regime with concepts of transitional *justice*. Nevertheless, the *Machtergreifung* of 1933 has to be included in any account of German dealings with problems of social transformations, as National Socialism clearly transformed the German society profoundly. The reaction of the new regime towards the old, from its perspective deeply illegitimate order of the first german republic was to keep the bulk of officials, while staging reckless purges against political opponents and the victims of their racist ideology. Many victims of these purges did not only lose their positions, but were punished for their perceived misdeeds as well, without trial and often with the utmost brutality by incarcerating, torturing, and killing them in concentration camps.

The reaction to state crime after 1945 is widely reported and has been the object of many studies. The crimes that potentially had to be dealt with by institutions of transitional justice were horrendous. They included among others the mass murder of Jews, Gypsies, handicapped people, or homosexuals; political terror; the pursuit of a war of aggression that caused millions of deaths and included war crimes of terrible scale; and massive atrocities against civilian populations in the occupied territories, most notably in Poland and Russia.

The first institution of transitional justice supposed to deal with these crimes was of course the Nuremberg trials. The period of 1945–1952 showed some further prosecution of Nazi crimes, first the measures of denazification by the Allies that differed widely in severity from occupied zone to occupied zone, and ceded in the long run to other strategic interests of the unfolding Cold War. The German authorities gained more and more responsibility for the prosecution of past crimes. From 1952 till around 1958, the numbers, however, dropped rapidly. The General Attorney of Frankfurt and veteran prosecutor of Nazi crimes, Fritz Bauer, commented on the reasons for this development that the judiciary thought to conclude legitimately from various official actions and pronouncements, that according to Parliament and the executive, the judicial prosecution of crimes of the past had ended (Bauer 1965). Only after spectacular cases like the *Ulmer Einsatzgruppenprozess* in 1958, instigated by a police officer seeking reemployment by court action that made evident that the officer was involved in the killing of 4000 Jews, did new interest arise. This interest led to a better institutionalization of the prosecution of Nazi crimes[6] and further trials like the Hanauer trial of the crimes in the ghetto of Czenstochau in 1959, or the trials dealing with the crimes in the concentration camps of Auschwitz, Belzec, Treblinka, Sobibor, Chelmno, or Majdanek in the early 1960s and later on.

A special case is formed by crimes of the judiciary. There have been at least 15 trials and 2 sentences of professional judges (Rottleuthner 1992), which is noteworthy and to be kept in mind when discussing the problems of transitional justice after 1989, as the misadministration of justice forms a major group of actions prosecuted in this time.

A very problematic chapter of transitional justice after 1945 concerns the periods of limitations. In 1955, the period of limitations ended for all criminal actions, with the exception of manslaughter, murder and severe bodily harm. In 1960, the period of limitations for manslaughter and severe bodily harm ended. Attempts of the Social Democrats in Parliament to prolong this period, in order to keep open the possibility of further prosecution, failed. After long and bitter debates in 1965 and 1969, the prolongation of the period of limitations was achieved for the only criminal offence left to be prosecuted: murder.[7] In consequence many crimes of the Nazi period were never tried because they were statute-barred. Part of the Nazi crimes was, in addition, the object of amnesties, for example in 1949 and 1954.

All in all, the follow-up trials and the prosecution by the West German authorities led to 106,496 criminal investigations and 6497 convictions. Apart from 13 death sentences, there were 166 sentences to life imprisonment, 6201 prison sentences, 115 pecuniary fines, and 1 reprimand because of juvenile delinquency. About 2036 cases were still pending in 2000, the latest statistic of the Federal Ministry of Justice.[8] There have been massive campaigns pardoning many of the convicted: there are estimates that between 1945 and 1951, about 5000 people were pardoned, due to the influence of a "pardoning lobby" (Kempner 1986: 386–99). Given the nature of the crimes in question, these numbers are not impressive and underline the skeptical résumé of many perceptive commentators on transitional justice after 1945 in West Germany, who contend that despite important exceptions and considerable efforts, all in all, justice has not been done.

In East Germany, about 13,000 sentences have been reported up to 1989 (Wieland 1991: 50),[9] including, however, many cases where principles of due process of law were violated using the trials for political purposes of the communist state, which of course delegitimized the claims of the GDR to do what

West Germany was not doing, namely to prosecute consequently the crimes of the past. As to the special case of the judiciary, GDR officials reported 149 convictions of Nazi judges.

Transitional justice after 1989

In 1989, the political context and results were different. One of the most interesting features of transitional justice after 1989 was the unwillingness of the democratically legitimated Parliament of unified Germany to tackle this problem of great importance for the country itself, even though this task was clearly linked to the identity of the new republic. It was of great importance how the East Germans were treated in this respect, as this treatment had the potential to be taken as a symbol for the general spirit of reunification, whether it would be organized in the terms of a vindictive West overwhelming the East, or in the terms of reconciliation and a minimum degree of mutual respect. The Parliament, however, remained silent on the question of transitional justice. (Unlike, one might add, on the question of the capital of Germany that stirred a passionate debate.) The only question regulated was the question which penal code would be applied in these cases: in the framework of the Unification Treaty between East- and West Germany, Sec. 315 of the Introductory Act to the Criminal Code regulated that Sec. 2 of the Criminal Code of West Germany should be applicable to actions of the past by East Germans. Sec. 2 of the Criminal Code regulates the principle that if, subsequent to the commission of a criminal offence, the law provides for a lighter penalty, that penalty shall be applicable. In consequence, the only question the Parliament regulated was which of the two norms of the East or the West German penal code should take precedence in case of different sanctions. There were no regulations of material questions of transitional justice and no regulation of the question of an amnesty of at least some potentially criminal acts that was the topic of many debates in the public sphere at that time. One of the rare examples where the Parliament took action in this domain was the parliamentary act declaring the judgments of the *Waldheimer Prozesse* as void.[10]

In many other areas of equal interest beyond the criminal law, the German legislature created differentiated legal instruments, and felt clearly itself not unable to solve, at least to a certain degree, the problems of transitional justice. Examples are the policies of employment of former officials in the civil service of reunified Germany or the way the educational system was reformed. An important topic is the regulation of pensions, too. Another topic of interest in the context of transitional justice are the problems posed by the restitution of property in East Germany to former owners who fled, for example, to the West, who were expropriated by the GDR or were the victims of aryanizing by the Nazis, as these cases were not solved by the GDR after the war due to the official doctrine that the anti-fascist GDR was not the heir of the collapsed German Reich. The difficult questions of these areas beyond the criminal law will not be pursued here. This outline of the attempts to establish transitional justice in Germany will focus on criminal offences which form a core area for the problems discussed, as the criminal law is the most severe tool of the state and a symbol of its attitude towards the past.

As we will see, the silence of the legislature meant the delegation of the task of transitional justice to the judiciary, more precisely the West German judiciary that quickly replaced the East German institutions. On the background of this silence one can only make informed guesses. It might not be too far-fetched to assume that it was the German political parties' lack of political courage to deal with these problems in the public sphere that motivated this course of affairs—sometimes in the disguise of scruples against openly enacting retroactive law. Instead of parliamentary action, one relied on the considerable reputation of the judiciary to solve this problem successfully. This course of events reiterates to a certain degree the patterns of transitional justice of the post-1949 period. Here, the courts were the core agents of developing normative standards for dealing with the crimes of the past as well. As far as penal prosecution is concerned, the legislation restricted its activities to issuing statutes of limitation.

To sum up the jurisdiction of the German courts in some rough outlines, it might be useful to distinguish four topics of this jurisdiction.

The limitation of prosecution to severe human rights violations – The German courts pursued a line that amounted to a limitation of sentencing to human rights violation of some severity. The first and most important group of cases in this respect is formed by the killings at the German border. The amount of deaths is not quite clear yet and depends on the definition of victims. The highest number given including all deaths somehow related to the border is 957.[11] Estimates that are based only on cases with intervention and responsible action of a second party lead to 421 deaths.[12] According to the law of East Germany, these killings were justified according to Sec. 27.2 of the Border Act. The German Federal Criminal Court ruled a famous decision in 1992 that this justification was invalid because of a contradiction with superpositive norms of justice concretized by international human rights covenants and international human rights standards that were incorporated in the law of East Germany.[13] The latter argument found some legitimate legal critique as interpreting the laws of the GDR against what they meant in reality.

The German Federal Constitutional Court upheld this ruling in a landmark decision with a however slightly modified argumentation. Its decision rests on two grounds. The core legal problem is of course the principle of the prohibition of retroactive punishment in Article 103.2 of the German Basic Law. The court argued that the punishment of the border guards did not violate this principle because firstly, the foundation of the prohibition of retroactive punishment is in the view of the court the special legitimate trust that citizens can have in a democracy that only those deeds are criminal offences that are punishable according to the existing laws. In an authoritarian system like the GDR, the citizens cannot legitimately have this trust, as the laws are not democratically created. Secondly, the citizens had no legitimate ground to trust the existing criminal laws in the GDR on material grounds: these laws contradicted the basic tenets of international human rights standards. Therefore, the court argued, it was legitimate to punish even though it contradicted the prohibition of retroactive punishment.[14] These decisions have been upheld by the European Court of Human Rights.[15]

The second large group of cases relevant for questions of transitional justice were cases of misadministration of the law (*Rechtsbeugung*) (cf. Hohoff 2001). These cases actually formed the bulk of the criminal investigations instigated after 1989: 70% of the criminal investigations were concerned with this kind of cases (Marxen and Werle 1999: 236). These investigations led to 62 sentences until 2001 (Hohoff 2001: 20). In comparison with the reaction to the misadministration of justice in the Third Reich, this seems on first view a very considerable number, given the high amount of criminal investigations in this area. However, it is rather the indication of something else: the courts ruled that the misadministration of law had to violate severely the human rights of a person, and had to be in consequence considered as arbitrary, as an illegal misadministration of the law.[16] This excluded most of the cases the many investigations were concerned with and limited criminal prosecution considerably. As GDR law was applied in these cases, the courts reinterpreted it by incorporating in it the application of human rights standards. This seems to be another example of reinterpreting GDR norms against the reality of its legal system.

A third group in which the limitation of prosecution to severe human rights violation played a role are the cases of political denunciation. Sec. 241a of the West German Criminal Code[17] (Political Denunciation) was only applied if evident and severe human rights violations had to be feared as a result of the denunciation.[18] The same line was pursued for false imprisonment.

Further state crimes – An important group of cases relevant for questions of transitional justice are the actions of the *Ministerium für Staatssicherheit*, the so-called *Stasi*. A wide range of action could potentially be regarded as criminal offences. To take some examples: bugging telephones was not regarded as punishable, as there was no prohibition of bugging in the penal code of the GDR. Opening letters as the secret entering into private rooms was regarded as not punishable due to an unavoidable error as to the prohibited nature of the act. The extraction of money and goods from the mail by the *Stasi* was not regarded as embezzlement, as there was no norm prohibiting this if not done for the own profit of the actor instead of—as in the *Stasi* cases—the profit of the state. The legal norms concerning embezzlement have changed in this respect since unification. The harassment of citizens of the GDR wanting to leave the country was potentially punishable as unlawful compulsion or blackmail, depending on the nature of the case.

Other cases concerned physical abuse in GDR prisons or—a group of cases with very high media attention—doping cases. Finally, an important group is formed by the problems of espionage. There was a long battle in the legal sciences and in the courts how to deal with these cases, as West Germany had evidently—as any other state—spied on the GDR as well.[19] The German Federal Constitutional Court ruled in a decision which gained considerable attention that, according to the principle of proportionality, acts of espionage against West Germany could not be prosecuted if these acts were perpetrated from the territory of the GDR alone.[20]

The statutory period of limitation was prolonged twice for deeds of middle severity without much discussion. This is worth mentioning, as one of the very troubling chapters of the prosecution of Nazi crimes—as we have seen—was the regulation of the period of limitation. Here, the prolongation happened only after difficult political debates and was in the end limited to murder.

The continuity of prosecution – A further important guideline of the court reaction to the problems of transitional justice was the continuity of prosecution. Most of the prosecution of cases of election fraud, most notably during the communal elections of 7 May 1989, abuse of official functions, criminal breach of trust, and theft from letters were started during the last months of the GDR in the aftermath of the peaceful revolution of 1989. About 40% of the final sentences concerned these cases (Marxen and Werle 1999: 233). 11 of 21 members of the *Politbüro* were arrested at the time (Marxen and Werle 1999: 233). These investigations were continued by the newly formed judiciary after reunification. Other crimes, like the misadministration of justice, abuse by prison guards, doping, and espionage were prosecuted only after reunification. The same is true for the killings at the border. There were, however, a few reluctant measures by the East German prosecutors to take action in this respect, mostly as a reaction to reports of East German citizens to the police that demanded prosecution. Among these cases is the prosecution of Erich Honecker that was initiated for the abuse of power, criminal breach of trust, and other offences at the end of 1989, and that was later extended to the killings at the border in summer 1990, at a time of increasing influence of the West German judiciary on the prosecution in the East, but apparently without direct interference from the West (Rummler 2000: 18–21).

The intensity of prosecution – All in all, there have been 62,000 criminal investigations with about 100,000 people concerned (Marxen and Werle 1999: 234)—a number to a certain degree comparable to the number of criminal investigations after 1945 in West Germany. Even though far fewer persons in the GDR were potentially concerned than in the German Reich, the relevant period in which criminal deeds could have happened was much longer in the former case. The investigations, however, dealt with incomparable crimes. There were about 300 sentences (Marxen and Werle 1999: 234). Most of the trials have ended and there are estimates that there will be not more than 500 convictions. The amount of pecuniary fines was, at about 30%, below the average of 80% in other cases (Marxen and Werle 1999: 238). 90% of the prison sentences were, however, suspended on probation. This is about 20% above the average compared to other cases (Marxen and Werle 1999: 238). The rate of conviction was about 20% below the rate in normal criminal trials (Marxen and Werle 1999: 235).

Summary

When trying to summarize transitional justice in Germany after 1989, it is obvious that the standards applied after 1945 in West Germany were not the standards applied after 1989. After 1945/49, the threshold for prosecution was *cum grano salis* the killing of a person. The prosecution after 1989 was much more stringent and strict, even though the crimes concerned were of course dwarfed by the crimes of Nazi Germany. This discrepancy between post-1945 and post-1989 should not be forgotten in order to avoid any moralistic righteousness as to the achievements of transitional justice in Germany.

As to court action, it has to be underlined that the task of the courts was difficult indeed. The courts were confronted with a legislature that left the task of finding solutions to the intricate problems of transitional criminal justice to other institutions. The courts had to solve this problem in the historical context of reunified Germany, and heavy and still persisting social tensions between the former West and East German citizens. They had to find a way between the demands of the victims of state crimes in East Germany to address the injustices they had endured, and the demands of the East German citizens not to be made the prey of a vindictive action of the West. This context turned court action into something qualitatively different from a technical problem for the legal system. It made the jurisdiction a political statement as to the capability of the new state to integrate the East on the basis of respect and a minimum amount of dignity.

Compared to normal criminal cases, the jurisdiction of the courts leads to lower intensity of sanctions. There were whole groups of cases where this jurisdiction practically amounted to a silent amnesty, for example in the cases of misadministration of law, political denunciation, or espionage—at least if one compares the small number of convictions with the number of prosecutions. Between the models outlined in the previous section, the jurisdiction followed a twisted course between the application of natural law or universalistic legal ethics, international human rights standards, the application of internal standards of the GDR, and the reinterpretation of norms of the GDR that seems to have little to do with what these norms really meant in the East German judicial system. Examples of the latter strategy are the Federal Criminal Court's judgment on the killings at the border or some decisions on the misadministration of the law.

In Jon Elster's terms, transitional justice in Germany was mostly *exogenous* (Elster n.d.), that is, administered by a different legal order, as it was a judiciary dominated by staff from West Germany operating within the framework of a legal system taken over from the West that was the institutional agent of transitional criminal justice in unified Germany. Notable and quantitative significant exceptions to this were the prosecution of election fraud, abuse of official functions, criminal breach of trust and theft from letters, and to a certain extent the killings at the German border. The initiation of these prosecutions was part of an *endogenous* transitional justice, that is, an administration of justice from within the society concerned that should not be ignored.

Transitional justice can be reconstructed only to a limited degree in terms of contract theory. Most importantly, one can hardly say that, as far as transitional justice in criminal cases was concerned, its basis was a social contract that established its normative guidelines. Quite to the contrary, as we have seen, even the Parliament as a representative of the people felt unable to act in this area and left the problems and responsibilities to the courts.

As has been pointed out, the German courts did not follow a clear line between natural law or a universalistic legal ethics, the application of West German or East German norms to the actions tried by the legal system. It is clear, however, that in leading decisions like the decision of the Federal Constitutional Court on the prohibition of retroactive action, thoughts of universal standards of morality played a decisive role. The position of contract theorists like Hobbes or their deconstructivist heirs like Derrida, that values are dependent on and constituted by a given, historically contingent social order was thus not the leading normative intuition of transitional justice in Germany after 1989.

THESES

1. It is defensible to apply universalistic standards of morality as a final test of conduct. Core tenets of these standards are today positivized in human rights catalogues. It is equally defensible *in principle* to sanction *certain* actions *ex*

post that were legal in a social order that ceased to exist due to historical change, if these actions violate the universalistic standards of morality.

2. "Winner's justice" is surely prone to be, but is not necessarily, unjust. "Winner's justice" does not inevitably mean that the winner takes biased revenge but can mean that real justice is done. One should not forget that there are alternatives to dealing with state crimes of the past: historically the most common manner might be summary executions, lynching, forced exile or amnesty. Therefore, it is an important step to use court procedures to do justice. The Nuremberg trials—with all their shortcomings—are an important example for that.[21]

The precondition for justice being done even by a winner—admittedly a rather unusual achievement historically—is the principled use of the means of the rule of law and the awareness of its point in legal civilization.[22] Historical relativizations of the principles of the rule of law do not serve this end very well.

3. There are good reasons not to resort to criminal sanctions for the purpose of transitional justice, depending on the political, historical and social circumstances. These circumstances can make other means such as, for example, truth commissions a better tool.[23]

4. Retroactive action has to have the highest degree of legitimacy possible. Its standards have to be fixed in consequence by democratic organs, for example the Parliament. Its normative basis should not be left to be determined by the courts alone.

5. There has been serious criticism of the idea of dealing with state crimes in the ordinary courts. One of the positive effects, however, of these kinds of trials is that they underscore the individual dimension of guilt and responsibility that tends to disappear in some accounts of how transitional justice should be done, that take recourse to systemic functions or even historic fate—with the potentially unpleasant consequence of the prolongation of the (with rare exception traditional) impunity of agents of state crimes.

6. It is an important task for the international legal community to develop codes and institutions that fix and effectively administer standards of transitional justice and of state crimes.

7. As to the concrete case of Germany after 1989, there is much to be criticized in detail about the jurisdiction of the courts as outlined above. One can, however, hardly say that its jurisdiction was in general developed in a spirit of revenge and political bias against the citizens of the east. The jurisdiction of the courts limited the cases significantly despite the fact that surely many citizens in East Germany felt that injustice had been done in other cases as well that were—according to the developed jurisdiction— not regarded as a criminal offence. The continuity of prosecution seems

to be without alternative. The new state could surely not afford to disregard these initiatives by East German authorities after 1989 to do transitional justice themselves. The sanctions were generally hardly too severe.

There is, nevertheless, a major flaw of the administration of transitional justice in Germany: it is not the court action itself but that the courts were the core agents of transitional justice as to criminal offences in the first place. It was clearly a political task for the legislature to decide about the yardsticks and principles of transitional justice (see thesis 2 above). Such action by Parliament would have without doubt stirred the necessary public debate about these questions. Action by Parliament would have been surely the more difficult and potentially more painful way to solve problems of transitional justice in Germany. It would, however, have increased the democratic legitimacy of the process significantly.[24] In a democracy, this kind of political legitimacy seems to be without alternative.

NOTES

1 For a critique of Luhmann's autopoetic theory of history, compare Mahlmann 2000.

2 An often discussed example is Beck 1986.

3 As in Hobbes' theory, compare Hobbes 1986 [1651].

4 As in Locke's theory, compare Locke 1991 [1690].

5 The demonstrations in Leipzig for example, started under the slogan "Wir sind *das* Volk" (We are *the* people) before changing into "Wir sind *ein* Volk" (We are *one* people).

6 On 5 October 1958, the *Zentrale Stelle der Landesjustizverwaltungen zur Aufklärung nationalsozialistischer Gewaltverbrechen* was founded, first with a rather small staff and limited financial means.

7 On the special and infamous case of the reform of Sec. 50.2 of the Penal Code and its consequences for the prosecution of Nazi crimes, see Rottleuthner 2001.

8 Communication of the Federal Ministry of Justice, April 2002. The Federal Ministry collects the data from the German *Länder*. This is the reason for the delay in updating the statistics.

9 For an early report, compare Generalstaatsanwalt der DDR 1965, p. 27.

10 These trials that took place in 1950 concerned officially only Nazi crimes. They are widely regarded as a prime example of Stalinist jurisdiction. Section 1.2 of the *Strafrechtliches Rehabilitierungsgesetz*, BGB 1.I, 1814. Generally, a criminal sentence is annulled if it violates "essential principles of a liberal rule of law," Section 1.1. Section 1.2. declared that to be the case for the *Waldheimer Prozesse*.

11 The *Arbeitsgemeinschaft 13. August* gives this number, see in the *Frankfurter Allgemeine Zeitung,* 12 August 2000.

12 The *Zentrale Ermittlungsstelle Regierungs- und Vereinigungskriminalität* counts 421 deaths, see in the *Frankfurter Allgemeine Zeitung,* 12 August 2000. Klaus Marxen and Gerhard Werle give the number of 264 deaths as known to the prosecutors (Marxen and Werle 1999: 8).

13 *Bundesgerichtshof in Strafsachen* (Federal Criminal Court), 3 November 1992, Official Collection, Volume 39, p. 1. The argumentation has been criticised for the different

strands of argumentation that are not clearly connected. For an overview of the huge discussion, compare Karl Lackner and Kristian Kühl, *Strafgesetzbuch*, 23rd edition, Sec. 2, paragraphs 16 and 16a; Alexy 1993.

14 *Bundesverfassungsgericht* (Federal Constitutional Court), 24 October 1996, Official Collection, Volume 95, p. 96.

15 European Court of Human Rights, case of Streletz, Kessler, and Krenz v. Germany (applications nos. 34044/96, 35532/97, and 44801/98), 22 March 2001, http://www.echr.coe.int/Eng/Judgments.

16 *Bundesgerichtshof in Strafsachen*, 13 December 1993, Volume 40, pp. 30 and 41; 15 September 1995, Volume 41, pp. 247 and 253. The court formed several groups as paradigmatic examples, for example, the intention to repress political enemies.

17 Here, West German criminal law was applied because the German Federal Court interpreted a special provision of international criminal law, Sec. 5, number 6 of the Criminal Code, to the effect that it applied to cases happening in East Germany to East Germans. Compare *Bundesgerichtshof in Strafsachen*, 29 April 1994, Volume 40, p. 125.

18 *Bundesgerichtshof in Strafsachen*, 29 April 1994, Volume 40, pp. 125 and 133.

19 Compare for an overview Thiemrodt 2000.

20 *Bundesverfassungsgericht*, 15 May 1995, Volume 92, p. 277.

21 It was Stalin who prevailed with his proposal of courts in Teheran against the competing strategy of Churchill and Roosevelt aiming at executions of top Nazi leaders. The background might have been his "good" experience with courts during the thirties.

22 For some comments on this questions, see Krygier 2001.

23 For a good overview of the different ways to deal with state crime of the past in an international comparative perspective, compare Eser and Arnold 2000.

24 Hart's important defence of the advantages of openly retroactive legislation in his discussion with Radbruch still merit attention, compare Hart, "[a] case of retroactive punishment should not be made to look like an ordinary case of punishment for an act illegal at the time" (Hart 1961: 206).

BIBLIOGRAPHY

Alexy, Robert. *Mauerschützen* [Border guards' shouting at the Wall]. Göttingen: Vandenhoeck and Ruprecht, 1993.

Bauer, Fritz. "Im Namen des Volkes. Die strafrechtliche Bewältigung der Vergangenheit" [Dealing with the past by criminal law] in *Die Humanität der Rechtsordnung* [The humanity of legal order], ed. Bauer, Fritz (Frankfurt and New York: Campus, 1965), pp. 77–90.

Beck, Ulrich. *Die Risikogesellschaft: auf dem Weg in eine andere Moderne*. Frankfurt: Suhrkamp, 1986.

Derrida, Jacques. "Force of Law: The Mystical Foundation of Authority" in *Deconstruction and the possibility of justice*, eds. Cornell, Drucilla, Michel Rosenfeld, and David G. Carlson (New York and London: Routledge, 1992), pp. 3–67.

Elster, Jon. *A framework for the study of transitional justice*. Manuscript on file with the authors, n.d.

Eser, Albin and Jörg Arnold, eds. *Criminal Law in Reaction to State Crime*. Freiburg: edition iuscrim, 2000.

Generalstaatsanwalt der DDR, ed. *Die Haltung der beiden deutschen Staaten zu den Nazi- und Kriegsverbrechen*. Berlin: Staatsverlag der Deutschen Demokratischen Republik, 1965.

Hart, Herbert L. A. *The Concept of Law*. Oxford: Clarendon Press, 1961.

Hegel, Georg Wilhelm Friedrich. *Grundlinien der Philosophie des Rechts* [Philosophy of right]. Frankfurt am Main: Suhrkamp, 1976 [1821].

Hobbes, Thomas. *Leviathan*. London: Penguin, 1986 [1651].

Hohoff, Ute. *An den Grenzen des Rechtsbeugungstatbestandes* [Limits of preservation of justice as a legal offence]. Berlin: Verlag Arno Spitz, 2001.

Kant, Immanuel. *Metaphysik der Sitten* [Metaphysics of morals]. Berlin: Walter de Gruyter, 1968 [1797].

Kempner, Robert M. W. *Ankläger einer Epoche* [Prosecutor of an epoch]. Frankfurt: Ullstein, 1986.

Kersting, Wolfgang. *Die politische Philosophie des Gesellschaftsvertrags* [The political philosophy of the social contract]. Darmstadt: Wissenschaftliche Buchgesellschaft, 1994.

Krygier, Martin. "Transitional Questions about the Rule of Law: Why, What and How?" *East Central Europe/L'Europe Du Centre Est* 28, no. 1 (2001): 1–34.

Locke, John. *Two Treatises of Government*. Cambridge: Cambridge University Press, 1991 [1690].

Luhmann, Niklas. *Die Gesellschaft der Gesellschaft* [The society of society]. Frankfurt: Suhrkamp, 1997.

Macpherson, Crawford B. *The political theory of possessive individualism. Hobbes to Locke*. Oxford: Oxford University Press, 1962.

Mahlmann, Matthias. "Katastrophen der Rechtsgeschichte und die autopoietische Evolution des Rechts" [Catastrophies in legal history and the autopoietic evolution of law] in *Paradoxien des Rechts. Zeitschrift für Rechtssoziologie* [Paradoxes of law. Journal of legal society], ed. Teubner, Günther (Sonderheft, 2000), pp. 247–77.

Marx, Karl. "Einleitung zur Kritik der politischen Ökonomie" [Introduction to the critique of social economy] in *Karl Marx, Friedrich Engels, Werke Vol. 13.* [The collected works of Karl Marx and Friedrich Engels, Volume 13]. Berlin: Dietz, 1859.

Marxen, Klaus and Gerhard Werle. *Die strafrechtliche Aufarbeitung von DDR-Unrecht. Eine Bilanz* [Dealing with the criminality of the GDR—a balance]. Berlin: de Gruyter, 1999.

Rottleuthner, Hubert. "Kontinuität und Identität—Justizjuristen und Rechtslehrer vor und nach 1945" [Continuity and identity—judiciary and legal scientists before and after 1945] in *Recht und Rechtslehre im Nationalsozialismus* [Law and legal science under Nazism], ed. Säcker, Franz J. (Baden-Baden: Nomos, 1992), pp. 241–54.

——. "Hat Dreher gedreht?" *Rechtshistorisches Journal* 20 (2001): 665–79.

Rousseau, Jean-Jacques. *Discours sur l'inégalité. Oeuvres complètes, Vol. III* [Discourse on inequality. Collected works, vol. 3]. Paris: Gallimard, 1964 [1755].

——. *Du contract social. Oeuvres complètes, Vol. III* [Social contract. Collected works, vol. 3]. Paris: Gallimard, 1964 [1762].

Rummler, Toralf. *Die Gewalttaten an der deutsch-deutschen Grenze vor Gericht* [Violent acts at the German-German border before the courts]. Berlin: Verlag Arno Spitz, 2000.

Schwengler, Walter. *Völkerrecht, Versailler Vertrag und Auslieferungsverträge* [Public international law, the Treaty of Versailles and extradition treaties]. Stuttgart: Deutsche Verlagsanstalt, 1982.

Thiemrodt, Ivo. *Strafjustiz und DDR-Spionage* [Criminal justice and espionage by the GDR]. Berlin: Verlag Arno Spitz, 2000.

Wieland, Günther. *Ahndung von NS-Verbrechen in Ostdeutschland 1945–1990* [Sanctioning Nazi crimes in Eastern Germany 1945–1990]. Neue Justiz, 1991, pp. 49–53.

Restitutive Justice, Rule of Law, and Constitutional Dilemmas

Grażyna Skąpska

Introduction:
A Constitutional Dilemma

For the postcommunist, as well as any other postdictatorial, or postcolonial societies, not only the future, but above all the past also presents a test of new governments' will to fulfill promises of the rule of law. One such past issue is that of restitution, also called reprivatization.

It is argued that reprivatization "offers a principal means to redress some of the worst and most heinous injustices of the past" (Pogany 1997: vii). Reprivatization in Poland presents an important step in the endeavor known as "facing the past." In this it is similar to decommunization, that is, cleaning upper rank communist officials out of the public sector, and lustration, that is, screening individuals' past in order to exclude from public offices persons who collaborated with the communist secret police. However, whereas the decommunization and lustration procedures are focused mostly on perpetrators and instigators, restitution is a procedure focused on victims. As a matter of fact, restitution presents an important indicator of the new government's will to redress past human rights abuses and compensate for losses, as well as to re-establish trust in state and law.

As the author of the initial citation observes, property restitution in East Central Europe is a consequence of great human rights abuses. It is not only because of the installation of communism, but because of the close effects of World War II and the Shoah, and the great displacement of peoples due to geopolitical changes and political decisions (Pogany 1997: ch. 2).

Hence, for the governments in East Central Europe restitution poses a most difficult issue. Because of the scope and number of possible claims, restitution is enormously costly. In fact, in those countries the costs of restitution are either not debated at all, or estimates vary so greatly, that any public debate on them makes no sense. In many cases, the task of restitution is enormous because of the previously mentioned geopolitical changes after World War II, and also after 1989. As a result of World War II, some countries lost their territories but also gained new ones. The change of territories, as well as some conclusions of the Yalta and Potsdam Treaties, resulted in a great displacement and deportation of people: millions of Poles, Germans, Ukrainians, and others had to leave their homelands and property behind. Hundreds of thousands were simply displaced as a result of political decisions and deported elsewhere. After 1945, hundreds of thousands did not come back because they were afraid of communist authorities backed by the Soviet army and Soviet political police, whose cruelty they experienced too well during World War II, or because they did not want to come back to territories on which the Shoah took place, or because they were met with hostility and abused.[1] The geopolitical changes after 1989, especially the dissolution of the former Soviet Union, led to the formation of new states: Lithuania, Latvia and Estonia, Ukraine, and Belarus. There were also "velvet divorces," and the unification of Germany.

The introduction of communism brought about the nationalization of all property: private and communal, property belonging to civic organizations and to the churches, together with nationalization of banks and insurance companies. It is worth noting that some of these nationalizations only legitimized nationalizations carried out by the Germans during World War II, or legitimized the expropriations undertaken by the indigenous pro-Nazi governments, as is indicated by countries which were not hostile, or which collaborated with Nazi Germany. It also led to further displacement, because many fled from the new communist states and many did not come back. The Shoah turned East Central Europe, especially the Polish territories, into the grave of the European Jews. It also led to further displacements.

Thus, for the governments, restitution of property presents a multidimensional dilemma. It is a dilemma of financial costs of restitution versus the social sense of justice and trust in the new governments. The new governments also have to deal with the vested interests of various social actors: former owners, victims of nationalization and confiscations, and the new owners. They have to consider extremely complex matters in deciding what belongs to whom and how the losses should be compensated, or how the property rights shall be defined.

Notwithstanding the costs and the scope of restitution, the new governments are bound by the principles of the rule of law, or rather *Rechtsstaat*, which was enshrined in all postcommunist constitutions as their opening norm, by the constitutional guarantees of property rights protection, and perhaps even more importantly in the perspective of their possible membership in the European Union, by the ratified European Convention on Human Rights and Fundamental Freedoms of 1950, not to mention the Universal Declaration of Human Rights of 1948, that, next to other ratified covenants, pose a part of their constitutional and legal orders.[2] They are also under the constant and great pressure of foreign countries, notably, but not uniquely, of the United States' House of Representatives.[3]

Moreover, restitution poses an important issue in the adjudication of the European Court of Human Rights in Strasburg, as well as of the United Nations Human Rights Committee decisions. These verdicts and decisions are of great relevance to the implementation of the binding rule of law principle.

Restitution of nationalized property has also an important meaning for societies in East Central Europe. In individual terms, in many difficult cases the issue of restitution is linked with the very concept of full citizenship, human rights, and human dignity. In collective terms, the issue of restitution is closely linked with the re-establishment of ethnic, religious, and national identities. Thus, the legal dilemma has an important human aspect, and restitution of property presents a deeply sensitive issue for individual persons and society as well. It is a dilemma of economically and legally bound reasoning versus moral considerations focused on human dignity protection, empathy towards political victims, and the fulfillment of the promise to respect a "higher law" on which, in East Central Europe, the legitimization of the system change rested. In East Central Europe these issues are of even greater importance, since the societies whose moral bonds were destroyed during the last half of the twentieth century are experiencing a lack of moral justifications and the discursive resources to face the challenges brought about by the regime change. Restitution of the nationalized or confiscated property has such a potential for revitalization of a "moral impulse."[4] It makes people consider and discuss moral issues and think about the victims of the former system, but also about the public good, as important justifications for the newly introduced constitutional principle of the rule of law.

Last, but not least, there are important political issues: the strong interests on both sides, but especially on the side of the opponents of restitution who often form a considerable part of the electorate. There are those who either gained because of nationalization and confiscations, or these who profit by the lack of restitution.

The big question is the following: how the promise of the rule of law is to be fulfilled in these complex and costly legacies of the past? My chapter will be devoted mainly to the human dimension of this question as an important aspect of the postcommunist rule of law promise. I will debate the involvement of the restitution issues with very personal concerns and with the expectations of individual persons and of large social groups that "justice shall be done." In my view, these human aspects are decisive for the re-conceptualization of the rule of law after the collapse of totalitarianism or a dictatorship. In such a view, restitution presents not only a "cost-efficient" legal mechanism, but it is also linked to "life-worlds" and "moral impulses" of societies undergoing transformation, to the "intangibles" and "imponderables" of this process. As I will try to demonstrate, the conventional, legal approaches to restitution put in question the very promise of the rule of law. Of importance are the mentioned intangibles and imponderables of the rule of law formation and application after the collapse of a dictatorial regime: the hopes, emotions, dignities, values, moral expectations, and cultural identities of persons and groups engaged in the processes, on the one hand, and in the symbolic, cultural, discursive, or rhetorical aspects of the rule of law, on the other.

In order to develop my argument, I will outline the scope and range of expropriations mostly in Poland, but with reference to other East Central European countries. These past events and the measures undertaken to compensate for them provide a sort of lens through which the new governments and the rule of law promise are perceived. Then, I will reflect upon the motives of expropriations as linked with concepts of society and law, but also with interests of those who profited from them. Then I will outline the legal measures aimed at restitution and discuss them in view of the currently ongoing and implemented restitution policies. Finally, I will debate property restitution in East Central Europe as a challenge to the conventional rule of law conceptualizations.

EXPROPRIATIONS: LEGAL AND EXTRA-LEGAL
FRAMEWORKS AND MOTIVES[5]

The most thorough expropriations in East Central Europe took place mostly after 1944, after the change of the political regimes imposed by the Red Army, and they were nearly completed by the early 1950s. However, expropriations started long before 1944 and they did not end in the 1950s. In Germany, the first mass-scale expropriations were due to the series of statutes and decrees issued in 1933–1938 aimed at expropriations of Jewish property, and also confiscation of the property of political opponents of the Nazi regime. In the countries that collaborated with Nazi Germany, similar decrees or statutes were issued in the early 1940s. For instance, in Hungary the final expropriation of Jewish property was due to a statute issued in 1944 before the Red Army entered that country (Pogany 1997; Paczolay 1999). In Poland and other countries occupied by Nazi Germany, the Nazi occupants first and foremost took property which belonged to Jews, but also to other Polish citizens, regardless of their ethnic or other characteristics, if that property was of any use for the occupants. From the point of view of ongoing restitution, these expropriations are of importance, because they were often legalized by the new governments.[6]

The expropriations did not end in the 1950s. In fact, as the comparative Polish-German research indicates, there were great efforts of the communist governments aimed at nationalization—directly or indirectly, for instance by the levy of taxes or other payments. Such measures were characteristic of the

1970s, and the last statutes or other regulations aimed at expropriations were issued in the late 1980s.[7]

Expropriations took place not only due to the regime change, but also to the war. In the case of eastern Polish territories, as well as in the Baltic countries, the great expropriations started after the Red Army entered these territories in 1939 and started deporting the people who were there. The wave of expropriations was due to the change of borders after the political treaties of Yalta and Potsdam. As a result of the Yalta and Potsdam Treaties, Poland lost 30% of her former territories behind the river Bug in the east, and was given the former German territories in the West. From the latter, the German population was deported to Germany. The Germans were also deported from the western Czech territories. Expropriations and deportations also took place in other countries.[8]

The Shoah, and the events which came later decided that many of those who found themselves in the West did not return to their homelands. If they did not indicate the will to take the property into their possession—which during Stalinism could be quite dangerous—their property was qualified as "abandoned," in order to be nationalized after the prescriptive periods elapsed.

However, the most thorough expropriations were due to the regime change. Those expropriations had strong constitutional foundations and legitimization. In all communist constitutions modeled unanimously on the Soviet Constitution of 1936, the so-called "Stalin constitution," one of the first provisions declared the annihilation of "exploitative classes," land owners, and productive property owners.

In order to implement these constitutional provisions, the expropriations and nationalization of property went on from 1944, directly or indirectly, by means of law, in the shadow of law, and by purely illegal means, that is, by political blackmail or provocation. (Skąpska 1998).

Expropriations reflected several motives and various meanings of property and property rights, and of law as an instrument of social change. The law was used as an homogenizing and dehumanizing instrument brutally applied. Since the societies in question were often considered backward, and the nationalized, state-owned and state-administered property to be more efficient and rational than the private, the nationalization laws were also used as a means of brutal and ruthless modernization and rationalization.

The first characteristic feature of such instrumental law was abstraction and categorization. The subjects of expropriations were Jews, national and ethnic minorities (Ukrainian, Polish, German, Silesian, and others), and the very broadly defined category of the exploiting class.

The second, after de-individualization, posed the "dehumanization," that is, the denial of humanity proper of the victims of the totalitarian regime, which had several degrees. In the extreme case, the subjects of expropriation were not treated as human beings at all, and expropriation posed the first step to the "final solution" of their case, that is, their deprivation of the fundamental right to life. This is the case of Jews who were deprived of their property in Germany between 1933–1938 and in the occupied countries after 1939, before they were murdered. To strip the Jews of their property before they were annihilated also meant to deprive them of their individual and collective identity, to deprive them of material witnesses and evidence of their personal achievements, achievements of their families, and of family histories incorporated in material property. Characteristically, the language of political propaganda was full of descriptions of Jews (but also of Poles, for instance) as "worms," or "vermin." not to mention "pigs." The lower degree of dehumanization consisted in treatment of subjects as an inferior class or category of human beings, who cannot possess property but rather work on the property of others (Poles, and generally the Slavic peoples).

Expropriations were also linked with identities, national, religious, and ethnic, and consisted in nationalization of collective property of churches, communal religious and cultural organizations, objects of art, and other collectively possessed property important for preservation of collective identity, as for instance of synagogues, and also forests in the case of the Polish minority of Lemkos. Especially the case of Lemkos, as before the case of Jews, illustrates close links between expropriations and an attack on identities, not only individual, but also collective.[9]

The fourth characteristic feature of expropriation consists in its close links to the concept of citizenship and civic rights. If one defines property rights primarily as civic rights and as an important component of active citizenship, then expropriations lead either to deprivation of citizenship, or to a redefinition of citizenship as fully dependent on economic resources of the state. Obviously, the Nazi-led expropriations of Jewish property were based on the conviction that Jews could not be treated as citizens. Expropriations of the property of national or ethnic minorities in all East Central European countries often took place prior to their displacement.

Expropriations could have many motives, apart from racist, economic, and ideological ones. They could present a means of punishment, especially punishment for treason to the country; they could be a means of some form of social—as distinct from ideological—justice, as indicated by the case of land reform. The striking feature of many expropriations in East Central Europe, predominantly based on the example of pre-World War II Germany, was that they were used also as a means of ethnic cleansing, of homogenization of culture and its subordination to the dominant one by nationalization of collective cultural objects and changing their meanings. The late example of such expropriations is here provided by the Greek Orthodox or Uniate churches in Poland, which were turned into Catholic churches, or the example of churches and synagogues which were turned into something else. Nazi and communist expropriations were used for elimination of civil society autonomous organizations, and finally, elimination of property was used as a means of elimination of individual and collective autonomy and limitation of social differentiation. It was a condition for formation of a society that was totally state-dependent and undifferentiated, homogeneous racially, economically, ethnically and/or ideologically. Finally, expropriations were used by the communist government as a most important ideological imperative to create a classless society.

EXPROPRIATIONS IN THE MEMORIES OF VICTIMS AND BENEFICIARIES

Expropriations are still vivid in the memories of victims as something opposite to their concept of the rule of law. These memories play an important part in efforts to regain property rights or to be compensated for the lost property. In interviews with former owners, or their successors, as well as in documents presented in restitution proceedings, such motives as pride in the family past, pride in the former achievements of close relatives (fathers and grandfathers), or pride in the past of a society or social group, are referred to. As the rabbi of Kraków argued, for the Kraków Jews, as well as the Polish Jews more generally, the expropriation of collective, commmunal property meant the destruction of the material evidence of Jewish identity and culture, and even symbolic restitution would have been of great meaning, as it would document the 700 years of history of Jews in Poland and the development of the flourishing Jewish culture on the territory of Poland.[10] Similar concerns with restitution as a means of restoration of collective identity were expressed by the representatives of the Lemkos—the ethnic group subjected to severe persecutions and displacements by the communist authorities of Poland. Characteristically, these memories have been rather private in Poland. Until recently, expropriations were seldom publicly tackled there. The tacit acknowledgment of expropriations and the lack of public discourse about them had an ideological source—it was generally claimed the expropriations posed an answer to the claims for more social justice, and the nationalized property was given to the public use, either in the form of state-owned companies, or in other forms of public property (museums, schools, hospitals, etc.), or in the form of cheap housing, or it was used for the long-awaited land reform. The atrocities committed were just swept aside and they represented, until very recently, a public *taboo*. However, the *tabooing* of expropriation issues may also be related to the fact that they had not only their victims but also their perpetrators and beneficiaries, and the memories, individual and collective as well, could be quite shameful.

Despite the long lasting propaganda on the social justice of expropriations, or the arguments that everybody lost something during communism, for victims expropriations still represent dramatic and even traumatic events: they affected the lives of nearly two generations. For many, expropriations presented the first step to further dramatic events in their lives, to their deportations to ghettos, or labor camps, to the death of their closest family members; they brought about the loss of all that was collected during generations and had given a sense of stability and safety. Expropriations were linked with humiliation, even with a deep humiliation, as the owners—the Jews, the "inferior" persons, the "traitors," and the members of "exploitative classes"—were exposed to scornful treatment, even—according to personal recollections—mocked and ridiculed at the time when they had to leave their property. Afterwards many of them saw their property—companies and enterprises, manor houses, farms—taken over by new owners, or ruined under state management.

The legalization of Nazi expropriations in Poland by the new government brought about a dramatic disappointment with the new reality and the new Polish state after years of Nazi occupation, and contributed greatly to the deep distrust toward the state and law.[11] For many former owners, individual and collective, expropriations meant deprivation of something that was "sacred": churches, forests, land.[12] For Jews owners, or the successors of murdered owners expropriations, especially expropriations which were conducted or legalized after World War II, are often identified with the prolongation of the Nazi policy of racial cleansing and even genocide after the war ended, by new governments.[13]

There were many different types of persons and organizations which benefited from the past expropriations. The biggest direct beneficiary of communist nationalization was the state treasury. After the reforms of 1989, especially after the reforms of administration and government at the beginning of the 1990s, and communalization of state-owned assets (that is, when the owners became local governments), the beneficiaries are local governments since much of their income comes from the former state-owned assets. Thus, for instance in Poland, local governments have recently become the greatest opponents of restitution.

There were also indirect beneficiaries of confiscations and nationalization: all those who received the rights to use public property, like schools, hospitals, kindergartens, etc., but also those who received a right to use directly a state-owned or even a still private property for a very small rent (mostly, they received a right to occupy an apartment in an apartment house). For these persons the issue of restitution is an ambiguous one, as is the issue of the past expropriations. At least, as they argue, the expropriations were conducted without their active participation, so in their conscience they feel "absolved."

There are however also other beneficiaries, who would not refer to history at all, not because it was so dramatic and the memories are so traumatic, but because it was shameful. The interested persons would like to forget about the past, or to get rid of its burden as fast as possible. They are those who profited by the Holocaust simply by taking Jewish property and helping with expropriations in a deep belief that the owners would never return and claim the property back. Often they were neighbors of the expropriated property or employees in the confiscated company, which they could buy very cheaply after expropriation. In the occupied countries they were those who suddenly turned out to be Germans (persons who signed the so-called *Volksliste* as ethnic Germans), local blackmailers, and other persons who simply used the opportunity to enrich themselves.

Others profited by the expropriations of property from ethnic minorities, or of the "exploitative classes." The former is the case of the Lemkos, whose farms were sold very cheaply to Poles. Some of those new owners, according to the Lemkos, took the homes and things which were inside these homes even in the former owners' presence. The most ugly example of such private and direct profit from expropriations presents in Poland the so-called *shaber*, that is, looting of the property allegedly German, but many times also property belonging to the Silesian minority, by semi-organized gangs of persons from central Poland. That looting took place at the end of the 1940s. The considerable looting of personal property, furniture, objects of art, clothing etc. took place after land reform, that is, the parceling out of land, but also after legal and illegal nationalization of buildings and manor houses as part of the land reform. The looting had strong ideological support in the state propaganda. In Poland it was supported by the propaganda that the owners were traitors to the Polish nation in the case of Silesians, defined as Germans, that Lemkos were Ukrainians involved in an anti-Polish Ukrainian conspiracy, by the created hate for "capitalists" and land-owners, and by anti-semitism. Such arguments live long in social memories, and they are handy in reducing shame.

Not only private persons were beneficiaries of expropriations, but also institutions. In the former communist countries they were the state-owned companies which suddenly became enriched by equipment taken (illegally) from the private owners; the communist parties and the political police. Functionaries of these institutions who received the right to use buildings, luxurious villas, and hotels from the state as if they were their own, were also beneficiaries.

Finally, states were special sort of beneficiaries: they displaced peoples who lived on their territories and took over their belongings as well as the belongings of whole ethnic groups and nationalities, their objects of art, historical buildings, companies.

BETWEEN "ZERO-OPTION" AND
FULL RESTITUTION: A BRIEF OVERVIEW OF RESTITUTION
LAWS IN EAST CENTRAL EUROPE

As has been emphasized, the opening norm—usually Article One or Two— in all postcommunist constitutions declares the rule of law. In view of that, one may ask whether the promises of the rule of law are fulfilled.[14] One may also ask whether these past expropriations have any meaning today and whether law, directed to the future, should bother with the individual and collective memories of past dramatic events. Maybe it would be best, that is, least costly and most feasible for future reforms, especially economic and legal reforms, to forget, to accept some kind of a zero-option, as is argued; to start anew.

The answers given to such questions are important in the investigation of the restitution policies and formation of the rule of law in East Central Europe after 1989. The answers differentiate among the meaning and functions of restitution policy. If that policy is subordinated to purely economic, efficiency-focused considerations and used as a means of expeditious and efficient privatization, thus if governments are focused on economic reform, then it seems not to be practical at all to develop an elaborate restitution policy and evoke past atrocities. On the other hand, restitution could be a policy focusing on the victims of the former regime undertaken in order to prevent inhumane practices in the future, to re-establish the dignity of victims as an important component of the rule of law concept, and to restore trust in law and the state. The brief and very superficial presentation of the regulation of restitution claims in East Central Europe outlined below does not pretend to be a full analysis of restitution. Its aim is rather to illustrate the issue of rule of law formation in an empirical situation of system change.

In order to implement restitution of property rights or compensation for lost property, the governments in East Central Europe adopted various approaches. One should however emphasize that these approaches cannot be fully evaluated. Restitution laws are still changing or have not been comprehensively regulated yet. The latter is the case in Poland, where no comprehensive restitution law was proclaimed, although restitution is possible since 1984 on the basis of administrative procedural law, thus, since many years before the regime change.

The approaches to restitution and restitution policies vary with respect to the time, the entitled subjects, and the contents of restitution. Closer investigation of the ongoing application of the restitution policies not only indicates that the establishment of the rule of law faces considerable impediments, but also that restitution policies, law application, and interpretation of law depends not only on legal or economic considerations, but also on other factors, including vested interests.

If one evaluates efforts aimed at the establishment of the rule of law, the German restitution policies are quite unique in their full acknowledgment of claims and in the comprehensiveness of the policies. As a result of them, in united Germany, in the year 2001, nearly 95% of all restitution claims were solved. Policies of other East Central European countries are very different, and responses to important questions with which the new governments are faced vary along different lines. Therefore, it is very difficult to evaluate the level of the solved restitution claims.

The most difficult question faced by the postcommunist governments was, and still is, the question of time limits. From when are restitution claims valid? This question is important, since in reality it is a question about the legality of laws issued by the communist governments, and continuity of law. So, firstly, it is a question "how far back in the past," but also "shall we give back everything taken by communists because of the illegality of their regulations"? Responses to these questions vary. In Germany, the time limits were marked by the Nuremberg statutes on confiscation of Jewish property, that is, the year 1933. Those statutes were proclaimed illegal. Restitution, regulated by the Unification Treaty of 1990, encompassed all illegal confiscations and expropriations which took place after 1933. Since the united Germany adopted the German Basic Law of 1949 and the West German legal order, they are all illegal expropriations according to the standards set in the Basic Law (currently the constitution of the German Federal Republic). Such expropriations are considered invalid.

The second type of answers to the time limits question was given by governments of the Baltic States, the former Soviet Republics. In these states, all nationalization laws became invalid. The date of the German invasion was set up as a restitution time limit in the Czech Republic. However, in the Czech Republic controversies still exist regarding the first nationalizations of big enterprises, and property belonging to churches (that is, nationalizations undertaken after 1944).

The third type of answers was given by those governments which—like Poland (and Hungary to some extent)—accepted the first nationalizations and land reforms as valid, and generally did not question the laws introduced by communist authorities. There are, however, several exceptions characteristic of the latter approach. In Poland, the unique exception is the regulation of Catholic church property restitution, issued in 1989, just before the collapse of the former regime. In this regulation no time limits were defined. As a result of that clear legislative mistake, the Catholic church acquired the right to claim property which it lost at any time, even centuries ago. In practice, the Church uses this right quite extensively. Statutes regulating other types of restitution, notably the law of 1997 and the restitution of Jewish religious organizations' property extend time limits to the date of the German invasion of Poland, that is, 1 September 1939. The last governmental project of comprehensive regulation of restitution in Poland also set the time limits to the year 1939. Similar are these verdicts of the Polish Highest Administration Court, which regulate the compensation of property left behind the river Bug, that is, compensation for the lost property of persons who had to leave the former Polish, and afterwards Soviet, territories (now territories of the Ukraine, Belarus, and Lithuania). According to the innovative Hungarian regulation, the expropriations were generally not invalidated, but the victims, also victims of the Holocaust, and owners who lost their property before 1944, were equally, although symbolically, compensated.

The next important question is the question about who is entitled to restitution. Answers to this question are also very different, from those which are fully comprehensive to others which introduce some limits and exclude some categories of subjects from restitution. Examples of the fully comprehensive approach to the subjects of restitution are, again, Germany, the Baltic states, and, in a quite innovative way, Hungary. At the opposite pole are located those governments which introduced some limitations, predominantly of citizenship, sometimes also of residence. Also here an answer to the question who is entitled is extremely difficult, because of the great displacement of people and the changes of state borders.

According to the German regulation, all owners who were illegally deprived of their property or heirs of these owners shall regain it, regardless of citizenship or the place of residence, unless they were already compensated. According to the Hungarian solution, everybody was deprived of something during communism, not only the owners of property, so the owners were granted only a small, indeed a symbolic compensation for the lost property in the form of bonds which could be turned into shares of privatized companies. This solution caused great controversy and protest among the persons who were also victims of the Holocaust, and they were advised to refuse compensation.

In the Czech Republic, apart from the already mentioned questions which concern big companies and property which belongs to churches, citizenship represented a very controversial issue. In the first restitution law, non-citizens were excluded from restitution. After the decision of the U.N. Human Rights Commission,[15] and due to the verdict of the Constitutional Court, displaced Germans, that is, Germans who had to leave Czechoslovakia after 1945 (collectively defined as "traitors to the Czechoslovak nation") as a result of the so-called Beneš Decree, are excluded from restitution, but not persons who actually do not possess Czech citizenship.

In Poland, according to the current law, that is, the administrative procedural law, all former owners from whom property was taken illegally, that is, if expropriation violated the law issued after 1944, are entitled to restitution. Polish administrative procedural law foresees no exceptions related to any general criteria, that is, criteria of citizenship or the place of residence. However, because of the recognition of the nationalization laws introduced after 1944, the current law excludes from restitution owners of big company and land estates, and all those owners who lost their property in a legal way, that is, in a way set up by standards of the first communist decrees and statutes on nationalization of companies and other regulations conforming to these statutes. In light of the Polish law, the full restitution in nature shall be granted if the nationalization or expropriation consisted of a "shocking breach of law." The question of displaced Germans who collaborated with Nazi Germany and signed the *Volksliste* is in Poland considered to be fully and sufficiently regulated in the Potsdam Treaty. In contrast to the binding law, nearly all proposals for the comprehensive regulation of restitution presented to the Polish Parliament, including the last proposal of 2001 vetoed by the president, had foreseen exclusion of non-citizens, and the last proposal also the retroactive exclusion of persons who are not residents of Poland for over five years.

Finally, there is the question concerning the form of restitution, that is, a question whether the property shall be given in nature, or whether the loss of it shall be somehow compensated. That question regards not only the form, but in fact is closely related to the great tasks of economic reforms with which the new governments are faced. Generally it was argued that it would be feasible to replace restitution in nature by financial compensation if the priority was given to economic reforms. However, the new governments are too poor, and the state of nationalized property is often very bad, so this *prima facie* easy dilemma presents another issue that is not at all easy. There are also other important, constitutional and in a deeper sense pragmatic approaches to this question regarding the form of restitution.

The German approach to restitution *vis-à-vis* the reform of the East German economy was based on the assumption, often stressed by German politicians and lawyers, that in order to make the reform successful one should create trust in the prospective investors, that is, give a clear sign that property rights are fully protected. Above all, however, in the united Germany one should protect the constitution in order to create a democratic, unified society from the divided two: West and East German. Therefore, in Germany from the very beginning of the unification process, that is, from the Unification Act of 1990, the priority of restitution before privatization was set, next to the priority of restitution in nature before compensation, unless the first was not possible, that is, unless there was an other *bona fide* right to the property (that is, roughly, a right of a buyer who bought the property from the state, before the unification).

Generally, this model was followed by other postcommunist countries, with some exceptions. In Hungary, as previously mentioned, all owners were symbolically compensated and the restitution policy was closely subordinated to privatization. In Poland there are no clear guidelines, and much depends on the policies of the national and local governments. In light of the binding law, the owners shall be compensated in nature. Considering the impossibility of such compensation in many cases, notably when the property lies behind the river Bug, or when there are other *bona fide* owners, the government tries to find some other forms of compensation. However, implementation of these solutions (for instance, in the form of preemption rights to assets being sold by the government) depends on the actual government policy and also on the policies implemented by local governments. The restitution policies are also impeded by the close links of restitution with privatization, what is reflected in the very concept of reprivatization. As we see, even formal conditions promised by the constitutional provisions which relate to the rule of law vary greatly with respect to all dimensions of restitution: time limits, recognition of communist law, entitled subjects, the restitution form.

IMPLEMENTATION OF THE RULE OF LAW IN THE CASE OF RESTITUTION

It is obvious, at least for a sociologist of law, that one cannot reduce the concept of the rule of law to its formal, statutory characteristics. The rule of law is the rule of the actually applied law, it is closely related, in fact it consists in, actual implementation and in law enforcement. This recently was strongly emphasized by the European Court of Human Rights in Strasburg (in verdicts made with regard to several petitions of Polish citizens who accused Polish courts of procedural delays).

Evaluated from this perspective of applied law and of law enforcement, the actual restitution policies in East Central Europe are even more differentiated and confusing for their participants than the actual statutory regulations. From hearings of witnesses and involved parties before the U.S. Congress Commission, one learns that even in cases in which—according to the verdicts issued by the courts of law—property should be given back to its owners, it is still occupied by the local governments, other authorities, and even sometimes sold to other parties.[16] Those accusations concern the Lithuanian, Estonian, and Latvian cases, regardless of the comprehensive, indeed model, statutory regulations adopted in these countries. In Hungary the unique and quite ingenious regulation is contested by Jewish owners, who protest the small amounts of compensation for their losses, greater than the losses of other Hungarian citizens, not to mention the disappointment on the part of other owners and their successors who were compensated symbolically, that is, received bonds which presented a symbolic amount of money. In Poland—because of the lack of a comprehensive regulation—one can speak more particularly about different and competing concepts of the rule of law. These various concepts are promoted by various institutions involved in reprivatization and privatization. Policies implemented by the government, but especially by local governments, are often based on the full recognition of the communist nationalizations, and priority of economic reform and concerns with profits from privatization of state-owned assets. Different policies are supported by the Spokesman for Civil Rights, in whose petitions the protection of human rights is also emphasized as an important factor for the establishment of the rule of law. Policies represented in the verdicts of the highest courts (the Administrative Supreme Court, the Supreme Court of Poland, and the Constitutional Tribunal) are based on the formal concept of the rule of law, that is, on the recognition of the nationalization laws and decrees. But they are also quite strongly influenced by the Spokesman for Civil Rights and currently also by international covenants. The Parliament plays the role of a most obstinate brake upon attempts to regulate restitution comprehensively.

The actual success of the plaintiffs in restitution cases, according to their evaluation, rests very deeply on their good connections with the governmental agencies responsible for the restitution policies on the one hand, and on the expertise of an honest lawyer on the other. The failures are, if one summarizes very roughly the findings of the research, caused either by other important actors and interests, public and private, or by mere corruption. Both observations do not regard such situations in which the governments are interested in getting rid of property because it is ruined and they lack resources to restore it.[17]

All those differentiated approaches to restitution result from the seemingly impossible task of reconciling rule of law requirements, the great economic tasks faced by the new governments and the need to deal with the complexity of restitution (Skąpska 2000). If the comprehensive regulation proves to be too difficult and if it is so politically contested, as in Poland, or if it is not enforced, or if it represents only an economically "symbolic" solution, arguments appear that maybe it would be better to solve the restitution claims on a pragmatic case-by-case basis, within a framework created by general regulations, that is, general clauses, and with some discretion granted to the law-applying officials who could respond to the existing dilemmas in a given case and consider all relevant factors.[18] It would mean developing some form of "responsive law" as a most adequate form of law at the time of accelerated social change.

This approach promoted and discussed during the research with the governmental officials responsible for decision-making in restitution cases in Poland proved to be very difficult to implement. Indeed, the findings of the empirical research indicate that case-by-case decision-making led to further deterioration of the rule of law, and further social disappointments. It is a fairly trivial observation that responsive law, and all forms of reconciliation of conflicting priorities by discretionary decision-making, require some strong background and resolve to protect individual and collective rights on the part of officials, or some important other assets on the part of former owners seeking "justice," for instance negotiating skills. When this resolve is lacking, and when temptations to break, bend, or circumvent the law are too strong (and they are very strong if one considers the multi-million dollar value of properties in dispute), not the rights of property owners, but vested interests start to play a considerable role in restitution proceedings, that is, interests of those who profit by the lack of general and comprehensive restitution policies based on clear criteria.

APPROACHES TO THE PAST AS STIMULI
TO RESTITUTION

Restitution policies indicate that even if the countries in the region began transformation with fairly similar opening balance sheets, their approaches to the past as well as institutions shaping the future, that is, privatization policies, differ considerably. To elucidate these differences, three factors which contribute to the righting wrongs of the past, internal and external, apart from pragmatic economic reform oriented considerations, will be outlined here. With respect to all three factors, the memories of the past play an important part as stimuli for actions and as a context in which regulations of restitution are formed, and indeed, the rule of law principle takes a meaningful shape.

As it has been stressed above, Germany presents a unique model of restitution regulation and policy. In light of empirical findings, there the efforts to get rid of the burden of the past are so great that even such cases which could awaken some doubts (suggesting that maybe the property was sold for a fair price), are not even tackled or considered by officials responsible for decision-making. With respect to the German case, one sees the great role of the state in formation of public memories, supporting public discourses about the past, and in taking off the burden of shame from the society by means of effective, unquestionable and comprehensive restitution policy.

The past is a serious determinant in individual cases in other countries of the region and decides on efforts undertaken by individuals, collectivities, and institutions to claim the property, to introduce new laws, or to amend old ones. The common past of whole social categories deprived of their property is instrumental for the formation of civil society organizations, which push for restitution from below and have had some success.[19]

The past also motivates individuals and associations who send complaints to international or supranational law-applying institutions. This external, inter-, or supranational factor plays an even greater role in East Central Europe, as indicated by the verdicts of the European Court of Human Rights on the rule of law concept, the decision of the Human Rights Committee on the exclusion of non-citizens in the Czech restitution law, and the proceedings against the Polish government mentioned above. In light of that, to seriously implement the rule of law principle, governments should seriously consider in their policies not only their internal situation, but also the impact of external factors, and external verdicts in cases initiated by individual citizens or associations. In all of these cases, but especially those which are raised against governments, the factor of the past, and of memories of the past, is used by lawyers in order to justify the cases.

"ALIENATING FORMAL JUSTICE" OF THE ONGOING RESTITUTION, OR A NEW CONCEPT OF THE RULE OF LAW AFTER COMMUNISM? CONCLUDING REMARKS

Notwithstanding some successes, for many of the victims of the former expropriation, the ongoing restitution presents a form of "alienating justice." The idea of alienating justice was present also in debates among some others interested, that is, those who were "touched" by restitution as for instance tenants who had to leave their cheap apartments or to consider the growing rents. The concept of alienating justice is borrowed from the new system analyses of Gunther Teubner (Teubner 2001). However, in this paper this concept is applied also in a meaning closer to the practical problems with which the restitution efforts in East Central Europe are faced.

According to the original idea of Teubner, the concept of the alienating justice of a legal system refers to "conflict alienation" as an alleged property of law. It consists in the inevitable incongruence of social conflicts and law, when the internally developed legal rules and doctrines are exposed to external, that is, social constraints. In light of such a conceptualization, the law could never solve social conflicts, because it subordinates them to its own formal requirements and in this way deprives conflicts of their important social qualities, indeed of all their social, moral, cultural, ideological, but also economic characteristics. The law is here presented as a subtle *instrumentarium*, a machinery of dealing with legal questions in its own way, in a nearly total autonomy of law from the society in which the law operates. As such, the machinery transforms conflicts into disputes, and then regulates these disputes according to its internal, formal rules (one of them being the rule of internal coherence). The concept of alienating justice has some relevance where the idea of the rule of law is reduced to "legalism" or *Rechtsstaatlichkeit*, that is, where the state law is not questioned, and the duty of lawyers consists in the defense of legal coherence and autonomy, regardless of moral, social, and political considerations. If applied to the existing empirical situations, such issues as collective and individual memories, the traumatic individual recollections of the past, the trust in law and the state, but also rights as some sort of "higher law," have no legal relevance at all.

The concept of "alienating justice," but first and foremost the concept of the *Rechtsstaat* or legalism has relevance where there is some continuation of law, that is, where the legal machinery had time to grow and produce internal rules of self-reproduction and limitation of external influences, that is, internal rules which could protect legal autonomy.

"Alienating justice," that is, the concept of the purely formalistic rule of autonomous law cannot be applied, where the regulations are clearly subordinated to some criteria 'higher' than law, that is, protection of human rights; in this respect, the rights of property owners. Hence, the German restitution and its application clearly presents a test to the "alienating justice" proposition at least in respect to owners. If one considers the arguments of the opponents of the German comprehensive approach, however, then the idea of justice becomes questionable. According to them, not a "higher law" and rights, but the law imposed "from above" by the winners, that is, West Germans, the vested interests of owners, and the economic considerations of West Germans decided on the restitution (Offe 1994).

Quite unexpectedly, the alienating justice idea and the formal concept of *Rechtsstaat* finds some empirical illustration where concerns with the stability and autonomy of law resulted in very slow changes of the inherited communist law, and law's continuity was not put into question. With regard to such issues, empirical researches give a lot of evidence of clashes between expectations of persons who were expropriated of their property, and the binding law which offered no chances for a just solution subordinated to some "higher" principles than the formal, written law. There are examples of owners who were expropriated of their property for instance by the Nazi occupants and, as was mentioned, those expropriations were legalized afterwards because they were compatible with the existing law (that is, if the property was taken for public use). There are examples of abandoned property with no consideration of the fact that owners were simply afraid to come back having in mind the severe persecutions of others who did. There are examples of owners who had to leave their houses because they were located within an estate subjected to land reform, whereas their neighbors, whose houses were located outside it, could either retain them, or regain their property now. All such persons and other owners express a deep criticism of law. They cannot understand why some former owners can regain their property, whereas others—in empirically, but not formally, similar situations—cannot. On the other hand, the law is subjected to manipulations and one looks for some tricks in order to produce evidence that the property was nationalized with a shocking breach of law (for instance to produce evidence that the company had only forty-nine and not fifty employees working during one shift, therefore should not be subjected to nationalization). This is but one example of empirical situations in which gains of some mean losses to others due to the written law, and not a principle to protect rights.

It could, however, be plausibly denied that preservation of the old, or the very slow changes of the old law not only produces uncertainties in novel situations, but above all disguises some vested interests of those who were profiting by it: the beneficiaries of expropriations or of the lack of comprehensive restitution. The adherence to a formal legalism so understood would present only a mere facade for the actual big interests at stake: of the state, of the local governments, of the institutions and agencies which manage the state property, of those who profit from cheap housing, or of those who are intelligent enough to seek loopholes in the existing law to their own advantage, or smart enough to take advantage of the considerable discretion of officials responsible for restitution. This has been substantially corroborated by empirical findings. Here, the "alienating justice" leads to "alienating injustice," and to the growing distrust of new governments and new constitutions, as simply another edifice of purely symbolic, declarative legalism.

The feelings of "alienating justice" are even deeper here, where the law promises more than it could fulfill, that is, it promises full restitution, but in reality does not enforce it either because the resources are too small, or the law enforcement agencies are weak (which is a direct consequence of the small resources), or because there are vested interests at stake, and state agencies are corrupted enough to give them a priority, notwithstanding the binding law, constitutional regulations, and international covenants.

However, one may plausibly look for the solution to an initial question mentioned earlier, which to a great degree contributes to all others and which gives some substance to the idea of 'alienating justice', that is, incompatibility of the promise to protect the rule of law and rights, and the resources to fulfill this promise.

If one considers the restitution and protection of property rights, one should change the meaning of the rule of law, first and foremost by not debating property rights in purely economic terms. In a complex and indeed difficult process of restitution of property and compensation of victims of nationalization or confiscation, it would be important to reconsider other than economic aspects of property rights, and to define them not merely as commodities. In fact, the opinions of the former owners stressed many such non-economic aspects of property rights and property, aspects important for identities, culturally bounded, even "sacred." It seems also plausible to suggest the redefinition of the rule of law in this situation, in which the full financial compensation or the full restitution of property in nature—which itself could be a blessing in disguise—is no longer possible.

Perhaps a good direction was indicated by the rabbi of Kraków, cited earlier. In an interview with the Polish daily *Gazeta Wyborcza*, he pleaded for important symbolic compensation and, with regard to communal buildings previously owned by the Jewish community in Kraków, for a sign that they belonged to the great Jewish inheritance, in the form of an inscription on the buildings that they belonged to Jews as hospitals, schools, libraries, and orphanages in order to commemorate the long lasting, not only physical, but also cultural, presence of Jews in Poland. Certainly, such an approach seems to be appropriate only in cases in which full restitution is not possible or could prove too difficult to implement. Another approach was taken by the Polish landowners who, during their meeting in Warsaw in February 2001, after long and heated discussion, resigned from claims for full compensation and approved a partial compensation for their losses after considering the public good, that is, the state of the economy in Poland.

As a concluding remark of this paper, let me cite Jeremy Waldron and repeat that past events have moral (and constitutional—G.S.) content for the present, to the extent that the present was shaped by this past (Waldron 1992: 7). To this one can add that this morally important past could give the present an innovative impulse.

This paper is based on results of two research projects. The first, "Property Restitution in the Post-1989 Transformation Process in Germany and Poland," was carried out between 1999–2001. The project was sponsored by Volkswagen-Stiftung. The principal investigators were Mark Blacksell from the University of Plymouth, Hartmut Haeussermann from the Humboldt University, Berlin, and Grażyna Skąpska, Jagiellonian University, Kraków. Karl-Martin Born from the University of Plymouth, Birgit Glock, and Carsten Keller from the Humboldt University, Grzegorz Bryda and Jarosław Kadyło from the Jagiellonian University also participated in the project. The aim of the project was to assess the nature and scale of property restitution, to compare the policies and agendas for property restitution, and to evaluate the extent to which restitution policies in Germany and Poland contributed to consensus on justice.

The second research project was carried out between 1992–1995. The project was devoted to the formation and implementation of totalitarian law in East Central Europe (Eastern Germany, Poland, Czechoslovakia, Hungary). The project was coordinated by the Max Planck Institute for the European Legal History in Frankfurt, and sponsored by the German Research Council and the European Union.

I am also presenting here some data gathered during my stay at the American Bar Foundation, within a framework of a project on restitution and citizenship. It was possible for me to gather these data thanks to the generous sponsorship and encouragement of colleagues in the American Bar Foundation, and of the Polish Consulate in Chicago.

NOTES

1 Jews and Germans, ubiquitously present throughout East Central Europe before the World War II, were no longer there or were radically reduced in numbers in the postwar era. They were an urban population *par excellence*. An important nucleus of the middle class was removed from the region as a consequence of their disappearance. Between 1939 and 1943, more than thirty million Europeans were transplanted, deported or dispersed, and from 1943 through 1948 another 20 million were "on the move." In place of 2.5 million expelled Sudeten Germans, 1.8 million Czechs and Slovaks were transferred into the area. In Poland, 4 million settlers were sent to the "Regained Territories" taken from Germany. In Germany, a steady westward flow of refugees from the Soviet zone took place (see Gross 1991: xvii, xix).

2 Ratified international treaties and covenants not only make up a part of internal law in the European continental constitutional orders. The high position of ratified treaties and covenants is guaranteed by constitutional provisions, according to which all internal laws must be accommodated to the contents of ratified treaties and covenants.

3 See Commission on Security and Cooperation in Europe, Testimony from the Hearing on "The Long Road Home: Struggling for Property Rights in Post-Communist Europe (http://www.house.gov/csce). This Testimony and the U.N. Human Rights Committee decisions are of interest to the U.S. House of Representatives, as well as American Senate resolutions (http://www.restitution.org/us/scr73.960927.htm).

4 On moral impulse, see Bauman 1993: 15.

5 This part of my paper is mainly based on the research on implementation of totalitarian law (Skąpska 1998).

6 In Poland, the German expropriations were legalized mostly, but not uniquely, in those cases in which the property was taken from its owner for public use. Indeed, in the view of historians, the etatization of the economy and nationalization of private property and central planning were initiated by German occupants on a considerable scale.

These expropriations were later legalized, and their public use meant often that attractive buildings were turned to holiday resorts for party apparatus or communist political police, or simply given for usage to the high-rank party members.

7 The expropriations in Germany also took place as late as after 1984, on the basis of the law on provision of land for prefabricated housing buildings, and in Poland after 1962 on the basis of the regulations on state investment and renovation worth amounts greater than 50% of property value, and after 1984 after the new law on land surveying and urban planning.

8 Moreover, during the wartime, all countries of East Central Europe, except Yugoslavia, experienced a shift from being multiethnic to becoming nationally fairly homogeneous. That shift was completed (with the exceptions of Slovakia and Romania) during the first years of Stalinism.

9 The Lemkos lived in South East Poland as a Polish-speaking minority of the predominantly Greek Orthodox denomination. After World War II, the Lemkos were accused of collaboration with the anti-communist Ukrainian Liberation Army. As a result of these accusations—which were vehemently denied by the Lemkos—, their property, individual and collective, was confiscated in the years 1948–1949 due to the laws of 1947. Their churches were given to the Catholic Church. Together with the Ukrainians, they were deported to the western part of Poland where they were settled in various locations, under the close supervision of the political police. This policy—and it is argued that the policy itself resulted from the incomplete, earlier efforts to deport all Ukrainians to the Soviet Ukraine—was aimed at the destruction of the collective identity of the Lemkos. They were defined as a Ukrainian minority, which they were not, and they were deprived of material indicators of their own identity as an ethnic group: churches and forests.

   Another example is the Silesians—a loosely defined ethnic minority that lives in the southwest of Poland. The Silesians were collectively accused of collaboration with Nazi Germany. In fact many of them demonstrated a heroic resistance to cultural germanization and Nazi occupation. After 1945, the Silesians were subjected to harsh persecutions undertaken by the Polish authorities and by private people: the new settlers. The latter simply were given a free hand to loot Silesian property.

10 See the interview in *Gazeta Wyborcza*, 25 August 1999.

11 Nazi expropriations in the occupied territories during World War II varied with respect to the status of territories, that is, whether they were annexed and incorporated into the Reich, or occupied under German administration. In the first case, the large industrial, commercial property and agricultural land was nationalized (that is, put in the trust of the German *Treuhandstelle*), then the medium-sized and small properties (shops, hotels, cafes) were confiscated together with private houses, and even with personal property of persons expelled from the annexed territories. In the territories under German administration, the property, if not confiscated, was simply looted by the German army and officials (see Lucas 1986: 27–33).

12 During our research, property was quite often referred to as "sacred": the Lemkos in the focus group discussion agreed that forests are sacred, since "they were given to the Lemkos by God": Silesians regarded tools as sacred, because they are used for work. Generally private owners mentioned the "sacred law of property," and Polish peasants have long treated their farmland and family farms as "sacred."

13 Motives of racial cleansing were strongly stressed in two cases against Polish government pending in the United States: in the case of Haven vs. the Republic of Poland, in Chicago (The United States District Court for the Northern District of Illinois, and

the United States Court of Appeal for the Seventh Circuit), and in the case of Gorb vs. the Republic of Poland (The United States District Court, Eastern District of New York).

14 This section is based on the following works: Appel 1995; Bender and Falk 1998; Brunner 1998; Eizenstat 1997; Koźmiński 1997; Mielke 1994; Pogany 1997; Schwartz 1974.

15 See the already cited Adam vs. the Czech Republic, Human Rights Committee, U.N. Doc. CCPR/C/57/D/586/1994 (1996).

16 According to the hearings of the Commission on Security and Cooperation in Europe, Testimony from the Hearing on "The Long Road Home: Struggling for Property Rights in Post-Communist Europe" (http://www.house.gov/csce), the governments are consciously limiting restitution independently of adoption of comprehensive restitution laws. Such cases were reported with regard to Lithuania and Slovenia. Such policies are also characteristic of Poland, especially with regard to compensation for the property left behind the eastern Polish border. A grand-scale example is that of 50 apartment houses in Kraków, which were allegedly given back to their former owners, but as it became clear, were sold to other persons on the basis of falsified documents and false witnesses, with no efforts on the part of officials to investigate documents or witnesses.

17 In such cases, as in the case of the Polish spa Szczawnica, the municipal government handed over the whole small city to the former owners. See the report on this case in the Polish newspaper *Rzeczpospolita*, 17 September 2001.

18 Beneficiaries of the lack of comprehensive restitution in Poland are local governments, various state agencies who are trustees of property, and persons who have connections and can buy the property very cheaply from the local governments or the agencies mentioned. Such is a case of an ethnic Polish American citizen, whom the local government proposed should buy his property back, and after he refused, sold the property for half of the formerly proposed price to a local banker.

19 Such is the case of Lemkos, or persons who left their property behind the river Bug. There are also civic society organizations which represent interests of landowners, apartment house owners, and tenants.

BIBLIOGRAPHY

Appel, Hilary. "Justice and the Reformation of Property Rights in the Czech Republic." *East European Politics and Society* 9, no. 1 (1995): 22–40.

Bauman, Zygmunt. *Post-modern Ethics*. Oxford: Clarendon Press, 1993.

Bender, Gerd and Ulrich Falk, eds. *Recht im Sozialismus. Band I: Enteignung* [Law in socialism. Vol. I: Expropriation]. Frankfurt: Vittorio Klostermann Verlag, 1998.

Boekner, Frank and Claus Offe. "Die moralische Rechtfertigung der Restitution des Eigentums: Ueberlegungen zur einigen normativen Problemen der Privatisierung in postkommunistischen Oekonomien." [Moral justification of property restitution: Considerations of some normative problems of privatization in postcommunist economies.] *Leviathan: Zeitschrift für Sozialwissenschaft* H, no. 3 (1994): 313–75.

Brunner, Georg. "Verfassungsrechtlicher Eigentumsschutz und Restitution enteigneten Vermoegens in Osteuropa" [Constitutional protection of property and restitution of expropriated property in Eastern Europe] in *Wandel der Eigentumsordnung in Mittel- und Osteuropa* [Change of property order in Central and Eastern Europe], eds. Manssen Georg and Bernd Banaszak (Berlin: Spitz, 1998), pp. 43–67.

Eizenstat, Stuart. "Restitution of Communal and Private Property in Central and Eastern Europe." *Eastern European Constitutional Review* 2, no. 3 (1997): 50–52.

Gross, Jan T. "Foreword" in *The Establishment of Communist Rule in Poland*, ed. Kersten, Krystyna (Berkeley: University of California Press, 1991), pp. iv–xv.

Koźmiński, Andrzej. "Restitution of Private Property: Re-privatization in Central and Eastern Europe." *Communist and Postcommunist Studies* 30 (1997): 95–106.

Lukas, Richard. *Forgotten Holocaust.* New York: Hippocrene Books, 1986.

Mielke, Kai. "Der vermoegensrechtliche Restitutionsgrundsatz." [Principle of restitution in the perspective of property law.] *Kritische Justiz* 27 (1994): 200–13.

Offe, Claus. *Der Tunnel am Ende des Lichts* [The channel at the end of light]. Frankfurt: Suhrkamp, 1994.

Paczolay, Peter. "Traditional Elements in the Constitutions of Central and Eastern European Democracies" in *The Rule of Law after Communism*, eds. Krygier, Martin and Adam Czarnota (Ashgate: Dartmouth, 1999), pp. 109–30.

Pogany, Istvan. *Righting Wrongs in Eastern Europe.* Manchester: Manchester University Press, 1997.

Schwartz, Walter. *Rueckerstattung nach den Gesetzen der Aliierten Maechte. Die Wiedergutmachungnationalsozialistichen Unrechts durch die Bundesrepublik Deutschland* [Restitution in light of the Allied Powers laws. Reparations of nationalsocialist lawlessness by the Federal Republic of Germany]. München: C. H. Beck, 1974.

Skąpska, Grażyna. "From Rights to Myths" in *Western Rights? Post-Communist Application*, ed. Sajó, András (The Hague, London, and Boston: Kluwer, 1996), pp. 81–100.

——. "Eigentum und Staatsanwaltschaft in der Volksrepublik Polen. War Totalitarismus ein gesteuerter Rechtsnihilismus?" [Property and State Prosecutor's Office in the Peoples' Republic of Poland. Was totalitarianism a steered legal nihilism?] in *Recht im Sozialismus. Band I: Enteignung* [Law in socialism. Vol. I: Expropriation], eds. Bender, Gerd and Ulrich Falk (Frankfurt: Vittorio Klostermann Verlag, 1998), pp. 79–98.

——. "Regulation of Restitution as a Part of Polish Transformation." *Working Paper Nr. 3.* Plymouth: Media Services, 2000.

Teubner, Gunther. "Sprawiedliwość alienująca. O dodatkowej wartości dwunastego wielbłąda" (Alienating justice and the added value of the twelfth camel). *Ius and Lex* 1 (2002): 107–32.

Waldron, Jeremy. "Superseding Historic Injustice." *Ethics* 103 (1992): 4–28.

Constitutional Courts and
the Past in Democratic Transition

Renata Uitz

> *"... there is a degree of sleeplessness, of rumina-*
> *tion, of the historical sense which is harmful and*
> *ultimately fatal to the living thing, whether this*
> *living thing be a man or a people or a culture."*
>   Friedrich Nietzsche[1]

While democratic transition is about institution-building for a better future,
the political and intellectual context of this institution-building is heavy with
attempts to handle the past. Handling the past has various meanings in the
context of democratic transition, some of which might reflect or result in
conflicting agendas. Among other things, handling the past might mean coming to terms with the past, doing justice about past injustices and, also, transforming inherited societal and institutional structures. Measures may be designed to achieve one or more of these objectives. Also, some measures might
appear more symbolic than others: opening up archives of secret services is
as much part of the process of handling the past as reforming health-care or
broadcasting systems. The relationship of measures with the past is context-
dependent and might not be apparent at the outset. For instance, taking care
of flood victims appears to be an issue that has little to do with handling the
past. Taking care of flood victims becomes burdened by the past if settlements flushed by the flood were created upon the housing policies of the previous non-democratic regime.[2]

In many democratic transitions, constitutional review fora had a significant
role in shaping legislative measures which were aimed at handling the past
for the purposes of democratic transition. The position of judicial review fora
is especially interesting: in emerging democracies, constitutional courts were
brought along with other measures of democratic institution-building and, at
the same time, the task of the newly created constitutional courts was to
enforce constitutionalism and the rule of law. Newly enacted legislative measures designed for handling the past directly (for example, retroactive justice
laws, lustration, restitution, and compensation legislation), however, are at
least dubious under the standards of non-transitional constitutionalism.[3]

The South African constitution do expressly call for measures for settling
accounts with the past. Thus, when reviewing legislation foreseen by the constitutions, the South African Constitutional Court had a sound textual and normative constitutional basis to act upon. On the other hand, while the preamble

of the Hungarian Constitution expressly declares it to be the charter of democratic transition, the constitution itself does not contain any specific provisions on orchestrating such transition. While the South African and the Hungarian constitutions represent two extremes of constitutionalizing transition, the jurisprudence of the two constitutional courts has one common feature dominating decisions concerning the constitutionality of legislation directed at handling the past. Interestingly enough, neither the South African nor the Hungarian Constitutional Court examined the relevant past tackled by the legislation in detail.[4] The paper does not attempt to provide a comprehensive account of transitional justice decisions in these jurisdictions; rather, it concentrates on a few, delicate aspects of these judgments, while being aware that numerous significant considerations are not even mentioned in the following pages. It is still believed that such an approach might help us explore whether an inquiry into the relevant past matters for the purposes of the constitutional review of transitional justice legislation at all; or, rather, if ignorance is becoming not a shield but a sword in the hands of constitutional justices.

SOUTH AFRICA: THE FORCE OF A CONSTITUTIONAL MANDATE

Amnesty: the constitutional mandate reaffirmed
Constitutions and other founding instruments do often refer to their past and to the history of their making in express terms.[5] The rebellious colonies provided the Crown with an elaborate description of events and actions which made them part: because the "[h]istory of the present King of Great Britain is a History of repeated Injuries and Usurpations" in the United States Declaration of Independence, 1776.

Many contemporary constitutions tend to follow a similar approach. Some refer to past ordeals in general terms, while others mention or elaborate on past days of glory and trial.[6] Constitutions of newly independent countries tend to mention previous periods of independence and flourishing, as if to demonstrate their worthiness for a better future.[7] Some documents, like the Argentinean, do not go beyond mentioning posterity, or the common destiny of the peoples of the nation, as in the case of Kazakhstan. Others offer more detailed accounts of the past and suggest that the past may be controlling the future of the nation.[8] While it might be far-fetched to argue that these texts are the bearers of a strong consequentialist line of argument, it is fair to say that they at least represent a claim for constitutional continuity, if not as strong and explicit as the preamble of the 1958 French constitution.[9]

Although constitutions fairly frequently contain references to the past or to the future in general terms, most of these passages remain unnoticed in constitutional adjudication. This indifference might be attributable to the language of these opening declarations: after all, a historical exposition referring to the past has little normative character, even if contained in a constitution.[10] The lengthy epilogue (or postamble) of the South African interim constitution entitled "National Unity and Reconciliation" elaborates on the need to come to terms with the past for building a better future and mentions amnesty in express terms.[11] In the AZAPO case,[12] the South African Constitutional Court had to decide about the constitutionality of the amnesty legislation enacted upon the constitutional authorization of the epilogue.[13] In the case, the Constitutional Court was in the position to review legal measures designed to cope with a shameful and repressive past despised by the present regime, and to draw (normative) consequences from the past for the purposes of the future.

Petitioners in the AZAPO case were families of some of apartheid's most-known victims, who wanted to prevent granting amnesty to the murderers (Webb 1998: 270). They challenged numerous provisions of the Promotion of National Unity and Reconciliation Act of 1995. The Act granted amnesty for acts committed with a political objective—as defined in s.20(3) of the Act—during the apartheid regime, in exchange for full disclosure of all relevant facts pertaining to the offence.[14] The amnesty procedure was to be administered by the Committee on Amnesty, one of the three committees of the Truth and Reconciliation Commission. The Committee on Amnesty is not a court of law, but an independent tribunal composed of five members and its chairperson shall be a judge.[15] In Kader Asmal's words the "objective of this Act was to deepen our country's factual and interpretative grasp of its terrible past, going back to 1960" (Asmal 2000).

First, petitioners argued that granting amnesty violates the victims' right of access to judicial process (s.22, interim constitution). The Constitutional Court noted the right of access to judicial process was subject to the general limitation clause—s.33(2) of the interim constitution (para 10). Furthermore, since the epilogue contains an express authorization for amnesty legislation, amnesty constitutes a constitutionally mandated limitation on the right to access to justice (para 11). It was in this respect that the Constitutional Court established that the epilogue was of no lesser status than any other provision of the interim constitution, and, that the government indeed was under a constitutional obligation to enact amnesty legislation (para 14).

It is important to note that the Constitutional Court understood the petitioners' challenge as an issue of rights limitation, and not as a matter of contradiction (collision) within the text of the constitution. In this respect it is interesting to draw a comparison with the Hungarian Constitutional Court's approach, in its decision to abolish capital punishment.[16] In this case, the Hungarian court faced a collision between two constitutional provisions. Article 8(2), the general limitation clause of the Hungarian constitution prohibits any limitation on constitutional rights which encroach upon the "essential content" of the right.[17] On the other hand, Article 54(1) of the Hungarian constitution did not foreclose all deprivations of the right to life, only the instances of arbitrary deprivation were prohibited. The Hungarian Constitutional Court found that these two provisions of the Hungarian Constitution were in conflict and said that it was the duty of the constitution maker (the legislature in the Hungarian case) to resolve this tension. Nonetheless, the Constitutional Court found that all deprivations of life amount to arbitrary deprivation, therefore any deprivation of life constitutes an infringement of the essential content of the right to life and is thus unconstitutional. Justice Schmidt filed a dissenting opinion arguing that it was not for the Constitutional Court to resolve the inconsistencies of the constitutional text.[18]

As János Kis pointed out, it is possible to interpret both provisions of the Hungarian constitution in a consistent manner, since a narrow reading of the two conflicting constitutional provisions would not result in a collision (Kis 2000: 58). Such a reading, however, does not preclude the constitutionality of capital punishment. In the case, the Hungarian Constitutional Court found it appropriate to resolve a collision within the constitutional text. The point made by Kis, however, suggests that in the capital punishment decision the Hungarian Constitutional Court resolved a constitutional collision generated by a reading attributed to constitutional provisions by the court itself. In the Hungarian case, this strategy (that is, framing and resolving a constitutional collision) was essential for creating a context in which the Constitutional Court was in the position to abolish capital punishment.

As suggested by the petitioners, a similar opportunity was also traceable in the text of the South African interim constitution. The South African Constitutional Court, however, avoided such a path. Instead, the South African court reaffirmed the status of the epilogue and, thus, the constitutional prescription to pass amnesty legislation. At the same time, this approach shifted the center of the South African court's analysis from the terrain of "rights review" to testing whether amnesty rules were in conformity with the constitutional mandate in the epilogue of the interim constitution. This approach presents many challenges to a constitutional review forum. In a primary, and rather technical sense, the South African Constitutional Court was to determine the standards applicable to testing the constitutionality of the amnesty provisions. An analysis of this aspect of the case reveals the court's understanding of the relevance of handling past injustice in democratic transition, and the means found to be appropriate in performing this task. In a more general sense, the decision provides an opportunity to examine the operation of a constitutional review forum in a highly exposed and politically charged setting in handling a case under an explicit but general constitutional provision.

The scope of amnesty: hidden premises?
In the AZAPO case, the petitioners' most serious challenge concerned not amnesty legislation *per se*, but the scope of amnesty granted by the act.[19] Petitioners argued that although amnesty legislation is authorized in the epilogue of the interim constitution, the amnesty provisions of the act are too "far reaching" and are beyond the scope of constitutional authorization (para 15). The epilogue, although it expressly provides for amnesty, does not describe the details of exempting offenders from the consequences of their actions. In its decision, the Constitutional Court refused to test the wisdom of the legislation, and noted that the court was only concerned about its constitutionality (paras 21 and 43).[20] When reviewing the amnesty rules, the Constitutional Court interpreted the provisions of the epilogue on amnesty in the light of the more general constitutional mandates on transition, reconciliation, and on coming to terms with the past. As broad and undetermined as these aids of interpretation might sound, they are all contained in express terms in the epilogue of the interim constitution.[21] Indeed, in its decision the Constitutional Court relied on almost all phrases of the epilogue, referring to it not only as a set of constitutional rules, but also as a repository of principles of constitutional interpretation (Davis et al. 1994: 129).[22]

In addition, the decision of the Constitutional Court rests on two implicit premises, which—although they might be connected to the words of the epilogue—are not prescribed by it. The first premise underlying the decision of the Constitutional Court is that the amnesty provision is future oriented: the point of amnesty is to pave the way for the transition to a "new future." The second premise on which the Constitutional Court relied heavily is the *quid pro quo* of full disclosure. The Constitutional Court outlined the considerations that were central to testing the constitutionality of the amnesty legislation on the basis of the language of the epilogue and these two related premises.

When testing the constitutionality of the amnesty legislation, the Constitutional Court took a purposive approach. According to the ccourt, the purpose of the amnesty legislation was to reveal the past for the purposes of a "new future" (para 21).[23] The Constitutional Court noted already in the opening remarks, that the new constitutional order was based on the premise of "a firm and generous commitment to reconciliation and national unity. It was realized that much of the unjust consequences of the past could not ever be fully reversed. It might be necessary in crucial areas to close the book on that past" (para 2). The Constitutional Court used the epilogue's metaphor of walking the "historic bridge" between past and future to describe the transition process. Amnesty was perceived as an attempt to erect this bridge (paras 18–19). Tying peaceful transition, reconciliation and amnesty in this constellation is crucial for the purposes of the decision. According to the Constitutional Court, the interim constitution is intended to bring reconciliation and transition in an effective manner (para 42). The court argued that it is impossible to build a lasting future based on retaliation and revenge, since "[f]or a successfully negotiated transition, the terms of the transition required not only the agreement of those victimized by abuse but also those threatened by the transition to a 'democratic society based on freedom and equality'" (para 19). If viewed from the perspective of the future, no matter how unjust it may be, the past is transformed into as a set of historical facts, a set that may be closed upon the completion of research into the past.[24] As Justice Didcott remarked in his concurring opinion: "Once the truth about the iniquities of the past has been established and made known, the book should be closed on them so that the catharsis thus engendered may divert the energies of the nation from a preoccupation with anguish and rancor to a future directed towards the goal which both the postscript to the Constitution and the preamble to the statute have set" (para 59).

In the AZAPO decision—unlike in other cases[25]—, the Constitutional Court did not engage in analyzing the details of the relevant past, despite the ambiguity concerning the scope of the actions covered by amnesty. It is disputed whether amnesty is limited only for those actions which constituted a crime under the law as in force during apartheid. In addition, the amnesty rules apply to acts committed by the apartheid government as well as by liberation movements, among them the ANC. John Dugard argues that this "even-handedness" was unfortunate to the extent that it created a "moral equality" of perpetrators and victims of apartheid (Dugard 1998: 295–96).[26]

Reading the decision of the Constitutional Court one may find that petitioners did not challenge these aspects of the amnesty provisions, therefore it might even have been beyond the powers of the court to address them. In defense of the Constitutional Court's approach, one may also submit that such considerations belong to the "wisdom" of the amnesty rules, a consideration that the Constitutional Court refused to review.[27] Thus, in this respect the Constitutional Court was deferential towards the legislature's choices.

It might be a question whether it is acceptable for a judicial review forum to be willfully incognizant of the past when deciding about the constitutionality of legal norms designed to institutionalize that past. Skeptics may note that the work of the TRC "involved making that knowledge officially sanctioned, part of the historic record" (Villa-Vicencio 1999–2000: 175). One may, however, argue that it was not for the Constitutional Court to analyze the amnesty legislation's appropriateness in the light of the actual events of the past, as there are no judicially enforceable standards to provide a basis for such a review. Thus, when not entering this field, the South African Constitutional Court defined an important aspect of its powers and self-perception. The justices were indeed fully aware of the details of apartheid history and the lack of constitutional and legal standards to review the appropriateness of the amnesty legislation from the perspective of that history: the court distinguished comparative sources on amnesty with reference to the uniqueness of apartheid in South Africa (para 24).[28]

While the Constitutional Court exercised self-restraint in the case with respect to the appropriateness of the amnesty legislation as far as the relationship of amnesty and the relevant past is concerned, the justices did have a clear view as to the purpose and role of amnesty legislation in the overall context of reconciliation. It is in this regard that the second premise of the Constitutional Court's argument becomes apparent. For the court, the main reason that makes amnesty legislation acceptable is that it grants amnesty for full disclosure (in particular paras 17, 20, and 32). In essence, the Constitutional Court regarded amnesty as a means of learning about the past for the purposes of reconciliation (para 36). The court's argument might be seen as a policy-cushioned position (Dugard 1998: 302; Burnham 1997: 30), or as a restatement echoing the epilogue's language contrasting "understanding" with "vengeance."

Thereupon, the court reviewed the amnesty provisions to see if amnesty was a suitable means of discovering the truth about past injustice. In its judgment, the Constitutional Court said that although granting amnesty to past offenders was discomfiting, there was no better solution in the circumstances (paras 17 and 21). The court argued that individual prosecutions would not help reveal the truth about the past. On the one hand, it would be impossible to gather sufficient evidence to conduct such a trial properly. On the other hand, the Constitutional Court argued that "truth, which the victims of repression seek so desperately to know is, in the circumstances, much more likely to be forthcoming if those responsible for such monstrous misdeeds are encouraged to disclose the whole truth with the incentive that they will not receive the punishment which they undoubtedly deserve if they do" (para 17). In relation to this premise, the court presupposed that what the victims of past repression want is the unveiling of the truth about the past (see para 17). Dugard, who is critical about the court's position, submitted that "[r]econciliation, however, does not follow automatically or even easily from knowledge. On the contrary, knowledge may produce bitterness and a desire for revenge on the part of victims, or, on the part of unknowing supporters of the previous regime, resentment that blame is attached to silent acquiescence" (Dugard 1998: 308).

Indeed, in some native African cultures, taking revenge is a must: "Only by so doing will the ancestors be appeased... Reconciliation is only possible after revenge."[29] The reconciliation process was meant to offer an alternative for coming to terms with the past, which restores the dignity of those who were deprived of their rights during apartheid (Asmal 1995: 27).

According to Dullah Omar, the Minister of Justice of the democratic government, the wounds of the people must be recognized, wounds suffered by the participants on all sides (Omar 1995). While the amnesty process was aimed at revealing the truth about the past for the purposes of reconciliation, applicants seeking amnesty are not required to apologize. "Archbishop [Desmond] Tutu, the head of the Commission, publicly announced that amnesty applicants do not need to show remorse and may even express pride in their actions" (McCarthy 1997: 248).[30] Whether reconciliation is possible without any apology or forgiveness, and whether forgiveness may be secured by legal means are questions which cannot be explored here in detail. Note, however, that a recent study suggests that "many of the presuppositions underlying the truth and reconciliation process are incompatible with the ways ordinary South Africans attribute blame, as well as the ways in which their blame judgments affect their views toward amnesty" (Gibson and Guows 1999).[31]

The main argument used by the Constitutional Court in support of amnesty as a means of achieving full disclosure is noteworthy. According to the court, the perspective of amnesty is more likely to promote the offender to reveal the full truth than the perspective of future prosecution. At this point it would still be too early to seek a comprehensive analysis of the overall effects of the amnesty process or of the appropriateness of the logic and psychology of the court. Many key players did not appear to seek amnesty, among them former apartheid presidents de Klerk and Botha. Others did not apply for amnesty in the hope of remaining unnoticed, although this way they are risking future prosecution. In general, many were against the TRC for fear of disruption of progress (Dyzenhaus 1998: 13). Thus, one may question whether the amnesty process was able to reveal the full record of the past.

In this respect, it is important to consider a further point, namely that many of the abuses revealed by the TRC process might have been known to the victims and the perpetrators. What makes the search for truth different is the distinction between private knowledge and public acknowledgement by the government. Priscilla Hayner adds an important consideration suggesting that "[o]fficial acknowledgement can be so powerful precisely because official denial has been so pervasive" (Hayner 2001: 26–27). As Alex Boraine noted, "the process will not be complemented until all South Africans who benefited from apartheid confront the past, accept the uncomfortable truth of complicity, give practical expression to remorse, and commit themselves to a way of life which accepts and offers the dignity of humanness" (Boraine 2000: 9).

What is relevant for the purposes of the present discussion is that, except for emphasizing the importance of full disclosure, the Constitutional Court did not set any conditions determining the constitutionality of amnesty. What the court suggested was that "blanket amnesty" would not satisfy the requirements of a constructive transition (para 32). Note that while full disclosure of the truth is a stringent standard, it is a requirement initially established by the legislature in the act on amnesty and not a requirement set by the court. Thus, in essence, the Constitutional Court transformed the standard established by the legislature into a condition of the constitutionality of amnesty legislation.

The justices used the premise of amnesty as a means of learning the truth about the past to support this outcome. The words of the Constitutional Court suggest that the court did not equate knowing the past with reconciliation. Instead, the court argued that uncovering the past was a necessary precondition of reconciliation: "[T]ransforming anger and grief into a mature understanding and creating the emotional and structural climate essential for the 'reconciliation and reconstruction' which informs the very difficult and sometimes painful objectives of the amnesty articulated in the epilogue" (para 17). The justices, however, did not attempt to define further conditions or preconditions in this respect.

The Constitutional Court's premise about amnesty as a means of discovery or learning is a naive or at least an idealistic one. Although the wording of the epilogue of the constitution on reconciliation and the need to understand the past is sufficiently broad, the Constitutional Court did not draw further obligations from this wording. "Amnesty for full disclosure" is certainly not mentioned in the epilogue. It must be noted, however, that when accepting this standard, the Constitutional Court certified the choice made by the legislature. Thus, when adopting this approach, the Constitutional Court did not impose new obligations on the legislature or on the Amnesty Commission. Viewed from a slightly different perspective, however, one may see that the decision of the Constitutional Court—while legitimizing the legal framework of amnesty—drove the amnesty process back to the Amnesty Commission, to the courts, and to public discourse. In this regard it is worth mentioning that while some of those applying for amnesty might have evaded prosecution, the numbers show that the vast majority of amnesty applications was rejected.[32] In case an application was rejected, the wrongdoers are facing prosecution. Also, in the procedure before the Amnesty Commission, victims had strong participatory rights, a lot more than in ordinary criminal procedures (McCarthy 1997: 188).[33]

The constitutional boundaries of reconciliation and amnesty were not set very tight in the epilogue. Nothing in the interim Constitution precluded the Constitutional Court from passing judgment about the injustices of the apartheid regime on a large scale, and the AZAPO case requesting the court to test the constitutionality of amnesty legislation presented an excellent opportunity. Nonetheless, in that case the Constitutional Court did not substitute its judgment on the past and the justices' vision of proper reconciliation and amnesty for that of the legislature. The case was decided on the basis of a constitutional provision inviting an inquiry into the past, and the facts of the case did also present an opportunity for the court to condemn the past in the name of the present or the future. Instead, the decision of the South African Constitutional Court demonstrates how a judicial review forum may refrain from passing judgment on the past even in such circumstances.

If viewed in this way, the decision of the South African Constitutional Court not only approved the legal regulation of amnesty, but also enabled the participants in the discourse to shape the reconciliation process themselves. Also, it is not only by chance that a reminder of past injustice was preserved in the preamble of the final constitution. When the inclusion of this reference was challenged, in the certification judgment the Constitutional Court emphasized that the preamble puts the need to heal past injustice in the broader context of building national unity.[34] In this regard, Nietzsche's words are all the more interesting and alarming: "To determine [the] degree and therewith the boundary at which the past has to be forgotten if it is not to become the gravedigger of the present, one would have to know exactly how great the plastic power of a man, a people, a culture is: I mean by plastic power the capacity to develop out of oneself in one's own way, to transform and incorporate into oneself what is past and foreign, to heal wounds, to replace what has been lost, to recreate broken moulds" (Nietzsche 1874: 62).

HUNGARY: A TRANSITIONAL CONSTITUTION?

The locus of transition: retroactive criminal justice cases
At this point, it is interesting to contrast the South African Constitutional Court's approach with the jurisprudence of the Hungarian Constitutional Court on measures concerning transitional justice. In Hungary, the main issues of legislative measures concerning the injustices of the pervious regimes were property restitution, lustration, and criminal prosecution for offences committed in the name of the previous regime. Being aware of the complexity of these issues, the following analysis will focus on the problems indicated in connection with the AZAPO case, concentrating on the role of the Hungarian Constitutional Court in judging the past (if at all), and the effects of the decisions of the Constitutional Court.[35]

In Hungary, the textual background for deciding the cases concerning the handling of the past was profoundly different than under the interim constitution of South Africa. In South Africa, the interim constitution contains express provisions on facing the legacy of the past when it prescribes legislation on amnesty in the epilogue. In addition, both the interim and the final constitution provide for property restitution.[36] While the Hungarian constitution "constitutionalizes" transition, it does not provide for special legislation with regard to coming to terms with the past. The strongest textual hint in this regard is contained in the preamble of the Hungarian constitution: the preamble calls for "a peaceful transition to a rule of law state based upon a multi-party system, parliamentary democracy and social market economy."[37] According to its preamble, the Hungarian constitution itself was established in the light of these aims. Still, despite a constitutionalized commitment to transition, the Hungarian constitution does not provide expressly for settling accounts with the past.

The phrasing of the preamble of the Hungarian constitution is very vague. While petitioners often referred to the preamble in cases in relation to transition to market economy, the Constitutional Court was reluctant to attribute normative force to the provisions of the preamble (Sólyom 1994: 229). Although one may note that nothing in the French constitution of 1958 suggested that its preamble contains obligations and the drafters intended the preamble not to be binding, still, the *Conseil constitutionnel* turned the preamble into a primary source of constitutional rights protection.[38] While the position of the Hungarian Constitutional Court on the status of the preamble was clarified only as late as in 1994, and the justices did refer to the preamble in the restitution cases, in its decisions the Hungarian Constitutional Court primarily relied on the specific provisions of the constitution, and not on the preamble or broader principles derived from the contextualization and interpretation of the past. Due to the nature of the claims—the legal norms tested by the Constitutional Court—, restitution cases are capable of shedding light on the role of the constitutional text and constitutional argument in a discourse haunted by the past.

A second major distinction between the South African and Hungarian jurisprudence regarding the rules on coming to terms with the past is also connected with their respective constitutional backgrounds. While the South African process is centered around the notion of reconciliation, the main concepts framing the review of transitional legislation in the jurisprudence of the Hungarian Constitutional Court are legal continuity and the rule of law (Article 2 (1), Hungarian constitution) (Paczolay 1993). The Hungarian constitution does not establish a requirement of legal continuity. It is a jurisprudential concept which was developed in response to the government's attempt to lift the statute of limitations for crimes which were not prosecuted for political reasons in the previous regime (retroactive criminal justice cases).[39] Upon the preliminary review petition of the president of the republic, an unanimous Constitutional Court abolished the retroactive criminal justice bill in its entirety.[40]

In retrospect, one may believe that the application of the constitution for measures of transition, and for the legal norms of the new as well as the old legal regime, is not so surprising, as the preamble refers to the constitution

as a facilitator of peaceful transition. Note, however, that in the case the
Constitutional Court did not refer to the preamble at all. Instead, the decision of the Constitutional Court in the retroactive criminal justice case is
based on the premise of legal continuity and the rule of law.[41] The Constitutional Court found that the "old law remains in force. As for validity, there
is no difference between norms 'from before' and 'from after' the Constitution.
The legitimacy of the various regimes of the past 50 years is irrelevant in this
respect, more precisely, it has no significance in constitutional analysis."[42]

Revolutionary as it may sound, this ruling of the Constitutional Court did
not do more than summarize the *status quo* for the purposes of constitutional analysis. On the one hand, in Hungary "all of the political forces ensured
that the political changes would be peaceful and that there would be an agreement with the Soviet Union. From a narrow constitutional point of view,
scrupulous attention was paid to ensure that changes were carried out within the constitutional and legal systems" (Paczolay 1993: 561). In addition, the
Constitutional Court did test the constitutionality of norms enacted under
the previous regimes many times before this holding. Still, it is true that unlike
in South Africa where the constitution expressly provides for keeping the old
laws in force and reaffirming the supremacy of the constitution over them,[43]
there is no such rule in the Hungarian constitution.

The Hungarian Constitutional Court clearly said that it is not willing to
subject transitional rules to a "transitional standard" of constitutionality.[44]
Thereafter, the justices outlined the constitutional principles applicable to
criminal law in a rule of law state. Still, talking in abstract terms, the court
emphasized that *ex post facto* rule-making was prohibited in criminal law.[45]
Based upon the concepts outlined in general, the Constitutional Court entered
a detailed constitutional analysis in all respects indicated in the president's
petition. The Constitutional Court's decision was rendered in abstract terms.
The opinion of the court does not contain references to the immediate context of the case. Indeed, based upon the decision of the Constitutional Court,
it would be very hard to tell that when drafting the bill annulled by the justices, "[o]f the crimes committed, those perpetrated against Hungarian citizens during the attempted revolution of 1956 were uppermost in the legislators' minds" (Zifcak 1995). The rehabilitation of Prime Minister Imre Nagy
was an emblematic event for retroactive criminal justice attempts in transition. Over the years, the "Imre Nagy narrative" shifted from being a victim
narrative to a perpetrator narrative, and was then inflated into an alibi to
support political endeavors.[46]

In the retroactive criminal justice case, the Hungarian Constitutional Court
avoided passing a judgment on the remote and recent history behind the
case.[47] Earlier, in one of the restitution cases, the Constitutional Court argued
that the uniqueness of the measures of reconstruction shall be part of the

context upon which the constitutionality of these measures is determined.[48] In the retroactive criminal justice case, however, the Constitutional Court established in clear terms that "the historical circumstances shall be considered within the requirements of the rule of law and for the purposes of its establishment. It is not acceptable to refer to historical circumstances and to justice under the rule of law in order to circumvent the safeguard of the rule of law. It is impossible to build a rule of law state against the rule of law."[49] When the Hungarian Constitutional Court rejected arguments based on the exceptional historical circumstances and insisted on testing the constitutionality of the retroactive criminal justice bill against rule of law considerations, the justices extinguished the grounds for natural law arguments (Kis 2000: 62). This approach is especially noteworthy in the light of the German "Mauerschutzen cases," where the German Federal Supreme Court said the following: "Especially the time of the National Socialist regime in Germany taught that... in extreme cases the opportunity must be given for one to value the principle of material justice more highly than the principle of legal certainty"[50] (Teitel 2000: 16–17). The German Federal Supreme Court's emphasis on material justice is in direct opposition to the Hungarian Constitutional Court's rejection of natural law considerations.

In this respect it is important to emphasize that when stressing the importance of legal continuity, the Hungarian Constitutional Court did not intend to diminish the political or historical significance of democratic transition. The justices made it clear that their emphasis on continuity is not to suggest continuity with the previous political regime. Instead, it is continuity for the purposes of constitutional analysis, in order to protect the integrity of the legal system (Holló 1997: 66). Also, the court's emphasis on legal continuity was not to acknowledge the legitimacy of the previous regime (Paczolay 1993: 562). Rather, the approach chosen by the justices enabled them to deliver a principled opinion regarding retroactive criminal justice, the decision relying on a "more neutral and formalistic understanding of the rule of law" (Sólyom 2000: 38). This approach allowed the Constitutional Court to avoid passing a judgment on the past, and submerging in the public discourse on punishing the real perpetrators of 1956.[51]

Also, it is important to note that while the Constitutional Court analyzed the retroactive criminal justice bill in a number of respects, the justices did not indicate any solution which would provide a constitutionally acceptable scheme for prosecuting the offenders targeted by the bill. This is remarkable as it was very likely that the justices did not say the final word on prosecuting the perpetrators of the previous regimes. After reviewing two other bills on retroactive criminal justice, the Constitutional Court finally ruled that lifting the statute of limitations is constitutional to the extent that (1) the statute of limitations under Hungarian law did not apply to the offence at the time it was committed; or (2) the said offence constitutes a crime under international law and the statute of limitations does not apply under international law.[52] The Constitutional Court ended the saga of retroactive criminal justice, attaching these conditions to the future application of the act.

Rules, exceptions or double standards: restitution cases

Despite the above differences concerning the constitutional background of the two review fora, one fundamental similarity may be traced in the jurisprudence of the two constitutional courts in cases on settling accounts with the past. Independent of the number of cases decided, one may find that both constitutional courts intended to decide about the constitutionality of legal measures dealing with the past without letting the past influence their judgment, in a sense both courts intended to be neutral about the past. The courts intended to restrict themselves to deciding about the constitutionality of the legislature's treatment of the past, but not about its rightfulness or appropriateness in terms of history. When reviewing legislation they were determined not to give way to "special measures" justified with reference to the evil of the past, at least not in cases where the courts reviewed the constitutionality of the legislative schemes at large. The South African Constitutional Court relied on the premise of reconciliation, while the Hungarian Constitutional Court found the baseline in the requirements of the rule of law and legal continuity.

While this approach seems to be the most appropriate one in avoiding revenge under the veil of constitutional transition, it is not without problems. A few examples taken from the jurisprudence of the Hungarian Constitutional Court might highlight the major points. As was already mentioned, the Hungarian constitution does not contain express provisions about dealing with past injustice. The Hungarian Constitutional Court reviewed the constitutionality of measures of transition under the "ordinary" provisions of the constitution. As a matter of principle, the Hungarian Constitutional Court did not accept special standards for reviewing the constitutionality of legislation handling past injustice.[53] The following passages explore whether the justices of the Hungarian Constitutional Court succeeded in their pronounced effort of not applying a special standard when reviewing transitional legislation.

In Hungary, property restitution fits into the broader context of privatization and economic reconstruction.[54] "Privatization was connected with nationwide expectations that 'unjust' expropriations of the 1940s and 1950s would be reviewed and made retroactive or that the earlier owners would be fully compensated" (Sólyom 2000: 26). The basic principles of restitution defined by the Constitutional Court are the following: restitution takes place *ex gratia* and not as of right;[55] restitution may be partial and may be provided in installments;[56] the government has a wide discretion in determining what constitutes a ground for compensation and the amount of restitution;[57] treatment of persons as subjects with equal dignity.[58] These principles were applied to compensation for moral (non-material) harms accordingly.

The first problem the Hungarian Constitutional Court faced was with regard to determining the title upon which restitution was offered. The communist regime almost annihilated private property, and in this process various legal means were used. It was accepted as a baseline that in that process previous owners suffered harm. However, the idea of full compensation to all previous owners was not even raised.[59] The Constitutional Court accepted the proposition of the government on partial restitution in its very first restitution decision.[60] The title for restitution of harms in property was identified by the justices as *novatio* (renewal). The court reasoned that property restitution was based on the government's gesture of renewing its old obligations on new grounds, as a new title in property.[61]

The Constitutional Court used the concept of *novatio* in a sense different from the one attributed to it in Roman law. This aspect is relevant because the understanding of *novatio* was strongly influenced by the notion as used in Roman law and, then, later in Hungarian civil law. In Roman law, *novatio* was a concept in the law of obligations, referring to the creation of a new obligation on the basis of an old one, while extinguishing the old obligation.[62] When discussing *novatio* under the Civil Code in force (Act No. 4 of 1959), Eörsi points out that *novatio* is a means to revive obligations which are not enforceable anymore because of the statute of limitations (Eörsi 1992: 122). It is important to point out that under the Roman law and contract law understanding of *novatio*, while the renewal of the obligation creates a new title, *de facto* performance does not change. The Constitutional Court saw property restitution as a means of performing the unique and historic task of restructuring the system of ownership.[63] The concept of *novatio* used by the Constitutional Court gave a "new content" to the obligation, that is, it altered the extent of *de facto* performance. One may find that property restitution based on *novatio* is future oriented.[64] Indeed, in order to avoid further misunderstandings the Constitutional Court stated expressly that it used the term *novatio* as a shorthand reference for a novel concept developed by the court, and not in the sense used in civil law.[65]

The concept of *novatio* is best understood in the context of the group which was affected by it. The concept underlying property restitution is that of "previous owners."[66] The rules on restitution created the group of "previous owners" as a homogeneous group, on the basis of one common denominator. The common characteristic of previous owners is that at a point government deprived all of them of their property. The Constitutional Court agreed that for the purposes of being a "previous owner" in the context of restitution, the means of deprivation of property and the holder of the new title are irrelevant. Still, while the property of some was expropriated or confiscated, the property of others was transformed into agricultural cooperatives with some compensation. Those who did not receive compensation were entitled to be compensated by the state as of right. In spite of the diversity of titles and methods of deprivation, however, the Constitutional Court found that creating a homogeneous group out of these "previous owners" did not give rise to equal protection concerns. According to the court, *novatio* extinguishes all claims, including the right to compensation, and replaces them by rules of property restitution.[67]

Paradoxically, this approach may be the result of a complete disregard of the past, or, also, of the complete awareness of past reality. It might result from a fear of opening the book of the past, taking the advice of *non novere*. However, it might also result from knowing the past too well. Indeed, the court argued that the right to civil law compensation in the previous regime was not a real right, since it was impossible to assert a claim for compensation due to the lack of legal regulation.[68] This, however, suggests that the book of the past was not closed before the renewal of the obligations of the state but exactly as a result of *novatio*. It suggests that there were existing, if dormant, claims for full compensation which were transformed via *novatio* into a claim for partial compensation. Also, although one may insist that the standard of review was relaxed not because of historical consideration but pursuant to the fiction of *novatio*, it shall also be seen that *novatio* is acceptable because of the extraordinariness of the task, that is, because of history. The basic problem with the concept of *novatio*, however, is that it is not sensitive to the past itself.

Partly due to the different history of deprivations of property, the South African constitutions have a different approach to property restitution. Indeed, the first attempt to introduce apartheid was the Native Land Act of 1913. As Jenkins notes, the "Native Lands Act apportioned South Africa's lands giving most of it, ninety-three percent, to whites, while allocating only seven percent to blacks for use as reserves. The Act also restricted blacks' access to white land by making it illegal for any African to be on European land who was not a hired servant. The Act uprooted black families from land that had been in their families for generations and forced them to sell their successful farms to white farmers and move to the 'reserves'" (Jenkins 1996: 469). Thereafter, the apartheid government made further steps to achieve the physical distancing of black South Africans by confining them to assigned tribal homelands (Jenkins 1996: 470–71). In South Africa, there was one shared feature of deprivations of property which was regarded so fundamental, that it was made the basis of property restitution: deprivation of property via racial discrimination.[69] The obvious challenge against this definition is not that the group is not homogeneous enough, but that the solution is openly retroactive. After all, it provides for the application of the new constitution's concept of racial discrimination on the old regime's discriminatory measures. The Constitutional Court, however, did not deal with the issue of retroactivity, as "[l]egislation to provide for this is specifically sanctioned, and indeed required, by the... Constitution. It is clear from these provisions that existing rights of ownership do not have precedence over claims for restitution."[70]

While both the Hungarian and the South African solution interfere with existing rights in property, there is one crucial distinction between the two positions. In South Africa, the respective measures of property restitution were expressly authorized in the constitutions, thus, as long as the rules on restitution stayed within the confines of the constitutional authorization, they were in conformity with the constitution, despite their retroactivity. On the other hand, in Hungary—due to the lack of express provisions in the constitution—legal rules on property restitution were submitted for review to the Constitutional Court. Thus, while in South Africa the exception allowing restitution for past injustices was contained in the constitution, in Hungary the exception was created by the Constitutional Court.

Another important aspect of the property restitution legislation is related to the rights of present owners. In the Hungarian restitution process, the state was distributing its own property and also the property of agricultural cooperatives (collective farms),[71] that is, the property of others.[72] Those entitled to receive agricultural lands were granted an "option of purchase" which could be used to acquire arable land in the amount of restitution received (in restitution bonds) owned by agricultural cooperatives.[73] The Constitutional Court did not find this limitation of the property right of cooperatives unconstitutional. The justices referred to the wide discretion of the government in reconstructing the system of ownership and said that this is a necessary burden of transforming the Hungarian economy.[74] Indeed, it was suggested that the Constitutional Court was not looking for a constitutionally acceptable justification for the property limitation, rather, the decision was based on the exceptional nature of the situation (Sajó 1992: 197).

In this respect, it is interesting to compare the Hungarian case with the South African Constitutional Court's decision on the rights of landowners, whose lands were distributed in the land restitution process. In South Africa, the applicant for land restitution shall file a request for restitution, describing the piece of land the restitution of which is sought under the Land Rights Act of 1994. If the Land Commission is satisfied with the request, the Commission of Restitution of Land Rights posts a notice on the claim. Landowners challenged the constitutionality of the act because it did not provide them with special participatory rights in the administrative process redistributing their lands.[75]

The South African court said that posting a notice shows that the land is subject to a claim for restitution. However, according to the South African Constitutional Court the "owner remains free to alienate or deal with the property and other interested parties are free to assert their rights. Registration is no more than notice to the world at large that the land in question is subject to a claim under the Act, information which the landowner would in any event have been obliged to disclose to any potential buyer or mortgagor."[76] The Constitutional Court said that the procedural rights of the owners were not extinguished by the fact that the legislation on land restitution does not mention them expressly, as in this regard general rules of administrative procedure apply. Nonetheless, the court declined to decide what sort of involvement of landowners procedural fairness required.[77] As the notice of the claim for restitution indicates to any willing buyer that the land has a former owner with a reasonably clear title for restitution, it is difficult to accept the argument of the Constitutional Court suggesting that a notice is not a real limitation on property rights. Indeed, the Hungarian and the South African cases suggest that the level of constitutional protection of property was reduced in an attempt to justify a measure of correcting past wrongs, if not taking revenge for them.[78]

Based upon the above it seems that despite the lack of a strong textual support for transitional justice legislation in the Hungarian constitution, the Hungarian Constitutional Court tested legislation on settling accounts with the past many times, at great length. The involvement of the Hungarian court is primarily due to the fact that almost all bills were submitted to the Constitutional Court preliminary review for approval. As a matter of principle, the Constitutional Court rejected all measures of retroactive criminal justice as a means to punish offenders who were not prosecuted in the previous regimes. In the field of restitution, however, the Constitutional Court emphasized the great discretion of the legislature. Despite this, many legislative attempts were rejected. The court did not preclude legislation on settling accounts with the past *per se*, and legislative measures of transitional justice could not be exempted from review. Nonetheless, the court emphasized that it is not going to establish special standards for transitional legislation. In practice this means that the Hungarian Constitutional Court applied the provisions of the constitution and relied extensively on two concepts which were developed in response to the demands of transitional justice. While the Constitutional Court emphasized legal continuity and the rule of law, it denied that restitution for past injustice has any other ground than the political decision of the government to give it. This premise of the *ex gratia* nature of restitution became the baseline of compensating moral and material damages.

The second premise developed by the Hungarian Constitutional Court is *novatio*. While the premise of the *ex gratia* nature of compensation granted the government wide discretion in both taking property for the purposes of restitution and distributing it, the premise of *novatio* allowed the Constitutional Court to detach the past from the future. In this sense, *novatio* is about discontinuity. In practice, these two premises enabled the Hungarian Constitutional Court to test and uphold transitional legislation, even measures which would not have passed scrutiny lacking the extraordinary circumstances of transition. The problem inherent in these two concepts is that as they both translate into "wide discretion," they give rise not to rules but to exceptions. And indeed the Hungarian Constitutional Court used these concepts extensively to justify deviations from constitutional rules and standards applicable in unextraordinary circumstances. When establishing the concept of the *ex gratia* nature of compensation and *novatio*, the Hungarian Constitutional Court created the functional equivalent of the South African "historic bridge."[79]

At this point it is important to see that the epilogue of the South African interim constitution and its provisions on land restitution create exceptions from the ordinary, to facilitate constitutional transition. One may argue that the Hungarian Constitutional Court created exceptions to be able to give way to legislation on remedying past injustice. The court was taking a deferential position. One may also add that the exceptions based on the *ex gratia* nature of restitution and *novatio* were not used outside transitional justice cases. There is, however, a fundamental difference between an exception created by a constitutional court and the constitution itself, even if it leaves way to the legislature's decision. In the context of democratic transition, this difference also places the courts in a different position on the past-present-future continuum. While the South African Constitutional Court was enforcing the measures of the new regime (the new constitution) against the real-world heritage of the past, the Hungarian Constitutional Court was in the position of curbing the efforts of the new regime to settle accounts with the past and repair past injustice. This is so, even if both courts are untainted by the past, since they were established in the course of democratic transition.

CONCLUSION

Transitional justice cases brought the past to the courts in a concentrated form, and the imprint of the authoritarian regime and its heritage are long going to be noticeable both on legislation and on constitutional challenges. The examples in Hungary include the Constitutional Court's review of the government's austerity package in 1995 intending to abolish the communist scheme of welfare benefits, a series of decisions concerning the restructuring of the broadcasting system, and guarantees in the law of civil and criminal procedure. The South African Constitutional Court had to decide whether the government has an obligation to finance minority education for Afrikaans children,[80] whether the right to medical treatment included the right to receive life saving renal dialysis,[81] whether differences in water tariffs for black and white residents and the differences in the enforcement of the tariff-rules constitute "unfair discrimination,"[82] or whether in addition to common law damages, "constitutional damages" should also be available against the state for the infringement of constitutional rights.[83]

At least at first sight, these cases do not seem to be concerned with legislative attempts intending to settle accounts with the past, and these cases do not seem to call for the exceptions developed for transitional justice legislation. It is, however, important to see that all the cases listed—and a vast number of other cases not mentioned above—involve constitutional concerns about legal rules preserved from the previous regimes or concerns about newly enacted legislation which alters or affects the *status quo* established during the previous regimes. These constitutional cases involve more than abstract constitutional questions.

In some cases democratic regimes are facing problems of withdrawing services or benefits that were provided by the previous regime, while in other cases the new governments have to eliminate disadvantages created and maintained by the previous regime. What is the legal and constitutional status of such services and benefits in a constitutional system? How long and on what grounds can property rights be limited in the name of transforming an inherited property-structure? How long and on what grounds can an inherited welfare system be protected by constitutional means? What does equality command in a constitutional regime following apartheid? What is the extent of the government's constitutional obligations to provide for socio-economic rights following complete deprivation by the previous regime?

When responding to such questions, constitutional review fora often determine the standard of constitutionality with regard to the respective past. This willingness does not mean that constitutional courts always enter into a detailed analysis of the relevant past. Rather, it means that constitutional courts account for the *status quo*. However, there is a difference between taking the inherited state of affairs as facts, as opposed to deriving legal rights or constitutionally protected interests from the *status quo*. The line between the two approaches might be fine but the difference in effect is fundamental. In the former case the past or the remnants of the past gain consideration among other facts and may shape constitutional standards accordingly. In the latter case, however, the institutional structures as inherited from the previous regime become part of the normative order of the new constitutional regime under construction.

These findings are not that surprising to the extent constitutional courts are expected to explore the facts relevant to deciding the case before them, segments of the past being one aspect of the relevant facts. Also, respect for long-preserved institutions might be explained with the legal mind's temptation to defer to the *status quo*. Nonetheless, as a result such an approach might also mean that constitutional courts impose—often unforeseen—obligations on new governments in the name of the past. Indeed, there is a potential that the judicial activism of the constitutional courts of transition-to-democracy countries results in preserving the institutional structures of the previous, despised establishment.

Other than preserving the inherited institutional structures in the name of protecting the *status quo*, respect for the past might result in the development of constitutional standards which cannot be distinguished as constitutional measures facilitating transitional justice. Exceptions made in order to allow for the reconstruction of the system of ownership may become part of the property jurisprudence of a constitutional court, the concept of government-conferred benefits as vested rights may not vanish as fast as deadlines for requesting property restitution or compensation for non-material damages expire.

More precisely, such exceptions—initially made to enable a constitutional court to uphold legislation handling the past—may be preserved in the jurisprudence of constitutional review fora and, thus, may be invoked in any future case depending on the discretion of the constitutional court. In addition to the relaxed standard of constitutional protection, this aspect adds further concerns, as the emergence of future cases triggering the altered (lowered) standard of constitutional protection are not foreseeable with sufficient certainty. To the extent constitutional standards which were developed in order to cope with the past are preserved for the purposes of everyday (non-transitional) constitutionalism, it is possible that everyday constitutionalism is at risk in constitutional adjudication, long after transition to democracy was believed to be over.

APPENDIX

The epilogue to the interim South African constitution reads as follows:

> This Constitution provides a historic bridge between the past of a deeply divided society characterized by strife, conflict, untold suffering and injustice, and a future founded on the recognition of human rights, democracy and peaceful co-existence and development opportunities for all South Africans, irrespective of color, race, class, belief or sex. The pursuit of national unity, the well-being of all South African citizens and peace require reconciliation between the people of South Africa and the reconstruction of society. The adoption of this Constitution lays the secure foundation for the people of South Africa to transcend the divisions and strife of the past, which generated gross violations of human rights, the transgression of humanitarian principles in violent conflicts and a legacy of hatred, fear, guilt and revenge. These can now be addressed on the basis that there is a need for under-

standing but not for vengeance, a need for reparation but not for retaliation, a need for ubuntu but not for victimization. In order to advance such reconciliation and reconstruction, amnesty shall be granted in respect of acts, omissions and offences associated with political objectives and committed in the course of the conflicts of the past. To this end, Parliament under this Constitution shall adopt a law determining a firm cut-off date, which shall be a date after 8 October 1990 and before 6 December 1993, and providing for the mechanisms, criteria and procedures, including tribunals, if any, through which such amnesty shall be dealt with at any time after the law has been passed. With this Constitution and these commitments we, the people of South Africa, open a new chapter in the history of our country.

NOTES

1 Nietzsche 1983 [1874]: 62.
2 See the facts in the Republic of South Africa vs. Grootboom and Others, CCT 11/00 (2000). See also the subsequent case of the Republic of South Africa vs. Kyalami and Others, CCT 55/00 (2000).
3 Of course, handling the past in democratic transition is not only about creating or transforming institutions, but also about the players preserved from the past who might still be around to preserve their stake. Although it would be naïve to ignore this factor altogether, these aspects are not going to be explored in detail. In addition, this is not to suggest that the past of long-standing constitutional regimes is always untainted.
4 Cf. the Czech Constitutional Court's decision on property restitution (Decision Pl. U.S. 14/94), in which the Czech Court took a clear stand on the legal status of the "Beneš Decrees." The Czech decision provides a prime example of a constitutional court considering history in detail.
5 For exceptions, see the constitutions of Belgium, Canada, Finland (1999), Germany, Greece, Italy, or Romania. Certainly, this is not to mean that these constitutions do not bear the imprints of history.
6 See, for example, the constitutions of Algeria, Cambodia, China, Croatia, Indonesia (1945), Iran (1979), Ireland, Liberia, or Macedonia.
7 Examples can be found in the constitution of Belarus, the Latvian Declaration of Independence, or the Czech, Georgian, Lithuanian, Slovak, or Polish (1921) constitutions.
8 For example, the constitutions of Albania (1998), Armenia, Azerbaijan, Estonia, or Poland (1997).
9 See Rivero submitting that the French *Conseil constitutionnel*'s freedom of association decision of 16 July 1971 (71–44 DC) relying on the preamble re-established constitutional continuity in France (Rivero 1990: 157). Note that the *Grundgesetz* also contains provisions on religious freedom transplanted from the Weimar constitution of 1949 (Article 140 of the *Grundgesetz* lists the so-called "Weimar articles").
10 For the purposes of an analysis of techniques of constitutional interpretation, the problems raised by the normativity of historical references in constitutional argument shall be distinguished from the question of normativity of constitutional provisions referring to the past.

11 For the text of the epilogue, see the Appendix. Both the interim and the final constitution contain express provisions for legal measures to facilitate democratic transition. Issues of land restitution are discussed below in comparison to the Hungarian Constitutional Court's jurisprudence, where relevant.

12 Azanian Peoples Organization (AZAPO) vs. the President of the Republic of South Africa, Case CCT 17/96 (1996). Justice Mahomed wrote for the court. Justice Didcott wrote a separate concurring opinion. References are to the judgment of Justice Mahomed, unless noted otherwise.

13 The original draft constitution had no provisions on amnesty, as amnesty was an issue for closed door negotiations (Geula 2000: 61–62).

14 The relevant period was specified in the act, and was subsequently extended along with the deadline for applications. Cf. the Hungarian Constitutional Court's decision in the retroactive criminal justice case (11/1992 (III. 5.) AB decision). The bill challenged in the case lifted the statute of limitations for crimes committed during the previous regime but "not prosecuted for political reasons." In its decision, the Constitutional Court found that this condition was unconstitutionally vague, since it is impossible to determine its scope. ABH 1992, 92–93.

15 S.3(3)(b), Promotion of National Unity and Reconciliation Act of 1995. Dugard concludes that unlike the rest of the TRC, the Committee on Amnesty was a quasi-judicial organization. In practice, the TRC procedures turned into trials (Dugard 1998: 294, 298).

16 23/1990 (X. 31.) AB decision.

17 Cf. Article 19(2) of the *Grundgesetz*.

18 23/1990 (X. 31.) AB decision, ABH 1990, 94–95.

19 For a summary of the petitioners' argument, see AZAPO, Mahomed, J., para 8.

20 For critical reactions, see Brice Dickson calling it a politically charged decision (Dickson 1997: 563), or Jeremy Sarkin arguing that the court dismissed access to justice considerations without sensitivity and criticizing the court's treatment of international law (Sarkin 1998: 198). Cf. Burnham arguing that "[i]f the AZAPO case is result-driven, its approach can be justified by the urgency of navigating a safe passage over the bridge to the future South Africa" (Burnham 1997: 54).

21 "[I]n reaching its decision, the Court went to great lengths to endorse the Act's rationale as essential to successful democratic transition" (Burnham 1997: 52).

22 Various justices of the Constitutional Court relied extensively on the epilogue when it abolished capital punishment in the State vs. Makwanyane, CCT 3/94 (1995).

23 The preamble of the act provides that "it is deemed necessary to establish the truth in relation to past events as well as the motives for and circumstances in which gross violation of human rights have occurred, and to make the findings known in order to prevent a repetition of such acts in future."

24 Note that "closing the book" in the above sense is essentially different from legislating amnesia. For contrasting the two positions, see Asmal 1997: 27.

25 See, for example, the City Council of Pretoria vs. Walker, CCT 8/97 (1998), where the court examined the effects of long-lasting racial segregation in the context of utility fees; In re: dispute concerning the constitutionality of certain provisions of the school education bill of 1995, CCT 39/95 (1996), where the court analyzed the effects of racial segregation in education and interpreted "minority education" in its historical context (para 51).

26 Note that two out of three non-governmental commissions of inquiry were appointed by the ANC itself between 1992 and 1993. They found that the ANC did commit torture and other forms of human rights violations. Also Geula 2000: 63–64.

27 Note that the Hungarian Constitutional Court in an essentially similar situation refused

to interfere with the legislature's determination of history (time periods) considerable for restitution on a large scale.

28 "[T]he case favoring restraint in the Court's use of comparative constitutional analysis is more compelling in AZAPO than in the Gauteng Provincial Legislature opinion because of the special role of the Truth Commission in the context of South Africa's divisive history'" (Webb 1998: 210). For a detailed analysis of South African Constitutional Court decisions using comparative sources, see Webb 1998: 276–83.

29 The account of a Kenyan woman on the work of the TRC, quoted in Villa-Vicencio 1999–2000: 167.

30 Also Minow 2000: 1403.

31 Also Hayner 2001: 133–53.

32 The Committee on Amnesty received 7112, amnesty was granted in 849 cases and denied in 5394 cases. See http://www.doj.gov.za/trc/amntrans/index.htm (last visited April 30, 2002).
Note that a considerable number of petitions were filed by prison inmates, who had nothing to lose by applying (McCarthy 1997: 190).

33 Or, at least one may find that the "Commission focused the nation's attention on the victim rather than the need to punish the perpetrator" (Villa-Vicencio 1999–2000: 175). Teitel notes that the amnesty process in South Africa contained a "promise of reparation" for the victims (Teitel 2000: 128).

34 See Certification of the Constitution of the Republic of South Africa, 1996, Case CCT 23/96 (1996), para 205.

35 In an even broader sense, measures to settle accounts with the past also include the abolition of the old rules on takings—27/1991 (V. 20.) and 66/1992 (XII. 17.) AB decisions— and the abolition of the rules on the universally applicable personal identification number—15/1991 (IV. 3.) AB decision. See also 20/1990 (X. 4.) AB decision abolishing Act No. 3 of 1990, which required the leaders of new political parties and non-governmental organizations to make disclosures on their possessions. Cf. 1154/B/1990/5 (1991) AB decision, upholding constitutionality of Act No. 73 of 1990, requiring "certain civil organizations attached to the previous regime" to make a disclosure on their properties.

36 See Articles 121–23 of the interim constitution and Article 25(7) of the final constitution.

37 Act No. 20 of 1949, as amended by Act No. 31 of 1989, the first comprehensive democratic amendment to the constitution.

38 Note that the French *Conseil d'Etat* used to be one of the first interpreters of the preamble of the 1946 constitution, and it has applied the preamble to invalidate norms which had been enacted before the entry into force of the 1946 constitution (see Stirn 1992: 215).

39 11/1992 (III. 5.) AB decision. The bill lifted the statute of limitations for crimes the prosecution of which was already barred. In addition, it extended the statute of limitation with respect to crimes the prosecution of which was not barred yet. In further cases, the bill restarted the limitations period. This scheme was supposed to make all crimes prosecutable retroactively. The sponsors of the bill argued that "the rule of law cannot be used to shield injustice" (Kis 2000: 61).

40 For an analysis, see Paczolay 1993: 570–73; also Trang 1995.

41 The Constitutional Court submitted that from a political perspective the transition was revolutionary, still, the new regime came about pursuant to the rules prescribed by the old legal system. 11/1992 (III. 5.) AB decision, ABH 1992, 81.

42 11/1992 (III. 5.) AB decision, ABH 1992, 81.

43 See s.229 of the South African interim constitution, keeping in force all legal norms which were in force prior to the commencement of the interim constitution. In addition, s.4(1) provides that that the interim constitution shall be the supreme law of the land and apply to all laws and acts, unless to those which are expressly exempted.

Cf. Article 4 of the Singapore constitution, providing that the constitution applies to the constitutionality of those statutes only which were enacted after the entry into force of the new constitution.

44 See also 11/1992 (III. 5.) AB decision, ABH 1992, 83; Holló 1997: 66; Sólyom 2000: 26.

45 11/1992 (III. 5.) AB decision, ABH 1992, 84–87. The Constitutional Court provided a detailed elaboration on the principles of *nullum crimen sine lege* and *nulla poena sine lege* from a constitutional perspective.

46 According to Kovács, this transformation (inflation) was fueled by revenge (see Kovács 2000: 35).

47 In his concurring opinion in the death penalty case, Chief Justice Sólyom stated that the court abolished the death penalty based upon general principles and not as a symbolic reaction to the evils of a political regime which used human lives for its own purposes. 23/1990 (X. 31.) AB decision, ABH 1990, 99–100, Sólyom, Ch. J., concurring opinion.

48 28/1991 (VI. 3.) AB decision, ABH 1991, 84.

49 11/1992 (III. 5.) AB decision, ABH 1992, 82.

50 Teitel adds an important detail to the borderguards' cases: the prosecution campaign led to the conviction of many low level borderguards, while there was almost no accountability for the shootings at higher levels (Teitel 2000: 45; see also Quint 1997: 196–205).

51 Cf. Zifcak 1995 on the approach of the Czech Constitutional Court in the retroactive criminal justice case (Decision Pl.US 19/93).

52 53/1993 (X. 13.) AB decision, the third retroactive criminal justice case. See also 42/1993 (VI. 30.) AB decision, the second retroactive criminal justice case.

53 Note that in the course of the German unification process, the drafters of the Unification Treaty did create exceptions from ordinary constitutionalism in order to facilitate unification, that is, transition. See Article 143 of the *Grundgesetz*. The two most touchy issues were abortion and *Bodenreform*. For further details on the latter, see Quint 1997: 136–44; Kommers 1997: 256–57.

54 See the preamble of Act No. 25 of 1991 on the restitution of damages caused by the unjust actions of the state. Also 1/1995 (II. 8.) AB decision, ABH 1995, 43. For an overview of the economic environment and circumstances of privatization in Hungary, see Frydman et al. 1993: 95–147.

55 21/1990 (X. 4.) AB decision, ABH 1990, 76–77; 16/1991 (IV. 20.) AB decision, ABH 1991, 57.

56 16/1991 (IV. 30.) AB decision, ABH 1991, 59. Restitution in installments shall be foreseeable. Restitution in installments refers to the enforcement of restitution. 28/1991 (VI. 3.) AB decision, ABH 1991, 92.

57 28/1991 (VI. 3.) AB decision, ABH 1991, 89.

58 28/1991 (VI. 3.) AB decision, ABH 1991, 87. Note that the standard of constitutionality is lower than in a discrimination analysis because the distinction is not made with regard to a constitutional right.

59 See Klingsberg presenting the concepts of various political parties on restitution (Klingsberg 1992: 81–85).

60 21/1990 (X. 4.) AB decision, ABH 1990, 76–77.

61 16/1991 (IV. 20.) AB decision, ABH 1991, 59; applied in 27/1991 (V. 20.) AB decision, 28/1991 (VI. 3.) AB decision, 15/1993 (III. 12.) AB decision, 16/1993 (III. 12.) AB decision, 1/1995 (II. 8.) AB decision, and 4/1996 (II. 23.) AB decision.

62 Digest 46.2.1.pr, Ulpian. Also Brósz and Pólay 1991, para 1087.

63 15/1993 (III. 12.) AB decision, ABH 1993, 117.

64 According to Teitel, "it serves a forward-looking economic interest" (Teitel 2000: 130).

65 15/1993 (III. 12.) AB decision, ABH 1993, 117–18.

66 Art. 2(2) of Act No. 25 of 1991 on the restitution of damages caused by the unjust state actions.

67 28/1991 (VI. 3.) AB decision, ABH 1991, 87–88; 15/1993 (III. 12.) AB decision, ABH 1993, 118.

68 28/1991 (VI. 3.) AB decision, ABH 1991, 88.

69 S.8(3)(b) of the interim constitution. Ss. 121–23 of the interim constitution provided for the restitution of land rights, and established the Commission of Restitution of Land Rights and its basic tasks.

70 Transvaal Agricultural Union vs. Minister of Land Affairs and Another, CCT 21/96 (1996) Chaskalson, Ch. J., para 33. 65,000 claims were launched under the restitution scheme before the cut-off date (December 1998). "Although the hope is to redistribute 30% of the country's farmland by 2014, only 0.81% had been transferred to blacks until the end of [2000]." Note that a mere 6% of farmland is sold in South Africa in ordinary commercial transactions. (In 1997 the government introduced a tenure reform program. Restitution seems to be a little more successful if conducted out of courts. This solution is supported by the government.) "South Africa Survey," *The Economist,* 24 February–2 March 2001, no. 5.

71 By the 1980s, over 60% of arable lands were owned by agricultural cooperatives, and less than 10% belonged to the state (Swain 1999). Indeed, the "land fund" created out of the lands of the cooperatives for distribution in the course of restitution included almost half of the arable lands owned by the cooperatives.

72 16/1991 (IV. 30.) AB decision, ABH 1991, 57. The Constitutional Court said that it is not *per se* unconstitutional if the state includes the property of cooperatives among the resources distributed via restitution.

73 On the concerns of constitutionality of the option of purchase see Sajó arguing that the option of purchase indeed constitutes taking (Sajó 1992: 190–209).

74 28/1991 (VI. 3.) AB decision, ABH 1991, 95/96.

75 Transvaal Agricultural Union, Chaskalson, Ch. J., para 13.

76 Transvaal Agricultural Union, Chaskalson, Ch. J., para 28.

77 Transvaal Agricultural Union, Chaskalson, Ch. J., para 30.

78 Note that agricultural cooperatives were often created against the free will of the landowners.

79 See Teitel arguing that transitional constitutions create interim periods (Teitel 2000: 197–98).

80 In re: dispute concerning the constitutionality of certain provisions of the school education bill of 1995, CCT 39/95 (1996).

81 Soobramoney vs. Minster of Health (Kwazulu-Natal), CCT 32/97 (1997).

82 City Council of Pretoria vs. Walker, CCT 8/97 (1998).

83 Fose vs. Minister of Safety and Security, CCT 14/96 (1997).

BIBLIOGRAPHY

Asmal, Kader. "Fears and Hopes" in *The Healing of a Nation?*, eds. Boraine, Alex and Janet Levy (Cape Town: Justice in Transition, 1995), pp. 26–30.

——. "International Law and Practice, Dealing with the Past in the South African Experience: The Second Annual Grotius Lecture." at http://education.pwv.gov.za/-Media/Articles/Grotius_Lecture.htm, 5 April 2000 (last visited 15 January 2004).

Boraine, Alex. *A Country Unmasked, Inside South Africa's Truth and Reconciliation Commission*. Oxford: Oxford University Press, 2000.

Brósz, Róbert and Elemér Pólay. *Római jog* [Roman law]. Budapest: Tankönyvkiadó, 1991.

Burnham, Margaret A. "Cultivating a Seedling Charter: South Africa's Court Grows Its Constitution." *Michigan Journal of Race and Law* 3 (1997): 29–58.

Davis, Dennis, Matthew Chaskalson, and Johan de Wal. "Democracy and Constitutionalism: The Role of Constitutional Interpretation" in *Rights and Constitutionalism, The New South African Legal Order*, eds. Van Wyk, Dugard David, Bertus de Villiers, and Dennis Davis (Cape Town: Juta, 1994), pp. 1–130.

Dickson, Brice. "Protecting Human Rights through a Constitutional Court: The Case of South Africa." *Fordham Law Review* 66 (1997): 531–66.

Dyzenhaus, David. *Judging the Judges, Judging Ourselves: Truth, Reconciliation and the Apartheid Legal Order*. Oxford: Hart Publishing, 1998.

Dugard, John. "Reconciliation and Justice: The South African Experience." *Transnational Law and Contemporary Problems* 8 (1998): 277–311.

Eörsi, Gyula. *Kötelmi Jog. Általános rész* [The law of obligations: general part]. Budapest: Tankönyvkiadó, 1992.

Frydman, Roman, Andrzej Rapaczynski, and John Earle, eds. *The Privatization in Central Europe*. Budapest: CEU Press, 1993.

Geula, Marianne. "South Africa's Truth and Reconciliation Commission as an Alternate Means of Addressing Transitional Government Conflicts in a Divided Society." *Boston University International Law Journal* 18 (2000): 57–84.

Gibson, James L. and Amanda Guows. "Truth and Reconciliation in South Africa: Attributions of Blame and the Struggle over Apartheid." *American Political Science Review* 93, no. 3 (1999): 501–17.

Hayner, Priscilla. *Unspeakable Truths, Conflicting State Terror and Atrocity*. New York and London: Routledge, 2001.

Holló, András. *Az Alkotmánybíróság, alkotmánybíráskodás Magyarországon* [The constitutional court, constitutional review in Hungary]. Budapest: Útmutató, 1997.

Jenkins, Daisy M. "From Apartheid to Majority Rule: A Glimpse intro South Africa's Journey to Democracy." *Arizona Journal of International and Comparative Law* 13 (19996): 463–90.

Kis, János. "Az első magyar Alkotmánybíróság értelmezési gyakorlata" [The first Hungarian Constitutional Court's practice of interpretation] in *The Constitution Found? The First Nine Years of Hungarian Constitutional Review on Fundamental Rights*, ed. Halmai, Gábor (Budapest: Indok, 2000), pp. 48–98.

Klingsberg, Ethan. "Judicial Review and Hungary's Transition from Communism to Democracy: The Constitutional Court, the Continuity of Law, and the Redefinition of Property Rights." *Brigham Young University Law Review*, vol. 1 (1992): 41–144.

Kommers, Donald P. *The Constitutional Jurisprudence of the Federal Republic of Germany*. 2nd ed. Durham, N.C.: Duke University Press, 1997.

Kovács, Éva. "'Íme az Istennek ama báránya, aki elveszi a világ bűneit': Etüd a rendszerváltó mítoszokról" [Essay on the myths of transition]. *Világosság* 41, nos. 6–7 (2000): 28–37.

McCarthy, Emily H. "South Africa's Amnesty Process: A Viable Route toward Truth and Reconciliation?" *Michigan Journal of Race and Law* 3 (1997): 183–253.

Minow, Martha. "The Role of Forgiveness in the Law." *Fordham Urban Law Journal* 27 (2000): 1394–419.

Nietzsche, Friedrich. "On the Uses and Disadvantages of History for Life" in *Untimely Meditations*, trans. Hollingdale, R. J. (Cambridge: Cambridge University Press, 1983 [1874]), pp. 57–123.

Omar, Dullah. "Introduction to Justice in Transition. South Africa Truth and Reconciliation Commission." at http://www.doj.gov.za/trc/legal/justice.htm, 1995.

Paczolay, Péter. "Constitutional Transition and Legal Continuity." *Connecticut Journal of International Law* 8 (1993): 559–74.

Quint, Peter E. *The Imperfect Union, Constitutional Structures of German Unification.* Princeton: Princeton University Press, 1997.

Rivero, Jean. "Les libertes" [Liberties] in *La continuité constitutionnelle en France de 1789 a 1989, journées d'études des 16–17 mars 1989* [Constitutional continuity in France between 1789 and 1989, collection of papers, 16–17 March 1989], ed. Association Français de Constitutionnalistes (Paris: Economica, 1990), pp. 153–60.

Sajó, András. "A részleges kárpótlási törvény által felvetett alkotmányossági kérdések" [Concerns of constitutionality raised by the act on partial compensation]. *Állam- és Jogtudomány* 34, nos. 1–4 (1992): 190–209.

Sarkin, Jeremy. "The Effect of Constitutional Borrowings on the Drafting of South Africa's Bill of Rights and Interpretation of Human Rights Provisions." *University of Pennsylvania Journal of Constitutional Law* 1 (1998): 176–204.

Sólyom, László. "Alkotmányosság Magyarországon. Értékek és tények" [Constitutionalism in Hungary: values and facts] in *Nizsalovszky Endre emlékkönyv* [Nizsalovszky festschrifts], eds. Mádl, Ferenc and Lajos Vékás (Budapest: ELTE ÁJK, 1994), pp. 218–36.

——. "Introduction to the Decisions of the Constitutional Court of the Republic of Hungary" in *Constitutional Judiciary in a New Democracy: The Hungarian Constitutional Court*, eds. Sólyom, László and Georg Brunner (Ann Arbor: University of Michigan Press, 2000), pp. 1–64.

"South Africa Survey." *The Economist*, 24 February–2 March 2001, no. 5.

Stirn, Bernard. "Le tradition republicaine dans la jurisprudence du Conseil d'Etat" [The republican tradition in the jurisprudence of the Conseil d'Etat] in *La Republique en droit Francaise* [The republic in French law], eds. Bertrand, Mathieu and Michel Verpeaux (Paris: Economica, 1992), pp. 213–20.

Swain, Nigel. "Agricultural Restitution and Co-operative Transformation in the Czech Republic, Hungary and Slovakia." *Europe-Asia Studies* 51 (1999): 1199–219.

Teitel, Ruti. *Transitional Justice.* Oxford: Oxford University Press, 2000.

Trang, Duc V. "Beyond the Historical Justice Debate: The Incorporation of International Law and the Impact on Constitutional Structures and Rights in Hungary." *Vanderbilt Journal of Transnational Law* 28 (1995): 1–43.

Villa-Vicencio, Charles. "The Reek of Cruelty and the Quest for Healing." *Journal of Law and Religion* 14 (1999–2000): 165–87.

Webb, Hoyt. "The Constitutional Court of South Africa: Rights Interpretation and Comparative Constitutional Law." *University of Pennsylvania Journal of Constitutional Law* 1 (1998): 205–83.

Zifcak, Spencer. "Retroactive Justice in Hungary and the Czech Republic." at http://www.austlii.edu.au/au/special/alta/alta95/zifcak.html, 1995 (last visited 15 January 2004).

PART THREE
Rule of Law

Rethinking the Rule of Law
After Communism

MARTIN KRYGIER

Long before there were written constitutions, and before law was considered a way of purging problematic pasts and fashioning successful futures, the Western legal and political tradition knew demands for the rule of law. The concept, though not always the specific verbal formulation, embodies ideals that have been central to political and constitutional discourse at least since Aristotle. And though the meaning and worth of the rule of law have long been contested, the major claims of its partisans have equally long been quite clear: that law can and should contribute in salutary, some say indispensable, ways to channeling, constraining, and informing—rather than merely serving—the exercise of power, particularly public power.

Not only are the goals of the rule of law venerable, so too are what are taken as the proper ways of implementing them. Readers of the standard jurisprudential literature might be forgiven for thinking that they know pretty well what these involve: general rules rather than or superior to particular edicts, that are public not secret, prospective not retrospective, relatively clear and precise rather than ambiguous or vague, relatively stable, not always up for grabs, consistent with each other, and administered by legally authorized agencies in accordance with knowable and non-arbitrary interpretations of their terms. With some variations, these are familiar themes. Of course, any realistic exponent of the rule of law knows that these institutional achievements are not simple to attain, and that typically they are likely to be satisfied only to greater or lesser degrees, rather than completely or not at all. Still, these are general truths about the institutionalization of virtually any ideals, rather than problems peculiar to the rule of law. And realists know that differences of degree matter. We know, then, what the rule of law is for, we know what is needed for it, and different legal orders have had more or less success in realizing it. End of story; or so it has often seemed.

So, in any event, it seemed in 1989. For, as several observers noted at the time and since, 1989 ushered in a new sort of revolution, at the same time extraordinarily ambitious and deliberately unadventurous. Ambitious because no one had ever moved from "really existing socialism" to where the most prominent revolutionaries professed to want to go: democracy, the rule of law, a market economy. Unadventurous because these bold spirits all claimed to have seen the future in the past and present of other countries.

They wanted "no experiments," a "normal" country, just as one finds in liberal democracies of the West. As Timothy Garton Ash captured the sentiment, "[i]n politics they are all saying: There is no 'socialist democracy,' there is only democracy. And by democracy they mean multi-party, parliamentary democracy as practiced in contemporary Western, Northern, and Southern Europe. They are all saying: There is no 'socialist legality,' there is only legality. And by that they mean the rule of law, guaranteed by the constitutionally anchored independence of the judiciary" (Ash 1990: 21).

If, as this book suggests, the experience of over a decade of postcommunism gives grounds for rethinking the rule of law, one implication is that there is more to the story than this. That might be for at least two reasons. On the one hand, that experience might cast fresh light on old beliefs or beliefs about old things, adding to or in some way altering our appreciation of the rule of law where we thought we knew it. Alternatively, there might be distinctive features of this new phenomenon which elude models, or lessons, or parallels that we thought would apply to it. Of course, both reasons might operate.

TRANSITION

Postcommunist reformers have almost universally, and at least rhetorically, been committed to implementing the rule of law, a *Rechtsstaat*, a "law-governed state." So, given the apparent clarity of the goal, and the widespread common understanding of the means to it, it must have seemed plain at the start what was necessary to achieve it. Of course, realistic reformers knew that where it had not existed before or had been systematically denied, achieving the rule of law was not a simple matter. Nevertheless, at least the criteria by which achievement might be judged seemed evident to many.

> On one interpretation of the significance of postcommunist transitions, however, it would be simplistic in the extreme to believe this. To borrow Wojciech Sadurski's coinage, on a "fancy" understanding of post-dictatorial transitions, among them postcommunist ones, they involve social, political, and legal transformations which have unprecedented, *sui generis* aspects, aspects which cannot be captured in the simple identikit portraits we have inherited of what law, the rule of law, and constitutionalism should be like.

Nowhere has the distinctive character of the transitional moment, the *situation of transition*, been more strongly and effectively delineated than in the work of Ruti Teitel, particularly in her book, *Transitional Justice* (2000), and in her chapter in this collection, which distils that book's guiding lines. In this chapter, as in the book, Teitel seeks to offer a legal "phenomenology of liberalizing transition."

She suggests that transitions are *sui generis*, "extraordinary," periods, for several reasons that might be worth distinguishing. One is that they are periods of great "flux"; typically, as the song has it, "the joint is rocking." Much more so than in times of "ordinary" politics when business goes on more or less as usual. Second, not only are they flux-full, but the flux is not just tumultuous but directed, that is, it is aimed to move away from the past and to something different. Third, not just different, but different in a specific way. At least the end-of-millennial, postdictatorial transitions involve a "normative shift," that is, roughly a shift from a now-derided despotism to a now-desired democracy and the rule of law.

All these elements and special tasks, Teitel insists, make it wrong to assimilate the role of law in such periods to "ideal" models of legality drawn from flux-free moments. Indeed: transitions imply paradigm shifts in the conception of justice; thus, law's function is deeply and inherently paradoxical. In its ordinary social function, law provides order and stability, but in extraordinary periods of political upheaval, law maintains order even as it enables transformation. Accordingly, in transition, the ordinary [more usually Teitel writes of "our ordinary"] intuitions and predicates about law simply do not apply... It does not mean that ideals of rule of law are irrelevant to transitions, but rather that they are inapplicable to these exceptional circumstances without making a variety of adjustments, both to the context of transition, and to the particulars of that state's political conditions. In dynamic periods of political flux, legal responses generate a *sui generis* paradigm of transformative law (Teitel, this volume).

According to Teitel, in such periods law has a special, extraordinarily constructive role, in that it doesn't merely provide settled guidelines for the present but exercises its "transformative potential" to engender the putatively different future which will come at the end of a "bounded period, spanning two regimes." The tension between these two functions Teitel calls the "rule-of-law dilemma." Law is involved in this dilemma because legal institutions are peculiarly apt to 'mediate normative shift' in a gradual, measured, and non-violent manner and so, unlike the law of "ordinary times," become preferred sites and vehicles of social, political, and ideological transformation. Thus, "[i]n modern political transformation, it is through legal practices that successor societies make liberalizing political change, for, in mediating the normative hiatus and shift characterizing transition, the turn to law comprises important functional, conceptual, operative, and symbolic dimensions" (Teitel 2000: 221).

This has profound consequences for the nature of "transitional justice," according to Teitel. Since the transition is special it should not be judged according to presuppositions derived from "normal" conditions. On the contrary, circumstances of transition generate "a distinctive conception of justice and rule of law in the context of political transformation" (Teitel, this volume). While the envisaged future is actually described in rather familiar liberal fashion, the pasts which transitional regimes seek to undo are seen to vary markedly from each other. Since they do, so will the character of the law which is doing the undoing.

Where "ordinarily" the rule of law is prospective, transitional rule of law "is both backward- and forward-looking, as it disclaims past illiberal values, and reclaims liberal norms" (Teitel, this volume). Where punishment is traditionally conceived as an individualized response to individual wrongdoing, "[i]n the transitional context, conventional understandings of individual responsibility are frequently inapplicable, and have spurred the emergence of new legal forms: partial sanctions that fall outside conventional legal categories" (ibid.). Where traditional rule of law stabilizes expectations in an existing liberal order, transitional rule of law is often intended to destabilize existing expectations in order to construct a future order; "the hope of change is put in the air" (ibid.).

In consequence of all these variable peculiarities, Teitel does, and by implication we should, eschew "idealized theorizing about the rule of law in general" (Teitel 2000: 12), and instead recognize "the tension between idealized conceptions of the rule of law and the contingencies of the extraordinary political context. Struggling with the dilemma of how to adhere to some commitment to the rule of law in such periods leads to alternative constructions, constructions that mediate conceptions of transitional rule of law" (ibid., p. 15). We must recognize that in transitions "the rule of law is ultimately contingent" (ibid., p. 11), "partial, contextual, and situated between at least two legal and political orders" (ibid., p. 9). So much so, that "in transition, the ordinary intuitions and predicates about law simply do not apply. In dynamic periods of political flux, legal responses generate a sui generis paradigm of transformative law" (ibid., p. 6).

What characterizes law in this transitional epoch is its "liminal" quality— "it is the law between regimes"—and its "limited form... limited and symbolic—a secular ritual of political passage" (Teitel, this volume). Through such and other means, and drawing upon the "canonical language, and the symbols and rituals of contemporary political passage," "a new course is charted" (ibid.). And this charting, the construction of a "collective liberal narrative," is "transitional justice's main contribution" (ibid.). It retells the despotic past and foretells the liberal future, not merely passively as record and prediction, but actively as denunciation and redemptive prophecy, and as "the leading ritual of modern political passage"; "[t]ransitional accounts themselves construct a normative relation, as they connect the society's past with its future" (ibid.).

This ties in well with Jiří Přibáň's theme, the importance of constitutional symbolism in distinguishing and at the same time bridging the past, present, and future of postcommunist transitions. For him, too, where other systems are in turmoil, law becomes particularly important, since "[t]he symbolic function of legal rationality... becomes extraordinarily strong in the process of a revolution which depicts itself as a constitutional and legal transformation" (Přibáň, this volume). In this period, says Přibáň like Teitel, "law operates both as a mechanism of social stabilization and change. It has the double function of being the stabilizing symbol and being the instrument of the coming changes. It helps to minimize the risk that the future of a revolution would get beyond control. At the same time, it speeds up the abandonment of the condemned past because it legislates new political conditions and thus constitutes its own present which, from a temporal point of view, is still in the future and yet to be achieved" (ibid.).

All transitional states face these dilemmas. Different states with different pasts deal with them in different ways. Přibáň illustrates these demands on law, and their strains with traditional conceptions of the rule of law, suggestively and with detailed discussion of a number of central challenges, among them how to deal with the past legally, whether to insist on or deny legal continuity, how to rebuild political identity and (re-)constitute civil society, whether and how to combine or choose between ethnic and civic traditions in determining the specific character of the *nation* that is to be constitutionally enshrined. In all these examples, he seeks to demonstrate that and how "[t]he ethical issues of historical justice, political identity and national history were channeled by the legal and constitutional modes of communication" (Přibáň, this volume).

These explorations of the specificities and peculiarities of transitional law are well taken. They alert us to the inevitable tensions among demands placed on law in such circumstances and times, and the often novel ways that have been devised to resolve them in matters of criminal, historical, reparatory, administrative, and constitutional justice. Above all, Teitel's and Přibáň's stress on the intermediary and dynamic role of law in transition and the influence this exerts upon the form it takes, are particularly illuminating. While it is now fashionable and often useful to question the implicit teleology in transition talk, there is no doubt that where you came from, where you stand, and where you hope to end up, deeply affect what you do, what you should do, the way you do it, and the consequences as well. And when you are trying to depart from where you came from and end up in a very different place, odds are that you will ask different things of your institutions than you would if you just wanted to stay, safely and securely, where you are.

All this is important to acknowledge, particularly by contrast with apparently simple and commonly unsuccessful "off-the-shelf blueprint" (Jacoby

1999: 62) approaches to legal transplantation and development. These latter have been plentiful among reformers and international legal "experts" and their results are not covered in glory. And that should not be surprising. For it is not only postdictatorial "transitions" which differentiate the contexts in which the rule of law might be sought. Law never means everything in people's lives, and it rarely means nothing either. But to speak sensibly of the rule of law as a significant element in the life of a society, the law's norms must be socially *normative*. They must make a difference. How that difference-making capacity might be generated is something for which we have few universal prescriptions worth offering.

For it is a general truth, and not merely a transitional one, that we have few recipes for producing the legal normativity in a society on which the rule of law depends. Its ingredients vary, some don't travel well, some turn out on arrival to depend upon others which were not noticed at home let alone packed, resources and equipment in some places are more welcoming than in others. And that is not even to mention *tastes,* which everyone knows are beyond discussion. And if this is all true of the conditions that legal orders need to satisfy to generate the rule of law, it is much more so of the particular institutions and practices that might satisfy such conditions. Here the variety is enormous. This is true both in a positive sense: there are many ways in which comparable achievements can be arranged (Selznick 1999); and negatively: the same institutional arrangements work differently, even counterproductively,[1] and some don't work at all, in different places.

And yet, it might be misleading to insist on too fancy a distinction between transitional and more general understandings of the rule of law. For the more fancy one gets, the more vulnerable one becomes to at least two sorts of criticism. First, the key explainer and differentiator, "transition" is too blunt an instrument to do the work asked of it. And second, too heavy an emphasis on the *sui generis* character of the transitional rule of law runs the risk of a somewhat "po-mo" relativism or localism that can be misleading and unhelpful.

First, the bluntness of the instrument. A lot is happening in postcommunist or postdictatorial societies more generally, law has to deal with a great deal of it and *transition* is arguably too meager a concept to explain it all. A concept that explains everything is in danger of explaining nothing. Perhaps there are other forces in play than the desire to escape a dingy past and enter a sparklingly transformed future.

Transition is a situation, a condition, a predicament if you will, on a kind of indeterminate but Whiggishly-inclined trajectory from hateful past to liberal future. But in that space people make decisions, mistakes, seek to serve their interests, etc., for many reasons some concerned with that trajectory, others not much or at all. For example, elite theory, which is quite popular these days, focuses on one category of such people. But elites have many purposes, some of them arguably not related merely to getting us from disreputable point A in the transition to liberal destination B.

Think, for a moment, of David Stark and László Bruszt's *Postsocialist Pathways* (1998), full of people not especially interested in the transition and its normative change, but in making a buck, even a killing, with the resources and connections and opportunities at their disposal. It might turn out that differences between approaches in different "transitional" countries have as much to do with different elites choosing different solutions, for different reasons, even where observers might see common problems, as they do with the exigencies of the transitional moment.

But what if elite purposes, or the purposes of other key legal actors, really are dominated by transitional ambitions? What reason do we have to expect that the *explanation*, still less the *results* of what actually occurs to and in law faithfully reflect those ambitions and purposes? One reason I am uneasy with "transition" as the unmoved mover of all this is the way in which Teitel's and Přibáň's chapters seem to slide between saying what a transitional situation might require to imputing that as the purpose and explanation of actual arrangements as they have developed. And not only do these arrangements get explained by the needs of transition; they seem uncommonly successful in satisfying those needs: "the language of the law imbues the new order with legitimacy and authority," "legal practices enable successor societies to make liberalizing political change"; "[a]s the question of transitional justice is worked through, the society begins to perform the signs and rites of a functioning liberal order"; "transitional jurisprudence emerges as a distinct paradigmatic form of law responsive to and constructive of the extraordinary circumstances of periods of substantial political change" (Teitel, this volume). This is the language of success, to which a skeptic might respond, well maybe, sometimes, maybe not, sometimes not.

Are we talking of individuals' purposes which may or may not be achieved, transitional "needs" which may or may not be satisfied, or end-states that are actually and successfully achieved, and the achievement of which explains what went before? It makes a difference. What threatens is a sort of circle, common and tempting in a lot of functionalist explanation. One postulates an overarching social need or function-necessary-to-be formed, say transition to the rule of law. People do whatever they do, what happens happens. And one concludes that whatever they do, regardless of what happens, it occurs to fulfill that function for the transition, so it is what the law does and it is the reason why law does it. This circle is even more tightly closed by the assumption that transitions are *sui generis*, indeed each transition is in its own way, since that robs an observer of standards with which to assess what's going on. I'll return to this point presently.

Secondly, there is a larger point to be made about the allegedly *sui gener-*

is nature of the rule of law. In her book, Teitel several times acknowledges that transitions do not raise unique issues, or rather, as she puts it, "these periods are not fully discontinuous [from the normal, I presume] but, instead, vividly display in exaggerated form, problems that are ordinarily less transparent in more established justice systems" (Teitel 2000: 67). She does little with this point, however, which indeed cuts across the grain of much that she says elsewhere. But the observation has implications.

Elsewhere I have advocated a teleological approach to the rule of law (see Krygier 2001a; Krygier 2001b; Krygier 2002). First, ask what the *point* of it is, why bother, what's the fuss? The answer to that teleological question might be quite general in form—for example to reduce arbitrary exercise of power—as might questions about why anyone should value that: *protection* against arbitrary power and *facilitation* of confident interaction are my simple answers. Only *then* should one go on to ask how best, in particular circumstances, times, societies, legal traditions, to achieve these ends. I take the first question to travel further than the particular answers developed or tried in particular places and I recommend this procedure for every occasion, transitional, transformational, consolidat*ing*, consolidat*ed*, solid as a rock.

And so, it is no doubt true that if we try to use law in periods of transition, "our" domestic intuitions will often be confronted, if not assaulted. But this does not mean that in the lands of transition nothing general can be said about the rule of law, that all is "partial" and "contingent." Rather, it simply confirms that wherever you are, the rule of law should be approached with a combination of its *purposes* in mind (and yours, which may not be the same), acquaintance with various attempts to ground and institutionalize them, *together with* a great deal of reflected-upon local knowledge. It should never be regarded as an occasion to impose imported institutional recipes and *idées fixes* about how precisely they must be fulfilled. And so, I would dispute Teitel's claim made in this chapter and in her book, that "in transition, the ordinary intuitions and predicates about law simply do not apply" (Teitel, this volume). Instead, I would want to endorse and to generalize to other contexts the footnote appended in this chapter to that claim: "[this] does not mean that ideals of rule of law are irrelevant to transitions, but rather that they are inapplicable to these exceptional circumstances without making a variety of adjustments, both to the context of transition, and to the particulars of that state's political conditions" (ibid.).

Whatever the particular context in which one might seek the rule of law, it is always sensible to *start* with the experience of countries which have rich experience of the rule of law, since that experience is often larded with trial, error and reflection, but one must, also always, be open to the need to move beyond that experience in the face of different trials, newfound errors, and further reflection.

It is doubtless true that in the West, the distance between purposes, intuitions, and institutions is generally smaller than in countries undergoing unprecedented regime transitions. But this is just to say that when things are established, familiar, and change little, it is easier to know what to do than when they are novel, strange, and/or change a lot. But changes, novelties, and surprises confront "normal" countries, too, sometimes dramatically. It may be altogether more dramatic and unprecedented after the collapse of dictatorships, but everywhere, reflections about what we want from law will not automatically tell us how in particular circumstances it might be got. Everywhere, we should try to resist being forced to choose between the clichés of parochial "intuitions" and the conviction that in matters of transitional justice, it all just depends. Everywhere we need to exercise judgment, not follow recipes.

The point is not that the particular "transitional" considerations that fancy theory addresses are of no account. They are important and one learns a great deal about them from writers, such as Ruti Teitel, Jiří Přibáň, Kim Lane Scheppele, Cindy Skach, and others. It is rather that, in reacting against an impoverished "off-the-shelf blueprint" (Jacoby 1999: 62) approach to the rule of law, one must guard against so boosting the uniqueness of transitions that one severs their moorings in institutional possibilities and limitations, and more broadly in the human condition and more general human purposes. That not only limits one's repertoire of possibility needlessly, and risks time-consuming reinvention of wheels, but it also makes it hard to know when purposes are achieved or criticism is appropriate. For where would standards of appraisal or criticism come from in a world of truly *sui generis* events?

We know, more or less, what the rule of law is about, but we can more easily state the values it serves, and recognize violations of it, than we can specify the particular institutions and practices that will promote it, with any combination of generality, detail, and ability to travel. What might go to accomplishing (or thwarting) it will vary with time, place, history, and tradition. Since the ideal of the rule of law is important, we should keep that ideal clearly in view, but we should avoid identifying it with, still less reducing it to, particular incarnations or institutional arrangements. These are general truths made particularly apparent in transitional contexts. They are not merely "transitional truths."

CORRUPTION

If a theme of the first two chapters in this part of the book is that we have not always understood what will serve the rule of law in circumstances of transition, then a theme of Ivan Krastev's intriguing and often counter-intuitive chapter is that we equally overrate our understanding of what most threatens the rule of law and how best to guard it.

The rule of law, Krastev contends, has become "the white myth of transition. After some years of flirting with the ideas of democracy and market economy now rule of law is the magic phrase in Eastern Europe. It is rule of law and not democracy that brings foreign investors, it is rule of law that secures development and protects rights" (Krastev, this volume). Pitted against this "white myth" there is an even more widespread "black myth": corruption, "the explanation of last resort for all failures and disappointments of the first postcommunist decade" (ibid.). It is not only that the rule of law is taken to be good and corruption bad, but that they are believed to be precisely each other's "Other"—if one rises, the other must fall. And so the promotion of the rule of law is sought through anti-corruption campaigns, corruption is fought by measures claimed to build the rule of law, and these campaigns become a currency of political virtue. While corruption is allegedly everywhere and the rule of law nowhere, who speaks for the former or against the latter?

Krastev's provocative thesis is that most of us who talk of corruption literally do not know what we are talking about. More to the point, we do not know *why* so many people are talking about it in countries in transition, and why so many of them are convinced it is continually increasing. These anxieties are, he insists, not explained by an increase in corrupt practices, the evidence of which is at best equivocal. Nor, on the other hand, is it simply explained by media "beat-ups" of corruption. Rather it stems from a change in the quality of corruption—from an "economy of favors" to an economy of bribes—and represents public unease at the new forms of inequality that attend an economy which monetarizes even its corrupt practices. The new economy breaks down the intimacies and communities involved in what Adam Podgórecki used to call fellowships of "dirty togetherness" (1994: 51, 115, 131–32) which could link people in various places in former hierarchies, and leaves in their place the power of money, to which many have little access. *Blat* was socially acceptable because it combined friendship, mutual assistance, and a kind of social equality. Monetarized corruption does none of these things and it corrodes the power of resources which once were useful and at the same time did not appear simply venal. So the problem is not the existence nor the scale of corruption, as it is often interpreted, but its kind and what it represents.

Nevertheless, so great is its hold on the public mind that nowadays the call for anti-corruption campaigns is well-nigh irresistible: "[i]f in the beginning of the campaign the suspicion is that corruption is almost everywhere, already in the middle of the campaign the suspicion is that corruption is almost everything. The final stage is the conviction that almost everybody is corrupt" (Krastev, this volume). Krastev is skeptical about this development for many reasons, among them their inability to deliver their loudly proclaimed goal, the rule of law. Since corruption is very hard to prove, the determination to prosecute in ever-increasing circles for corruption exposes the legal system to ridicule: if everyone is corrupt and so few are convicted for corruption, then what is wrong with the legal system? And if the legal system is remodeled on the best Transparency International models, and still everyone is corrupt, what hope for the rule of law? Rather than promote the rule of law, obsession with corruption might just undermine the possibility of it.

This argument gibes with a deeper issue raised at several places in this book, and especially this part. Is the rule of law to be regarded as a primarily legal institutional achievement, judged by the forms and properties of legal institutions, or is it rather to be seen as a complex social and political state of affairs in which the law *counts*? Such a state of affairs depends in part, to be sure, on legal institutions, but on much else as well, and familiar institutional recipes are not self-evidently either necessary, or sufficient to produce it. The argument in this book has been that the second interpretation is the more useful, and that one should not get carried away with formal-legal prescriptions at the expense of social and political realities. To do so is to mistake means for ends, and at the same time threaten those, and perhaps other, valuable goals, in whose name one is purporting to act. So, just as corruption is not necessarily reduced by an obsession with it, nor is the rule of law necessarily served by such an obsession. And mechanistic attempts to institutionalize the rule of law fall under similar suspicion to those voiced by Krastev about anti-corruption campaigns; "what postcommunist societies need are policies that reduce corruption but not a rhetoric that leads to corruption-centered politics" (Krastev, this volume).

EUROPE

The last chapter in this part and this book, fittingly, concerns a development only recently consummated but one whose effects are likely to be profound for all the questions with which we have been concerned. For Neil Walker's chapter analyzes the club which all our postcommunist states are anxious to join: the European Union. And that, too, is a work-in-progress, indeed a *sui generis* transformation if ever there was one, arguably more so than even postdictatorships face. For the latter still talk of wanting to become states with democracy and the rule of law, and, however much the transiters might deviate from them, we have examples of those things. But no one knows what a united Europe will be like, since among other things, it is unlike any state we have known and statehood has been the unexamined presupposition of the transitions hitherto embarked upon. The EU "lacks... a generalizable

template and background presumption of settled political form," and equally "the strong cultural ties of common language, traditions, history, affective
symbols, and developed civil society and public sphere, which, in various
mixes, are central to many national or pluri-national state identities" (Walker, this volume). Whatever the Union ends up to be, the process of its formation, and the form it ultimately takes will have profound effects on the
countries we have been discussing.

Notwithstanding the unprecedented nature of this transformation, Walker
does not think that this means everything is particular or contingent, but rather
he develops his argument from a conception of the goals of constitutionalism
and the ways in which constitutions contribute to the achievement of those
goals. The means to be adopted, however, he regards to be contingent, dependent on circumstance and so on. That, as I have suggested, seems to me the
proper way to think about the attainment of many of the things we value.

The substance of Walker's argument is that contrary to the common belief
that the enlargees are at the mercy of the enlargers in Europe, the truth might
be quite different, since the process of enlargement significantly assists Europe
in approaching some of the conditions of successfully creating the unprecedented constitutional entity that a united Europe would be. As a result, Walker
suggests that the enlargees are important, at its highest perhaps even indispensable, to the negotiation of a successful European constitution and constitutionalism, and that "the current constitutional transition in the EU offers
a context within which it is possible, though far from guaranteed, that the
underlying asymmetry of power between two distinct regional constituencies
of West and East—between old and new—will become less pertinent to the
project of European polity-building" (Walker, this volume).

His argument is strong, and his self-conscious posture of "studied optimism" seems to me the appropriate one to adopt when countries are playing
for high stakes, and the future is not closed. However even at its strongest,
Walker's case may not yet be the one he imagines he has made. Asymmetry
might remain, albeit of a different sort. Max Weber, everyone knows, considers
that bureaucracy was indispensable to modern society; whatever forms its polity took. And in some of his political writings he clearly feared that *German*
bureaucrats, for particularly German reasons, were also too powerful.

But at a theoretical level, he insisted that the power of bureaucracies was
an open question, which their contemporary indispensability did not close or
decide. For, he insisted against, among others, Robert Michels, indispensability and power are conceptually and often empirically distinct. The ancient
Greek slaves, he said, were indispensable to the Greek polity, but they were
not at all powerful. And so, some Hungarian, let alone Romanian, might be
intrigued and persuaded by Walker's argument that they are much more
important to the rest of Europe than they realized, but still worry that they

might not be more powerful than they already thought. That might paradoxically mean that the enlargees are more important to the shape of the enlargers than we thought they might be, while the power of the latter over the former continues not much diminished. Whether that is "win-win" or "lose-lose," it is too soon to tell. Whatever the outcome, however, Walker has identified the matrix within which the next stage of struggle with the problems at the heart of this book will take place.

NOTES

1 See, for example, András Sajó's observation, based on experience in postcommunist Europe, particularly Hungary: "[w] here the cabinet is endowed with its own anti-corruption police, that police will investigate those whom the majority in the cabinet dislike. The rule of law will be stabbed in the back by a partisan and arbitrary knife, although the use of that knife was originally authorized to protect the rule of law" (Sajó 1998: 46).

BIBLIOGRAPHY

Ash, Timothy Garton. "Eastern Europe: The Year of Truth." *New York Review of Books*, 15 February 1990.

Jacoby, Wade. "Priest and Penitent: The European Union as a Force in the Domestic Politics of Eastern Europe" *East European Constitutional Review* 8, nos. 1–2 (1999): 62–67.

Krygier, Martin. "The Rule of Law" in *International Encyclopaedia of the Social and Behavioural Sciences*, eds.-in chief Smelser, Neil J. and Paul B. Bates (Oxford: Elsevier Science, 2001a), Vol. 20, pp. 13404–408.

Krygier, Martin. "Transitional Questions about the Rule of Law: Why, What and How?" *East Central Europe/L'Europe de Centre-Est* 28, no. 1 (2001b): 1–34.

Krygier, Martin. "The Grammar of Colonial Legality: Subjects, Objects, and the Australian Rule of Law" in *Australia Reshaped: 200 Years of Institutional Transformation*, eds. Brennan, Geoffrey and Francis C. Castles (Cambridge: Cambridge University Press, 2002), pp. 220–59.

Podgórecki, Adam. *Polish Society*. Westport, Connecticut: Praeger, 1994.

Sajó, András. "Corruption, Clientelism and the Future of the Constitutional State in Eastern Europe" *East European Constitutional Review* 7, no. 2 (1998): 37–46.

Selznick, Philip. "Legal Cultures and the Rule of Law" in *The Rule of Law after Communism*, eds. Krygier, Martin and Adam Czarnota (Ashgate: Aldershot, 1999), pp. 21–38.

Stark, David and László Bruszt. *Postsocialist Pathways. Transforming Politics and Property in East Central Europe*. Cambridge: Cambridge University Press, 1998.

Teitel, Ruti. *Transitional Justice*. New York: Oxford University Press, 2000.

Transitional Rule of Law

Ruti Teitel

Introduction

My remarks attempt to provide a distillation of arguments that are more fully elaborated in my book (Teitel 2000).

In recent decades, societies throughout much of the world—Latin America, Eastern Europe, the former Soviet Union, Africa—have been engaged in transition: postcolonial changes, and the overthrowing of military dictatorships and totalitarian regimes, for greater freedom and democracy. In these times of massive political movement from illiberal rule, one burning question recurs: how should societies deal with their evil pasts? What, if any, is the relation between a state's response to its repressive past and its prospects for creating a liberal order?

For about two decades now, the point of departure in the transitional justice debate is the notion that the move toward a more liberal democratic political system implies a universal norm. Indeed, this methodological question is the subject of a paper by one of the editors of this book (Krygier 2001). Yet, I suggest this way of framing the debate is too stark. Instead, my remarks propose an alternative way of thinking about the relation of law to political transformation. Exploring an array of experiences describes a distinctive conception of justice and rule of law in the context of political transformation.

The problem of transitional justice arises within the distinctive context of transition—a shift in political orders, and more precisely, of change in a liberalizing direction. Understanding the problem of justice in the transitional context requires entering a distinctive discourse organized in terms of the profound dilemmas characteristic of these extraordinary periods. The threshold dilemma arises from the context of justice in political transformation: law is caught between the past and the future, between the backward-looking and the forward-looking, between the retrospective and prospective. Transitional justice, therefore, is that justice associated with these political circumstances. Transitions imply paradigm shifts in the conception of justice; therefore, law's role appears deeply paradoxical. In ordinary times, law provides order and stability, but in extraordinary periods of political upheaval, law maintains order, even as it enables transformation. Accordingly, in transition, the ordinary intuitions and predicates about law simply do not apply. What this means is further elaborated in the chapter. It does not mean that ideals of rule of law are irrelevant to transitions, but rather that they are inapplicable to these exceptional circumstances without making a variety of adjustments, both to the context of transition, and to the particulars of that state's political conditions. In dynamic periods of political flux, legal responses generate a *sui generis* paradigm of transformative law.

What emerges is a conception of justice that is contextualized and partial: it is constituted by, and constitutive of, the transition. The very notion of what is just is contingent, and informed by prior injustice. As a state undergoes political change, legacies of injustice have a bearing on what is deemed transformative.

Indeed, at some level, one might say that the legal responses create transition. In transition, the rule of law is historically and politically contingent, elaborated in response to past political repression that had often been condoned. While the rule of law ordinarily implies prospectivity in the law, transitional rule of law is both backward- and forward-looking, as it disclaims illiberal past values, and reclaims liberal norms.

PUNISHMENT OR IMPUNITY

In the prevailing view of transitional justice, the core debate as it takes as its point of departure ordinary times, frames the relevant question as whether or not to punish the predecessor regime. This is the so-called "punishment or impunity" debate. Punishment dominates our understandings of transitional justice, and of the related rule of law. In the public imagination, transitional justice is generally linked with the trials of ancient regimes. The enduring symbols of the English and French revolutions from monarchic to republican rule are the trials of Kings Charles I and Louis XVI. A half century after the events, the leading monument to the Nazis' World War II defeat remains the Nuremberg trials. The contemporary wave of transitions from military rule, throughout Latin America and Africa, as well as from communist rule in Central Europe and the former Soviet bloc, has revived the debate over whether to punish. While trials are thought to be foundational, and to enable drawing a bright line demarcating the normative shift from illegitimate to legitimate rule, the exercise of the state's punishment power in the circumstances of radical political change raises profound dilemmas. Transitional trials are few and far between, particularly in the contemporary period. The low incidence of successor trials reveals the real dilemmas in dealing with systemic wrongdoing by way of the criminal law. In the transitional context, conventional understandings of individual responsibility are frequently inapplicable, and have spurred the emergence of new legal forms: partial sanctions that fall outside conventional legal categories.

This harshest form of law is emblematic of accountability and the rule of law; yet, its representation far transcends its actual exercise.

TRANSITIONAL RULE OF LAW AND THE LIMITED CRIMINAL SANCTION

Despite the call for justice in the abstract, transitional practices over the last half-century reveal the recurring problems of justice as a result of the norm shift characterizing transition. These compromised conditions of justice mean that there are real limits on the exercise of the punishment power in periods of political transition. These real rule of law dilemmas help explain why, despite the dramatic expansion in criminal liability in the abstract, enforcement lags far behind. Indeed, transitional practices reveal a pattern of criminal investigations and prosecutions, often followed by little or no penalty. While ordinarily punishment is conceptualized as a unitary practice that includes both the establishment and penalizing of wrongdoing, in the transitional criminal sanction, the elements of investigation and condemnation have become somewhat detached from one another. It is this partial criminal process I term the "limited sanction" that distinguishes criminal justice in transition.

The "limited criminal sanction" constitutes compromised prosecution processes that do not necessarily culminate in full punishment: and that imply differentiation of the phases of establishing responsibility, and ascribing penalty. Depending on just how limited the process, investigations may or may not lead to indictments, adjudication, and conviction. Convictions are often followed by little or no punishment. In transition, the criminal sanction may be limited to an investigation establishing wrongdoing.

The limits of the transitional criminal sanction are well illustrated throughout history: in post-World War I and World War II cases, in the postmilitary trials of Southern Europe, as well as by the contemporary successor criminal proceedings in Latin America and Africa, and in the wave of political change in Central Europe, following the Soviet collapse. Though it is often repressed, post-World War II successor justice illustrates the limited criminal sanction. In the midst of the Allied Control Council No. 10 follow-up trials, the International Military Tribunal began the reversal of the Allied punishment policy. Between 1946 and 1958, a process of reviews and clemency culminates in the mass commutation of sentences for war criminals. In Germany's national trials, a similar sequence unfolds. Out of the more than one thousand cases tried between 1955 and 1969, fewer than one hundred of those convicted received life sentences, and fewer than three hundred received limited terms. Years later, in Southern Europe, a similar sequence unfolds. Greece's trials of its military police culminate largely in suspended or commutable sentences. A similar pattern appeared in the transitions out of military rule in Latin America. In the 1980s, soon after the Argentine junta trials, began the limits on the follow-up trials. Ultimately, pardons would be extended to everyone convicted of atrocities, even the junta leaders. Amnesties became the norm throughout much of the continent: Chile, Nicaragua, and El Salvador.

The story repeats itself in Central and Eastern Europe after the communist collapse. Ten years after the revolution and the real story is the transitional limited criminal sanction. In unified Germany's "borderguards" trials, suspension of sentences is the norm. This was also true of the few prosecutions in the Czech Republic, Romania, Bulgaria, and Albania. The course of developments reflects a limiting of the final phase of punishment policy. Sometimes the limiting of the criminal sanction is used strategically, as an incentive to achieve other political goals, such as cooperation in investigations or other political projects; in Chile, a law, exempting its military from prosecution, was conditioned on officers' cooperation in criminal investigations relating to past wrongdoing under military rule. Penalties were dropped up front and on condition of confession to wrongdoing, in postapartheid South Africa, with the amnestying of crimes deemed "political" on conditions of participation in the truth and Reconciliation Commission. This left a window open for investigations into past wrongs, a practice which could also be understood as a limited prosecutorial process.

Other contemporary legal responses occurring in the region, such as the _ad hoc_ International Criminal Tribunal established to adjudicate genocide and war crimes of the former Yugoslavia, reflect similar developments. The common problem of securing custody over the accused, as well as the lack of control over the evidence, as well as the many other constraints relating to war crimes prosecutions—means that the International Tribunal has often had little choice but to investigate and indict—but to go no further.

The "limited criminal sanction" constitutes the pragmatic resolution of the core rule of law dilemma of transition: namely, the problem of attempting to attribute individual responsibility for systemic wrongs perpetrated under repressive rule. The basic transitional problem is whether there is any theory of responsibility that can span the move from a repressive, to a more liberal regime. Indeed, the emergence of the limited sanction suggests a more fluid way to think about what punishment does: namely, clarify and condemn wrongdoing, without necessary attribution of individual blame and penalty. The transitional sanction prompts rethinking the theory of punishment, namely to think about punishment's justification as more closely connected to discrete stages of the criminal process. The emergence of the transitional sanction points to an alternative sense of the retributivist idea. Though this sanction is characterized by its limited character, transitional practices suggest that core retributive purposes of recognition and condemnation of past wrongdoing are vindicable by diminished—even symbolic—punishment. The sheer recognition and condemnation of past wrongdoing has transformative dimensions. Where wrongdoing is publicly established, it liberates the collective in a measured process of transformation. Mere exposure of wrongs can stigmatize and disqualify affected persons from entire realms of the public sphere, and relegate them to a predecessor regime. In extraordinary circumstances of radical political change, some of the purposes ordinarily advanced by the full criminal process are advanced in the sanction's more limited form.

Practices in such periods suggest the transitional limited sanction is that mediating form. The absence of traditional plenary punishment in periods of political transition suggests that more complex understandings of criminal responsibility emerge in the application of the principle of individual responsibility in the distinct context of criminal justice associated with systemic crimes in shifts out of repressive rule. Rule of law within a liberalizing state is commonly equated with individual accountability, individual responsibility central to law in the liberal state. Yet, this perspective on punishment does not account well for its role in times of radical political flux, where the transitional criminal form is informed by values related to the distinctive project of political change. Ordinarily, criminal justice is theorized in starkly dichotomous terms, as animated by either a backward-looking concern with retribution, or a forward-looking, utilitarian concern with deterrence, considered internal to the justice system. In transition, however, punishment is informed by a mix of retrospective and prospective purposes: whether to punish, or to amnesty, to exercise or restrain criminal justice is rationalized in overtly political terms. Values such as mercy and reconciliation commonly treated as external to criminal justice are an explicit part of the transitional deliberation (Teitel 2000). The explicit politicization of criminal law in these periods challenges ideal understandings of justice, and yet turns out to be a persistent feature of jurisprudence in the transitional context.

The extraordinary transitional form of punishment I term the "limited" criminal sanction is directed less at penalizing perpetrators, than it is at advancing the political transformation's normative shift. The limited sanction is well illustrated historically, not only in postwar policy, but also in the course of punishment following more recent cases of regime change, during which the sanction performs important operative acts—formal public inquiry into and clarification of the past, the indictment of past wrongdoing—, advancing the normative shift central to liberalizing transition. Even in its arch limited form, the limited sanction is a symbol of rule of law that enables expression of a critical normative message.

What distinguishes transitional criminal measures is their use to construct normative change. This is plainly seen in the way transitional responses' focus varies from country to country to "undo" rationalized past political violence, through procedures of inquiry and indictment, rituals of collective knowledge that enable isolation and disavowal of past wrongdoings. Where the prior regime was sustained by persecutory policy rationalized within a legal system, this policy rationale is addressed by the transitional critical legal response. Critical responses to past persecution express the message that the policy is manmade, and, therefore, reformable. The transitional criminal sanction by isolating knowledge of past wrongdoing and individuating responsibility enables the potential of liberalizing change, in this way liberating the successor regime from the weight of states' evil legacies. Through ritualized legal processes of appropriation and misappropriation, of avowal and disavowal, of symbolic loss and gain, allowing the perceptions of transformation, societies begin to move in a liberalizing direction.

Criminal justice in some form, transitional practices suggest, is a ritual of liberalizing states, as it is these practices that publicly construct rule of law norms. Through these processes, a line is drawn, liberating a past that allows the society to move forward. While punishment is conventionally considered largely retributive in its aim, in transition, even punishment's purposes become largely corrective, going beyond the individual perpetrator to the broader society. This function is seen in the primacy of systemic political offenses, for example, in the persistence of prosecutions of crimes against humanity—the archetypal offense of persecutory politics, constituting a critical response to illiberal rule through the criminal law. Moreover, whereas ordinarily punishment is thought to divide society, in transition, wherever punishment is exercised, it is done in a limited fashion, to allow the possibility of return to a liberal state. As such, criminal processes have affinities with other transitional exercises of rule of law.

THE PARADIGMATIC TRANSITIONAL RULE OF LAW RESPONSE

The operative effects advanced by the limited criminal sanction, such as establishing, recording, and condemning past wrongdoing, display affinities with other legal acts and processes constructive of transition. The massive and *systemic* wrongdoing characteristic of modern repression implies a recognition of a mix of individual and collective responsibility. There is a pronounced overlap of punitive and administrative institutions and processes. Individualized processes of accountability give way to administrative investigations and commissions of inquiry, the compilation of public records, official pronouncements and condemnation of past wrongs. These are often subsumed in state histories commissioned pursuant to a political mandate for reconciliation. However, whether bureaucratic forms of public inquiry and official truth-tellings are desirable, and will signify liberalization, is contingent on the nature of the state legacies of repressive rule. To illustrate, one might compare, in this regard, postmilitary Latin America with the postcommunist bloc on the social meaning of state history and accountability. As is elaborated further on, the diversity in their historical responses reflects their disparate histories of repression.

The paradigmatic affinities discussed here bear on the recurrent question in transitional justice debates concerning what is the right response to repressive rule, towards supporting a lasting democracy. The subtext of this question assumes a transitional ideal and that normative concerns somehow militate for a particular categorical response. However, this is simply the wrong question: there is no one right response to how to deal with a state's repressive past, and to liberalize for the future. This question should be reframed. Among states, the approach taken to transitional justice is politically contingent, nevertheless, it is worth distinguishing between states undergoing juridical transitions, where there is an established rule of law tradition and those where there is not. At the same time, there appears to be a paradigmatic transitional response in the law. Transitional constitutionalism, criminal justice, and the rule of law share affinities in the contingent relation that these norms bear to prior rule, as well as in their operative work in the move to a more liberal political order.

Transitional constructivism

I will now turn to the constructive role of law in transition. How is transition constructed? What is law's role in political passage? The paradigmatic form of the law that emerges in these times operates in an extraordinary fashion, and itself plays a constructive role in the transition. It both stabilizes and destabilizes. In these circumstances, law's distinctive feature is its mediating function, as it maintains a threshold level of formal continuity, while enabling transformative discontinuity. The extent to which formal continuity will be maintained depends on the modality of transformation, while the content of the normative shift will be a function of history, legal culture, and political tradition, as well as the society's receptiveness to innovation.[1] What this also implies, of course, is that states with more established rule of law traditions will have an easier time to reestablish.

Just what do transitional legal practices have in common? Law constructs transitions through diverse processes, including legislation, adjudication, and administrative measures. Transitional operative acts include pronouncements of indictments and verdicts; the issuing of amnesties, reparations, and apologies; and the promulgation of constitutions and reports. These transitional practices share features, namely, they are ways to publicly construct new collective political understandings. Transitional processes, whether taking the forms of prosecution, lustration, or inquiry, share this critical dimension. These are all transitional actions taken to manifest change by publicly sharing new political knowledge. Law here works on the margin, as it performs the work of separation from the prior regime, and integration with the successor regime. Transitional law has a "liminal" quality, it is law between regimes. The peculiar efficacy of these salient transitional legal practices is their ability to effect separation and integration functions—all within continuous processes.

Transitional rule of law often implies procedures that do not seem fair or compelling: trials lacking in regular punishment, reparations based on politically driven and arbitrary baselines, constitutions that do not necessarily last. What characterizes the transitional legal response is its limited form, embodied in the provisional constitution and purge, the limited sanction and reparation, the discrete history and official narrative. Transitional rule of law is, above all, limited and symbolic—a secular ritual of political passage.

The legal process has become the leading transitional response for its ability to convey publicly and authoritatively the political changes that constitute the normative shift between regimes. What is constructed through these processes is the relevant political difference between illiberal and liberal regimes. In its symbolic form, transitional jurisprudence reconstructs the relevant political differences through changes in status, membership, and community. While the relevant critical difference is necessarily contingent, it is recognized as legitimate, in light of a given successor society's past legacies. Moreover, the language of law imbues the new order with legitimacy and authority.

In modern political transformation, legal practices enable successor societies to make liberalizing political change. By mediating the normative hiatus and shift characterizing transition, the turn to law comprises important functional, conceptual, operative, and symbolic dimensions. Law epitomizes the liberal rationalist response to mass suffering and catastrophe; it expresses the notion that there is, after all, something to be done. Rather than resignation to historical repetition, in the liberal society, the hope of change is put in the air. By their engagement in transitional justice debates, successor societies signal the rational imagining of a more liberal political order.

Legal rituals offer the leading alternative to the violent responses of retribution and vengeance in periods of political upheaval. The transitional legal response is deliberate, measured, restrained, *and* restraining; in their transitional form, ritualized legal processes enable gradual, controlled change. As the question of transitional justice is worked through, the society begins to perform the signs and rites of a functioning liberal order. Transitional law transcends the "merely" symbolic to be the leading ritual of modern political passage. Ritual acts enable the shift between two orders: of the predecessor and successor regimes. In contemporary transitions, characterized by their peaceful nature and occurrence within the law, legal processes perform the critical "undoings," the inversions of the predicates justifying the prevailing regime, through public processes that produce the collective knowledge constitutive of the normative shift. Legal processes simultaneously disavow aspects of the predecessor ideology, and affirm the ideological changes constituting liberalizing transformation.

These are various ways in which the new democracies respond to legacies of injustice. Patterns across legal forms constitute a paradigm of "transitional jurisprudence," rooted in prior political injustice. Law's role is constructivist: transitional jurisprudence emerges as a distinct paradigmatic form of law responsive to and constructive of the extraordinary circumstances of periods of substantial political change. In transitional jurisprudence, the conception of justice is partial, contextual, and situated between at least two legal and political orders. Legal norms are multiple, the idea of justice pragmatic. Transitional jurisprudence centers on the law's paradigmatic use in the normative construction of the new political regime.

TRANSITIONAL RULE OF LAW AS LIBERAL NARRATIVE

Transitional justice's main contribution is to advance the construction of a collective liberal narrative. Its uses are to advance the transformative purpose of moving the international community, as well as individual states in transition, towards greater liberalizing political change. Consider law's potential in constructing a story that lays the basis for political change. Let us begin with the trial, though observe that the transformative dimension is also advanced in other legal responses.

Law's history
One of transitional criminal justice's primary roles is historical. Trials have long played the arch role in transitional historymaking. Criminal justice creates public, formal shared processes that link up the past to the future, the individual the collective. Criminal trials are the historical, ceremonial form of shared memory-making in collectives, a way to work through a community's events in controversy. Even the ordinary criminal trial's purposes are not only to adjudicate individual responsibility, but also to establish the truth about an event in controversy in a society; this is even more true of the trial's role in settling historical controversies characteristic of periods of transition. Transitions follow regime change, and periods of heightened political and

historical conflict; therefore, a primary purpose of successor trials is to advance a measure of historical justice.

What sort of "truths" are established in such periods? They are "transitional critical truths"; namely, shared political knowledge critical of the ideology of the prior regime. Through the trial, the collective historical record produced both delegitimizes the predecessor regime, and legitimizes the successor. While military or political collapse may bring down repressive leadership, unless the bad regime is also publicly discredited, its ideology often endures. An example is the trial of King Louis XVI, which served as a forum to deliberate over and to establish the evil of monarchic rule (Walzer 1974). Leading trials, whether of the major war criminals at Nuremberg, or the public trials of Argentina's military junta, are primarily remembered, not for their condemnation of individual wrongdoers, but, instead, for their roles in creating lasting historical records of state tyranny, and for representing political shift.

Transitional criminal processes enable authoritative accounts of past evil legacies and collective historymaking. There are many representations: the recreation and dramatization of the repressive past in the trial proceedings, in the written transcript, trial records, and the judgment. Radio and television reportage add to the many representational possibilities (consider The Hague today). One might add the Internet.

The contemporary post-Cold War period has given rise to even more complex and disaggregated understandings of responsibility, as well as to a problematizing of the public and the private realms. Consider the growing focus on the role of the multinationals in World War II, and other monetary settlements that attempt to legitimate the transforming global private regime.

The connections between law in the production of history discussed above adverts to the broader role of law in constructing what I have termed the "narrative" of transition. The next part explores the distinct narrative structure of transitional rule of law.

Narratives of transition
Narratives constructed in transitions, whether trials, administrative proceedings, or historical commissions of inquiry, make a normative claim about the relation of a state's past to its prospects for a more democratic future. As is explained further on, the very transitional narrative structure propounds the claim that particular knowledge is relevant to the possibility of personal and societal change. Narratives of transition offer an account of the relation construction of the political knowledge bears to the move away from dictatorship, as well as to the potential of a more liberal future.

Transitional narratives, I claim, follow a distinct rhetorical form: beginning in tragedy, they end on a comic or romantic mode. In the classical understanding, tragedy implicates the elements of catastrophic suffering by individuals, whose fate, due to their status, implicated entire collectives, and was followed by some discovery or change from ignorance. In tragedy, knowledge seems only to confirm a fate foretold. Contemporary stories of transitional justice similarly involve stories of affliction on a grand scale. While such narratives begin in a tragic mode, in the transition they switch over to a non-tragic resolution; there is a turn to what might be characterized as a comic phase. Something happens in these accounts; the persons enmeshed in the story ultimately avert tragic fates to somehow adjust and even thrive in a new reality. In the convention associated with transitional accounts, change necessitates a critical juncture, where, as opposed to tragic structure, knowledge's revelation actually makes a difference. The country's past suffering is somehow reversed, leading to a happy ending of peace and reconciliation.

The transitional narrative structure manifests itself in fictional and nonfictional accounts of periods of political transformation. National "truth" reports read as tragic accounts that end on a redemptive note. Suffering is somehow transformed into something good for the country, to a greater societal self-knowledge, that is thought to enhance prospects for an enduring democracy. Thus, after "Night and Fog" disappearance policies throughout much of Latin America, bureaucratic processes were deployed to set up investigatory commissions. Beginning with their titles *Never Again*, the truth reports promise to deter future suffering. Thus, the prologue to the report of the Argentine National Commission on the Disappeared declares the military dictatorship "brought about the greatest and most savage tragedy" in the country's history; but history provides lessons. "[G]reat catastrophes are always instructive." "The tragedy which began with the military dictatorship in March 1976, the most terrible our nation has ever suffered, will undoubtedly serve to help us understand that it is only democracy which can save a people from horror on this scale." Knowledge of past suffering plays a crucial role in the state's ability to make liberating transition.

Confrontation with the past is considered necessary to liberalizing transformation. The report of the Chilean National Commission on Truth and Reconciliation asserts that knowledge and disclosure of past suffering is necessary to reestablishing the country's identity. The decree establishing Chile's National Commission declares "the truth had to be brought to light, for only on such a foundation... would it be possible to... create the necessary conditions for achieving true national reconciliation." "Truth" is the necessary precondition for democracy. This is also the organizing thesis of the El Salvador Truth Commission. This story line is seen in the report's title: *From Madness to Hope* tells a story of a violent civil war, followed by "truth and reconciliation." According to the report's introduction, the truth's "creative consequences" can "settle political and social differences by means of agreement instead of violent action." "Peace [is] to be built on [the] transparency of ... knowledge." The truth is a "bright light" that "search[es] for lessons that would contribute to reconciliation and to abolishing such patterns of behavior in the new society." Even where the reporting is unofficial, the claim is similar, that the revelation of knowledge—in and of itself—offers a means to political transformation. In the preface to the unofficial Uruguayan *Nunca Mas* or *Never Again* report writing, in and of itself, constitutes a triumph against repression. The claim is that the transitional truth-tellings will deter the possibility of future repression. It is the lack of "critical understanding which created a risk of having the disaster repeated... to rescue that history is to learn a lesson... We should have the courage not to hide that experience in our collective subconscious but to recollect it. So that we do not fall again into the trap."

In transitional history making, the story has to come out right. Yet this implies a number of poetic leaps. Was it the new truths that brought on liberalizing political change? Or was it the political change that enables restoration of democratic government, and reconsideration of the past?

Despite ongoing processes of political change, without some form of clarification of the deception and ensuing self-understanding, the truth about the evil past is hidden, unavailable, external, foreign. In the postcommunist transitions characterized by struggling with the accumulated past state archives, the region's transitional accounts begin with the story of invasion and popular resistance; the foe represented as foreign outsider, progressing to the ever more troubling discovery of collaboration, closer to home and pervasive throughout the society. In the narratives of transition, whether out of a repressive totalitarian rule in the former Soviet bloc, or, out of authoritarian military rule; whether Latin America's truth reports, or postcommunist "lustration," transitional stories all involve a "revealing" of supposedly secreted knowledge. What is pronounced is the tragic discovery.

What counts as liberalizing knowledge? These productions are not original, or foundational; but contingent on state legacies of repressive rule. Successor truth regimes' critical function is responsive to the repressive practices of the prior regime. For example, after military rule, where the truth was a casualty of disappearance policies, the critical response is the "official story." While, after communist rule, the search for the "truth" constituted a matter not of historical production as such, as previous uses of official history had been deployed as instruments of repressive control; but, instead, a matter of critical response to repressive state histories, to the securing of private access to state archives, to the privatization of official histories, and to the introduction of competing historical accounts.

Knowledge's exposure means that the possibility of change is introduced through the potential of human action. The very notion of a knowledge objectified and exposed suggests somehow that there was "logic" to the madness, and intimates now that there is something to be done. The message propounded the notion that, had the newly acquired knowledge been known then, events would have been different. And, moreover, that now that the truth is known, the course of future events will indeed be different. Processes that illuminate the possibility of future choice distinguish the liberal transition. In the transitional accounts lie the kernels of a liberal future foretold. The revealed truth allows the switch from the tragic past to the promise of a hopeful future. A catastrophe is somehow turned around, an awful fate averted by the introduction of a magical switch. Transitional justice operates as such a device: legal processes incorporate persons vested with transformative powers, judges, lawyers, commissioners, experts, witnesses with special access to privileged knowledge. Reckoning with the past enables the perception of a liberalizing shift.

Narratives of transition suggest that minimally what is at stake in liberalizing transformation is a change of interpretation. In this process, political and truth regimes have a mutually constitutive role. Societies begin to change politically when citizens' understanding of the ambient situation change. As Václav Havel has written, the change is from "living within a lie to living within the truth." Consider that the Eastern European literature of the period such as Bernard Schlink's *The Reader*; Ivan Klima's *The Ultimate Intimacy*; Pavel Kohout's *I am Snowing* and *The Confessions of a Woman of Prague* are stories of precisely this move, from "living within a lie," to the revelation of newly gained knowledge and self-understanding, effecting a reconstitution of personal identity, and of relationships. These tales of deceit and betrayal, often stories of longstanding affairs, appear to be allegories of the citizen/state relation, shedding light on the structure and course of civic change.

What emerges clearly is that the pursuit of historical justice is not simply a response to, or, representation of political change, but itself helps to construct the political transformation. Change in the political and legal regimes shapes and structures the historical regime. New truth regimes go hand in hand with new political regimes, indeed, they support the change. Transitional accounts themselves construct a normative relation, as they connect the society's past with its future; narratives of transition are stories of progress, beginning with the backward-looking reflection on the past, but always in light of the future. The constructive fiction is that, had the knowledge now acquired been known then, the tragedy would have been avertable. New societies can be built on this claim about knowledge. It is this change in political knowledge that allows the move from an evil past, to a sense of national redemption.

Transitional narratives follow a distinct structured form. Revelation of knowledge of truth occurs through switching mechanisms, critical junctures of individual and societal self-knowledge. There is a ritual disowning of pre-viously secreted knowledge, a purging of the past, as well as an appropria-tion of a newly revealed truth, enabling corrective return to the society's true course. A new course is charted.

The practices in such periods suggest that the new histories are hardly foundational, but explicitly transitional. To be sure, historical narrative is always present in the life of the state, but, in periods of political flux, the nar-rative's role is to construct perceptible transformation. Transitional histories are not "meta"-narratives, but discrete, "mini"-narratives, always situated within the state's preexisting national story. Transitional truth-tellings are not new beginnings, but build upon preexisting state political legacies. Indeed, the relevant truths are those implicated in a particular state's past political legacies. These are not universal, essential, or metatruths; a marginal truth is all that is needed to draw a line on the prior regime. Critical responses nego-tiate between historical conflict in contested accounts. As political regimes change, transitional histories accordingly offer a displacement of one inter-pretive account or truth regime for another, so preserving the state's narrative thread.

Transitional law transcends the merely symbolic to be the leading ritual of modern political passage. The legal response epitomizes the liberal secu-lar rationalist response to mass suffering and catastrophe; and expresses the notion that there is something to be done. Rather than resignation to histori-cal repetition; in the liberal society, hope is put in the air. Ritual acts enable the passage between the two orders, of predecessor and successor regimes. In contemporary transitions, characterized by their peaceful character with-in the law, legal processes perform the critical undoings of the predicate justifications of the prior regime, through public procedures that produce constitutive collective knowledge transformative of political identities. The paradigmatic feature of the transitional legal response is that it visibly advances the reconstruction of public knowledge, comprehending operative features that enable the separation from the past, as well as integration pro-cesses. The importance of establishing a shared collective truth regarding the past repressive legacies has become something of a trope in the discourse of transitions. The meaning of "truth" is not universal, but rather is largely polit-ically contingent to the transition. Accordingly, the paradigmatic transition-al legal processes rely on discrete changes in salient public political knowl-edge for their operative transformative action. Legal processes construct changes in shared public justifications underlying political decision-making and behavior that simultaneously disavow aspects of the predecessor ideol-ogy and justify the ideological changes constituting liberalizing transforma-tion. What is politically relevant to transformation is plainly constituted by the transitional context, as well as by the legacies of displacement and succession of predecessor truth regimes.

Legal processes are ways of changing public reasoning in the political order, for these processes are predicated on authoritative representations of public knowledge. So it is that transitional legal processes contribute to the interpretive changes that create the perception of political social transformation. At the same time, transitional legal processes also vividly demonstrate the contingency in what knowledge will do the work of constructing the normative shift underpinning political regime change. The normative force of transitional constructions in public knowledge depends on critical challenges to the policy predicates and rationalizations of predecessor rule and ideology. Accordingly, what the relevant "truths" are in transition is discrete and yet of disproportionate significance. These reinterpretations displace the predicates legitimizing the prior regime, and offer newfound bases for the reinstatement of the rule of law.

Law offers a canonical language, and the symbols and rituals of contemporary political passage. Through trials and other public hearings and processes, legal rituals enable transitionally produced histories, social constructions of a democratic nature with a broad reach. These rituals of collective historymaking publicly construct the transition, they divide political time into a "before" and an "after." Transitional responses perform the critical undoings that respond to the prior repression: the letting go of discrete facts justificatory of the predecessor regime, critical to political change. The practices of historical production associated with transition often publicly affirm only what is already impliedly known in the society, transitional processes bring forward and enable a public letting go of the past.

Whether through trials or other practices, transitional narratives highlight the role of knowledge, agency and choice. Though the received wisdom on historical responses to past wrongs is that these are popular in liberalizing states emphasizing structural causation, transitional histories are complex accounts, dense layered narratives that weave together and mediate individual and collective responsibility. By introducing the potential of individual choice, the accounts perform a transitional liberalizing function. By revealing "truths" about the past, these accounts are distinctive narratives of progress, as they suggest that the course of events might have been different—had this knowledge been previously known—adverting to the potential of individual action. The message is of avertable tragedy. This expression of the hope for prospective individual freedom and human action goes to the core of liberalism and its rule of law discourse.

Notes

1 It is worth observing that, notwithstanding Martin Krygier's comments to the contrary, the context of the legal transformation is not only defined by the project or aims of the transition (see Krygier 2001: 25–26), but rather is also shaped by the mix of past and present variables that are almost definitional of transition.

Bibliography

Krygier, Martin. "Transitional Questions about the Rule of Law: Why, What, and How?" *East Central Europe—L'Europe du Centre Est. Eine wissenschaftliche Zeitschrift* 28, no. 1 (2001): 1–34.

Teitel, Ruti. *Transitional Justice.* New York: Oxford University Press, 2000.

Walzer, Michael, ed. *Regicide and Revolution: Speeches at the Trial of Louis* XVI. trans. Marian Rothstein. New York: Cambridge University Press, 1974.

Constitutional Symbolism and Political (Dis)continuity: Legal Rationality and Its Integrative Function in Postcommunist Transformations

Jiří Přibáň

> *"As I ran, I saw a future history in advance, compacted into a moment."*
>
> Ben Okri[1]

> *"... in the civil society among demons..."*
>
> Jáchym Topol[2]

Symbolic power of law, political discontinuity and revolutionary times

The modern form of legislation and the codified system of law have been established against traditional sources of law. Legislation has, of course, become the main vehicle both of social change and integration in modern society. In addition, the concept of judge-made law as respecting the traditions and moral fabric of a political community has almost disappeared in the period of modernity and the judiciary has started to regard itself as an institution and force for social change.[3] Legislative process, a special example of which is the constitution-making process, modifies the future quality of social life and any change of law, apart from other consequences, means the abandonment of existing legal regulations. Nevertheless, law is not a matter of social experimentation. It acknowledges reasoned public opinion and the political commonsense which expresses already existing customs and public morals. The innovative function of legislation and adjudication is heavily influenced by existing political interests and power struggles (see especially Sumner 1960: 86). The constitution-making process and legislation always reflect present and past experiences. New normative frameworks are, therefore, closely tied to the existing social reality, its past developments and changes.

As a result, social changes and political discontinuities including revolutions must be analysed, apart from structural, semantic and functional aspects, in their *temporal dimension*. The temporal dynamic of a revolutionary change is typically one of complete condemnation of the political present and past. The present condition is unsustainable and those who favour the *status quo* lose support for their political actions. The condemned past is the past controlled and determined by the present which is being replaced by revolution.

The present only represents a political deadlock because it has lost the crucial power to shape and control the future. The political future "must happen" but it cannot happen under the rules and procedures enacted in the present condition. In short, revolutions are complex social changes in which political expectations of the future cannot be facilitated and controlled by the political present.

Modern revolutions have a primarily *prospective nature*. A new political order must completely replace the old one and the expectations of what is yet to come are extremely high. The political past framed by the existence of the condemned political regime must be abandoned. New sources of legitimation for the revolutionary changes must be established in the name of the future. This condemnation of the present order contradicts the political needs of stability, continuity and predictability supplied by the legal system. The modern state is perceived as a social institution securing political stability and defining the limits of political actions. Stability takes precedence over uncontrolled changes in politics. The rational normative nature of modern law is considered to be the ultimate source of such stability. Political change and novelty are to be channelled by the legal normative framework and thus controlled by the existing political order. Revolutionary changes, therefore, indicate that this framework has lost its power to provide social stability and accommodate political changes and developments.

In the process of revolutionary change, the present is already perceived as the abandoned past as the future emerges as a part of the present. The modern social experience of the future as something designed, yet not existing in the present, is given a radical expression in a revolution (Toffler 1971). Making the future in the present always involves the risk of failure because the future may emerge differently from its present designs. To avoid the political nightmare of a failed revolution, the revolutionaries may introduce a number of mechanisms of social and temporal stabilization in order to maintain control over the revolutionary process. The symbolic function of legal rationality, therefore, becomes extraordinarily strong in the process of a revolution which depicts itself as a constitutional and legal transformation. In a political community undergoing revolutionary discontinuity, law may become an important symbol of unity and provide an integrative framework for political fractures (Arnold 1935). In this way, law operates both as a mechanism of social stabilization and change. It has the double function of being the stabilizing symbol and being the instrument of the coming changes. It helps to minimize the risk that the future of a revolution would get out of control. At the same time, it speeds up the abandonment of the condemned present because it legislates new political conditions and thus constitutes its own present which, from a temporal point of view, is still in the future and yet to be achieved.

In this chapter, I will seek to analyse the temporal aspect of the 1989 revolutions and the subsequent constitution-making processes in Central Europe. The postcommunist transformations are typical of a highly selective and ambivalent dealing with the past. One (communist) past was condemned while the other (civic, liberal democratic, nationalist etc.) became a source of legitimation of the new political regimes. One past was treated by means of retributive justice, while the other outlined a new symbolic political framework. I will, therefore, start by addressing the problem of retroactive justice and its compatibility with the principles of constitutionalism and the rule of law as reviewed by the constitutional courts in Hungary, Poland and the Czech Republic. After this analysis, I will focus on the symbolic power of the constitutions during the process of rebuilding national and civic identities. Finally, I will analyse the constitutional links and tensions between civil society values and the revitalized ethnic nationalisms in Central Europe.

REVOLUTIONS BETWEEN PAST AND FUTURE

Political and constitutional transformations of the postcommunist societies are good examples of the *revolutionary differentiation of the present and future*. The speed of the social, political and legal changes in the various postcommunist countries have made many prognoses and research conclusions about the postcommunist developments look almost embarrassingly wrong and naïve (see, for example, Krygier 1999). The main consequence of this speed of transformation is that the future of postcommunist countries is more open and diverse than it seemed to be in the past.

In the late 1980s, communist elites in Poland and Hungary had already realized that their rule had become unsustainable. In those countries, the communist governments and the opposition, encouraged by international changes in the late 1980s and in particular the Soviet policies of *perestroika* and *glasnost*, gradually engaged in a process of political negotiations through the Roundtable Talks. The primary aim of the talks was to maintain political stability while fundamentally changing the constitutional, political and economic foundations of those countries. The Roundtable Talks were an instrument for securing political stability while facilitating complex political changes. A strong emphasis was placed on political negotiations governed by rules accepted by all participants in order to strengthen the idea of "the rule of law," although this principle was, in fact, one of the principal goals to be achieved by the political transformation.

The countries in which Roundtable Talks played a fundamental role in the process of political transformation established a strong, yet somewhat paradoxical, idea of "revolution by rules."[4] The present control of the political future was facilitated by the quasi-legal rationality of roundtable talks. The meta-normative and provisional character of roundtable talks had a strong symbolic value which channelled the revolutionary changes and gave a pragmatic strength to the coming constitutional and legal transformations. They supported the notion of legal continuity between the old communist and the new democratic systems and significantly weakened all attempts to implement retroactive criminal justice for the punishment of the political crimes of the past.[5]

Roundtable talks were a typical example of provisional control of the present political situation by the future political goals. However, revolutionary changes had not been established only by the differentiation of the political present and future. The *differentiation of the present and the past* played an important a role in the revolutionary process as the differentiation of the present and future. The prospective nature of the revolution was accompanied by the retrospective condemnation of the present. The political present was blamed for the unjust past and the first demands were to get rid of the existing regime, "heal the wounds" and deal with the political crimes committed in the name of this regime. The revolution, which took over the political present, had to come up with its own differentiation of the past and the future. The prospective work of the roundtable talks and constitutional transformations had to be accompanied by a retrospective justice and dealing (legal or non-legal) with the past.

The emerging democratic public discourse was originally fragile and threatened to collapse back into the past, but it was also vital and necessary for future political institutions and stability. In this public discourse, a new political identity was confronted with unjust political history and law became one of the most important discursive and integrative techniques. Prospective hopes and efforts to (re)construct liberal democratic conditions and the rule of law were haunted by past injustices, political oppression and violence. The emerging political and legal structures were trapped between the past and future. They were facing the dilemma of *dealing with the past in order to make the future happen.* They had to deal with the past both in political and legal terms and to establish specific forms of retrospective justice in order to proceed with the transformation of the legal and political systems.

LEGAL (DIS)CONTINUITY, RETROACTIVITY
AND CONSTITUTIONAL JUSTICE

The new present required the following *archive imperative*: record all past political injustices, reveal them to the re-emerging public and organize them in the form of a memento to the future generations. Using the criterion of retributive justice, this imperative can have either a minimal form avoiding legal solutions, or a maximal form seeking to prosecute all crimes and injustices of the past. The minimal form avoiding punitive justice was typical of the various truth and Reconciliation Commissions emerging after the collapse of authoritarian and illiberal regimes in Latin America or South African apartheid. In general, the postcommunist reality was different and the new governments did not give up punitive justice in the hope of achieving political stability and national unity. Indeed, there are several examples of the archive imperative strategies which went beyond normal criminal justice and the purpose of which was to judge and condemn the past regime by other than criminal legal means. One of them was the decision of the German Parliament to hold a formal inquiry into the causes and consequences of the communist dictatorship in the former German Democratic Republic (GDR). The Parliament set up a commission with the task of reviewing the past 40 years of the GDR. Between May 1992 and May 1994, the commission, consisting of 16 parliamentary members, 11 academic advisers, and a number of administrative staff, conducted a series of public hearings and closed sessions and debated various political topics in the history of the GDR. Its findings were received positively by the legislator and the commission's job was renewed for another round of investigations in the spring of 1995.[6]

The Czech government chose a slightly different method when it set up a special Office for Documentation and Investigation of the Crimes of Communism.[7] The Office, which is part of the Ministry of Interior, seeks to carry out both the historical task of mapping all injustices, atrocities and crimes related to the communist regime and the criminal justice task of prosecuting individuals who still are subject to criminal liability. It became a common routine of the Office to submit individual cases to the prosecution office. In accordance with the logic of publishing all the atrocities of the communist secret police, the Czech legislator also enacted a law granting public access to secret police files.[8]

Recently, Poland also came up with its own minimalist version of the archive imperative by setting up the Institute of National Remembrance in July 1999. The institute's job is to gather documentation on Nazi and communist crimes, political repression and persecution. Like the Czech Office for Documentation and Investigation of Communist Crimes, the Polish Institute of National Remembrance is to investigate and file individual cases and, therefore, can access the communist secret police files and make them available to victims. However, the findings of the Polish institute do not have the criminal law consequences which are an intrinsic part of the jurisdiction of the Czech Office.

From the perspective of temporality, the archive imperative may lead to a *confrontation* with the past or to an attempt to achieve a new *consensus* and hope for the political future. The social and political consequences of the archive imperative depend on its relationship to the instruments of retributive justice. Some scholars asserted that the application of criminal justice or administrative discrimination against former communist officials, such as lustrations, divided societies and caused social and political tensions and confrontation.[9] However, criminal justice leading to the prosecution of political crimes, administrative measures taken against officials of the communist regime such as lustrations, and other coercive and supposedly confrontational methods were not necessarily anti-consensual because the affected social groups constituted only a fragment of political society. The majority of citizens even thought that this was, in principle, the correct line to take against people directly or indirectly responsible for the injustices and persecutions organized by the communist regime.

That retribution is a constitutive part of the concept of justice has been accepted since ancient times (see, for instance, Kelsen 1946). *Lex talionis,* the norm of retribution, formed an important link of causality between human actions and rewards or punishments for them in early notions of justice. Since the ancient Greek times, retribution has been regarded as "a kind of trade in which good is exchanged for good and bad for bad" (Kelsen 1946: 193). Justice is established on the notion of compensation for human actions either in the form of reward or punishment. It is closely tied to the concept of a political order as harmony protected by laws. The main goal of law is to protect harmony and establish balance between harmful acts and their punishment. Retribution re-establishes a disturbed balance by either negative or positive compensation for harmful acts. Justice without retribution lacks compensation and represents only a partial concept of justice. In spite of being possibly controversial, retributive criminal justice constituted an integral part of the revolutionary transitional processes in postcommunist societies because it sought exactly to establish a balance between past political crimes and their just punishment, and as such was one of the most important bridges over the gap between the political past and future.

Analysing the concept and different use of retributive criminal justice, it is important to distinguish the following strategies: prosecution of criminal acts which, though not prosecuted under the communist system of justice, could have been prosecuted under the existing provisions of criminal law; retroactive legislation which would lead to the prosecution of past crimes and acts of political terror in those circumstances when the existing criminal law provisions could not be applied; and non-criminal forms of legal punishment for the abhorrent political activities of individuals under the communist rule. Postcommunist countries generally did not apply the politics of impunity and reconciliation. They sought to prosecute communist political crimes, but this turned out to be very difficult or even impossible in many cases. Institutional failure and reluctance on the part of the old judiciary and prosecutors to deal with the criminal past was common. The fruits of using criminal justice were even poorer in Czechoslovakia, Poland and Hungary than they were in unified Germany. This politically and morally frustrating situation lent support to the idea that special legal measures such as *retroactive legislation* had to be taken to deal with past communist crimes. The prohibition of retroactive criminal justice and the principles *nullum crimen sine lege* and *nulla poena sine lege* are, of course, essential to the democratic constitutional states established after the fall of communism in Central European countries. However, the legal rationality of the constitutional and democratic rule of law also involves the principle that no individual is above the law and all criminal acts shall be prosecuted. This implied that the new democratic authorities had a moral and legal duty to bring to criminal justice those whose political position effectively protected them from prosecution for acts otherwise classified as criminal even by the communist law.

The problem of retroactive justice haunted legislative bodies, constitutional courts, politicians and the public. Its strong symbolic power made it a cornerstone of the democratic rule of law discussions in all postcommunist Central European societies which perceived the process of constitutional and legal transformations as the *return* to constitutional democratic rule (Brzezinski and Garlicki 1995: 13). The principle of *lex retro non agit* was often taken by politicians, lawyers and judges in postcommunist countries as an untouchable pillar constituting the democratic rule of law and criminal justice. However, the jurisprudence and philosophies of the democratic rule of law do include politically more reflexive and socially more responsive attitudes towards retroactive justice. While acknowledging the fact that retroactive law, in principle, is incompatible with the rule of law, Lon L. Fuller argues that there are special political and historical circumstances in which retroactive law in fact supports the rule of law (Fuller 1969). Fuller uses the example of Nazi Germany to show that there are political discontinuities so radical as to call for imagination and invention in the application of constitutional and legal principles. Similarly, Hans Kelsen and Herbert L. A. Hart argue that every revolution involves an element of political and legal discontinuity. A new constitution and legal system subsequently define a new normative framework which may be more or less distant from the former framework. This discontinuity may take either the form of the most radical departure from the old system and complete revolutionary destruction of its normative framework, or the form of peaceful transition which gradually incorporates new elements and principles into the existing legal system and thus eventually transforms it into an entirely different one (Hart 1994: 118–20; Kelsen 1961: 117ff, 219ff).

Constitutional and legal discontinuity is entrenched in the very logic of revolution which is prospective by being destructive in relation to the past. Retroactive justice is revolutionary justice and we may distinguish two main methods of giving effect to retroactive justice: retroactive legislation enacted by representative bodies and retroactive decision-making applied by the courts. In the following analysis, I will focus on retroactive legislation and its review by the constitutional courts in Hungary, Poland and Czechoslovakia/-Czech Republic.

Legal continuity: the formalistic perspective of the Hungarian Constitutional Court

The Hungarian Constitutional Court formulated its strong doctrine of legal continuity when dealing with the Act of Parliament (the "Zétényi-Takács law") which opened up the possibility of prosecuting serious political crimes committed between 21 December 1944 and 2 May 1990. The court ruled the law unconstitutional on the basis that it lifted the penal code limitations that had been in effect at that time. The law was declared unconstitutional exactly because it represented retroactive *ex post facto* legislation. In the decision, the court even summarized basic statements on the change of regime in Hungary and on legal continuity. It ruled that "there is no substantive distinction between legal rules enacted under the Communist regime and since the promulgation of the new Constitution. Consequently, there is no double standard in adjudicating the constitutionality of legal norms... The Constitution and the basic laws that introduced revolutionary changes from a political point of view were enacted without formal defects according to the rules of lawmaking of the old regime and deriving their binding force from them" (Paczolay 1993: 34).

Further, the court refused to compromise its commitment to the fundamental principles of the rule of law by acknowledging the needs of historical justice and specific circumstances that may require a specific legal approach. According to the court, "legal certainty based on objective and formal principles takes precedence over justice, which is generally partial and subjective" (Paczolay 1993: 35).

The court also recognized strict limitations on retroactively undoing communist unconstitutional interferences with citizens' property rights, although its judgments in these property rights cases display a more flexible reasoning than its judgments concerning retroactive criminal justice (Klingsberg 1992a: 94–95). The court refused to recognize the current validity of rights violated by the communist legal acts and thereby eschewed any attempt to remedy unconstitutional interferences with those rights. It generally refused to affect the ownership right of the state based on nationalization, but the court's doctrine of legal continuity was not determined by a golden rule in property rights matters. The court admitted that retroactive judicial interference and remedy might take place if there were important interests of legal security or of the petitioner involved in the matter (Klingsberg 1992a: 81, 116).

The formalistic and legalistic understanding of the rule of law adopted by the Hungarian Constitutional Court has a strong symbolic role because it excludes the demands of historical justice from the present state of the rule of law. History is described as only a partial and subjective matter while the present is constituted by legal rationality as objective and impartial.

Legal continuity limited: Polish constitutional justice

In August 1990, the Polish Constitutional Tribunal ruled that the principle of non-retroactivity of laws is one of the basic components of the rule of law clause legislated in the constitutional amendment in Article 1 of the Polish constitution in 1989. According to the tribunal's judgment in a case concerning the lowering of state pensions of former communist officials, legislative enactments introducing retroactive justice are inconsistent with Article 1 and therefore may be declared unconstitutional and void.[10] It is noteworthy that this reasoning is surprisingly consistent with the early jurisprudence of the communist Constitutional Tribunal which itself ruled that the principle of non-retroactivity of laws "represents a fundamental principle of legal order. It finds its foundation in such values as legal security, certainty of legal transactions and protection of vested rights."[11]

The Polish Constitutional Tribunal formulated a very strong doctrine of *legal continuity* between the old and new regime which was nevertheless weakened by its later judgment regarding the prosecution of Stalinist crimes committed between 1944 and 1956. In this ruling, the tribunal imposed limits on the application of the principle of non-retroactivity of law, but it warned that "any departure from the principle of *lex retro non agit* in order to achieve justice demands a very precise definition of the specific crimes addressed."[12] Although the Constitutional Tribunal of Poland did not rule out the possibility of a departure from the principle of non-retroactivity, such a departure was classified as an exceptional instrument which may be used only when the principles of justice would clash with the application of the principle of *lex retro non agit.*

In comparison with the formalism of the Hungarian Constitutional Court, the Polish Constitutional Tribunal gave greater weight to "historical subjectivity" and its judgments do not perceive the rule of law and historical justice as contradictory.

Constitutional and legal discontinuity: on substantive and formal legality

Following the rulings of other constitutional courts in the region of Central Europe, it is possible to discover more flexible attitudes towards the issues of historical justice and legal certainty granted by the principle of *lex retro non agit*. In the context of the Czechoslovak constitutional justice, this matter arose in connection with the Lustration Law. The process of *lustrations* in Czechoslovakia and, later, in the Czech Republic[13] is an administrative procedure for screening individuals holding certain public offices or positions of legally defined political or economic influence.[14] It was originally enacted as a provisional and only temporary protection of the new democratic regime.[15] The lustration statute lists two groups of positions and activities: the first one enumerates those offices and positions which are subject of lustrations, while the second one enumerates offices and activities held during the communist regime which disqualify individuals from taking positions listed in the first group. The law covered key positions in state administration, universities, judiciary, state-owned enterprises and media, military, police etc. It affected the secret police members (StB), their agents, members of the Communist Party militia, and former officials of the Communist Party. It did not affect former Communist Party members as such.[16] It also did not apply to positions for which individuals are elected by democratic vote. Democratic legitimacy took precedence over lustration procedures.

In spite of these limits to its scope, nobody can deny the simple fact that lustration involves elements of discrimination and thus violates the principle of equality of all citizens before the law which is fundamental to the democratic rule of law.[17] When the Czechoslovak Constitutional Court reviewed the Lustration Law, it accepted the common argument that lustrations serve the purpose of avoiding the destabilisation that threatened the developing constitutional order. Instead of following formalistic arguments, it generally upheld the Lustration Law (with the exception of some sections of the statute [Gillis 1999: 75–80]) on the basis that the making of the rule of law actually requires the abandonment of formal-legal and material-legal continuity with the totalitarian legal system, which is based on a differing value system. The court recognized formal normative continuity in the legal order of Czechoslovakia, yet it denied that legal norms may be interpreted without regard to the value system of the liberal democratic rule of law. The discrimination imposed by lustrations was only formal and, according to the court, the law ought not to be discarded as unconstitutional because it asserts and protects the principles and values upon which a democratic liberal state is founded.

In sharp contradiction to the formalistic approach of the Hungarian Constitutional Court, the Czechoslovak Constitutional Court and, after the splitting of Czechoslovakia, the Czech Constitutional Court favoured interpretation on the assumption of *political and substantive legal discontinuity* between the communist and post-1989 democratic legal systems. Constitutional laws enacted after 1989, especially the Charter of Fundamental Rights and Freedoms which was adopted in 1991 and later incorporated into the constitutional system of the independent Czech Republic, fundamentally changed the value system and the nature of the constitutional and legal system. Distinctions between formal legality (which involves elements of legal continuity) and substantive legality (which, due to the different value foundations and principles

of the democratic rule of law, involves discontinuity with the former totalitarian legal system) dominated the judgment of the Czechoslovak
Constitutional Court not only on the lustration statute but also on other matters throughout the mid 1990s.[18] Political discontinuity affects the values and
principles behind the constitutional and legal system. Formal legal continuity
must not, therefore, put limits on the developing democratic rule of law.

Revolution: constitutional discontinuity or amendment?
Postcommunist Czechoslovak politics primarily reflected the political and
constitutional discontinuity between the communist and the democratic systems. According to the Constitutional Court, the new constitutional framework was built on this discontinuity and symbolized it. On the other hand,
the approaches of the Hungarian Constitutional Court and, to a lesser extent,
the Polish Constitutional Tribunal were less reflective of discontinuity and
their decisions were backed by the principle of formal legal continuity. The
Hungarian Court explicitly eschewed pursuit of historical justice because of
its subjective and anti-universalistic nature. The negotiated goal of the *rend-
szerváltozás* (change of regime) assumed that the Hungarian political transformation would be conducted entirely by constitutional acts and democratic procedures.[19] The constitutional revolution in Hungary wished to avoid
political divisions and conflicts and to establish new national unity. As Peter
Paczolay pointed out, "[t]he basic concern of Hungarians has long been peaceful change, the shaping of a constitutional state, and the avoidance of any
possible conflict with the Soviet Union..." (Paczolay 1993: 25). The constitution was a symbol of stability and continuity, not of change and discontinuity. The Hungarian revolution was a transformation of communism into
liberal democracy controlled and shaped by the existing constitutional and
legal framework (Dahrendorf 1990). It had the nature of a *constitutional
amendment* corresponding very well to the concept of constitutional transition formulated by Herbert L. A. Hart. In Hungary, control of the future by
the constitutional present and past was much stronger than in any other country in Central Europe.

CONSTITUTIONALISM AND POLITICAL IDENTITY: ON CIVIL SOCIETY

The way a postrevolutionary constitution deals with the past is a part of the
more general normative issue of *rebuilding political identity*. Legality reconstituted its symbolic function as the ultimate language of modern politics as
it was able to mark continuity whilst legislating discontinuity. The rule of law
was re-established as a primary political commitment of the democratic and

liberal discourse. Legal rationality facilitated the establishment of such discourse. The constitution of the new political identities of Central European nations was phrased by legal language, procedures and principles.

This symbolic role of legality evokes the more general sociological and socio-legal problem of social integration, collective identity and the role of time and law as integrative social mechanisms. Identifying the problems and traumas of the past, people proceed in shaping their future. Norbert Elias wrote that timing "means connecting or synthesizing events in a specific way" (Elias 1992: 96). What is depicted as the past, present and future depends on the living generations of the present and their integrative manipulation with the concept of time. The system of time conventions is one of the most rigorously codified systems of social rules. The conventional and abstract nature of social time is what makes it very close to the concept of law in its most general sense. Collective memory and political identity are shaped by the temporal self-reflection of a political community which is then reconstructed in the form of codes and canons. Canons become the referential framework of a community (from ancient civilizations to modern nations), establish limits of repetition and interpretation of community's history, and therefore constitute a codified version of its collective memory and identity.[20] The social need for the codification of collective memories grows with the flow of time and gradual loss of experience of commonly shared historical events. Codes and canons replace historical experience by dogma. The collective memory then also operates as the interpretation and hermeneutics of the "legislated" history.

In this context, constitutionalism played an important role in legislating the limits of government and the boundaries of civil society. Associations, civil organizations and pressure groups were non-existent under communism, yet the concept of civil society was very popular among dissidents living under the communist regimes. The dissident concept of civil society heavily romanticized the spontaneous order of liberal societies and contrasted it to totalitarian surveillance, planning and political control. The prominent Hungarian dissident and writer György Konrád sought to transform the dissident experience of resistance into a more general argument of government limited and controlled by the activism of civil society. He called for an "antipolitics" which would permanently challenge existing governmental actions, ideology and control when he wrote that "a society does not become politically conscious when it shares some political philosophy, but rather when it refuses to be fooled by any of them. The apolitical person is only the dupe of the professional politician, whose real adversary is the antipolitician. It is the antipolitician who wants to keep the scope of government policy (especially that of its military apparatus) under the control of civil society" (Konrád 1984: 227).

Konrád's antipolitics had a broad appeal because its criticism embraced both the communist regimes and the political engineering and ideological control existing in the Western liberal democratic states. Comparing the concept of antipolitics with the concept of non-political politics popular in the Czech dissident movement, it is possible to detect striking similarities of intellectual elitism, the romantic critique of bureaucratic power-making processes, and a strong belief in the reconstructive ability of "parallel activism" driven by a sense of communal solidarity instead of by a struggle over power (Havel 1985: 27). Václav Havel and other former dissidents who became the new political leaders therefore considered the rejuvenation of the institutions and virtues of civil society to be the greatest problem confronting postcommunist countries (Klingsberg 1992b: 866–67). Their attention was directed to the past and their task was to revitalize what was suppressed by communists. The lost paradise was to be rediscovered (Havel 1992a: 6).

An important reason for the credibility of the civil society argument was the peaceful character of the revolutionary events, which did not end up in violence and civil war (Preuss 1990). "Civil disobedience" and "civilised negotiations" were the main revolutionary tools facilitating the political and constitutional changes. According to this view, the civil society elements incorporated in the anticommunist political dissent were principally responsible for the institutionalisation of the liberal democratic rule of law (Arato 2000: 70–80). They were able to exercise great influence over postcommunist constitution-making.

The difference between totalitarian and civil society constituted an important social distinction and identity referential framework after the fall of communism. Civil society was contrasted to the communist totalitarianism. It represented values and virtues such as individual freedom, cooperation, spontaneity, solidarity, public initiative, protest, intellectual critique, recognized political dissent, and many other aspects of communal life destroyed by communists. In the Polish context, "ever since the early 1980s, a majority of scholars and observers agreed that a crucial agent of change in Poland would be the emerging 'civil society'. The civil society was a growing network of underground organizations outside of communist control. In fact, it was the civil society that Solidarity represented at the Roundtable in Poland. A logical conclusion was that, with the end of communism, the civil society would evolve into pluralistic and democratic political structures" (Osiatyński 1991: 855).

The constitutional transformations were supposed to promote and protect the political virtues of civil society by the force of law. Constitutional rules were to impose limits on government and facilitate the development of the institutions of civil society institutions by ensuring the civil and political rights of citizens (Klingsberg 1992b: 894). Central European nations searching for their political identity after the 1989 revolutions looked for an alternative to the communist past and the concept of civil society formulated by dissidents provided the necessary referential framework for liberal and democratic politics (Přibáň 2002). The future was constructed by the past dissident ideals and alternatives to the communist totalitarian system. Constitutional laws were perceived as a vehicle for rebuilding the civil society and as the guardians of civic virtue. Due to this coeval symbolic power of the concept of civil society and constitutional legislation, constitutionalism achieved an almost heroic status because it secured a differentiated, spontaneous and well-ordered civil society.[21]

The values of civil society influenced postcommunist constitution-making, yet the need to institutionalise a market economy and a political society which would secure a democratic control of the new power structures was even more crucial. The establishment of democratic procedures, political parties, ideologies and power techniques and loyalties was essential for the emerging political system. Without the establishment of a market economy and democratic political society, the virtues of civil society would evaporate very soon after the fall of communism. Even the most convinced advocates of civil society admit that the maximum it can do is to operate as "the key to the possibility of innovation in the East Central European transitions and... [the concept of civil society] also points to the possible locus of reconciliation between economic liberalism and political democracy, both evidently necessary and yet in conflict in the difficult processes of transition" (Arato 2000: 36).

A postcommunist ideology of civil society was a central part of the codification of new political identities which was typical of the Central European countries in the first half of the 1990s. The codification of the new democratic and liberal spirit of laws and the redrafting of the persisting communist constitutions was in fact a re-codification of the political communities at the level of political and ethical virtues. In spite of the fact that the process of dealing with the past and retrospective justice heavily influenced the character of the postcommunist transformations, it must be re-emphasized that the temporal orientation of these transformations was primarily prospective. The codification of the political future preceded legal and political dealing with the unjust past. Nevertheless, the prospective role of legal rationality and the codification of new political identities have always been haunted by the spirits and demons of the past. In the final part of this text, I will therefore focus on one of them, namely the ethnic aspect of national identities in Central Europe.

CONSTITUTING A NATION: ETHNIC AND CIVIC TRADITIONS

The process of post-communist constitution-making is only one of a number of transformation processes which were designed to secure stability in the period of fundamental political and social changes. The liberal model of democracy as a system of constitutionally protected political procedures and civic liberties prevailed over the progressive model of democracy as a system of power decisions leading to substantive moral and economic improvement of humankind. Constitutions played an enormous role of *political stabilizers*, the primary role of which was to protect the *civic identity* of the new political community.

A liberal procedural model of democracy tamed by the constitution-based rule of law is nevertheless an insufficient stabilizer and it is necessary to look for a more cohesive and substantive supplement. As had previously happened in many other European political societies, Central European countries rebuilt their popular sovereignty and statehood on historically and culturally shared sentiments of national identity and ethnic unity.[22] *Democracy rediscovered nations in the course of postcommunist constitution-making.* The constitution-making processes consequently legislated national identity based on the idea of a culturally and ethnically defined community. The prospective job of constitution-making was strongly determined by national traditions. Rebuilding the *national identity* in the sense of the ethnic and cultural identity was another part of the process of rebuilding political identity. The revolution was not just an event of political discontinuity dismantling the communist system. It also reinstated cultural and political continuities and traditions suppressed or manipulated by the communist power. Canons and codifications of a new political identity had to be applied to the sphere of national history and traditions. In this context, three different phenomena relating to time, history and codes of society need to be distinguished: tradition, its code and its interpretation.

Tradition means all objects, patterns and practices of the past that have some meaning in and impact on the social present (Shils 1981). They are "transferred" in time and must be enacted and re-enacted by living human beings. Traditions spontaneously exert a historical influence on current social patterns, their duration representing a chain across a span of social time. The element of normativity is involved in the chain because behavioural patterns of tradition are entering the present life of a society with the purpose of producing affirmation and acceptance. This normative aspect of traditions must, nevertheless, be distinguished from social codes and codification. Unlike the spontaneous normativity of tradition, *codes and codifications* are the outcome of a rational "legislative" project of existing authorities which affect all spheres of social life, stretch into history and construct the future. Codes are not, therefore, only a matter of the legal system of a particular society. They emerge wherever social control and power are at stake. They are purposive acts intended to produce collective dogma which will integrate a society. The *interpretation* of a code or dogma is then an active process of enacting and applying their normative frameworks to everyday social reality. It must be inventive and imaginative because it reacts to social changes and new circumstances. It establishes the meaning of a code in present social conditions, and therefore is also affected by the spontaneous normativity of traditions.

Traditions can subsequently take the form of inventions of the new meaning of a code. Alternatively, new codes need to be codified in order to overcome traditions persisting and burdening the present social and political condition. Different traditions need to be rediscovered and codified. Codifications establish new traditions or correct and transform social meaning of the old ones because they turn out to be detached from existing social conditions. Rebuilding the political identities of Central European postcommunist political societies was then a complex interplay of the establishment of new political codes (constitutions), precommunist traditions and their present interpretations.

TRADITIONS AND NATIONS

Analysing the role of traditions, Edward Shils said that "the connection which binds a society to its past can never die out completely; it is inherent in the nature of society, it cannot be created by governmental fiat or by a 'movement' of citizens that aims at specific legislation. A society would not be a society if this bond were not there in some minimal degree. The strength or efficacy of the link can vary considerably, just as can the state of integration of a society at any point in time" (Shils 1981: 328).

It is necessary to acknowledge the significance of tradition and renewed bonds of different postcommunist national societies in constitutional and political transformations. Furthermore, it is important to explore the strength of those traditions and their ideological and integrative role in postcommunist society. Tradition is intrinsic even to contemporary societies and the present can never fully abandon the past. The present grows into the past. The role of the past in modern society is nevertheless very different from its role in traditional societies. The past *is* the present in traditional societies. It is not questioned, contested, or manipulated by present political actions. As opposed to this, in modern societies, tradition and the past are the subject of permanent challenge by the present: they must be presented. Tradition may be a starting point for new beliefs and actions (Shils 1981: 44), yet this point is determined by present pragmatics. The past is present in modern society, but no longer as its unquestionable and indisputable social foundation.

The different histories, traditions, nationalities and political cultures existing within the seemingly monolithic bloc of East European communist countries gained new dynamics after 1989. The very concept of Eastern Europe became dubious and subsequently useless for any profound constitutional, political and social analysis. After the revolutionary changes of 1989, postcommunist nations sought to revitalize their national heritages. Ernest Renan pointed to the mutual dependence of a nation's past and present in his *Qu'est-ce qu'une nation* (1882) when he said that "a nation is a soul, a spiritual principle. Only two things, actually, constitute this soul, this spiritual principle. One is in the past, the other is in the present. One is the possession in common of a rich legacy of remembrances; the other is the actual consent, the desire to live together, the will to continue to value the heritage which all hold in common" (Renan 1882: 26).

Memory establishes a nation's identity by reviving the common ground and mystery of historical unity. However, the unity must be based on this common historical existence permanently confirmed by the present. According to Renan, a nation is a unity of the collective memory and the forgetting necessary for constituting present identity. In postcommunist Central Europe, re-established and liberated collective memories addressed the question of national identity.

ETHNOS AND DEMOS

The constitutional concept of a sovereign nation has always been trapped between *demos* and *ethnos*. The concept of the nation is identified with the institution of the state. This means that the nation is regarded as a collectivity living in the state's territory and administered by the means of state's violence.[23] This definition subsumes the category of nation under the category of state. Nations are people under the control of modern, state administration. This definition is nevertheless haunted by the ethnic concept of the nation, which reflects tensions and differences among different collectivities living in the same state territory, their customs and history. The ethnic definition of a nation emphasizes the sense of belonging and the homogeneity of a particular group which is not restricted to the artificial borders and institutions of modern politics. It is rather common history, language, customs, traditions and other shared social facts which constitute nations (Connor 1978).

This difference, which is demonstrated in the modern histories of all European nations, was re-established as one of the major features of the new democratic liberal discourse in Central European political societies in the first half of the 1990s. The common understanding of the revival of national tradition and nationalism in postcommunist countries in the 1990s contrasts the ethnic and civic concepts of the nation and blames the emerging liberal democracies for the revival of ethnic hatred and national tribalism in Central and Eastern Europe. This is, however, a gross simplification of the postcommunist developments and a misunderstanding of the historical role of nationalism.

The ethnic self-understanding of the nation as an entity organically rooted and united in common history is politically very dangerous. Nevertheless, ethnicity is also an intrinsic part of modern liberal democratic politics. The organic and metaphysical perception of the nation as one sovereign body of people of the same racial and historical origin undoubtedly led to the establishment and legitimation of fascism (Connor 1978). Ethnicity certainly involves a high level of exclusive tribalism but it is the allying of this organic and socially conservative entity with the modern state, with its monopoly of violence and bureaucratic administration, which establishes the fascist totalitarian regime (Kohn 1945: 20). Ethnicity, therefore, cannot be blamed for all modern political wrongs and catastrophes.

It is necessary to emphasize the historical fact that the ethnic concepts of nationhood and popular sovereignty were not always necessarily anti-democratic and illiberal. Nationalisms in Central Europe were very different, from the Polish aristocratic resistant nationalism and the Hungarian aristocratic loyalist nationalism to the Czech competitive nationalism of the small bourgeoisie (for further details see, for instance, Sugar and Lederer 1969). Moreover, those nationalisms were often a revolutionary force challenging autocratic, illiberal regimes and aiming at the democratisation of politics, constitutional rights and popular parliamentary sovereignty. Liberalism and nationalism often did not contradict but rather complemented each other in the modern history of Central Europe (Sugar and Lederer 1969: 46–49). This history proves that ethnic nationalism could serve both the struggle for democracy and provide the legitimation framework for state violence and ethnic repression.

POPULAR SOVEREIGNTY AND NATIONAL IDENTITY

A substitution of "nation" for "state" as the basic administrative, territorial and legal unit is typical of modern political language and studies of constitutionalism and nationalism. The doctrine of popular sovereignty, which dates back at least as far as to the late seventeenth century, identifies the people as the political sovereign holding state power. The people were equated with the state and its sovereignty. During the nineteenth century, nation and the people or citizenry became two distinct categories and nations were gradually referred to more often as ethnicities. The concept of popular sovereignty became burdened by the political and constitutional question of "Who is the people?"

Postcommunist politics certainly suffered from the antidemocratic and illiberal effects of conservative and aggressive nationalism.[24] Due to this, it became a matter of priority to make ethnic national identity constitutionally and ideologically subject to the principles of civil society based on the legal concept of citizenship and not on a mythical community of blood and race. Constitutional patriotism was to contain and channel distinct national identities, prides and histories.[25] The patriotism of citizens established on the ideologies of civil liberties and democratic political rights played an important role in overcoming national hostilities and historical resentments, both inside national states (between a majority nation and ethnic minorities) and in new developing international relations (between sovereign nations).

This struggle was complicated by the legacy of communist nationalism, though this is hardly recognized by many Western scholars. The historical period of the late 1950s and 1960s is sometimes labelled as the period of "nationalist communism" (Osiatyński 1991: 847). After the decline of the centralizing ideology of Stalinism, national communist parties in the Soviet bloc countries ideologically shifted to a nationalist rhetoric in order to win more popular support. This shift was partly caused by the change of international political climate and partly by the generation struggles inside the national communist elites. National and ethnic intolerance were not, therefore, reinvented or reborn after the 1989 revolutions. They rather represent an interesting transformed continuation of communist policies mixed with pre-communist nationalist ideologies.

CONSTITUTIONALISM, THE CONCEPT OF A NATION AND POPULAR SOVEREIGNTY IN CENTRAL EUROPE

Turning our attention to the individual countries of Central Europe, the preamble of the Polish constitution represents an interesting mixture of civic and national patriotism. Unlike Hungary, Slovakia or the Czech Republic, Poland is hardly challenged by the coexistence of a majority nation and ethnic minorities. The constitution, therefore, re-establishes the national heritage as a source of political pride by stating that:

> Having regard for the existence and future of our Homeland,
> Which recovered, in 1989, the possibility of a sovereign and democratic determination of its fate,
> We, the Polish Nation—all citizens of the Republic,
> Both those who believe in God as the source of truth, justice, good and beauty,
> As well as those not sharing such faith but respecting those universal values as arising from other sources,
> Equal in rights and obligations towards the common good—Poland,
> Beholden to our ancestors for their labours, their struggle for independence achieved at great sacrifice, for our culture rooted in the Christian heritage of the Nation and in universal human values,
> Recalling the best tradition of the First and the Second Republic,

Obliged to bequeath to future generations all that is valuable from our
over one thousand years' heritage,
Bound in community with our compatriots dispersed throughout the
world.[26]

This is a clear example of the mixture of the civic and ethnic concepts of the
nation, full of references to history, traditions, religion, culture and national
territory. The reference to universal human values and civility treats them as
an intrinsic part of national identity. National patriotism is worthy of being
preserved because it aspires to universal humanity and civic culture promoted
and protected by the constitution.

Hungary provides a very different example of rebuilding national identity
through constitutionalism. Unlike the other Central European constitutions,
the preamble of the constitution of the Republic of Hungary is entirely prospective and surprisingly makes no references to history, culture, tradition or
religion. In terms of national identity and ethnicity, it nevertheless contains a
highly controversial and disputed Article 6/3 which reads: "[T]he Republic of
Hungary bears a sense of responsibility for the fate of Hungarians living outside its borders and shall promote and foster their relations with Hungary."

This constitutional commitment to ethnic Hungarians living abroad reflects
the fact that almost one third of people of Hungarian ethnicity live outside
the territory of the Hungarian state and constitute ethnic minorities in neighbouring states (Mediansky 1995: 108). At the same time, Article 6/3 stretched
constitutional sovereignty beyond the state borders and understandably
caused negative reactions from the neighbouring states with large Hungarian
minorities such as Romania and Slovakia.

Article 6/3 became a cornerstone of the Hungarian nationalist politics when
the first postcommunist Prime Minister, late József Antall, made a statement
that he regarded himself as a Prime Minister of 15 million Hungarians, the
number which includes the ethnic Hungarian minorities living abroad. After
the victory of the postcommunist left-wing opposition in subsequent parliamentary elections, the new Prime Minister Gyula Horn distanced himself from
this right-wing nationalism by commenting that he was only the Prime Minister
of the 10 million citizens of Hungary (see, for instance, Roth 1996: 282). The
ideological and political differences and struggles in Hungarian political life
symbolized by Article 6/3 were exacerbated by the ethno-nationalist policy of
the Hungarian Government of 1998–2002 under Prime Minister Viktor Orbán.
This government enacted legislation granting special access to social welfare
provided by the state of Hungary for ethnic Hungarians living outside its territory. This caused international tensions between Hungary and its neighbouring states once again and was criticized by the Council of Europe.[27]

Apart from other rights and entitlements, the law provides ethnic Hungarians from abroad with permission to work in Hungary for three months of each year. They also receive the Hungarian state's welfare benefits for that period. The law also provides financial assistance for ethnic Hungarian students in higher-education institutions while they are in Hungary and extends this assistance to ethnic Hungarians in their home countries. Foreign citizens who want to apply for any of these entitlements must obtain identity cards on the basis of a recommendation from foreign organizations of ethnic Hungarians recognized by the Hungarian government. The law was originally drafted even more extensively and was to create an "out-of-state-citizenship" based entirely on the blood and race principle. It was supposed to be a symbolic legal and political manifestation of the cohesion of ethnic Hungarians and their identification with the Hungarian state. It is then no surprise that the law was criticized even by moderate democratic leaders in Romania and Slovakia, and the Romanian delegation to the Parliamentary Assembly of the Council of Europe submitted a resolution calling on Hungary to suspend the implementation of the law. The resolution was supported by 26 other delegates and the law was described as discriminatory and violating the territorial integrity of other countries. Nevertheless, the law came into force on 1 January 2002, and shows how much the Hungarian constitutional and political transformation remains heavily determined by the divide between the civic and ethnic concept of a nation.[28]

The Czech and Slovak process of rebuilding the national identity by constitutionalism is even more theoretically fascinating than the cases of Poland or Hungary. The Czechoslovak constitution of 1920 purported to establish one Czechoslovak nation, which was a constitutional, political and cultural fiction partly reflecting the common history of Czechs and Slovaks and partly expressing a hope for political integration held by Czech and Slovak politicians of that time. The constitutional fiction of a Czechoslovak nation symbolized political unity and enhanced the chances of political homogeneity in the ethnically fragmented territory of Czechoslovakia. The project of multiethnic liberal democracy in Czechoslovakia was, of course, brought to an end by the Munich agreement of 1938 and the subsequent dismantlement of the state.

The problem of the coexistence of the different ethnic nations living in Czechoslovakia continued to preoccupy constitution-makers and politicians even during the communist era. After the transfer of ethnic Germans from the territory of Czechoslovakia in 1945, the whole matter was restricted to the mutual relations between the Czech and Slovak nations and the constitutional protection of ethnic and national minorities. The Constitution of 1960 limited the constitutional autonomy of the Slovak administration and shifted more power to central constitutional and political bodies. The Prague

Spring democratisation movement of 1968 introduced a federal system in Czechoslovakia. However, this system had no real impact on the lives of citizens because it lacked any capacity to express the truly democratic political will of Czechs and Slovaks, and this continued to be the case over the next two decades.[29]

After the fall of communism, the issue of constitutional transformation quickly became an issue of building an "authentic federation" and securing the rights of self-determination of the Slovak and Czech nations and of the other national minorities within the framework of the common state (Havel 1992b). The complicated process of redrafting the constitutional division of power and a system of checks and balances failed, and both nations subsequently drafted constitutions for the new, independent states of the Czech Republic and Slovakia. This failure is an example of the deadlock between ethnically established political entities living on the territory of a common state, leading to the state being peacefully split.[30]

The constitutions of both the Czech Republic and Slovakia legislate on the concept of a nation, and the two documents manifest fundamentally different understandings of nationhood. The Slovak constitution was criticized for marginalizing the constitutive role of ethnic and national minorities because its preamble referred primarily to the ethnically specified Slovak nation, its cultural heritage and political history.[31] This constitutional ethnic domination was abused by the 1994–98 government of Prime Minister Vladimír Mečiar. The Prime Minister and his government used historical resentment of and recent fears about Hungarian nationalism held by some of the ethnic Slovak population in order to isolate the Hungarian ethnic minority living in Slovakia from politics and public life.[32] On the other hand, the Slovak constitution contains a special section on ethnic and minority rights[33] which always enjoyed the attention of the Constitutional Court of Slovakia during its confrontations with Mečiar's ethno-nationlist policy. After the fall of Mečiar's Government in 1998, this section was used as the basis of a more balanced policy towards the protection of ethnic and national minorities.

The Czech constitution-makers merely reacted to political developments, and their lack of constitutional enthusiasm, which was so typical of constitution-making in Slovakia, even led to the suggestion that the constitution-making process could wait until after the independent Czech Republic came into existence on 1 January 1993. This opinion eventually did not prevail and the constitution of the Czech Republic was adopted in December 1992, just two weeks before it came into effect.

The merely reactive attitude of the Czech constitution-makers is well illustrated by their definition of a nation. After the adoption of the Slovak Constitution and subsequent criticism of its ethnicity-established definition of nationhood, the Czech constitution-makers enacted a document which begins as follows:

We, the citizens of the Czech Republic in Bohemia, in Moravia, and in Silesia,
At the time of the restoration of an independent Czech state,
Faithful to all good traditions of the long-existing statehood of the lands of the Czech Crown, as well as of Czechoslovak statehood,
Resolved to build, safeguard, and develop the Czech Republic in the spirit of the sanctity of human dignity and liberty,
As the homeland of free citizens enjoying equal rights, conscious of their duties towards others and their responsibility towards the community,
As a free and democratic state founded on respect for human rights and on the principles of civic society,
As a part of the family of democracies in Europe and around the world,
Resolved to guard and develop together the natural and cultural, material and spiritual wealth handed down to us,
Resolved to abide by all proven principles of a state governed by the rule of law,
Through our freely-elected representatives, do adopt this Constitution of the Czech Republic.[34]

Nationhood was exclusively defined in terms of citizenship, territoriality, state (not national) history and the universal values of human dignity, liberty, democracy and human rights. Like the Polish and Slovak constitutions, the Czech constitution retreats to a historical legitimating discourse, but it ignores the ethnic diversity existing in Czech society. Constitutional protection of ethnic and minority rights was secured by the Charter of Fundamental Rights and Freedoms which was incorporated into the newly established Czech constitutional order.[35]

Analysing the different constitutions put in place in Central Europe during the 1990s, it is possible to construct an interesting spectrum of constitutional definitions of a nation: entirely civic (Czechia); a patriotic mixture of civic and ethnic (Poland); internally civic combined with externally ethnic (Hungary); and entirely ethnic, defining the popular sovereignty as participation and cooperation between an ethnic majority and minorities (Slovakia). The legal and political consequences of this constitutional symbolism are not simple matters of causes and effects. A state established on the civic definition of popular sovereignty can have a discriminatory ethnic policy, such as Czech local authorities' policies towards the Roma/Gypsy in the mid-1990s. At the same time, the ethnic definition of a nation does not automatically rule out the possibility of a cooperative and inclusive ethnic policy. Dilemmas of the ethnic and civic concept of a nation and popular sovereignty go beyond the level of constitutionalism, pervade practical legal policies, and do not necessarily keep the same form when translated from the constitutional level to ordinary legislation and vice versa.

CONCLUDING REMARKS

The postcommunist political transformations manifest the symbolic power of constitutional and legal rationality. The constitution-making processes were instruments of both political change and stability and therefore had to deal with the problem of (dis)continuity outside the technical legal framework. Analysing the issues of retroactive justice and the constitutional definition of collective political identity, we detected specific normative frameworks which determined the character of constitutional transformations and established the background and limits of legal rationality. Law required a more general normative supplement in order to operate both as a stabilizing force and an instrument of the revolutionary changes. However, law and legal rationality also provided a specific codification of these normative frameworks and thus significantly influenced the way they were addressed in the emerging public discourse. The ethical issues of historical justice, political identity and national history were channelled by the legal and constitutional modes of communication.

The force of legal rationality codifying political time was required to eliminate the possible dangers arising from the political and ethical dealings with the past, present and future during the postcommunist transformations. Political and social discontinuities had to be legally interpreted and the legal consequences of these interpretations had to be established. The symbolic power of law often clashed with the technical limits of legality, yet legality remained the ultimate instrument of overcoming the politically condemned past. Legal rationality was stretched between past and future. It involved crucial questions of collective identity and choice of the political principles which were to govern the new democratic societies of postcommunist Central Europe.

The 1989 revolutionary changes in Central Europe also prove that the problem of collective identity is not merely an issue of social and political integration. It is also a process of discrimination and political differentiation between *us* and *them*. Analysing the temporal dynamics of the changes, it turned out that the complex constitution-making processes in different

Central European countries were governed by the logic of the difference between the communist past, referring to *them*, and liberal democratic future, referring to *us*. Specific legal definitions of this profound political discontinuity subsequently secured the integrative function of legal rationality in the postcommunist political and constitutional transformations. Temporal disintegration was a precondition of the political integration pursued by the postcommunist constitution-making processes.

NOTES

1 Okri 1992: 314.
2 Topol 2000: 92.
3 This change is manifested, for instance, in the jurisprudence of the legal realists. They generally supported Roosevelt's policy of the New Deal and emphasised the prospective, future-oriented instrumental role of legislation and judicial decision-making in the public policy. For more details, see, for example, Frank 1970.
4 For more information, see Přibáň 2002: ch. 3.
5 For political and theoretical difficulties with postcommunist "ex post facto political justice" see, for instance, Varga 1995.
6 For further details, see especially McAdams 2001.
7 The Office was set up from two different administrative offices under the Ministry of Interior on 1 January 1995.
8 Act 140/96 Sb. on the opening of the state secret police files, adopted on 26 April 1996.
9 See, for instance, Rosenberg 1995; for more scholarly and specific legal critique see Schwartz 1994: 398.
10 Judgement K 7/90 of 22 August 1990 Orzecznictwo Tryb. Konst. 42. In this judgement, the tribunal decided that lowering of state pensions did not violate the constitution.
11 See Judgement U 5/86 of 5 November 1986 Orzecznictwo Tryb. Konst. 7, at 46. Quoted from Brzezinski and Garlicki 1995: 36.
12 Judgement S 6/91 of 25 September 1991 Orzecznictwo Tryb. Konst. 290, 294. Translation from Brzezinski and Garlicki 1995: 38.
13 After the splitting of Czechoslovakia, the Lustration Law became an intrinsic part of the Czech legal system, while it was not applied in Slovakia.
14 The Act of the Federal Assembly of the Czech and Slovak Federal Republic n. 451/1991 Sb., on standards required for holding specific positions in state administration of the Czech and Slovak Federal Republic, Czech Republic and Slovak Republic, passed on 4 October 1991 and enacted from 1 January 1992. For the English translation, see Sklar and Kanev 1995: app. A.
15 The statute was originally enacted for five years, but its validity was later extended by the Czech Parliament and it is still a part of the Czech legal system which is widely believed to be incorporated into new law on civil service.
16 For details on the Czechoslovak Lustration Law, see especially Cepl 1992; Šiklová 1999; Gillis 1999.
17 All postcommunist constitutions in Central European countries legislated the principle of equality of all citizens before the law. See Article 1 of the Czechoslovak Charter of Fundamental Rights and Freedoms and the preamble of the Constitution of the

Czech Republic adopted on 16 December 1992; Article 57/1 of the Constitution of Hungary redrafted and enacted in October 1989; Article 32 of the Constitution of Poland adopted by Polish Parliament on 2 April 1997 and confirmed by referendum in October 1997; Articles 12, 46 and 47 of the Constitution of Slovakia adopted by the Slovak Parliament on 1 September 1992.

18 See especially its historically first judgement 19/93 Sb. on the Act of Lawlessness of the Communist Regime and Resistance Against It, which manifests strong argumentative continuity with the Czechoslovak Constitutional Court that ceased to exist in December 1992 after the split of Czechoslovakia.

19 For legal continuity and change of regime, see Klingsberg 1992a: 49.

20 For anthropological theories inspired by Halbwachs and his concept of collective memories, see, for instance, Assmann 1997.

21 For a theoretical position similar to the political and constitutional ambitions in postcommunist Central Europe, see Arato and Cohen 1992.

22 For this need of stability and the concept of nationhood see, for instance, Offe 1996: 256–57.

23 For this classification, see especially Giddens 1987.

24 See, for instance, anti-semitic nationalist pamphlets distributed by the Saint Crown organisation in Hungary in the early 1990s, nationalist populism within the Solidarność movement, or racist rhetoric of the extreme right-wing Republican Party in Czechoslovakia at the beginning of the 1990s. For further details on constitutionalism and nationalism, see Czarnota 1995.

25 Constitutional patriotism as remedy of ethnic national animosities and hatred is often promoted, for instance, by advocates of the civil society ideology such as Jürgen Habermas. See Habermas 2001.

26 The preamble of the Constitution of the Republic of Poland of 1997.

27 The Act of Parliament enacted on 19 June 2001, the so-called "status law." For the first comments in English, see *East European Constitutional Review* 10, nos. 2/3 (2001): 20.

28 Ibid.

29 For further details on the federal system of 1968 and the constitutional history of Czechoslovakia, see Cutler and Schwartz 1991: 519.

30 Former Yugoslavia would be an example of the violent dissolution of a common state, while Belgium may be used as an example of a crippled unity and continuing animosities between different nations under one federal rule.

31 See the Preamble of the Slovak Constitution.

32 Famous examples of this policy are the law on protection of the Slovak language and the electoral law adopted for the 1998 elections.

33 Part IV of the Constitution, Articles 33–34.

34 The Preamble of the Constitution of the Czech Republic.

35 See Articles 24–25 of the Charter.

BIBLIOGRAPHY

Arato, Andrew. *Civil Society, Constitution, and Legitimacy*. London: Rowman and Littlefield Publishers, 2000.

Arato, Andrew and Jean Cohen. *Civil Society and Political Theory*. Cambridge, Mass.: The MIT Press, 1990.

Arnold, Thurman. *The Symbols of Government*. New Haven: Yale University Press, 1935.

Assmann, Jan. *Die kulturelle Gedächtnis, Schrift, Erinnerung und politische Identität in frühen Hochkulturen* [The cultural memory, writing, recollection, and political identity in early civilisations]. München: C. H. Beck, 1997.

Brzezinski, Marek F. and Lech Garlicki. "Judicial Review in Post-communist Poland: The Emergence of a *Rechtsstaat?*" *Stanford Journal of International Law* 31 (1995): 13–59.

Cepl, Vojtěch. "Ritual Sacrifices." *East European Constitutional Review* 1 (1992): 24–26.

Connor, Walker. "A Nation is a Nation, is a State, is an Ethnic Group, is a..." *Ethnic and Racial Studies* 1, no. 4 (1978): 379–88.

Cutler, Lloyd and Herman Schwartz. "Constitutional Reform in Czechoslovakia: *E Duobus Unum?*" *The University of Chicago Law Review* 58 (1991): 511–53.

Czarnota, Adam. "Constitutional Nationalism, Citizenship and Hope for Civil Society in Eastern Europe" in *Nationalism and Postcommunism: A Collection of Essays*, eds. Pavkovic, Alexander, Halyna Koscharsky and Adam Czarnota (Aldershot: Dartmouth, 1995), pp. 83–100.

Dahrendorf, Ralf. *Reflections on the Revolution in Europe.* London: Chatto and Windus, 1990.

Elias, Norbert. *Time: An Essay.* Oxford: Blackwell Publishers, 1992.

Frank, Jerome. *Law and the Modern Mind.* Cloucester, Mass.: Smith, 1970.

Fuller, Lon L. *The Morality of Law.* Revised edition. New Haven: Yale University Press, 1969.

Giddens, Anthony. *The Nation-State and Violence: Volume Two of a Contemporary Critique of Historical Materialism.* Berkeley: University of California Press, 1987.

Gillis, Mark. "Lustration and Decommunisation" in *The Rule of Law in Central Europe,* eds. Přibáň, Jiří and James Young (Aldershot: Ashgate Publishing, 1999), pp. 56–81.

Habermas, Jürgen. *The Postnational Constellation: Political Essays.* Cambridge: Polity Press, 2001.

Hart, Herbert L. A. *The Concept of Law.* 2nd edition. Oxford: Clarendon Press, 1994.

Havel, Václav. "Paradise Lost." *New York Review of Books,* April 9 1992(a), p. 6.

——. *Summer Meditations: On Politics, Morality and Civility in a Time of Transition.* London: Faber and Faber, 1992b.

Keane, John, ed. *The Power of the Powerless: Citizens against the State in Central-Eastern Europe,* London: Hutchinson Press, 1985.

Kelsen, Hans. *Society and Nature: A Sociological Inquiry.* London: Kegan, Trench, Trubner and Co, 1946.

——. *General Theory of Law and State.* New York: Russell and Russell, 1961.

Klingsberg, Ethan. "Judicial Review and Hungary's Transition from Communism to Democracy: The Constitutional Court, the Continuity of Law, and the Redefinition of Property Rights." *Brigham Young University Law Review* 1 (1992a): 41–144.

——. "The State Rebuilding Civil Society: Constitutionalism and the Post-communist Paradox." *Michigan Journal of International Law* 13 (1992b): 865–907.

Kohn, Hans. *The Idea of Nationalism.* New York: Macmillan Press, 1945.

Konrád, György. *Antipolitics.* New York: Hartcourt, Brace, Jovanovich, 1984.

Krygier, Martin. "Traps for Young Players in Times of Transition." *East European Constitutional Review* 8, no. 4 (1999): 63–67.

McAdams, Arthur J. *Judging the Past in Unified Germany.* New York: Cambridge University Press, 2001.

Mediansky, Fedor. "National Minorities and Security in Central Europe: The Hungarian Experience" in *Nationalism and Postcommunism: a collection of essays,* eds. Pavkovic, Alexander, Halyna Koscharsky and Adam Czarnota (Aldershot: Dartmouth, 1995) 101–20.

Offe, Claus. *Modernity and the State: East, West*. Cambridge: Polity Press, 1996.

Okri, Ben. *The Famished Road*. London: Vintage, 1992.

Osiatyński, Wiktor. "Revolutions in Eastern Europe." *University of Chicago Law Review* 58 (1991): 823–58.

Paczolay, Peter. "The New Hungarian Constitutional State: Challenges and Perspectives" in *Constitution Making in Eastern Europe*, ed. Dick, Howard A. E. (Baltimore: Woodrow Wilson Center Press and John Hopkins University Press, 1993), pp. 21–55.

Preuss, Ulrich. *Revolution, Fortschritt und Verfassung* [Revolution, progress and constitution]. Berlin: Wagenbach Verlag, 1990.

Přibáň, Jiří. *Dissidents of Law*. Aldershot: Ashgate Publishing, 2002.

Renan, Ernest. *Qu'est-ce qu'une nation?* [What is a nation?]. Paris: Calmann-Levy Press, 1882.

Rosenberg, Tina. *The Haunted Land: Facing Europe's Ghosts after Communism*. New York: Vintage, 1995.

Roth, Stephen J. "The Effect of Ethno-Nationalism on Citizens' Rights in the Former Communist Countries" in *Western Rights?: Post-communist Application*, ed. Sajó, András (The Hague: Kluwer, 1996), pp. 273–90.

Schwartz, Herman. "The Czech Constitutional Court Decision on the Illegitimacy of the Communist Regime." *Parker School Journal of East European Law* 1 (1994): 392–98.

Shils, Edward. *Tradition*. London: Faber and Faber, 1981.

Sklar, Morton and Krassimir Kanev. *Decommunisation: A New Threat to Scientific and Academic Freedom in Central and Eastern Europe*. Report issued by the Science and Human Rights Program of the American Association for the Advancement of Science, September 1995.

Sugar, Peter F. and Ivo J. Lederer, eds. *Nationalism in Eastern Europe*. Seattle: University of Washington Press, 1969.

Sumner, William G. *Folkways: A Study of the Sociological Importance of Usages, Manners, Customs, Mores and Morals*. New York: Mentor Books, 1960.

Šiklová, Jiřina. "Lustration or the Czech Way of Screening" in *The Rule of Law After Communism*, eds. Krygier, Martin and Adam Czarnota (Aldershot: Ashgate Publishing, 1999), pp. 248–58.

Toffler, Alvin. *Future Shock*. London: Pan Books, 1971.

Topol, Jáchym. *Anděl* [The Angel]. 2nd revised edition. Praha: Labyrint, 2000.

Varga, Csaba. *Transition to Rule of Law: On the Democratic Transformation in Hungary*. Budapest: Hungarian Academy of Sciences, 1995.

Corruption, Anti-Corruption Sentiments, and the Rule of Law

IVAN KRASTEV

Postcommunist societies are simply obsessed with corruption. Corruption is the most powerful policy narrative in the time of transition. It explains why industries that were once the jewels of the communist economies have gone bankrupt. Corruption explains why the poor are poor and the rich are rich. For the postcommunist citizen, blaming corruption is the only way to express his disappointment with the present political elites, to mourn the death of his 1989 expectations for a better life, and to reject any responsibility for his present well being. Talking about corruption is the way the postcommunist public talks about politics, economy, about the past and the future.

Outsiders are even more obsessed with postcommunist corruption. For many observers corruption explains why some transition countries succeed and others fail, why reforms are endangered and democracy is at risk, why people are unhappy and the mafia is over-powerful. Richard Rose, William Mishler, and Christian Haerpfer argue that "corruption has replaced repression as the main threat to the rule of law" (Rose et al. 1997). Their multiple regression analysis suggests that the level of corruption is a more important determinant of attitudes towards "undemocratic alternatives" than the country's democratic tradition, its current level of freedom or its current economic performance. Corruption steals economic growth, erodes democracy, degrades society, and dooms the chances for the establishment of the rule of law society in Eastern Europe.

Corruption is the black myth of transition. It is the explanation of last resort for all failures and disappointments of the first postcommunist decade. Rule of law is the white myth of transition. After some years of flirting with the ideas of democracy and market economy, now rule of law is the magic phrase in Eastern Europe. It is rule of law and not democracy that brings foreign investors, it is rule of law that secures development and protects rights. It is the lack of rule of law that explains the spread of corruption and it is the march of rule of law that will guarantee success in the fight against corruption. What strikes one in this new rule of law orthodoxy are its formalistic and anti-political overtones. Rule of law is not portrayed as a society in which rules of the game are respected and the rights of the citizens are protected, but as a set of institutional devices and capacity building programs that should free people from the imperfections of democratic politics. And in this rule of law building exercise, the special role is reserved for anti-corruption campaigns. Anti-corruption campaigns designed to achieve transparent institutions, raise public awareness, and build institutional capacities are viewed by the World Bank and other external policy makers as the critical strategy for promoting the rule of law state. But are the anti-corruption campaigns the shortest cut to a rule of law culture and are we aware of the hidden risks of such campaigns? The major argument of this chapter is that the current policy-thinking misunderstands the effects of anti-corruption campaigns and in this way blurs the prospects for the establishment of a rule of law culture in Eastern Europe. The central reason for this misunderstanding is the misreading of the nature of the public's anti-corruption sentiments.

It is the analysis of the moral economy of the anti-corruption sentiments in the period of transition and a close reading of the attempts to create a socialist legal state in the early 1980s that can enlighten us to the dark side of the current obsession with fighting corruption.

The present chapter is not a study of corruption, nor a study of rule of law politics. It is an interpretation of the anxieties of transition. It is a reflection on the popular discourse on corruption and its role in making postcommunist society. Anti-corruption discourse is not simply a discourse on real or alleged acts of bribery or other forms of misusing public office for private gains. It cannot be reduced to the unarticulated public disappointment with the *status quo*. It is a discourse expressing the painful process of social stratification in the transition societies. It is a discourse on social equality and fairness. It is indeed a set of discourses, conflicting with each other and reconstituting the meaning of postcommunist corruption.

The anti-corruption pronouncements of the international financial institutions have almost nothing in common with the anti-corruption outcries hosted in the tabloid media, heard on the streets or captured in focus groups. What is corruption, who corrupts whom, what are the reasons for the rise of corruption and what should be done to curb it are among the questions that will receive different answers depending on whom you ask in postcommunist society.

"It would be impossible for an historian to write a history of political corruption in the United States," noted Walter Lippman in 1930. "What we could write is the history of the exposure of corruption" (ibid.). It would also be impossible for a historian to write a history of political corruption in postcommunist Eastern Europe. What we could write is the history of policy responses to corruption and what we can speculate on is the long-term effects of these responses.

THE CORRUPTION PARADOX

It was a commonplace among the ordinary citizens of the Soviet bloc to view corruption and privileges as the most disgusting features of "real socialism." Privileges were for the nomenclature, corruption was for the people. People complained about it, lived with it, and protested against it. In academic writing, communism was also described as highly corrupted. Dependence on bribes and contacts was notorious. Towards the end of the communist regime, a majority of respondents in Wayne DiFranceisco and Zvy Gitelman's survey of Soviet émigrés suggested that bribery or connections could be used to change an unwelcome work assignment or to get a dull child into a good university department (Miller et al. 2001).

A decade ago, both the public and scholars would have been shocked to learn that one day postcommunism would be seen as more corrupt than communism. It is this transformation of the "unexpected" into "unproblematic" in the perception of corruption that I refer to as the "corruption paradox."

THE NON-BANALITY OF POSTCOMMUNIST CORRUPTION

What is common between the successful Polish transition, the semi-successful Bulgarian transition, and the unsuccessful Russian transition? Not much, except that the majority of Poles, Bulgarians, and Russians are convinced that in their country there is more corruption today than in the days of communism.

The figures are striking because Polish, Bulgarian, and Russian public opinions sharply differ in the way they judge the success and the direction of the economic and political changes, the desirability of changes, and also their personal benefits and losses in the period of transition. The result is striking also because in the Corruption Perception Index of Transparency International for 1999, Poland ranks 44 on the level of corruption, while Bulgaria is at 66 and Russia at 82, and because corruption is figured out as a major social problem in Bulgaria and Poland, but not in Russia (Sajó 1998).

The claim that postcommunism is more corrupt than communism cannot be explained simply by the failure of market reforms. The success or failure of reforms can be a working explanatory model when we compare the scale of corruption in different countries, but it is a weak explanation when we compare "now" and "then." Culture, religion, and the length of the communist rule are also non-explanations. Poland is a Catholic society, Bulgaria and Russia are Orthodox countries. Russia has lived much longer under communism than Bulgaria and Poland. These countries differ significantly in their size and ethnic homogeneity, two other factors that affect the spread of corruption. They differ in GDP, attractiveness to foreign investment, availability of natural resources, and the level of economic optimism with respect to the future. The finding that Bulgarians, Poles, and Russians share the common view that postcommunism is more corrupt than communism is an unexpected finding, a non-trivial one. It is worth closer exploration.

Corruption cannot be studied directly. Indirect studies of corruption are also problematic. What do we claim when we assert that a certain regime or certain period is more corrupt than another? Do we claim that during this period the number of corrupt transactions has increased? Do we claim that the number of people involved in corrupt transactions has increased? Do we claim that corruption has reached the highest places of power? Do we claim that the social costs of corruption have increased? Do we claim that society as a whole is more tolerant to corruption, or do we claim all these together?

How can we know what exactly the respondent wants to tell us when judging that postcommunism is more corrupt than communism? Does he refer to the cost of corruption, to the ugliness of the grand political corruption, or to pervasive bureaucratic corruption? Is his judgment based on his personal experience with petty corruption, or is his claim based on media stories about the scale of political corruption? It is also well known that the popularity of corrupt practices increases the levels of their acceptability. If almost everybody is a practicing corrupter or corruptee, then corruption is a rule and not a deviation from the rule. Does it mean that communism looked less corrupt because everybody was part of corruption games?

And finally, is postcommunism really more corrupt than communism? The empirical data are too controversial and incomplete to sustain such a claim. In most of the communist countries, corruption was a taboo topic, so reliable data on perceptions of corruption or fact-based reports on the spread of acts of corruption are not available. The court and the police records cannot be a source of valid information. Most of them are silent with respect to corruption when it comes to the high-ranking communist officials. Communism was a political system based on virtue, so the regime was unwilling to demonstrate the human vulnerability of its outstanding members.

And what kind of definition will be adopted for the purpose of comparison? Should we consider only the corrupt acts that are criminalized in a given period? Should we count only acts that are perceived as corrupt by public opinion, what Arnold J. Heidenheimer called "white corruption" (Heidenheimer 1989), or should we adopt a more general public interest definition that will define as corruption all those acts that are viewed as corruption today? In interpreting corruption we should face all these and many other constraints.

THE DEBATE

In the current debate, various approaches compete in explaining and constructing the corruption phenomenon. They legislate how to think about corruption, what to think about corruption, and how to act against corruption. The dominant anti-corruption discourse of the IMF and World Bank is institutional in nature. For it, the claim that one political regime is more corrupt than another is not an empirical claim. It is a normative claim. The prevailing institutional discourse measures corruption through the corruption incentives created by various institutional environments. In the context of this approach, regime A is more corrupt than regime B if the discretionary power of public officials and the level of state intervention is higher in regime A in comparison with regime B.

The dissident or perceptionalist view on the rise of corruption is limited in its influence and is perceived by many as the last incarnation of the "apologists" of corruption. This discourse is not interested in the incentives for corrupt behavior that are made available by different political regimes. It starts with the assumption that there is no necessary link between the perception of the public that corruption is pervasive and the actual level of corruption. In the context of this school of thought, corruption perception is a product of a given media reality (in the broader sense) and not of any significant changes in the actual spread of corruption. Perception change in Germany in the wake of the "Kohl affair" is a powerful illustration of the fact that it is the corruption we know about and not the actual level of corruption that governs public sentiments. Germany after the Kohl scandal broke out is not more corrupt than Germany the day before the story was revealed, but the perception of the cleanness of the Berlin Republic has declined dramatically both inside and outside the country. The perceptionalist argument distrusts the consensus that corruption is on the rise. In their seminal study of street-level corruption in four Eastern European countries, William L. Miller, Åse B. Grødeland, and Tatyana Y. Koshechkina documented that citizens' actual experience of dealing with street-level corruption is far less negative than their perceptions (Miller et al. 2001).

My interpretation of the boom of corruption perceptions in Eastern Europe does not side either with the institutionalists or with the perceptionalists. It agrees that the link between corruption perceptions and the actual levels of corruption is highly problematic. But it suggests that when the public compares corruption "now" and "then," it does not simply "count" corrupt acts, nor does it "count" corruption-related media materials. The judgment on the rise or decline of corruption is mediated by reflections on its social functions. In interpreting the public opinion's claim that postcommunism is more corrupt than communism, we need to bring in the broader context of actors' experience of social change. Numbers and correlations are not enough for reading the public mind. It is in the course of the endless talks about corruption, the corrupted, and the government's failure to resist corruption that postcommunist citizens negotiate their attitude to the phenomenon. And in the course of these invisible negotiations, the consensus that postcommunism is more corrupt than communism is being reached.

WHEN LESS STATE DOES NOT MEAN LESS CORRUPTION

In arguing that the actual corruption in Eastern Europe has increased, political scientists and economists point to several recent developments. Internalization of trade and finance and the end of the grand ideological divide counts for external reasons for the "corruption eruption." But there are several "transition" arguments for the rise of corruption.

The communist legacy, and particularly the legacy of the interventionist state, is singled out as the critical domestic pre-condition for the rise of corruption. Postcommunist regimes as a rule have inherited a lot of license permission and discretionary power for state officials. The existence of these discretionary regimes is at the core of the institutional explanation of the corruption eruption (Tanzi 1998).

The crisis of legitimacy and low trust in public institutions is the other part of the explanation. The existence of corruption incentives cannot be directly translated into claims of more corruption. Values do matter. The Nordic countries that are known for the significant presence of the state in the economy are among the most corruption-free countries in the world. Corruption incentives increase the actual level of corruption only when they are in partnership with public tolerance of corruption and absence of professional bureaucracy and rule of law. Social norms are the independent variable in the corruption equation that constrains the ambitions of institutional reductionism.

However, not only big governments but also weak states contribute to the pervasive corruption in Eastern Europe. A weak state lacks the capacity to enforce rules and dramatically diminishes the risks connected with corrupt behavior. The weak state is at the heart of the argument developed by Andre Shliefer and Robert Vishny (Shliefer and Vishny 1993). In their article "Corruption" they suggest that postcommunist corruption is more inefficient than the communist one, and as a result, it is more costly. Communist corruption was centralized. It was enough to bribe the boss in order to set the chain in action. The model of postcommunist corruption is a model of independent monopolists. In order to make the transaction happen the corrupter should bribe almost everybody in the chain.

Another argument explaining the rise of corruption in the transition period is the argument of the Hungarian constitutionalist András Sajó (Sajó 1998). He suggests that postcommunist corruption is clientelistic in its nature and is closely connected with the forming of the political parties and re-distribution of state assets. Corruption is the hidden tax that society pays for the functioning of the multi-party system. Misrecognition of clientelism for corruption, and Western pressure for transparency, are the reasons for over-dramatization of the Eastern European corruption problem.

But it is large-scale privatization that dominates popular explanations for the rise of corruption in the time of transition. Theoretically, and in the long run, privatization is advertised as a corruption-reducing policy (Kaufmann 1997). But practically, and in the short run, privatization increases the level of corruption. The incentives for quick enrichment are so high that corrupt behavior is unavoidable. The Polish Minister of Privatization Janusz Lewandowski gave one of the best descriptions of the internal controversy of the process. "Privatisation," wrote Lewandowski, "is when someone who does not know who the real owner is and does not know what it is really worth sells something to someone who does not have any money" (quoted in Dunn 2003). Lewandowski's definition touches the three troubles with postcommunist privatization. The first is the pricing of the ex-socialist property. The prices of the socialist enterprises differ dramatically in the eyes of the market and in the eyes of society. The complaint that the state is selling "cheap" is the most popular complaint in the time of transition. In her study of workers' perception of privatization in one Polish food producing factory, Elizabeth Dunn underlines that the idea of the "bribe" here is the difference between two distinct measures of value: the supposedly "objective" measure set by Western accounting or by the market, and Alima workers' subjective opinion of the value of their lives and work under socialism, which were crystallized in the firm (Dunn 2003).

The second trouble is the buyers. Domestic buyers for big and even middle-sized enterprises did not exist in Eastern Europe. Real socialism was not a society of equal prosperity but in the beginning of transition many people still believed that it was a society of equal poverty. It was in the initial years of transition that some got access to credit and became buyers, and others remained on the side of the selling state. The past of the new owners intrigued public imagination much more than the future of the privatized enterprises. And the third trouble with privatization is that the very process of privatization was conceived by many as a form of corruption *per se*. The absence of effective control over the black and gray privatization practices acted as a catalyst in rising anti-corruption and anti-elite sentiments. One Czech study identified 33 cases of personal gain in the area of privatization in a 12-month period, totaling 25 billion Czech crowns, but resulting in only two prosecutions (Miller et al. 2001). The Bulgarian economist Rumen Avramov defined "privatisation of the profits and nationalisation of losses" as the major formula for creating the private sector in postcommunist Eastern Europe (Avramov 2001).

In explaining the "corruption eruption," the virtual school suggests different readings of the postcommunist obsession with corruption. A number of studies stress the fact that there is low correlation between respondents' personal experience with corruption and their judgment of the level of corruption in the country (Miller et al. 2001). Regular newspaper readers in Bulgaria estimate the country as more corrupt than do those who do not regularly read newspapers. Miller, Grødeland, and Koshechkina documented the fact that contrary to the proverb, familiarity bred trust rather than contempt. People tend to view as less corrupt those institutions that they know personally and as more corrupt institutions that are far away from their daily experience. As a result, the Parliament as a rule is viewed as more corrupt than the police. In a paradoxical way, the free media is an instrument for controlling and reducing corruption, but at the same time it increases corruption perceptions in the society.

The perceptionalist argument suggests that the boom in corruption perceptions is a result of the media's obsession with corruption and the role of corruption accusations in postcommunist politics. Corruption stories sell well. The public loves reading stories of degradation. But a commercial explanation is not sufficient. In the time of transition, when the grand ideological divide is already in history and when policy differences between the main political parties are negligible, corruption accusations are the major weapons of the opposition. To accuse government of being corrupt saves the need to offer an alternative to its policies. There is in Eastern Europe today a distinct prejudice in favor of those who make the accusations. The number of court verdicts on corruption charges is ridiculously small all over the region. The non-functioning legal system gives the media the role of both prosecutor and judge. In the postcommunist world anti-corruption rhetoric is the favorite weapon for anybody seeking power.

In the context of the institutional paradigm, the transition period creates high incentives for corrupt behavior and the weak postcommunist state constantly fails to respond efficiently. The virtual argument reduces the rise of corruption perception to the information asymmetry. Both arguments are vulnerable in their explanations as to why postcommunist public opinion is convinced that "today" is more corrupt than "yesterday."

Institutional arguments underestimate the role of social and cultural norms in restraining corruption. The virtual argument overestimates the lack of genuine information in the time of late communism. The fact that official channels of information were blocked does not mean that people were ignorant about the spread of corruption in their society. The unofficial discourse recorded many corruption stories. So, we need to include the perspective of the participant in order to offer a more convincing interpretation of the corruption paradox. The real question is not whether postcommunism is more corrupt than communism, but why public opinion judges postcommunism to be more corrupt than communism.

THE MORAL ECONOMY OF CORRUPTION — "NOW" AND "THEN"

The introduction of the actor's perspective in interpreting public opinion's view on corruption is the only alternative to institutional and virtual explanations. But the introduction of the actor's perspective is not an easy task. The data of anthropological studies and focus groups are contextual and heterogeneous and the risks of misinterpretation are grave. Respondents who claim that postcommunism is more corrupt than communism do not share a common view on what should be and should not be defined as corruption. They come from various social backgrounds and their tolerance with respect to corruption varies. Reconstructing individual motivations for blaming postcommunism for being more corrupt than communism is mission impossible. The general hypothesis of this chapter is that the claim expressed by the respondents that postcommunism is more corrupt than communism is not a factual claim. It is a value statement that includes in itself reflection on the social function of corruption.

Respondents do not simply "register" corruption, they judge the result of its work. The key factor explaining the new corruption sensitivity is that one specific type of corruption has been replaced by a radically different form of corruption. *Blat* was replaced by bribery. Interpretation of the "corruption paradox" necessarily presupposes comparison of respondents' perception of "blat" and "bribe" as the dominant forms of corruption respectively in the communist and postcommunist periods.

"DO ME A FAVOR SOCIETY" VERSUS "GIVE ME A BRIBE SOCIETY"

The mysterious and at the same time prosaic practices that Russians called *blat*, Bulgarians called "connections" and Poles called *załatwianie spraw* are known to be the secret key for understanding the communist society. A society in which, according to *Guardian* reporter Martin Walker, "nothing is legal but everything is possible" (quoted in Ledeneva 1998).

In her enlightening book *Russia's Economy of Favors* (1998), Alena Ledeneva defines blat as "the use of personal networks and informal contacts to obtain goods and services in short supply and to find a way around formal procedures" (Ledeneva 1998). All authors agree that blat is a typically Soviet (communist) phenomenon. Blat shares many similarities to premodern practices of gift giving and many theorists (like most citizens) are unenthusiastic to classify blat as corruption. "Adultery is not a crime and blat is not corruption" is the shared opinion among most of the participants in focus groups. But in its essence, blat is a classical form of misuse of public position for private or group gains. Blat works to the extent to which certain public officials betray their duties in order to favor their friends or friends of their friends.

In her remarkable book, Ledeneva presents a complex analysis of the phenomenon and its role in the survival and erosion of the Soviet system. In the context of my interest in revealing the moral economy of anti-corruption sentiments in Eastern Europe, several characteristics of blat are of critical importance. Blat was a widespread phenomenon all over the Soviet bloc. Living out of blat was a form of asocial behavior. Blat was an exchange of favors. Even when some gifts and money were involved in blat relations, it was the exchange of favors and not the bribe that was the driving force of the relations. In the words of Ledeneva, "blat is a distinctive form of non-monetary exchange, a kind of barter based on personal relations" (Ledeneva 1998). Blat was totally conditioned on the economy of shortages. It was a "survival kit reducing uncertainty in conditions of shortage, exigency and perpetual emergency, in which formal criteria and formal rights are insufficient to operate" (ibid.). Blat was condemned in the official discourse but, with the exception of extreme cases, it was not criminalized. Blat relations were not simple barter, they were not necessary dyadic. Blat transactions could be circular: A provides a favor to B, B to C, C to D, and D to A, and the last link in the chain might not have taken place. Blat exchange is mediated and covered by the rhetoric of friendship. In contrast, the relationship between corrupter and corruptee is centered on the bribe.

In the days of communism, blat coexisted with bribe and other classical forms of corruption. But blat was the most popular type of survival strategy. Blat was the paradigmatic form of corruption. Communism was totalitarianism moderated by the spread of blat and petty bribery. When respondents reflect on their communist experience, blat comes up as the form of corruption they associate with the old regime. Participants in different focus groups insist that the practice of "connections" was widespread in the old days, but acts of "real corruption" were much more limited than now.

In her book, Ledeneva even argues that blat should not be classified as corruption. Such a view can be also found when people tell their own blat experience. Personal friendship and readiness to help colored participants' blat memories. Ledeneva's argument is valuable in distinguishing blat from other forms of informal transactions. But it is also true that blat was perceived as corruption and that blat involves abuse of public office for private gains. Corruption was simply other peoples' blat. In the popular discourse, "other people's blat" was commented on and viewed as corruption. When a mother was telling the story of why her kid failed to enter university, when a customer complained about not "obtaining" valuable goods, privileges and "connections" were the explanations and they were judged as corruption.

The anti-corruption campaigns that were a common feature of the late days of the communist regimes best illustrate the fact that blat was perceived as a specific form of corruption and as a practice which erodes the public good. The citizen of communist society was aware of the social price of blat but he was also aware of the lack of any other realistic alternative for surviving.

The disappearance of blat is the key development for understanding the reality of postcommunist corruption. "Market conditions have changed personal relations and ruined many friendships," said one of the Russians interviewed by Ledeneva. "There is no room for blat as it used to be. It looks like blat won't be the same and the very word is going into oblivion" (quoted in Ledeneva 1998). Results of opinion polls show that blat is losing its significance (Ledeneva 1998; Miller et al. 2001).

The end of the economy of shortage and the rise of "real money" changed the rules of the game. The major process observed in all transition countries is the monetarization of blat relations and replacement of blat by bribe. The economy of favors was replaced by the economy of paid services. The transition rediscovered the unrestricted power of money. So, it is not surprising that former communist societies reacted to the monetarization of blat in the same way the pre-modern societies reacted in their earlier encounters with modernity (Avramov 2001).

In my interpretation, the perception inside the transition societies that postcommunism is more corrupt than communism is linked to the fact that bribes replaced blat as the dominant form of corruption. Blat networks are reorganized on market principles. Blat networks are transformed into classical corruption networks involved in the redistribution of the state assets, while other blat networks simply disappeared. Personal interests have become business interests. In the view of one of the participants in Ledeneva's survey, "finance, licenses, privileged loans, access to business information are the shortages of today" (quoted in Ledeneva 1998).

The critical question is what makes blat and bribe so different in the perception of the postcommunist public. Umit Berkman has stressed that corruption behavior is conditioned by the nature of the corrupt act (Miller et al. 2001). The non-monetary character of blat is critical in understanding its social acceptability. Citizens are easier offering presents than money. And officials more easily ask for favors than for money (Miller et al. 2001).

But the social acceptability of blat cannot be reduced to its non-monetary character. In the last years of socialism, bribe money was making its career in blat relations. It is the latent functions of blat and bribes in the communist and the postcommunist system respectively that explain the distinction. Blat is a socially acceptable form of corruption not simply because it is a non-monetary form but because it increases social equality in the communist society. It "allows" participants in blat transactions to misrecognize their activities as "help" and to cover it in the rhetoric of friendship.

In most of the studies, blat is analyzed as an exchange of services and information. Blat was the only channel for the unprivileged to obtain deficit goods. It was viewed as a form of protest against the communist regime. But what is even more important is that blat was also an exchange of social statuses. In the economy of deficit, the power status of the person was defined on one side by his position on the power hierarchy (being in or out of the nomenclature), but on the other side by access to deficit goods or information. Blat destroyed the dependence of consumption on one's place in the hierarchy. On the queue for a popular but deficit book, it is not the professor or the senior official but the friend of the bookseller who usually won the bid.

In its radical form, blat replaced the relations between public roles with relations between people. This redistribution of power sustained and subverted the system at the same time. It made life bearable, but it undermined power relations. Loyalty to one's blat network was higher than loyalty to the state. Using current jargon, blat empowered the powerless.

In the discourse of the majority of the people, "connections" were unfair but they were the only way to "humanize" the bureaucratic nature of the regime. The word "bureaucracy" had a connotation more negative than "connections." The discourse on corruption in communist times was a discourse of inclusion.

The social functions of the bribe in the postcommunist reality are contrary to the functions of blat. The bribe caused the inflation of the social capital defined as blat. Monetarization of social relations led to the inflation of the social investments that the ordinary citizen has put in their blat networks. Only blat networks of the powerful survived in the new conditions. The market deprived the bookseller of his power. The end of the shortage economy inflated the bookseller's shares in the blat cooperative. Now he has nothing to offer except his friendship. It is also much more costly to sustain previous blat networks. Blat was conditioned not only on the economy of shortages, but also on the low costs of communications, coffee, and the unrestricted availability of free time. Now it is not possible any more to spend long hours on the telephone talking about nothing and to leave the office any time your friend wants to see you.

The transition from blat to bribery was painful for postcommunist societies. Bribery cannot be covered under the rhetoric of friendship and this makes people feel morally uncomfortable. Bribery contributes to social stratification, making it easier for the rich to obtain what they want. "Corruption causes a distinction; in reality there should exist no difference," stated a participant in a focus group discussion in Sofia. Inequalities of wealth provide the means to pay bribes, while inequalities of power provide the means to extort them (Miller et al. 2001).

Why does public opinion in Eastern Europe perceive postcommunism as more corrupt than communism? This essay argues for a complex answer. The public judges corruption not by counting corrupt acts or corruption-related media stories. Judgment on corruption is mediated by the social functions of corruption in society. The dramatic change of corruption perception in Eastern Europe in the last decade cannot be explained simply by the actual rise of corruption or the boom of the media's interest in corruption. Anti-corruption sentiments in Eastern Europe were provoked by the fact that bribe has replaced blat as a paradigmatic form of corruption. Blat is viewed by the public as a socially more acceptable form of corruption. It was the non-monetary character of blat and its role in redistributing goods and power that made it look more legitimate in the eyes of public opinion. Bribery is less acceptable not only because it is more ugly (aesthetically), or because it is more risky (in legal terms). Bribery is less acceptable because it is a mechanism for producing social inequality. A World Bank report states that "inequality within the transition countries has increased at an alarming pace. In some countries of the region inequality has now reached levels on par with the most unequal Latin American countries" (World Bank 2000).

The popular anti-corruption discourse is not a discourse on transparency or good government, it is a discourse on the rise of inequality. This is the reason why anti-corruption discourse is the most popular discourse for criticizing market and democracy in a society in which market and democracy do not have an alternative.

THE RULE OF LAW PARADOX

In the early 1980s, three strange "criminals" shared a cell in Lefortovo prison in Moscow. They perfectly symbolized the three most dangerous enemies of the communist system. Lev Timofeev was a dissident and economist writing on corruption as an institutional problem in communist society. Vahab Usmanov was a top Soviet official, former minister of cotton in Uzbekistan, who in 1986 was executed for corruption and abuse of power. The third inhabitant of the cell was of less importance. He was a former university professor who was arrested for currency speculations and money extraction from his foreign students (Timofeev 2000). All three stayed in prison at the time when Soviet authorities inspired by Andropov tried to use anti-corruption campaigns and anti-corruption rhetoric as an instrument for replacing the ideological legitimization of the regime with a rational-legal legitimization. The ultimate goal was the creation of a socialist legal state (Holmes 1993). All three were skeptical about the chances of the undertaking. The ex-minister was struggling to understand why somebody should be put in prison for doing what all senior party officials usually do. It was true that Usmanov was taking bribes and he did not deny it, but was it possible not to take bribes when you should give bribes? The success or failures of Uzbek cotton production depended on the success of the bribe-mediated bargains in the Plan Committee and other federal institutions. For Usmanov, the anti-corruption campaign was a form of leadership war. Timofeev was also unable to grasp the logic of the undertaking. For him it was a mystery how the Soviet leadership was planning to fight corruption when the very existence of the Soviet system depended on the existence on the black markets of goods and power. The third prisoner did not have a specific argument for mistrusting the anti-corruption campaign but he did have a general argument: he mistrusted anything that the government did.

The prisoners were right in their skepticism. Andropov initiated an anti-corruption campaign and the officially tolerated anti-corruption rhetoric did not increase the trust in the government, but on the contrary, it contributed to the de-legitimization and the collapse of the communist system. In my view, there is also room for skepticism that anti-corruption campaigns are the shortest path to a rule of law culture in Eastern Europe.

An unavoidable trait of the anti-corruption campaign is the constantly expanding definition of corruption. If at the beginning of the campaign the suspicion is that corruption is almost everywhere, already in the middle of the campaign the suspicion is that corruption is almost everything. The final stage is the conviction that almost everybody is corrupt. The fear of corruption accusation paralyses the energy of government officials and the major objective of the policy makers to opt for solutions that look clean, notwithstanding whatever other disadvantages they have. Making "transparency" the ultimate policy incentive explains why the Bulgarian government in the last two years became in favor of the auction type of privatization. The criticism that such a type of privatization is not the best option for attracting strategic investors and preventing criminal money to enter the process have been ignored. For the government, it was more important to prove cleanness than to go for the better economic option.

The second disadvantage of the anti-corruption campaigns is that in focusing on corruption they contribute to the blurring of the lines between different political options. Corruption-centered politics in a way is the end of politics. It moralizes the policy choices to the extent that politics is reduced to the choice between corrupt government and clean opposition. Corruption-centered politics is one of the explanations for the transformation of Eastern European democracy into protest-vote democracies.

The third disadvantage of the anti-corruption campaigning that results in increasing de-legitimization of the political elite and public administration is that a number of young and talented people who in a different environment can choose politics or public administration as their vocation, under present conditions prefer to stay away from the realm of the corrupted. The claim that politicians are corrupt by definition is supported by the majority of respondents in public opinion polls in countries like Bulgaria, Romania, and Macedonia.

Bearing in mind that corruption is a crime very difficult to prove, the current focus on corruption leads to redistribution of powers in the direction of increasing the powers of investigating agencies. Loyal to the principles of the rule of law, courts face difficulty in producing sentences for corruption. There is a huge difference between the politicians accused in the media and the politicians sentenced in court. The pressure for spectacular verdicts in the war against corruption comes into conflict with the fact that corruption is one of the most difficult crimes to prove in court. In Bulgaria, practically all ministers who have been in office for the last ten years are investigated or have been investigated by the prosecution for corruption-related allegations, but there is no single minister in prison. The result is growing mistrust in the judicial system and growing accusations that the judicial system is totally corrupt.

Contrary to the expectations and intentions of the architects of the post-communist anti-corruption campaigns, the crusade against corruption can be as harmful to the emergence of rule of law culture in Eastern Europe as is corruption itself. The anti-corruption rhetoric creates expectations that cannot be met by the results of the anti-corruption policies, and the major reason for the vicious circle that emerges is the nature of the anti-corruption sentiments in the period of transition. Anti-corruption sentiments are driven not by the actual level of corruption but by the general disappointment with the changes and the rising social inequality. It is this weak correlation between the world of corruption and the world of anti-corruption sentiments that renders questionable the usefulness of the anti-corruption campaigns. What post-communist societies need are policies that reduce corruption, but not a rhetoric that leads to corruption-centered politics.

BIBLIOGRAPHY

Anticorruption in Transition: A Contribution to the Policy Debate. Washington DC: World Bank, 2000.

Avramov, Rumen. *Stopanskia XX vek na Bulgaria* [The 20th century Bulgarian economy]. Sofia: Centre for Liberal Strategies, 2001.

Coulloudon, Virginie. "The Criminalisation of Russia's Political Elite." *East European Constitutional Review* 6 (1997): 73–78.

De Sardan, Olivier J. P. "A Moral Economy of Corruption in Africa?" *Journal of Modern African Studies* 37 (1999): 25–52.

Dunn, Elizabeth. "Audit, Corruption, and the Problem of Personhood: Scenes From Postsocialist Poland" in *Negotiated Universals*, ed. Lepenies, Wolf (Berlin: Campus, 2003), pp. 127–45.

European Bank for Reconstruction and Development. *Transition Report 2000: Employment, Skills and Transition.* London: EBRD, 2000.

Grødeland, Åse B., Tatyana Y. Koshechkina, and William L. Miller. "Foolish to Give and Yet More Foolish Not to Take—In-depth Interviews with Post-Communist Citizens on Their Everyday Use of Bribes and Contacts." *Europe-Asia Studies* 50 (1998): 651–77.

Arnold J. Heidenheimer. "Perspectives on the Perception of Corruption" in *Political Corruption: A Handbook*, eds. Heidenheimer, Arnold J., Michael Johnston and Victor T. LeVine (New Brunswick, 1989), pp. 149–65.

Hellman, Joel S., Geraint Jones, and Daniel Kaufmann. "'Seize the State, Seize the Day': State Capture, Corruption, and Influence in Transition." Policy Research Working Paper 2444. Washington D.C.: World Bank, 2000.

Holmes, Leslie. *The End of Communist Power: Anti-Corruption Campaigns and Legitimation Crisis.* Cambridge: Policy Press, 1993.

Kaufmann, Daniel and Paul Siegelbaum. "Privatization and Corruption in Transition Economies." *Journal of International Affairs* 50 (1997): 419–59.

Ledeneva, Alena V. *Russia's Economy of Favors: Blat, Networking and Informal Exchanges.* Cambridge: Cambridge University Press, 1998.

Meny, Yves. "Fin de siecle Corruption: Change, Crisis and Shifting Values" in *Explaining Corruption*, ed. Williams, Robert (Cheltenham: Edward Elgar, 2000), pp. 309–21.

Miller, William L., Åse B. Grødeland, and Tatyana Y. Koshechkina. "How Citizens Cope with Postcommunist Officials: Evidence from Focus Group Discussions in Ukraine and the Czech Republic." *Political Studies* 45 (1997): 597–625.

——. "Are People Victims or Accomplices? The Use of Presents and Bribes to Influence Officials in Eastern Europe." *Crime, Law, and Social Change* 29 (1998): 273–310.

——. "Confessions: A Model of Officials. Perspectives on Accepting Gifts from Clients in Post-Communist Europe." Paper presented at the Coalition 2000 Conference in Varna, 19–20 June 1999(a).

——. "A Focus Group Study of Bribery and Other Ways of Coping with Officialdom in Postcommunist Eastern Europe." Paper presented at the Coalition 2000 Conference in Varna, 19–20 June 1999(b).

——. *A Culture of Corruption: Coping with Government in Post-Communist Europe.* Budapest: Central European University Press, 2001.

Mishler, William and Richard Rose. "Trust, Distrust, and Skepticism: Popular Evaluation of Civil and Political Institutions in Post-Communist Societies." *Journal of Politics* 59, no. 2 (1997): 418–51.

——. "Trust in Untrustworthy Institutions: Culture and Institutional Performance in Post-Communist Societies." Studies in Public Policy Number 310. University of Strathcylde, Glasgow: Centre for the Study of Public Policy, 1998.

Philp, Mark. "Defining Political Corruption" in *Explaining Corruption*, ed. Williams, Robert (Cheltenham: Edward Elgar, 2000), pp. 376–403.

Rose, Richard. "New Russia Barometer: Trends Since 1992." Studies in Public Policy 320. University of Strathclyde, Glasgow: Centre for the Study of Public Policy, 1999.

Rose, Richard and Christian Haerpfer. "New Democracies Barometer V: A 12-Nation Survey." Studies in Public Policy 306. University of Strathclyde, Glasgow: Centre for the Study of Public Policy, 1998a.

——. "Trends in Democracies and Markets: New Democracies Barometer 1991–1998." Studies in Public Policy 308. University of Strathclyde, Glasgow: Centre for the Study of Public Policy, 1998b.

Rose, Richard, William Mishler, and Christian Haerpfer. "Getting Real: Social Capital in Post-Communist Societies." Studies in Public Policy 278. University of Strathclyde, Glasgow: Centre for the Study of Public Policy, 1997.

Rose-Ackerman, Susan. "Reducing Bribery in the Public Sector" in *Corruption and Democracy*, ed. Trang, Duc V. (Budapest: Institute for Constitutional and Legislative Policy, 1994), pp.21–28.

——. *Corruption and Government: Causes, Consequences and Reform.* Cambridge: Cambridge University Press, 1999.

Sajó, András. "Corruption, Clientelism and the Future of the Constitutional State in Eastern Europe." *East European Constitutional Review* 7, no. 2 (1998): 37–46.

Shleifer, Andre and Robert Vishny. "Corruption." *Quarterly Journal of Economics* 108 (1993): 599–617.

Sztompka, Piotr. *Trust: A Sociological Theory.* Cambridge: Cambridge University Press, 1999.

Tanzi, Vito. "Corruption around the World: Causes, Consequences, Scope, and Cures." IMF Working Paper No. 63. Washington D.C.: International Monetary Fund, 1998.

Timofeev, Lev. *Institutcionalnata Korupcia* [Institutional corruption]. Moscow: Moscow State University Press, 2000.

Central Europe's Second Constitutional Transition: The EU Accession Phase

Neil Walker

Unlike the other chapters in this collection, the present chapter takes as its point of departure a supranational rather than a national constitutional episode or process. It examines the implications of the accession of various Countries of Central and Eastern Europe (CCEE) to the European Union at a time when the constitutional development of the EU itself is entering a critical phase. The relevance of the present chapter to the overall theme of the collection can be defended on at least three grounds. First, membership of the EU has now become an undeniable and increasingly salient fact of institutional life for many of the CCEE, one which has to be considered in order to understand the post-transitional phase in the round. Secondly, there is a close and complex relationship between the various national trajectories of constitutional transformation and the unprecedented supranational constitutional project of the EU. Each profoundly affects the other, even if, understandably enough, more attention has been paid until now to the ways in which national constitutional formations in the CCEE are affected by the European Union than vice versa. Thirdly, there are telling comparisons to be drawn between constitution-making in the various national contexts on the one hand, and in the supranational context on the other—comparisons that may serve to highlight certain significantly distinctive features of the two sets of processes. How the chapter orders and addresses these different focal concerns is explained below, following a scene-setting discussion of the broad political context of accession.[1]

THE UNEQUAL BARGAIN

Much of the voluminous literature on the current eastern enlargement of the European Union acknowledges, or at least presupposes, a significant asymmetry of power at the negotiating table. The reasons for this are not hard to seek. It is worth recalling, as the point is often lost in discussion of the particular motivations in play and interests at stake in securing or resisting enlargement, that the most basic reason for asymmetry is structural—to do with the very form of the agreement sought. Whether it be negotiation over new membership of a bowling club, a Trade Union, a political party or, as in the present case, a supranational polity, there is always a formal imbalance of power between those who are already in the club and those who want to join. The members set the conditions of membership, and when all is said and done, the aspiring members have to meet these conditions in order to qualify for membership. In this very basic sense, there is no difference between the present CCEE and the Mediterranean enlargement round and the three previous rounds that expanded EU membership beyond the original Six.

Yet the significance of this formal inequality depends upon particular circumstances. The existing members may be more or less keen on the candidates joining, while the candidates may be more or less interested in joining. The main contours of debate surrounding the current enlargement, however, suggest that the substantive terms of trade have reinforced rather than modified or reversed the formal inequality in favour of the existing members, and in a manner more pronounced than in any of the previous enlargements.[2] If we allow for a quick change of metaphor, this is well summed up by Heather Grabbe: "The EU... resembles a landlord reluctant to build an extension to his comfortable dwelling in order to house his poor relations. Might they be awkward, noisy and demanding? Might the new extension threaten the stability of the whole edifice? It is far easier to contemplate the renovation and refurbishment of the existing accommodation than embark on such bold new plans" (Grabbe 2001: 7).

For what reasons might the EU be jealous of its membership? Why might it have acted like a reluctant landlord in the pre-accession phase? While there has been a consistently high degree of acceptance in Western Europe, certainly amongst political elites, that the present enlargement project will pay a significant dividend in political and security terms—binding the postcommunist countries into a stable regional community of strong democracies and economies—, reluctance stems from a number of factors which impinge upon different national polities to differing degrees. These factors are well known. They include: the fiscal costs of enlargement in terms of increasing budget contributions and a decreasing share of subsidies, anxiety about wage competition, concern about increased immigration and decreased internal security, the effects of enlargement on the specific gravity of individual state voices and on a Union institutional structure already struggling to accommodate the size, diversity and complexity of the existing EU in a coherent and democratically accountable manner, not to mention a more general fear of change associated with an expansion program unprecedented both in scale and, perhaps, in the cultural diversity of its embrace (Vachudova 2000). For their part, the balance of costs and benefits of the accession states are quite different. Membership of the world's largest single market centred on the affluent economies of Western Europe has been an abiding incentive, while the security, freedom and democracy dividend of incorporation into the EU's stable supranational community appears all the more attractive against the backdrop of 70 years of political subjection and a decade of ethnic conflict in neighbourhood regions. Of course, there is another side to this coin. EU membership can be presented as a new form of subjection—a cheap and careless way of relinquishing a recently rewon sovereignty, while the economic benefits of membership may be viewed as only long-term and speculative, in contrast to the insistent reality of preparing national administrations and economies for membership with all the immediate burdens and hardships that entails. However, with certain exceptions at particular times and places, these counterarguments did not develop strong roots and support, for accession remained relatively solid throughout the pre-accession phase[3] and during the crucial period of the affirmative referenda on accession in the early months of 2003.

This brief synopsis of the terms of the debate helps us to answer one question, but raises another. Put crudely, the balance of power in favour of the existing members helps to explain why they felt confident in setting the criteria for membership in such exacting terms, and also why the accession countries accepted and responded to these terms. It explains why the EU felt able to set, and the accession countries were prepared to tackle the robust double hurdle of the 1993 Copenhagen political and economic requirements—with their broad emphasis upon stable institutions guaranteeing democracy, the rule of law, human rights and the protection of minority rights, a functioning and competitive market economy and an administrative capacity sufficient for the obligations of membership—and the adoption of the totality of the *acquis communautaire* numbering some 80,000 pages and divided, for negotiating purposes, into 29 chapters. But the asymmetry of incentives underpinning the imbalance of power also raises the question; why despite the grounds for its reluctance and lack of enthusiastic public backing or indeed of any concerted attempt to win such backing, and despite many fears and prognostications of wavering intentions, did the EU nevertheless maintain its commitment to enlargement after Copenhagen, manifest in its steadfast and ultimately successful projection of the end of 2002[4] as a point when negotiations with eight of the ten CCEE[5] and the two small Mediterranean countries[6] would be successfully concluded, and, ultimately, in its conclusion of an Accession Treaty with these ten states in April 2003[7] with these ten countries entering the EU in May 2004, to be joined in due course (probably 2007) by Bulgaria and Romania whose Acession Treaties were eventually signed in April 2005. As one commentator put it, the EU may have made "relentless but unenthusiastic headway towards absorbing onetime members of the vanished Soviet bloc" (Holmes 2000: 1) over the course of the last decade, but that merely begs the question, if so "unenthusiastic," why, then, so "relentless?"

The main thesis of the present chapter is that the answer to that question can (in some part at least) be found in examining the constitutional debate gathering momentum within the EU in recent years.[8] It claims, first, that if we look at the development of the EU in constitutional terms, this serves to augment and adjust our perspective on the dynamics of enlargement, and does so in a way which modifies our sense of the underlying asymmetry of power. It claims, secondly, that this is an ongoing process, that the current constitutional transition in the EU offers a context within which it is possible, though far from guaranteed, that the underlying asymmetry of power between two distinct regional constituencies of West and East—between old and new—will become less pertinent to the project of European polity-building. It claims, thirdly, that, on the contrary, the process of enlargement as it is interpellated within the discourse and practice of constitutional transition may offer a number of important cues for a more cohesive practice of polity-building. In making these points, the recent state constitutional transitions of the CCEE are given some attention, and for two reasons. First, it allows us better to appreciate the concerns which these states bring to the European constitutional table. In the second place, as mentioned at the outset there are in any case interesting analogies—and disanalogies—between the two classes of constitutional process, between constitutional transition in the statal context of Eastern Europe and the novel constitution-building process of the EU. A frame of analysis which embraces both types of process thus provides a good opportunity to tease out in what ways the EU constitutional transition—our main focus—is distinctive from the constitutional transitions of the CCEE themselves as examined elsewhere in the volume, and indeed from constitutional transition in the statal context more generally.[9]

THE SIGNIFICANCE OF THE CONSTITUTIONAL DIMENSION

In what ways, then, does the process of constitutionalization, and the accompanying deepening of constitutional*ism*—considered as a self-conscious discourse about the values involved in constitutionalization (see Walker 2002: especially 336ff)—in the EU unlock a new door to understanding the dynamics of enlargement? To answer this question we must first say something about the general functions that constitutionalization and constitutionalism perform in any polity—whether state-based or supranational.[10] Constitutionalization and constitutionalism can be seen to contribute to the three different but related dimensions of legitimacy within a political community. First, they may contribute to performance legitimacy—or what some writers call "output legitimacy" (Scharpf 1999: ch. 1). This concerns the capacity of the polity to produce effective and efficient performance in accordance with whatever criteria—economic success, fair distribution of resources and benefits, security from internal and external risk—are deemed relevant within that polity; that is with its capacity to "deliver the goods." Secondly, constitutionalization and constitutionalism may contribute to regime legitimacy. This concerns the extent to which there is a just arrangement of institutions in accordance with criteria of fair representation, appropriate protection of individual and minority interests, encouragement of an open and engaged political culture etc. Clearly, regime legitimacy and performance legitimacy are closely linked, in the sense that the very institutional matrix whose justness in design and operation is the measure of regime legitimacy is also an important variable in the nurturing of a policy-making environment conducive to the development of "good" policies and in the effective implementation of those policies which are developed. Thirdly, constitutionalization and constitutionalism may contribute to polity legitimacy. By polity legitimacy is meant the overall support for and stability of the polity in question as a self-standing "political community." So, to disaggregate this last notion into its two constituent terms, it embraces both a "political" and related legal dimension—a degree of autonomous political authority—and a "community" dimension—a sense of common attachment to and identification with the polity.

To some extent, polity legitimacy is a function of performance and regime legitimacy, in that a political community which is perceived to perform well in terms of policy formulation and delivery and which is perceived to have just institutions is more likely to win and sustain support as an autonomous polity. Yet clearly there is more to polity legitimacy than this, for performance and regime legitimacy are neither necessary nor sufficient conditions for polity legitimacy—at least in the sense of the minimum necessary for the achievement or survival of autonomous polity status. On the one hand, a polity which lacks current performance legitimacy and even regime legitimacy may on account of deep-rooted national and pluri-national identities nevertheless continue to attract significant loyalty as an autonomous polity. On the other hand, it is possible for a political system to be considered effective and just, yet, as with many sub-state political systems, to lack sufficient authority or, as with transnational systems such as the WTO or NAFTA, to provide an insufficient reference point in the political identity of those who comprise its putative "citizenry" to be conceived of as an autonomous polity.

How does constitutionalism contribute to these three dimensions of legitimacy? Just as there is a complex relationship between the three different dimensions of legitimacy, so there is a complex relationship between the three major functions of constitutionalism[11] and the satisfaction of these legitimacy dimensions. A first major function of constitutionalism may be termed community-mobilizing. Here we are concerned with "constitution as process" (Sadurski 2001: 466–72), with the way in which the making or reforming of the constitutional order defines, involves and commits those who are the subjects of the constitution also as its authors and, through their authorship, as members of the political community thus established. A second major function of constitutionalism is that of institutional design. This concerns the role of the constitution in the establishment of the institutional matrix and "power map" (Duchacek 1973) of government. A third major function of constitutionalism is that of polity-affirmation. This concerns the way in which the constitution contributes to the identity of the polity *qua polity* or "political community," both through its establishment of the boundaries or "authoritative space" of the polity and through its recognition or nurturing of the distinguishing and identifying political ideals or aspirations of the community who are members of that polity.

The community-mobilizing function clearly has a specific role to play in fostering the identity element in polity legitimacy, and also, through promoting the internal legitimacy of the constitutional framework generally, in enhancing the legitimating potential of the other major constitutional functions performed by that framework—namely institutional design and polity affirmation. Furthermore, as the experience in the candidate states attests, the mobilization of the community in a significant phase of constitutional reform, or even revolution, also has an important role to play in announcing and legitimating a new regime. The institutional design function clearly provides the blueprint on which regime legitimacy is founded, but also both serves as a facilitative framework for performance legitimacy and, through its provision of a derivative (that is, constitutionally-determined rather than constitution-determining) framework for political participation and representation, may complement the community-mobilizing and identity-forming work of the constitution-making process in the sphere of polity legitimacy. For its part, the polity-affirming function is more singularly concerned with polity legitimacy. To begin with, the very act of engagement in a self-defined constitutional discourse, because of the deep roots in the modern state tradition of the link between the possession of constitutional credentials and polity status, has important symbolic value in defining the authoritative space of the polity *as a* polity. Secondly, by defining "who we *are*" (Sadurski 2001: 461) through a set of ideals or a collective mission, and also, by defining the boundaries of its authoritative space (which people? what relationship to the international "outside" and the noncitizen "other"?), the constitution may contribute more actively to the definition of the identity of its citizens and the authority of its assertion of polity status.

EUROPEAN CONSTITUTIONALISM IN PERSPECTIVE

Different constitutional contexts offer different opportunities and impose different constraints on the potential of constitutional discourse and practice to achieve its various legitimizing functions and also indicate different legitimizing priorities for constitutional discourse and practice. *All* constitutions are more directly concerned with regime legitimacy and polity legitimacy than with performance legitimacy, whose relationship to constitutional function is complex, attenuated and intractably disputed. Yet, a brief comparison of the process of constitutional transition in the Accesion States on the one hand and the EU on the other demonstrates that in the different mix of opportunity, constraint and priority we can see quite different constitutional trajectories at work around the two major themes of regime and polity legitimacy.

In both cases—the Accesion States and the EU—, constitutional transition over the last decade or so has reflected and contributed to a period of significant social and political transformation, and has prompted a heightened emphasis on the active role of constitutionalism in both polity legitimacy and regime legitimacy as compared to "normal" periods of constitutional politics in established states with stable regimes. Beyond this very general baseline of similarity, however, there are important differences. Simply stated, the balance and relationship between regime legitimacy and polity legitimacy is rather different in the two cases, with somewhat greater emphasis on regime legitimacy over polity legitimacy in the Accesion States.

At first glance, this may seem a surprising conclusion, given the number of new states emerging in postcommunist Eastern Europe in general and in the Accesion States states in particular. So of the ten CCEE involved in the present wave of accession, six are new or "renewed" states—the three Baltic States, Slovenia, the Czech Republic and Slovakia, and so clearly the question of polity legitimacy was posed in these contexts. As Robert Elgie and Jan Zielonka comment, in these "new states, a new constitution was seen as a major and indispensable step in their process of state building" (Elgie and Zielonka 2001: 33). Yet, this still leaves four states (Poland, Hungary, Romania and Bulgaria)—four of the five largest in the region, moreover[12]—where the polity was basically continuous with existing boundaries and where, accordingly, no explicit state-building exercise was required. Additionally, even in the case of the new states, the identities and boundaries of the polity were already strongly suggested in cultural markers. That is to say, the "we feeling" and demarcation of authoritative space which are indispensable to legitimacy *qua* polity were facilitated by the legacy of pre-existing or strongly aspirational political identity, and so the symbolic work asked of the constitutional arrangements in the very process of state formation was minimal. The constitutional stamp may indeed have been "indispensable," but it was little more than that—an imprimatur of statehood rather than its agent.

If we turn, however, to regime legitimacy, constitutionalism had a much more urgent role to play in the CCEE. In all of these countries, the adoption of a new constitution or the substantial reworking of an existing[13] or even a precommunist model,[14] "was seen as a crucial symbolic break with the Communist legacy" (Elgie and Zielonka 2001: 33). While the process of community mobilization may often have left much to be desired in terms of its inclusiveness, the distinctiveness of its personnel and of its institutions of promulgation from those dominant in the *ancien régime,* and the independence and deliberative scope of its ratifying referenda (Elgie and Zielonka 2001: 37–42), it was nevertheless invariably seen as of great significance in expressing the aspiration towards a free and democratic order.[15] And even if the constitutional process was to some extent compromised by the very past from which it sought to distinguish itself, the product in terms of institutional design was surer in its announcement of a new regime. Guarantees of democracy and of judicial independence, detailed separation of powers, wide-ranging charters of fundamental rights; each contributed to an institutional matrix which promised social democracy rather than state socialism. Of course, there remains a variable implementation gap across the CCEE, in that while new political roles and relations have been created and respected, the degree of internalization of the new substantive constitutional discourse within the practice of politics, especially that concerning rights, remains limited (Sadurski 2001: 472–74). But this is only to indicate a local manifestation of an operational limitation of constitutional design applicable to all models and in all contexts. Indeed, to the extent that the implementation gap remains large in the CCEE, this points not to the marginality of constitutional influence but to the sheer scale of the task of institutional and discursive transformation and, it is submitted, to the abiding centrality of the new constitutionalism to its realization.

If we turn to the EU in *its* current transitional phase, here both regime and polity legitimacy are increasingly put in question, and the answer to these questions is increasingly sought in the constitutional domain. Performance legitimacy—whether the EU has the right priorities and policies and how well it pursues them—has always occupied an important place in the development of the European Union. As one analysis puts it, "[t]he possibility of utilitarian justification has always been central to the analysis and practice of European integration" (Beetham and Lord 1998: 94). The reasons for this are not obscure. Clearly, a major founding rationale for the European project was to achieve various economic purposes that required the member states to make common regulatory cause in the areas relevant to these purposes. Just as in the etiology of any international organization, regime factors were, at the outset, of secondary and derivative consideration, as the means to the achievement of these purposes, while any additional questions of "polity" legitimacy were barely, if at all, registered, as this would require the unlikely assumption that the European Union's Treaty predecessors had initially sought to construct, or succeeded in constructing, anything as grand as a "polity" (Chryssochoou 2001: ch. 4).

Yet, while performance legitimacy remains of profound significance, regime and polity considerations have, over the succeeding half century, become of increasingly central concern. As the performative scope and ambition of the EU has increased, clearly the legitimacy of the institutional regime which sustains it has becomes a salient consideration in its own terms, and not just as an instrument for performance delivery. The more the European Union's regulatory sphere has expanded to cover decisions bearing upon the allocation of key resources and the balance between fundamental political values, and the more it has come to challenge the dominance of the member states in these matters, the greater has become the concern that its institutional regime is fully and fairly representative of the range of constituencies affected by its actions.

Equally, the expansion of the performative and regulatory sphere has brought the question of the EU's status and legitimacy as a polity into sharp relief. It is well known and generally accepted that through its development of doctrines such as supremacy, direct effect and residual powers, the EU, in seeking to develop and sustain its performance and regime legitimacy, has increasingly assumed at least some of the authoritative attributes we associate with a state polity, but in so doing has neglected both the regime and the community or identitive aspects. That is to say, in formal legal terms it has increasingly taken on the shape of a federal polity, but without the democratic structures and social legitimacy or the sense of attachment that we associate with such a polity in its traditional statist mode (Weiler 1999: chs. 1–2).

Moreover, its difficulties in developing a self-standing institutional regime and a coherent and legitimate conception of its nascent polity status are not just a consequence of neglect—of the fact that its broader legitimation project is always playing "catch-up" with its performance-driven functional expansion. These are also a product of the genuine difficulties of translating the received wisdom of *state* polity building to the supranational context. In the so-called Westphalian world, states have provided the limiting case of regime choice and the paradigm form of polity, or political community.[16] Regimes of representative government and rights protection have traditionally been crafted with the model of statehood in mind. In contrast, as a regime which, unlike the institutionally self-contained Westphalian state, is implicated in a multi-level system of governance in which its institutional forms are required to articulate with the extant institutions of the state, the EU faces unprecedented problems of institutional design.[17] Further, at the level of political authority, as we have already noted, both the general idea of the state and particular state traditions and boundaries are deeply entrenched and have resilience which can withstand high levels of performance and regime illegitimacy. And at the level of political community, deep rooted national and even pluri-national identities (see Keating 2001) supply cultural substrata

that, again, may survive the iniquities, failures or abuses of particular performative aims or achievements, and regime forms. The EU, by contrast,
lacks both a settled template of political authority and the relatively "thick"
cultural identity of the national or pluri-national state (even if we also accept
that the idea that such a thick identity does, or should, rest on common ethnicity is widely and correctly discredited). The European Union is a new and
sui generis political formation, and, just because it is so, it cannot avoid or
answer questions about the type of polity it is, including, crucially, whether
it should be considered a separate polity at all, rather than a sophisticated,
but ultimately derivative, institutional outgrowth of state interests, by relying upon some general model, of which it is but one particular instance. It
lacks, in other words, a generalizable template and background presumption
of settled political form. At the level of identity, too, it is well-known and
much discussed that the European Union lacks the strong cultural ties of
common language, traditions, history, affective symbols, and developed civil
society and public sphere, which, in various mixes, are central to many national or pluri-national state identities (Beetham and Lord 1998: ch. 2).

We can now begin to think of these problems in constitutional terms. The
combination of an "institutional deficit"—which is in part the well-known
"democratic deficit" of the flawed representativeness of European institutions but also the deficit of effective decisional capacity which the complex
and unwieldy institutional structure is deemed to display[18]—and also of a
"polity deficit"—the lack of a coherently defined and generally agreed authoritative profile and the absence or fragility of a self-conscious "demos" or community of attachment within the citizenry of the putative polity—can also be
viewed as a "constitutional deficit." In Joseph Weiler's terms, the EU lives
with the legacy of "doing" before "hearkening," with a tradition of pragmatic
constitutional practice outrunning reflection on the broader implications and
direction of that practice: "It is a constitutional legal order the constitutional theory of which has not been worked out, its long-term, transcendent values not sufficiently elaborated, its ontological elements misunderstood, its
social rootedness and legitimacy highly contingent" (Weiler 1999: 8).

In turn, this begins to explain the recent development of an active constitutional debate within the European Union. Constitutional discourse, once
the preserve of the Court of Justice and academic inquiry, has gradually
infiltrated the broader political culture of the Union. The contemporary history of its constitutional debate is a busy and complex one, one which for
long had to struggle against vigorous opposition to the very idea of such a
debate by those Eurosceptic forces who feared, given the strength of the symbolic link between constitutionalism and polity-status, that the acceptance
that the EU needed such a debate was already to concede too much to more integrationist interests.[19] But at the institutional level, the constitutional

debate has now resolved itself into an extended post-Nice process; in the declaration attached to the Treaty of Nice of December 2000 of the wide-ranging reform agenda to be tackled in its wake (in anticipation of the conclusion of the next Intergovernmental Conference in 2004), in the subsequent Laeken Declaration on the Future of the European Union of December 2001,[20] in its launching of the Convention on the Future of Europe in the Spring of 2002 and, crucially, in the draft Constitutional Treaty produced by that body in the summer of 2003[21] for the examination of the Intergovernmental Council (IGC). For all that the Intergovernmental Council (for reasons to be discussed in the next section) subsequently refused to give final endorsement to the Draft Constitutional Treaty at Brussels in December 2003, and even when the IGC did reach final agreement in October 2004, the new document still had to negotiate the considerable hurdle of ratification by all 25 member states of the newly enlarged EU, this constitutional process already undoubtedly represents a landmark—a first explicit attempt by the European institutions to discuss the future of the European Union in constitutional terms, and one which seeks to harness each of the three main constitutional functions—institutional design, polity affirmation and community mobilization to the task of regime and polity legitimization.

This brings us, finally, to the crux of the matter. How has enlargement figured in this emerging constitutional discourse? And how, in particular, does this constitutional discourse help to explain and endorse the EU's commitment to the present enlargement, and to suggest that the notion of that enlargement as an unequal bargain between two quite distinct constituencies is becoming, or at least may become, less central as the transitional process unfolds? Let us tackle this question by looking at each of the three constitutional functions and themes of constitutional discourse—institutional design, polity affirmation and community mobilization—in turn. As we shall see, in each of these three areas, the enlargement process can undoubtedly be viewed as part of Europe's constitutional problem, but it may also tentatively be viewed as part of Europe's constitutional solution.

CONSTITUTIONALISM AND ENLARGEMENT

Institutional design
Heather Grabbe hinted at some important features of the enlargement process when she wrote in 2001 that "ever since 1989, eastward enlargement has seemed about five years way—and it still does" (Grabbe 2001: 1). In the light of the signing of the Accession Treaty in April 2003 this perception has at last been overtaken by events, but for a long time it held sway. In part, it spoke to a cynical view on the part of many in the East and some of enlarge-

ment's supporters in the West that enlargement was condemned to be kept tantalizingly just out of reach by the stalling tactics of the member states, forever disappearing over the horizon just as it was glimpsed. But it also spoke in a more subtle register to the role that the imminence of enlargement played in galvanizing and structuring the debate on the future of the Union, including the debate about institutional reform. Indeed, in the reform discourse of the 1990s, "the demands of the coming enlargement" served almost as a mantra to prompt and focus debate on reform of the institutional structure of the existing Union, rather than as a massive change in the shape of the Union which demanded attention for its own sake.

Of course there was a strategic, even cynical, side to this, too. Those who were, in general terms, on the intergovernmental side of the debate on EU institutional reform, in particular the British Conservative government in the 1980s and early 90s, saw enlargement as an opportunity to press their case for a looser, more state-centred institutional structure for the EU. An eastwardly enlarged EU of 25 or more member states, on this view, would create a structure of such size and heterogeneity that it could only function legitimately through a model which stressed the autonomy of its member states, including their power to veto or opt-out of decisions which would impose an unwelcome majoritarian view. "Wider" would necessarily imply "shallower." On the other hand, those who favoured a stronger centre for the EU, drew precisely the opposite conclusion from the same premise. Unless a Union of 25 or more was to succumb to gridlock, it would have to be reformed in a way that strengthened and streamlined the decision-making power of the Community institutions. On this view, "wider" necessarily implied "deeper" (see, for example, Walker 1998: 370; Wallace 1989; De Witte 2003).

Yet the role of enlargement rhetoric in this process was not merely one of serving opposing strategic gambits. After all, the debate on institutional reform *was* unavoidable regardless of enlargement, and enlargement merely served to increase its urgency. As the secular movement within the European institutional architecture towards majority decision-making indicates,[23] the structures put in place for the original Union of the Six were ill-adapted to a Union even of Twelve (as of 1986) and, certainly, of Fifteen (see, for example, Pentland 2000)—which figure the EU reached after Austria, Finland and Sweden joined in 1995. Yet because territorial expansion was paralleled by functional expansion in areas traditionally within the prerogative of national authority—such as Justice and Home Affairs, Foreign and Defence Policy, Economic and Monetary Union and a variety of "market correcting" (Scharpf 1999: 190–93) dimensions of social and economic policy where negative integration in accordance with the Four Freedoms threatened otherwise to leave a regulatory gap—concerns with the erosion of domestic sovereignty ensured that there could be no unopposed route towards the concentration of more power at the European centre. Especially after the Maastricht watershed when the expansionism of the Delors years and the renewed ambition of the Treaty on European Union provoked popular resistance in Danish and French referenda, as well as opposition on a smaller but still significant scale in states such as Germany and the United Kingdom, the macro-politics of European integration demonstrated a new and more visible polarization. Within this more charged atmosphere, genuine concerns for the democracy and the effectiveness of decision-making procedures were expressed both by those who feared intergovernmental gridlock and by those who cautioned against explicit concession or incremental drift towards the European centre. In these altered circumstances, then, the prospect of enlargement may be seen to have served not, or not just, as a strategic cloak under which states and EU institutions could prosecute their own particular self-interested views on the EU's institutional end-game. Rather, enlargement also provided a pressing "polity-centred" occasion for pursuing the institutional debate on the part of parties who risked becoming so divided on the substance of institutional reform, and on the proper register (constitutional or otherwise) in which this should be discussed, that they might otherwise have been unable to agree terms on which to have the debate at all.

It is no coincidence, therefore, that successive IGCs following Maastricht which culminated in the Treaty of Amsterdam in 1997 and the Treaty of Nice in 2000 were explicitly justified in terms of the pressing need for institutional reform in anticipation of enlargement. And while it is possible to interpret the reluctance with which this debate was mounted and its faltering progress as evidence of a lack of enthusiasm for enlargement, it is also possible, and perhaps more persuasive, to view the blockage on institutional reform as a reflection of deeper divisions and disengagements—with the projected institutional gridlock of enlargement both serving as a convenient scapegoat for these deep divisions while also, paradoxically, offering a common reason for staying at the negotiating table. So, while Amsterdam merely served to postpone the institutional debate, the Treaty of Nice could not avoid its insistent and increasingly urgent call and, for all its shortcomings, did succeed in reaching tentative agreement on limitation of the size of the Commission, on a modest further shift away from unanimity and towards qualified majority voting in the Council of Ministers, and towards a redistribution of voting power in the Council to correct the structural imbalance in favour of smaller countries.[24]

Of course, the mythical quality of this debate—that it was just or primarily about enlargement and would require to be *finally*[25] resolved in anticipation of enlargement—was very quickly exposed. Though the "no" vote in the first Irish referendum on Nice[26] was reversed in October 2002 so allowing the Treaty to be implemented, institutional reform did not then disappear from the agenda. The different commitments to and interpretations of democracy and the different analyses and projections of decision-making efficiency and effectiveness that underpin it are simply too deep rooted and complex to admit to any final solution. So the debate has continued in various forums, notably the Commission's much vaunted White Paper on Governance[27] and, subsequently, in the post-Laeken Convention on the Future of Europe itself. Laeken's Declaration on the Future of Europe had "more democracy, transparency and efficiency in the European Union" as one of its headline themes, and, therefore, the perennial questions of the relative power and inter-relationship of the Commission, the Council, the European Council, the European Parliament and national Parliaments were placed on the table yet again. What is more, it is the seeming intractability of the institutional design question that emerged as the major—or at least the most obvious—culprit for the initial failure of the IGC to endorse the draft Constitutional Treaty in December 2003, the question of the reform of the weights and thresholds of qualified majority voting in the Council[28] being the sticking point of disagreement amongst the national delegations. Despite this temporary impasse, and notwithstanding the fact that it was one of the enlargement states themselves, Poland, which, along with Spain, felt its interests to be sufficiently directly prejudiced by the Constitutional Treaty's proposed reform to block agreement,[29] it remains the case that the enlargement question did serve to concentrate on this vital issue of constitutional reform during a vital phase of "pre-constitutional" skirmishing when agreement on the very terms of the debate might otherwise have been unavailable. To that extent, enlargement did not merely serve as a pretext for a multitude of instrumental strategies and a cacophony of competing claims, but also provided a timely anchorage and indispensable frame for a collective debate.

Polity affirmation
According to Joseph Weiler, the EU has undergone a crisis of ideals in recent years (Weiler 1999: ch. 7). The founding values of peace and prosperity no longer have the resonance they did in the years of post-war austerity. "The culture of contentment" (Galbraith 1992) of the affluent majority in most EU states and the fading memory of the war in Western Europe has meant that just as Europe has reached a key stage in the polity-building phase, where its weight and scope of activity and its imposition of a level of legal discipline necessary to sustain that activity demand a stronger legitimating sense of identity and a more cohesive community of attachment, the very ideational roots which might supply this are in danger of withering.

Here, too, enlargement has played a role and continues to play a role in the task of polity-affirmation, including its constitutional dimension. The preamble to the original EEC Treaty in 1958 in which the founding states resolved themselves "to lay the foundations of an ever closer union among the peoples of Europe," proceeded to call "upon the other peoples of Europe who share their ideals to join in their efforts"—an exhortation backed up by the grant in the text of the Treaty (original Article 237 EEC Treaty) of a right on the part of "any European state" to apply for membership. These and similar promises have remained prominent in the Treaty structure as it has evolved in the succeeding half-century.[30] Frank Schimmelfennig has made a powerful argument to the effect that this original and resilient aspiration has provided a context of "rhetorical action" in which the enlargement debate has been conducted and through which it has been shaped (Schimmelfennig 2001).[31] His basic point is that the pan-European promise of the founding texts have provided a framework for the strategic use of norm-based arguments in the context of Eastern enlargement, so providing an additional explanation for enlargement which supplies the deficiencies of a purely interest-based "rationalist intergovernmentalism" (Schimmelfennig 2001)[32] on which the idea of the unequal bargain explicitly or implicitly draws. He emphasizes in particular the importance of "shaming" in this context, of the accession states holding Western Europe to its rhetorical promises on pain of its being exposed as insincere in its commitment to enlargement.

While this strategic point is well taken, Schimmelfennig's argument can also be cast in a somewhat more affirmative light. The strategic use of public normative commitments implies that even if the main motivation for such public declarations at one time or another or from one particular perspective or another is only or mainly strategic, these commitments will be taken sufficiently seriously by the significant audiences of such declarations—that is, by those who are in a position to judge and monitor and influence their authors—so as reflexively and recursively to influence the behaviour of the authors. In other words, it suggests that, even if this is only triggered in the context of strategic exchanges and secured by the commitments thereby made, norms *matter* in the context of collective action, structuring the mutual expectations and limiting the range of reasonable action on the part of those engaged in the normative discourse. In turn, this can be linked to the polity-affirming potential of constitutional discourse. Constitutional discourse and legal discourse more generally (see, for example, Kahn 1997) provides a particularly well-documented and solemn framework for rhetorical action. The symbolic association of constitutional discourse with polity-building means that its identification of defining values and objectives will provide a powerful context for the framing of rhetorical debate. Furthermore, in a self-reinforcing dynamic, the framing of the debate in these terms not only presupposes some kind of commitment to the norms in question but encourages action which has to be seen to take these norms seriously, so further consolidating that commitment and the sense of common identity which it fosters.

Of course, we cannot see this process as a closed hermeneutic (and unerringly virtuous) circle. The commitments in question can be derailed by other interests which are in tension with the collective values, and as Schimmelfennig notes, there have been many moments in the history of the current enlargement when this has threatened to happen (Schimmelfennig 2001: 66–76). Furthermore, the development and ongoing adjustment of a rhetorical discourse from a particular normative baseline has to be plausible to the parties to that discourse. In this respect, the fact that there was an open-ended commitment to a unified Europe in the original Treaty framework, and that the ideals of peace and prosperity, and indeed other plausible ideals which might ground the sense of Europe as a common political community such as human rights,[33] *are* so clearly pertinent to a region which has lacked the levels of affluence and of secure freedom of the West, has provided an amenable context for the development of the rhetorical commitment in the direction of enlargement.

In summary, the very constitutional ideals that have facilitated the enlargement process are also those which are crucial to the present polity-building phase of the EU in nurturing the sense of a common identity and of a community of attachment on which the legitimacy of the polity rests. Again, the debate continues. It is instructive that in the more explicit constitutional context of the Laeken Declaration, there were references to the pending "unification of Europe," to the overcoming of "artificial divisions," to the creation of "one big family, without bloodshed," and, indeed, to the prospect of including the "values which the Union cherishes" in any future formal constitutional text. It is instructive, too, that the debate over values did indeed find a significant place in the subsequent work and product of the Convention.[34] Again, then, the overblown rhetoric is not just that, but may be viewed as the continuation of a tradition of rhetorical action which is significant in structuring and animating the commitments vital to the development of a sense of common political community, a process in which enlargement has played an increasingly important role and which, to that extent, may become increasingly amenable to the influence of the enlargement states.

Community mobilization

Finally, let us turn to the influence of community mobilization. From the beginning of the accession negotiations, a significant point of tension was the absence of a voice for the enlargement countries in formulating and agreeing key new decisions that would nevertheless have a compulsory impact upon them as a condition of membership. As the example of recent IGCs (De Witte 2002b) and the process leading to the adoption of the Charter of Fundamental Rights in 2000 (Sadurski 2002) indicates, the enlargement countries may have occasionally managed to get one foot in the door, but they never achieved anything approaching full participating rights in the debating chamber. Rather, they were restricted to modest levels and narrow windows of consultation, and even these at the whim of the existing member states rather than as a matter of right. In this area, accordingly, there is not such a clear record as in the cases of institutional reform and polity affirmation of the European constitutional transition process being structured and facilitated in advance by the prospect of enlargement. Yet there is still an important trend at work in which the expectation of enlargement has played its part and which, more palpably than in the other two areas, promises increasing influence on the part of the enlargement states in the future.[35]

In the context of constitutional process, Europe has increasingly been affected by the problem of "self-reference" (Eleftheriados 2001: 22–24; see also Walker 2001). That is to say, the Intergovernmental Conference—the state-dominated Treaty reform process—has, since Maastricht, come more and more to be viewed as an inadequately narrow tool to pass fundamental reform, one which does little to mobilize the broader community whose common attachment to the EU polity is so important to its legitimacy, and, indeed, does little to help legitimize the mass of regulatory activity which takes place under the authority of the Treaties as periodically reformed. The IGC has continued to be used, nevertheless, because it is the *default* mechanism, the one provided for in the existing Treaty structure. Furthermore, it is a central feature of the paradox of "constitutional denial" (see Walker 1996) in the European Union that many who, in the cause of adherence to a traditional state-centred model of indirect democracy and of vicarious legitimacy, are most jealous of the retention of the IGC process, are also those who are most critical of the very sense of regulatory overreach of the EU that such an attenuated procedure of "constitutional" reform does much to sustain and even to exacerbate. On the one hand, then, much criticism of the constitutional development of the EU is precisely because of the thin procedural legitimacy of the IGC and its tendency to serve state interests in an environment of strategic bargaining. On the other hand, a new procedure requires both that these very state interests criticized as unduly dominant, and, paradoxically, also the source of much of the criticism of the legitimacy deficit of the EU that has supplied the impulse for the search for a new constitutional method in the first place, are prepared to divest themselves of power, and that there is sufficient agreement to legitimate an alternative mechanism.

The recent Charter of Fundamental Rights, which was approved alongside the new Treaty at Nice in December 2000, provided an unlikely catalyst for overcoming this bind. The deliberative procedure leading to the promulgation of the Charter was significantly more open-ended than the IGC, both in the formal sense of including national and European parliamentarians and the Commission as well as national government representatives, and in the informal sense of being much more open to sharing information and consulting with other groups from civil society (De Burca 2001). Perhaps the success of the Charter is due to two factors in particular. First, it was not envisaged as a solemn process of constitutional reform—and, indeed, this was reflected in the merely declaratory status of its end product. It was, accordingly, allowed a more experimental format precisely because it was not seen as a threat to the hegemony of the IGC. However, that it was successful in developing a substantially wide-ranging (if formally weak) Charter of Rights in a relatively short period of time and in garnering a high level of public and institutional support in so doing lent a retrospective legitimacy to its role. Secondly, contrary to some fears, the multi-party forum actually facilitated decision-making rather than producing gridlock. It broke the frame of pure intergovernmental bargaining, allowing a more fluid forming of alliances and a more nuanced representation of interests.

Thus the Charter proved to be highly influential as a procedural model for the new post-Laeken Convention, which of course had a far broader agenda of reform—including the incorporation of the Charter itself as a legally binding component of a more explicitly constitutional text.[36] Yet it would be naïve to set too much store by the prefigurative influence of the Charter. As noted, the paradox of self-reference was already vividly realized, the doubtful legitimacy of the IGC process in sustaining the ever more powerful claims to authority of the EU already a significant "pull" factor to which the Charter merely added a helpful "push." And clearly the prospect of enlargement; with the reception of over 100 million new citizens and their countless new interests; with the additional "gridlocking" potential of at least 10 more governmental parties—each of the 8 CCEE with a relatively traditionalist attitude to their newly regained sovereignty written into their renewed national constitutional order (see Albi 2003), and each also jealous that the central features of their much transformed domestic regime legitimacy should not be adulterated or diminished by external agents[37] within a consensus-based rather than majoritarian-based IGC process; and with the increasing insistence of the enlargement countries on their involvement in any further fundamental reform prior to their formal accession, was one factor in dramatizing the inadequacy of narrow intergovernmentalism—and so in *further* strengthening the "pull" towards reform. Moreover, if we recall how closely enlargement has been implicated in the recent constitutional politics of the EU, both as rhetorical anchor of the institutional reform debate and, more directly, as galvanizing ideal in the process of polity-building, it would have betrayed the Fifteen's own self-understanding and public portrayal of the animating forces behind the present grand constitutional debate if a constitutional process which sought to break the IGC mould so comprehensively had found no place for and allowed no voice to the candidate states.

The candidate states were duly "fully involved" in the deliberations of the post-Laeken Convention, even if not yet as full decision-taking partners and with their participation in the Praesidium—the pivot of the Convention machinery—only reluctantly granted.[38] Once again, then, we see a vital transformative phase in constitutional politics linked to the enlargement process. Unlike the other developments considered, however, in the case of the Convention and its exercise of community mobilization, we see in the interaction of constitutionalism and enlargement a direct promise of more influence—however ambiguous in form and uncertain in impact—to the enlargement countries themselves.

Yet it would be an inadequate conceptualization of the present interplay of enlargement and constitutionalism to see the Convention merely as an opportunity for the structural imbalance of power against the enlargement states to be somewhat redressed. As with the other developments discussed, the dynamic is more complex, the relationship one of mutual effect, the proper characterization of the relationship between constitutionalism and enlargement as (potentially) symbiotic rather than uni-causal. For as with the previous developments, if we look closely enough we can again see enlargement influencing EU constitutionalism just as much as EU constitutionalism has influenced enlargement. In this vein, we can discern the familiar outline of enlargement as a double-edged sword, as both a threat and challenge to the constitutional integrity of the EU and as an opportunity to help secure or deepen that integrity.

First, then, let us consider the threat. For in the post-Maastricht atmosphere of heightened concern over the fragile legitimacy of the European project and of deepening and more transparent division over the sources and mechanisms through which such legitimacy might be repaired or renewed, the method through which the aspiration to eastward enlargement hardened into a political commitment, however loyally continuous it might have been of the founding mandate of the European project, also highlighted the very deficiencies which had precipitated the sense of crisis. In the stark terms of Weiler, "the decision on this constitutional overhaul was adopted in a manner typical of the worst of Europe—white smoke emerging from the Copenhagen summit of 1993, wherein the Heads of States and Governments, like so many Princes, without a serious debate in any of the national parliaments, without a serious debate in the European parliament, and most importantly, without a serious debate in the European public space or in the European public spaces, just made it a *fait accompli*" (Weiler 2000: 239).

These words are a sharp reminder of a feature of the enlargement process sometimes neglected amidst concerns over the lack of voice amongst the candidates in deciding the terms of their own supranational destiny; namely, that the participant voices in the key decision of principle in the *existing* member states were themselves few and self-selecting. The political dangers of this omission were brought into vivid relief in the Irish "no" vote in the first referendum on the Treaty of Nice in June 2001 and in the concerted political effort subsequently required to rewin the cause of reform. Where previously popular ambivalence over enlargement was evident only in the grudging levels of support offered in opinion polls across the Union,[39] the first Irish vote showed the Eurosceptical mobilizing potential of a campaign which saw and portrayed the process and the outcome of enlargement less as the realization of a noble vision and more as an indicator of a Europe increasingly remote from its citizenry.[40]

On this view, the Convention—a "constitutional moment" (Ackerman 1989), the broad and open composition and the expansive polity-building and regime-transforming agenda of which is, as we have observed, complexly bound up with the enlargement process, offered an opportunity to redress the constitutional deficit on the member state side just as much as on the accession side. The wider constituencies who were denied their input at Copenhagen[41] at last had the opportunity to debate the complex institutional and polity-building ramifications of enlargement. They did so, moreover, in a setting where discussion was more fully informed and more comprehensively representative, where for the first time the "objects" of enlargement were also included as decision-making subjects. Here, furthermore, there was an opportunity for Europe's previous deficit of constitutional process to be turned to advantage in the politics of legitimation. For the candidate states were not latecomers to a discussion with high existing standards of democratic inclusiveness. Rather, their own first involvement in the constitutional process coincided and converged with what was arguably the first involvement of a reasonable range and balance of representative institutions on the member state side, too. In turn, this may have helped, in the context of the Convention at least, if not in the more traditional corridors of European power, (where, in particular, the intemperate reaction of the French President in February 2003 to the fact that some of the leading candidate states were supportive of the United States over the Iraq War served as a reminder that the power imbalance would persist until the Accession Treaty was signed and sealed),[42] to create a more level discursive playing-field and to help dispel the sense of entrenched division and deep disparity of influence between West and East, club member and applicant, landlord and tenant.

CONCLUSION

There is a sense, of course, in which the above analysis is an exercise in studied optimism. As the initial reluctance of the IGC to endorse the institutional
reform proposals contained in the Convention's draft Constitutional Treaty
highlights, and as is reinforced by the severe difficulties presently encountered in ratification of the Constitutional Treaty (as of April 2005, while six
countries had already ratified, many others were in danger of rejecting the
Treaty, including France and the UK, both of whom had decided to submit
the text to referendum) the formidable challenge of adapting an institutional system of already restricted effectiveness and limited democratic accountability to an even larger scale, and—what is more—of doing so "in the nick
of time and under heavy pressure" (De Witte 2003: 251), may not succeed.
The promise of extending and renewing the solidary mission of the fledgling
post-state polity to the circumstances of enlargement may turn out to be hol-
low—it may congeal into pious cant rather than flow through and animate
the decision-making structures and practices of the Union. History may con-
sign the Convention to the stature of a mouse rather than a "constitutional
moment" (Walker 2004), incapable of uniting its diverse forces in a powerful new constitutional message, and leaving a legacy of constitutional instability calculated to cause continuing anxiety to those who have come late to
the debate and who seek the security of membership of a stable entity.[43] Or,
even if successful, the coherence of the constitutional message finally agreed
may be purchased at the cost—aided and abetted by the still unequal rules
and climate of engagement which attended the pre-accession proceedings of
the Convention—of reassertion of old positions, and the increasingly deep
oppositions which these have generated, and marginalisation of the potential of any new approach less tied to vested national or institutional interests
and less constrained by the problems and solutions of an earlier era. Certainly,
even to the extent that it avoided these dangers, the Convention could not
hope to overcome the deep paradox of self-reference in one bold leap, and
any serious ambition to do so might have been self-defeating.[44] The best the
Convention could reasonably hope to achieve was to close the gap between
the IGC and any "ideal" alternative, appropriately by suggesting reforms in
both of the Union's decision-making structure and of the IGC process itself[45]
in the direction of a broader representation of the European "demos" which
the subsequent IGC would be prepared to contemplate seriously.

Yet studied optimism can still be defended against its two most obvious
criticisms—that it betrays objective analysis and that it neglects what is reasonably practicable in favour of wishful thinking. In the first place, objective
analysis of the relationship between constitutionalism and enlargement arguably leads precisely to the conclusion that matters are delicately poised

between the vindication of two quite starkly alternative readings and prognoses. Either the problems posed by the enlargement project and the divisions and legitimacy deficits to which the broader constitutional project responds are mutually reinforcing, each militating against the prospects of success of the other; or, with the help of the kind of historical reading suggested above, we can trace the outlines of a possible symbiosis of the two, one in which the post-Laeken Convention has played an important role. In the second place, then, the very starkness of these options refines our contextual understanding of what is reasonably practicable. Where the alternatives are a continuation and perhaps accentuation of the crisis of legitimacy and of orientation which has marked the post-Maastricht decade on the one hand, and on the other an attempt to utilize the polity-building potential supplied by the complex historical trajectory of enlargement in aid of restoring legitimacy—an attempt that the unprecedented contemporary phase of constitutional reflection at least provides a sufficiently open ideological climate and a viable institutional framework to pursue—then there is in effect *no* real choice. When the only other option is structural fatalism, our sense of reasonable practicability must embrace whatever might avail in getting off the ground a serious constitutional discussion that both captures and utilizes the imagination of the Union's enlarged public. And this search for a mobilizing dynamic cannot afford to exclude the perhaps wishful thought that the unprecedented centrality of the recurrent theme of enlargement may remind those engaged in the constitutional debate at all levels and from all corners of the best interpretation of the history of the European Union and so encourage them towards the best projection of Europe's collective identity.

NOTES

1 An earlier version of this chapter can be found in Walker 2003a.
2 As Pentland suggests (Pentland 2000: 281), the most closely comparable enlargement in terms of the balance of negotiating power favouring the EU was the second, "Mediterranean" phase of enlargement, encompassing Spain, Portugal and Greece.
3 To take but one snapshot from that period, see European Commission, *Applicant Countries Eurobarometer 2001*, which indicates on the basis of fieldwork carried out in October 2001 that 79% of eligible respondents in all 13 eligible countries (including Turkey whose eligibility was conceded after that of the other candidate states and whose progression towards membership remains in a slower lane) would presently vote in favour of joining the EU. The only country without a large majority in favour of accession was Malta, where only 53% would have voted positively. See http://europa.eu.int/comm/public_opinion. The figures in this and other polls are strikingly consistent with the figures which were in due course returned in the final referenda on membership in the 10 countries which signed the Accession Treaty with the EU in April 2003, including the narrowness of the Maltese majority.

4 A timetable agreed at the Laeken European Council in December 2001 and reconfirmed
   at the Seville European Council in June 2002 and at the Brussels European Council
   in October 2002, the last-mentioned summit confirming the objective of concluding
   accession negotiations at the forthcoming European Council in Copenhagen in December 2002 with a view to signing the Accession Treaty at Athens in April 2003; see
   Presidency Conclusions: Brussels European Council (24 and 25 October 2002) SN
   300/02. See also the influential report by the European Commission published just pri-
   or to the Brussels European Council, *Towards the Enlarged Union: Strategy Paper and
   Report of the European Commission on the Progress Towards Accession by Each of
   the Candidate Countries.* Brussels, 9 October 2002, COM(2002) 700 final.
5 Poland, Slovenia, Czech Republic, Slovakia, Hungary, Latvia, Estonia and Lithuania,
   but not Bulgaria or Romania, nor, of course, Turkey, whose candidate status was first
   recognized only at the European Council in December 1999 and with whom formal
   accession negotiations have not yet been opened. According to the European
   Commission annual reports on progress towards accession (see note 4 above), Bulgaria
   and Romania fulfil the political criteria but do not yet meet, to various extents, the
   economic and *acquis* criteria, whereas Turkey does not yet fully meet any of the three
   sets of criteria. However, the Brussels European Council of October 2002 (see note 4
   above) did at least set an indicative timetable for Bulgaria and Romania, expressing
   support for their efforts to achieve the objective of membership in 2007, and this
   timetable was reconfirmed as recently as the Brussels European Council of December 2003 and on. The question whether formal membership negotiations should be
   begun with Turkey is due to be decided by the end of 2004, while the matter of Croatia's
   candidature will also be addressed during the course of 2004.
6 Malta and Cyprus.
7 The Treaty of Accession was signed in Athens on 16 April 2003. See OJL 236, 23
   September 2003.
8 For a somewhat similar approach within the international relations literature which
   examines the tensions between, on the one hand, the "club" rationality of enlargement—emphasizing (Copenhagen-based) one-sided conditionality, and on the other,
   the rationality of constitutional finality—opening up the possibility of a more constructive and inclusive dialogue, see Wiener 2003.
9 This issue is explored in the following section.
10 For a fuller treatment, see Walker 2001.
11 A fourth function, which is not considered here, but which has played a not insignificant
   role in the EU constitutionalization process, is the technical function of clear communication of legal norms, with a documentary Constitution or, at least, a consolidated and simplified Treaty structure as a central point of reference. See Walker 2001,
   and, more expansively, Walker forthcoming (a) and Walker forthcoming (b).
12 Of course, polity-continuity is also true of the two Mediterranean candidates—Cyprus
   and Malta, and the 'thirteenth' Candidate, Turkey, although in these cases there is not
   of course the same recent history of *fundamental* political and constitutional transformation to a postcommunist order.
13 As in Hungary.
14 As in Latvia, where the old constitution of 1922 was readopted in 1992.
15 We should not, of course, overemphasize the similarity of the problems perceived and
   objectives sought across each of these transitional contexts. It is often remarked that
   constitutionalism differs significantly in the functions it performs between transitional and non-transitional contexts, and indeed the analysis here presented in some mea-

sure accepts this general premise. However, as Dryzek and Holmes remind us in their discussion of "four democratization roads" in postcommunist transition—namely the liberal, republican, participatory and statist roads—the idea of "a free and democratic order" also has very different inflections in different transitional contexts; see Dryzek and Holmes 2002, especially ch. 16. One of the notable symbolic dimensions of constitutional discourse is precisely its tendency, often consciously manipulated by constitutional actors, to obscure significant contextual differences and to suggest that there is one single paradigm of constitutional achievement to which any particular constitutional project conforms—a suggestion which can serve the purposes both of internal and of external legitimation. We should not forget the significant diversity of aspiration and achievement beneath the universalizing ideological gloss.

16 On the pre-Westphalian foundations of the ideas of polity (or *polis*) and constitutionalism, see, for example, Lane 1996: chs. 1–2.

17 On the problems of constitutional translation from the state to the postnational context more generally, see Walker 2003b.

18 On which see the Commission White Paper, *European Governance: A White Paper* Com (2001) 428, and see review essays collected in Joerges et al. 2001.

19 On the prevalence of such "constitutional denial" in the EU context, see Walker 1996: 278–79.

20 SN300/01 ADD 1.

21 OJC 189, 18 July 2003.

22 For discussion of the early efforts of the Irish Presidency of the European Council of the first half of 2004 to find a new basis for agreement in the IGC, see, for example, the monthly reports contained in the Federal Trust's EU *Constitution Project Newsletter* (constitution@fedtrust.co.uk). For the final text of the IGC's Constitutional Treaty, see OJ C310, 16th December 2004.

23 On the history of this movement, and the importance of the Single European Act as a catalyst towards a majoritarian decision-making system, see Weiler 1999: ch. 2.

24 See Treaty of Nice, 2001, Article 2 (for the relevant amendments to expand QMV); Protocol on the enlargement of the European Union Article 3 (concerning the reweighting of votes in the Council) and Article 4 (concerning reform of the Commission). For analysis, see De Witte 2002a and De Witte 2003.

25 On the importance of the metaphor of "finality" in the European constitutional debate, see Walker forthcoming (b).

26 For analysis, see Laffan 2001.

27 Com (2001) 428.

28 See draft Constitutional Treaty (hereinafter DCT) Article I–24.

29 Poland and Spain fared well in the reallocation of votes in the Council under the (as yet unimplemented) Nice formula, their weight of influence being significantly disproportionate to their population strength. By proposing to eradicate the whole system of weighted voting for individual countries, relying instead on a formula requiring a simple majority of member states who together account for at least 60% of the Union's population, Article I–24 of the Draft Constitutional Treaty eliminates that advantage. The compromise finally reached in Art I-25 of the Constitutional Treaty was to raise the threshold of majority voting in the Council to 55% of the Member States representing 65% of the population—so reducing anxieties about the increased hegenomy of the larger "old states."

30 The present Article 49 of the Treaty on European Union (TEU) states that *any* European state which respects the principles set out in Article 6(1) (that is, liberty, democracy, respect for human rights and fundamental freedoms rights and the rule of

law) may apply for membership of the European Union. More generally, in their preambles the present Treaties proclaim the need to achieve an "ever closer Union among the peoples of Europe" (EC Treaty) and "the historic importance of the ending of the division of the European continent" (TEU).

31 For similar analyses, see Sedelmeier 2000a and Sedelmeier 2000b.

32 He associates this position with Andrew Moravcsik in particular. See, for example, Moravcsik 1998.

33 Wojciech Sadurski has recently made the suggestive argument that the human rights discourse of the European Union, its profile tellingly enhanced by the promulgation of the new Charter of Fundamental Rights and Freedoms at Nice in 2000, may be vital in legitimating a sense of membership of a common political community within the enlargement states. Not just the general universalizing claim of human rights discourse, but also the particular collective memory of human rights-orientated intervention as a liberating rather than a repressive form of external "interference" in the domestic sovereignty of the CCEE during the communist era, together with a relative readiness to trust in judicial protection of rights as a counterweight to the all too familiar dangers of oppressive or corrupt political rule, may render the postcommunist candidate states peculiarly receptive to the idea of a broad human rights commitment as a significant bond of community in an enlarged Union: see his "Overcoming the Sovereignty Conundrum with Constitutional Rights" (unpublished manuscript). Furthermore, as a linked example of rhetorical commitment engendering new ties that bind, it is also noteworthy that the notorious "double standards" of which the EU has been accused in applying human rights criteria to accession countries and other external actors which it was not prepared to endorse internally has led to some, albeit hesitant, internal readjustment to answer the charge of hypocrisy, including the new Articles 6–7 of the Treaty on European Union promulgated at Amsterdam, and, at least on an expansive interpretation, the new Charter of Fundamental Rights and Freedoms itself; see in particular De Witte 2003.

34 Although not always in a manner which was favourable to an expansive view of the EU's potential for continuing enlargement. Well-publicized interventions on the nature of European values and identity were made by a number of key figures during the early stages of the Convention debate, including Jacques Chirac, Valéry Giscard D'Estaing and Pope John Paul II. This set a controversial tone for the Convention end-game, with the question of the recognition of Christian values in the constitutional text assuming a prominent significance, and with the question of "distance" from core European values becoming somewhat indistinct in some contributions from the question of territorial distance from the Western European core. In the final analysis, there was no strong proclamation of Christian values, or indeed any other particularly "thick" and exclusionary values, in the Draft Constitutional Treaty, either in the preamble or in the new values clause (Article I–2). Equally, and related, no significant change was made in the criteria for accession in the future—compare Article 49 TEU and Article I–57 DCT criteria. The fact remains, however, that the new register of debate on values may have changed the ideological climate in a way that increases the burden on the next wave of candidates—in particular Turkey—to prove their European credentials. See Walker forthcoming (b). For an interesting argument that closer constitutional recognition of the European Christian tradition may lead to a greater rather than a lesser toleration of reasonable differences of faith and worldview, see Weiler 2003.

35 Clearly, this influence is not restricted to the Convention process itself, or is even likely to have been most prominent there. One consequence of the conclusion of the Accession Treaty in April 2003 and the decision formally to admit the 10 new mem-

bers in May 2004, is that these new members, like the existing 15, will be required to ratify any agreement on the draft Constitutional Treaty emerging from the 2004 IGC before any such agreement may be formalized as law. At that later stage, then, the voice of the CCEE, by then full members of the EU, will become more prominent. It is arguable, of course, that awareness of this very institutional prospect also strengthened the hand of the CCEE representatives in the Convention itself, and, perhaps more pronouncedly, at the later IGC stage—by which point (after the Summer of 2003) the Accession Treaty had already been safely signed and delivered, and the question of ratification through national constitutional processes, and so of satisfaction of national constitutional audiences, was becoming more pressing. That, taken together, these factors have in fact permitted a more confident negotiating stance on the part of the accession countries but also encouraged this newly won negotiating confidence to be deployed in a manner assertive of national interests, might in part account for the increasingly forthright stance of Poland in the IGC in defence of its existing Treaty position on the question of QMV. See note 29 above.

36 The Charter was in fact duly incorporated, with minor amendments, as Part III of the draft Constitutional Treaty.

37 See the discussion of the importance of regime legitimacy in the postcommunist states in the section above.

38 The 105 member Convention included 39 representatives from the 13 accession states (one government and two parliamentary representatives per state), which is the same level of direct representation as the existing member states, although the latter could of course have additional indirect voice through the three-person Presidency or the 16 person European Parliament constituency or the two person Commission constituency. Under the terms of the Laeken Declaration, moreover, the full involvement of the accession representatives stopped short of the capacity to prevent the forming of a decisive consensus amongst the other members of the Convention—although the dynamics of the Convention ensured that this was never put to the test. As regards Praesidium membership, accession members were effectively excluded from candidature at the inception of the Convention, and it was only following pressure from all section of the Convention that the accession states were allowed to nominate one of their members as a participant in the Praesidium. For early details, see Nikolov 2002. For more general coverage of the work of the Convention, see Shaw 2002.

39 See, for example, *Eurobarometer 56* (European Commission, March 2002).

40 Laffan (2001) makes the interesting point that the "no" campaign did not directly oppose the "yes" campaign's assertion that enlargement remained a moral duty but instead emphasized, as well as specific short-term concerns (for example, increased immigration, reform of the Common Agricultural Reform), certain general anxieties about the loss of national sovereignty and democratic accountability in which the prospect of enlargement was clearly implicated. In other words, the argument about the EU's historical polity-building mission to enlarge showed a remarkable resilience even in a climate of heavy scepticism about the EU's propensity to erode national democracy and its own deficient democratic credentials, but, tellingly, the national sovereignty and democratic arguments still initially won the day.

41 This denial, of course, is even more egregious in the case of the three "third wave" enlargement countries—Austria, Sweden and Finland—whose own membership postdated Copenhagen and who, therefore, were denied even basic governmental participation in the key political decision on what was then the next-but-one enlargement.

42 For Chirac's comments about the need for the candidate states to keep their own counsel on geo-political matters in advance of accession, and his hints that enlargement

might otherwise be endangered, see http://www.eubusiness.com/imported/2003/02/-103745.

43 See, for example, the early reaction of Chirac and others to the failure of the December 2003 IGC to endorse the Convention's text, in particular their suggestion that the vacuum created by this failure might be filled by the establishment of a semi-autonomous pioneer group of states most favourable to further integration and best equipped to carry it out. Such a suggestion, even if it was quickly toned down in the months after December 2003, carries an implicit threat to new states, which by definition will be disadvantaged in terms of their capacity for immediate further integration. For discussion, see contributions to the Federal Trust's EU *Constitution Project Newsletter* (constitution@fedtrust.co.uk).

44 Indeed, one criticism of Giscard D'Estaing's chairmanship of the Convention was that the very boldness of his attempt to assert its status as a genuinely autonomous and foundational Constitutional Convention courted two dangers, one external and one internal. Externally, it threatened to provoke a reaction by the present Masters of the Treaties—the IGC—in the form of dismissal or marginalization of the Convention's work—and, here, subsequent events may to some extent have vindicated the critics. Internally, more immediately, and perhaps even more significantly, it may have led to the broad-ranging and open-ended discussion on which the legitimacy of the Convention as a community mobilizing process being sacrificed or compromised before the desire to conclude as expeditiously as possible a draft constitutional text.

45 In this regard, the proposed institutionalization of the Convention process itself as a staple of future cycles of reform, albeit still subject to IGC approval and national ratification in the final analysis, may be viewed as one of the successes of the Constitutional Treaty. See Article IV–443.

BIBLIOGRAPHY

Ackerman, Bruce. "Constitutional Politics/Constitutional Law." *Yale Law Journal* 99 (1989): 453–560.

Albi, Anneli. "Postmodern versus Retrospective Sovereignty: Two Different Discourses in the EU and the Candidate Countries" in *Sovereignty in Transition*, ed. Walker, Neil (Oxford: Hart, 2003), pp.401–22.

Beetham, David and Chris Lord. *Legitimacy in the European Union*. Cambridge: Polity, 1998.

Chryssochoou, Dimitris N. *Theorizing European Integration*. London: Sage, 2001.

De Burca, Grainne. "The Drafting of the EU Charter of Fundamental Rights." *European Law Review* 26 (2001): 126–44.

De Witte, Bruno. "Anticipating the Institutional Consequences of Expanded Membership of the European Union." *International Political Science Review* 23 (2002a): 235–48.

——. "The Closest Thing to a Constitutional Conversation in Europe: The Semi-Permanent Treaty Revision Process" in *Convergence and Divergence in European Public Law*, eds. Beaumont, Paul, Carole Lyons and Neil Walker (Oxford: Hart, 2002b), pp. 39–58.

——. "The Impact of enlargement on the Constitution of the European Union" in *The Enlargement of the European Union*, ed. Cremona, Marise (Oxford: Oxford University Press, 2003) pp. 209–52.

Duchacek, Ivo. *Power Maps: Comparative Politics of Constitutions*. Santa Barbara, California: ABC-Clio, 1973.

Dryzek, John S. and Lesley Holmes. *Post-Communist Democratization: Political Discourses across Thirteen Countries.* Cambridge: Cambridge University Press, 2002.

Eleftheriados, Pavlos. "The European Constitution and Cosmopolitan Ideals." *Columbia Journal of European Law* 7 (2001): 21–40.

Elgie, Robert and Jan Zielonka. "Constitutions and Constitution Building" *Democratic Consolidation in Eastern Europe, Vol. I: Institutional Engineering*, ed. Zielonka, Jan (Oxford: Oxford University Press, 2001), pp. 25–47.

European Commission. *Applicant Countries Eurobarometer 2001.* European Commission, 2001.

Galbraith, John K. *The Culture of Contentment.* London: Sinclair Stevenson, 1992.

Grabbe, Heather. *Profiting from Enlargement.* London: Centre for European Reform, 2001.

Joerges, Christian, Yves Meny, and Joseph H. H. Weiler, eds. *Mountain or Molehill? A Critical Appraisal of the Commission White Paper on Governance.* Harvard Jean Monnet Working Paper Series, No. 6/01, 2001.

Holmes, Stephen. "Introduction." *East European Constitutional Review* 9, no. 4 (2000): 1.

Kahn, Paul H. *The Reign of Law.* New Haven: Yale University Press, 1997.

Keating, Michael. *Plurinational Democracy: Stateless Nations of the United Kingdom, Spain, Canada and Belgium in a Post-Sovereign World.* Oxford University Press, 2001.

Laffan, Brigid. "The Nice Treaty, the Irish Vote." Unpublished manuscript, 2001.

Lane, Jan-Erik. *Constitution and Political Theory.* Manchester: Manchester University Press, 1996.

Moravcsik, Andrew. *The Choice for Europe: Social Purpose and State Power from Messina to Maastricht.* London: UCL Press, 1998.

Nikolov, Krassimir Y. "The Convention and the Accession States: Where do we Stand? Where do we Sit?" *Challenge Europe*, January 2002. http://www.theepce.be/challenge.

Pentland, Charles. "Westphalian Europe and Europe's Last Enlargement." *European Integration* 22 (2000): 271–98.

Sadurski, Wojciech. "Conclusions: On the Relevance of Institutions and the Centrality of Constitutions in Post-Communist Transitions" in *Democratic Consolidation in Eastern Europe, Vol. 1: Institutional Engineering*, ed. Zielonka, Jan (Oxford: Oxford University Press, 2001) pp. 455–74.

——. "The Charter and Enlargement." *European Law Journal* 8 (2002): 340–62.

——. "Overcoming the Sovereignty Conundrum with Constitutional Rights." Unpublished manuscript, n.d.

Scharpf, Fritz. *Governing in Europe: Effective and Democratic?* Oxford: Oxford University Press, 1999.

Schimmelfennig, Frank. "The Community Trap: Liberal Norms, Rhetorical Action and the Eastern Enlargement of the European Union." *International Organization* 55 (2001): 47–80.

Sedelmeier, Ulrich. "East of Amsterdam: The Implications of the Amsterdam Treaty for Eastern Enlargement" in *European Integration after Amsterdam: Institutional Dynamics and Prospects for Democracy*, eds. Neunreither, Karlheinz and Antje Wiener (Oxford: Oxford University Press, 2000a), pp. 218–38.

——. "Eastern Enlargement: Risk, Rationality and Role Compliance" in *The State of the European Union, Vol. 5: Risks, Reform, Resistance and Revival*, eds. Cowles, Maria Green and Michael Smith (Oxford: Oxford University Press, 2000b), pp. 164–85.

Shaw, Jo. *Process, Responsibility and Inclusion in EU Constitutionalism: the Challenge for the Convention on the Future of the Union.* London: Federal Trust, 2002.

Vachudova, Milada A. "EU Enlargement: An Overview." *East European Constitutional Review* 9, no. 4 (2001): 4–12.

Walker, Neil. "European Constitutionalism and European Integration." *Public Law* (1996): 266–86.

———. "Sovereignty and Differentiated Integration in the European Union." *European Law Journal* 4 (1998): 355–88.

———. "The White Paper in Constitutional Context" in *Mountain or Molehill? A Critical Appraisal of the Commission White Paper on Governance*, eds. Joerges, Christian, Yves Meny, and Joseph H. H. Weiler (Harvard Jean Monnet Working Paper Series, No. 6/01, 2001), pp. 33–54.

———. "The Idea of Constitutional Pluralism." *Modern Law Review* 65 (2002): 317–59.

———, "Constitutionalizing Enlargement, Enlarging Constitutionalism." *European Law Journal* 9, no. 3 (2003a) 365–85.

———, "Postnational Constitutionalism and the Problem of Translation" in *European Constitutionalism Beyond the State: A Festschrift to European Constitutionalism*, eds. Weiler, Joseph H. H. and Marlene Wind (Cambridge: Cambridge University Press, 2003b), pp.27–54.

———. "After the Constitutional Moment" in *The Draft Constitutional Treaty*, ed. Pernice, Ingolfe (Baden-Baden: Nomos, forthcoming [a]).

———. "The Idea of a European Constitution and the *Finalité* of Integration" in *The Emergence of a European Constitution*, ed. De Witte, Bruno (Oxford: Oxford University Press, forthcoming [b]).

Wallace, Helen. *Widening and Deepening: The European Community and the New European Agenda.* London: RIIA, 1989.

Weiler, Joseph H. H. *The Constitution of Europe.* Cambridge: Polity, 1999.

———. "Fischer: The Dark Side" in *What Kind of Constitution for What Kind of Polity? Responses to Joschka Fischer*, eds. Joerges, Christian, Yves Meny and Joseph H. H. Weiler (Florence: Robert Schuman Centre, 2000), pp. 223–35.

———. *Un'Europa Cristiana* [A Christian Europe]. Milan: Rizzoli, 2003.

Wiener, Antje. "Finality vs. Enlargement: Constitutive Practices and Opposing Rationales in the Reconstruction of Europe." New York University Jean Monnet Working Papers, No. 9/03, 2003. 3

List of Contributors

ADAM CZARNOTA teaches philosophy of law and sociology of law in the School of Law, the University of New South Wales in Sydney, Australia. He is co-director of the European Law Center at the same university. He is a member of the editorial board of *Ius et Lex*, a journal devoted to legal philosophy. Previously, he held positions at the Faculty of Law, Warsaw University and Faculty of Law and the Institute of Sociology, N. Copernicus University. He was a Visiting Fellow at Oxford University, the University of Edinburgh, and the European University Institute in Florence. He is a member of the Board of the Research Committee on the Sociology of Law and Chair of the Working Group on transformation of law in postcommunist societies. He has published extensively in Polish and English in the fields of sociology of law, legal theory, philosophy of law and history of ideas, and political theory. Currently he is working on a book on legal strategies of dealing with the past.

VENELIN I. GANEV is Assistant Professor of Political Science at Miami University, Ohio. He received his PhD in 1999 from the University of Chicago. His main fields of interest are postcommunist politics, democratization studies, and modern constitutionalism. He has published articles in the following journals: *East European Constitutional Review*, *American Journal of Comparative Law*, *Journal of Democracy*, *East European Politics and Society*, *Communist and Postcommunist Studies*, *Slavic Review*, and *Europe-Asia Studies*. He has also contributed chapters to several volumes that explore various aspects of institution-building in contemporary Europe. During 2003–2004, he was a National Fellow at The Hoover Institution, Stanford University.

LUC HUYSE was, until his retirement in 2000, Professor of Sociology and Sociology of Law at the Leuven University Law School (Belgium). He has written extensively on the consolidation of young democracies. His current research is on the role of retributive justice after violent conflict. He has been a consultant to governments and NGOs in Burundi and Ethiopia. He recently co-edited *Reconciliation after Violent Conflict. A Handbook* (Stockholm: IDEA, 2003).

IVAN KRASTEV is a political scientist and Chairman of the Centre for Liberal Strategies in Sofia, Bulgaria. He is the research director of *The Politics of Anti-Americanisms*, a project coordinated by Central European University. Since January 2004 he holds the post of Executive Director of the International Commission on the Balkans. His latest publications in English include the following: *Shifting Obsessions. Three Essays on Politics of Anti-Corruption* (CEU Press, 2004), "Missing Incentive: Corruption, Anticorruption, and Reelection" in *Building a Trustworthy State in Post-Socialist transition* (edited by János Kornai and Susan Rose-Ackerman, Palgrave Macmillan, 2004), *Nationalism after Communism, Lessons Learned* (co-edited with Allina Pippidi, CEU Press, 2004) and "The Anti-American century?" in the *Journal of Democracy* (April 2004).

MARTIN KRYGIER is Professor of Law at the University of New South Wales and the co-director of its European Law Centre. His work straddles borders between political, legal, and social theory. He has published extensively in academic journals and journals of public debate. His publications include *Between Fear and Hope: Hybrid Thoughts on Public Values* (Sydney, 1997), and as editor or co-editor, *Spreading Democracy in Europe?* (Berlin, 2005), *Community and Legality: the Intellectual Legacy of Philip Selznick* (2002), *The Rule of Law after Communism* (1999), *Marxism and Communism: Posthumous Reflections on Politics, Society, and Law* (1994), and *Bureaucracy: The Career of a Concept* (1979). A particular focus of his research is institutional and social development in postcommunist Europe.

MATTHIAS MAHLMANN is Assistant Professor of Law at Free University Berlin. He works in the fields of German public law, European law, practical philosophy, and legal sociology. His books include *Rationalismus in der Praktischen Theorie* (Baden-Baden, 1999), *Der Staat der Zukunft* (co-edited with C.-P. Calliees, Stuttgart, 2001), *Das neue Anti-Diskriminierungsrecht* (co-edited with B. Rudolf, Baden-Baden, 2005), and *Elemente einer ethischen Grundrechtstheorie* (forthcoming). Recent articles include "Dienstrechtliche Konkretisierung staatlicher Neutralität" in *Zeitschrift für Rechtspolitik* (2004) and "1789 renewed? The protection of Human Rights in Europe" in the *Cardozo Journal of International and Comparative Law* (2004).

CLAUS OFFE is Professor of Political Science at Humboldt University, Berlin. His main areas of research are welfare state and social policy, political sociology, democratic theory, and transitions from state socialism. He has published numerous papers and several books in these areas.

VELLO PETTAI (Department of Political Science, University of Tartu) received his PhD in Political Science from Columbia University. He was a regular contributor to the Constitution Watch section of the *East European Constitutional Review* for eight years. In addition to working on constitutional review, he has published articles on party development in the Baltic states, as well as comparative ethnopolitics. In 2003 he co-edited *The Road to the European Union: Estonia, Latvia and Lithuania* (Manchester University Press) with Jan Zielonka.

ULRIKE POPPE (Humboldt University, Berlin) is head of an adult education program on contemporary history with the Berlin Protestant Academy. She has been a civil rights activist and a prominent member of the opposition in the GDR. In late 1989, she was a representative of the opposition at the Roundtable Talks in Berlin.

JIŘÍ PŘIBÁŇ is Senior Lecturer at Cardiff Law School, Cardiff University and is Visiting Professor in philosophy and sociology of law at Charles University, Prague. He is the author and editor of numerous books in English and Czech, such as *Dissidents of Law* (2002), *Systems of Justice in Transition* (co-edited with P. Roberts and J. Young, 2003), *Law's New Boundaries* (co-edited with D. Nelken, 2001), and *The Rule of Law in Central Europe* (co-edited with J. Young, 1999). His main areas of research are social theory and law, jurisprudence, constitutional, EU, and human rights theory, and comparative law theory.

HUBERT ROTTLEUTHNER is a graduate of Frankfurt-am-Main University, with a degree in philosophy, law, and sociology. He received his PhD in 1972. In 1975 he was appointed Professor of Sociology of Law at the Free University Berlin, Faculty of Law. His fields of interest encompass judicial research, the role of law and lawyers (judges, practitioners, law professors, corporate counsel, and legislative counsel), efficacy research, Nazi law, law in the former East Germany (GDR), and the theoretical foundations of law.

KIM LANE SCHEPPELE is Laurance S. Rockefeller Professor of Public Affairs and the University Center for Human Values, and Director of the Law and Public Affairs Program, Princeton University. She works on "constitutions under stress," focusing on new constitutions in the former Soviet world and on reactions of constitutional democracies to September 11. Her work on Hungary is based on four years of fieldwork in Budapest during 1994–1998. Her work for the chapter in this volume was supported by grants from the (American) National Science Foundation, nos. SBE 94-11889, SBE 95-14174, and SBE 01-11963.

WOJCIECH SADURSKI is Head of Department of Law and Professor of Philosophy of Law and Legal Theory at the European University Institute in Florence, and Professor of Legal Philosophy at the University of Sydney, where he holds the Personal Chair in Legal Philosophy. He wrote extensively on the philosophy of law, political philosophy, and constitutional theory; his main English-language books include *Giving Desert Its Due: Social Justice and Legal Theory* (1980), *Moral Pluralism and Legal Neutrality* (1985), and *Freedom of Speech and Its Limits* (1999), all published in Kluwer's *Law and Philosophy Library*; and *Rights Before Courts: A Study of Constitutional Courts in Postcommunist States of Central and Eastern Europe* (Springer, 2004). His current research includes a study on the impact of the EU enlargement upon democracy and the rule of law in new member states.

CINDY SKACH is Associate Professor of Government at Harvard University, where she is also Faculty Associate of the Minda de Gunzburg Center for European Studies, the Davis Center for Russian Studies, and the Weatherhead Center for International Affairs. She is the author of *Borrowing Constitutional Designs* (Princeton), and several articles and book chapters on comparative constitutionalism. She was previously a Visiting Professor at the Center for Business, Government, and Society in the Department of Managerial Economics and Decision Sciences at the Kellogg School of Management.

GRAŻYNA SKĄPSKA is Professor of Sociology at the Jagiellonian University in Kraków, Poland. She has worked on the legal consciousness, *Social Background of Attitudes toward Law*, published in Polish in 1982; law and social change, *Law and the Dynamics of Social Change*, published in Polish in 1991; privatization as a part of postcommunist transformation, *A Fourth Way? Privatization, Property, and the Emergence of New Market Economies* (co-edited with G. S. Alexander, Routledge, 1994); postcommunist constitutionalism in light of contemporary social theories, "Paradigm Lost? The Constitutional Process in Poland and the Hope for a Grass-Roots Constitutionalism" (in *The Rule of Law after Communism*, edited by Martin Krygier and Adam Czarnota, 1999), and "Between Civil Society and Europe: Sociological Investigations of Constitutionalism after Communism," to appear in 2005. She has been a Vice-President of the International Institute of Sociology since 2001, and is a member of the editorial boards of *Droit et Societe* and *Ius et Lex*.

RUTI TEITEL is the first Ernst C. Stiefel Professor of Comparative Law at New York Law School, where she teaches international human rights, and comparative and U.S. constitutional law. An expert on Eastern European and Latin American post-totalitarian societies, Professor Teitel's extensive body of scholarly writing on comparative law, human rights, and constitutionalism encompasses articles published in some of the country's most prestigious legal journals, including the *Yale Law Journal* and the *Harvard Law Review*. She is a member of the Council on Foreign Relations and the Steering Committee of Human Rights Watch Europe/Central Asia, as well as of the Executive Advisory Board of the Boston College Law School's Holocaust/-Human Rights Research Project.

RENATA UITZ is Assistant Professor of Comparative Constitutional Law at Central European University (CEU), Budapest. At CEU she has been teaching various courses on European and American constitutional law, separation of powers, comparative constitutional review, legislative drafting, and transitional justice. She regularly publishes on constitutional review, protection of constitutional rights, and problems of democratic transition in English, Hungarian, and Russian. She was a long-time correspondent for the *East European Constitutional Review* and is now a correspondent for I-CON (International Journals of Constitutional Law). Her book exploring the relevance of accounts of history and traditions in constitutional adjudication is forthcoming with CEU Press.

NEIL WALKER has been Professor of European Law at the European University Institute since 2000, and before that was Professor of Legal and Constitutional Theory at the University of Aberdeen. He has written extensively on questions of constitutional law and constitutional theory in both national and transnational contexts. His recent books include two edited collections, *Sovereignty in Transition* (Hart, 2003) and *Europe's Area of Freedom, Security and Justice* (2004).

Index

Roth, Stephen J., 314
Rottleuthner, Hubert, 199,
207 n7, 373
with Matthias
Mahlmann, 130–31, 133
Rousseau, Dominique, 87
Rousseau, Jean-
Jacques, 191, 193, 195
Rousso, Henry, 142, 150
n11, 151 n15
with Eric Conan, 150
n11
Rummler, Toralf, 203
Rupnik, Jacques, 151 n23
Russia, 11, 54 n5, 55 n9, 56
n14, 193, 198, 325
Rustow, Dankwart, 146

Sadurski, Wojciech, 2, 86,
116, 266, 346, 348, 356,
365 n33, 374
Sajó, András, 4, 80, 251
n60, 251 n73, 277 n1,
325, 329
Sarkin, Jeremy, 257 n20
Sartori, Giovanni, 25, 29,
65
Schaal, Gary with Andreas
Wöll, 175
Schaefgen, Christoph, 177,
178
Scharpf, Fritz, 344, 353
Scheffer, Ronel with Alex
Boraine and Janet Levy,
148
Scheppele, Kim
Lane, 12–13, 14, 16,
19–20, 21, 23 n1, 23 n6,
24 n9, 24 n15, 53, 55 n7,
58 n32, 61, 116 n2, 273,
373
with Gábor Halmai 80;
with Antal Örkény 86
Schimmelfennig,
Frank, 355, 356
Schlink, Bernard, 291
Schmitter, Phillippe C.
with Guillermo
O'Donnell, 25

with Guillermo
O'Donnell and L.
Whitehead, 25
Schneider, Henrich, 117 n3
Schönherr, Albrecht, 187
Schöpflin, George, 64
Schorlemmer,
Friedrich, 188
Schwartz, Herman, 3–4, 24
n10, 61, 88 n17, 117 n6,
319 n9;
with Lloyd Cutler, 320
n29
Schwarz, Walter, 233 n14
Schwengler, Walter, 198
Scully, Timothy R. with
Scott Mainwaring, 65
Sedelmeier, Ulrich, 364
n31
Selznick, Philip, 88 n18,
270
Shaw, Jo, 366 n38
Sheehan, Reginald S. with
William Mishler, 71 n5
Shils, Edward, 309, 310
Shklar, Judith, 86
Shleifer, Andre with
Robert Vishny, 328
Shugart, Matthew with
John M. Carey, 29
Siegelbaum, Paul with
Daniel Kaufmann, 329
Šiklová, Jiřina, 319 n16
Sillamäe, 105–106, 115
Skach, Cindy, 14–15, 18,
19, 23, 23 n2, 24 n16, 61,
273, 374
Skąpska, Grażyna, 131–32,
133, 215, 225, 231, 231
n5, 374
Slagstad, Rune with Jon
Elster, 116 n1
Slovakia, 232 n8, 313, 314,
315, 316, 317, 319 n13,
319 n14, 319 n17, 347,
363 n5
Slovenia, 13, 233 n16, 347,
363 n5
Sobibor, 199

Solum, Lawrence, 82, 88
n13
Sólyom, László, 24 n13, 53,
80, 87 n4, 151 n19, 245,
247, 248, 259 n44, 259
n47; with Georg
Brunner, 24 n13
Sós, Vilmos, 4
South Africa, 1, 128, 132,
193, 236–60, 282
Southern Europe, 25, 266,
281, 282
Soviet Union, The, 32, 55
n8, 93, 104, 162, 180,
212, 246, 279, 305
Spain, 193, 362 n2, 364 n29
St. Petersburg, 56 n14
Stalin, Joseph, 208 n21
Stark, Christian with
Wilfried Berg and Bodo
Pieroth, 175
Stark, David with László
Bruszt, 271
Stepan, Alfred, 61;
with Juan J. Linz, 25, 72
n10, 116 n1
Suchocka, Hanna, 156
Sugar, Peter F. with Ivo J.
Lederer, 312
Sumner, William G., 295
Sunstein, Cass, 62, 63, 66,
72 n12
Swain, Nigel, 260 n71
Sweden, 353, 366 n41
Switzerland, 69, 70
Szczawnica, 233 n17

Tallinn, 101, 105, 111
Tanzi, Vito, 328
Tartu, 103, 118 n39
Teitel, Ruti, 2, 11, 65, 247,
258 n33, 259 n50, 260
n64, 260 n79, 266–68,
269, 271–72, 273, 279,
283, 374–75
Teubner, Gunther, 227
Thayer, James Bradley, 71
n3
Timofeev, Lev, 335–36